THE PILGRIM WAY

THE PILGRIM WAY

ROBERT MERRILL BARTLETT

A PILGRIM PRESS BOOK
PHILADELPHIA

The author wishes to express his appreciation to the many individuals, organizations, and publishers that have permitted him to
quote from their copyrighted works (acknowledged in Notes, page
347) and to reproduce illustrative material (acknowledged in List
of Illustrations, page ix).

Dedicated to
my wife, Sue Nuckols Bartlett,
inspirer and co-laborer
in all my endeavors,
and a true Pilgrim,
although she came earlier
to the Jamestown Colony

CONTENTS

LIST OF ILLUSTRATIONS
(illustration acknowledgments)

FOREWORD

The Pilgrim Way has in every respect fulfilled the need for a scholarly treatise on John Robinson. A fresh study of this foremost leader of the Pilgrims has been wanting for the past fifty years, since Walter Burgess published his *John Robinson, Pastor of the Pilgrim Fathers*. At the same time the appearance of Dr. Bartlett's masterly work justly reverses a trend in Pilgrim historiography, namely the recent tendency among some historians to concentrate almost wholly on the economic life, political development, and material culture of the Plymouth Colony, while minimizing the basic motivation of New England's first settlers.

Personalities and religious concepts that are seldom expounded in these days among students of the Old Colony provide the center of discussion in Robert Bartlett's volume. Robinson's relationship with seventeenth-century scholars like William Ames, Henry Jacob, Robert Parker, William Perkins, Paul Baynes, Robert Browne, Francis Johnson, John Smyth, Richard Clyfton, Henry Ainsworth, Jacob Arminius, Hugo Grotius, and others is unfolded. The profound issues of theological controversy are skillfully presented in readable and appealing literary style. The entire drama of the Pilgrim migrations and final settlement in New England is told with singular warmth and understanding.

John Robinson is the moving force in this Pilgrim epic, a man of remarkable tolerance in an intolerant age. His importance as theologian is exceeded only by his humanity as a pastor. His broad, humanistic views of a universal Christian fellowship, so important and so lacking in all ages, are set forth in the following pages. As Robinson wrote: "It is too great arrogancy for any man or church to think that he or they have so sounded the word of God to the bottom as precisely to set down the church's discipline without error in substance or circumstance." In another context he stated: "There is more truth and light yet to break forth from God's holy word."

The Pilgrim Society is proud to sponsor this most significant book on the occasion of the 350th anniversary of the landing of the Pilgrims and the 150th year of the Society's existence. Not only should this study make a vital contribution to scholarship, it should also help men to be more understanding of one another and to value human dignity above all things.

L. D. Geller, Director
The Pilgrim Society

ACKNOWLEDGMENTS

The author wishes to express his appreciation to the following for their inspiration and their help:

The Pilgrim Society, Plymouth, L. D. Geller, Director
The Congregational Library, Boston
The Congregational Historical Society
The Boston Athenaeum
Harvard University Library
Yale University Library
Plymouth Public Library
The British Museum, London
Dr. William's Library, London
The Congregational Society of England and Wales
Corpus Christi College, Cambridge, England
Cambridge University Library, Cambridge
The Rev. Edmund P. Jessup, All Saints, Babworth, England
The Rev. Billie James, St. Wilfrid's, Scrooby, England
The Rev. Ernest J. Weil, St. Helen's, Austerfield, England
The Rev. C. G. Pearce, John Robinson Memorial Church, Gainsborough, England
The Rev. L. R. R. Harris, St. Peter and St. Paul, Sturton le Steeple, England
The Pilgrim Fathers' Memorial Church, London
Dr. J. G. Hoenderdaal, Leyden University
Dr. A. G. H. Bachrach, Leyden University
Dr. B. N. Leverland, Archives of Leyden, Holland
Dr. W. Downer, Archivist, Leyden
The Pieterskerk, Leyden
Jack Bax, Director, Press and Information, Rotterdam
The Rev. Wiebe Vos, Pilgrim Fathers Church, Delfshaven
The Rev. James C. Gordon, English Reformed Church, Amsterdam
The Rev. John Russell, Scot Church, Rotterdam
Mrs. Douglas Wallace, a descendant of John Robinson
The Ellison Foundation
John Kendall
Mr. and Mrs. F. H. Ellenberger
Mrs. Elden L. Howe
Judson E. Fuller

INTRODUCTION

A good many years ago I was searching the *Plymouth Town Records* for information about the Bartlett House, built in 1660, in which I live. I read an intriguing little piece about Mercy Bartlett, youngest daughter of Pilgrim Robert Bartlett, who as a teenager created quite a stir at Plimoth Plantation.

The records of October 25, 1668 state:

> James Clarke complaineth against Sarah Barlow and Marcye Bartlett, in an action of slaunder and defamation, to the damage of two hundred pounds for reporting that they saw the said James Clarke kisse his mayde, and vse other uncuiell carriages that he acted towards her in the field vppon the Lords day.
>
> This was refered to be ended by the majestrates by mutuall consent of each of the pties, whose determination and judgment is as followeth:
>
> In reference to the complaint of James Clarke against Sarah Barlow and Marcye Bartlett, for defaneing him in makeing report of vnseemly familiarities between him and his mayde, the Court, haueing fully considered the matter, and compared the testimony relateing thereunto, and takeing notice how the pties that haue charged him haue, one or both of them, said and unsaid or greatly varyed in their relations about it, doe declare, that we judge they have defamed and slaundered him therein, because the things charged by them doth in noe measure appear by testimonie; and also their way of devoulging it was manifestly scanderlous, although there had bine some appaerences of truth in their report, and therefore for this theire misdemeanor doe amerce them ten shillings appece to the Kinge. (On the margin) This was non suited because the said Marcye Bartlett was found under couert barud.

The girls were reprimanded for gossiping, but the shillings were not collected because Mercy Bartlett was under court age. James Clarke suffered only embarrassment. And that was that.

Somehow this did not read like very stern Puritanism. Why didn't they throw James Clarke out of the church? Or why didn't the girls whip up a witch hunt like the hysterical teenagers in Salem? Later on I read that Mercy's brother, Joseph, had been

brought into the same court and fined for striking an Indian. Why make a fuss about that? In such a wilderness a man had to protect himself.

I noted in these two incidents an attitude of common sense and compassion that raised a question in my mind. I found my answer in John Robinson, the intellectual and spiritual mentor of the Pilgrims.

I have not attempted to write a history of the Puritan movement. I have dealt with one small and unique group in this great migration to America, namely the Pilgrims. I have tried to write about them in as clear and direct manner as possible, hoping that the book will appeal to the general reader who would like to know just what their story was all about. This is a study of the Pilgrim epic, from its English origin through its years in Holland and the final establishment of Plimoth Plantation. I have endeavored to portray the personality of John Robinson, the main character in that drama, and his influence on the first New England colony.

Having lived for thirty-five years in a house they built, sat in their chairs, read their writings, walked in their fields and paths, and cultivated their garden plots, I do not think of the Pilgrims as demographic statistics. They are very real people, and as such I would like to write about them, their human frailties, and their superhuman faith and courage. I can almost hear their footsteps in the creak of the old floorboards and their voices as I sit in the stormy sessions of Plymouth town meetings.

I will use the seventeenth-century style spelling of Plimoth throughout the text following the practice of the Pilgrim chronicler, William Bradford.

Robert Merrill Bartlett
Plymouth, 1971

The world is waking out of a long deep sleep. The old ignorance is still defended with tooth and claw, but we have kings and nobles now on our side. Strange vicissitude of things. Time was when learning was only found in the religious orders. The religious orders nowadays care only for money and sensuality, while learning has passed to secular princes and peers and courtiers.
—Desiderius Erasmus

1 "THE WORLD IS WAKING"

One summer day in 1588 a twelve-year-old boy named John Robinson heard an exciting story as he walked along the River Trent in Nottinghamshire, England. Fishermen had sailed down the Humber River from the North Sea where they reported sighting the ships of the Spanish Armada in retreat before the navy of Queen Elizabeth. The survivors of the 132 vessels that had crossed the channel in July to destroy the English fleet were being pursued up the east coast of England. From the North Sea they were chased north of Scotland and west of Ireland, and then back to their home ports in Spain.

It was an incredible report that set the village buzzing. Slowly through the ensuing weeks news crept into sleepy, little Sturton le Steeple, verifying the tale of the fishermen. Bold English mariners like Howard, Drake, Hawkins, and Frobisher had been the heroes of the victory.

John Robinson, his family, and neighbors had gleaned reports of the brutal war that Spain had been waging against the Low Countries from refugees who sought haven in East England. They were troubled by a shadowy fear that Spain might invade their homeland. Reports of Spanish intrigues had been passed on from the London court to the north country. But now, a surge of rejoicing swept through the byways of the kingdom. The England of Elizabeth was at last free from the threat of foreign tyranny. A new sense of pride was stirred in the British people because their seamen were exploring the oceans and discovering faraway lands.

John returned to his studies in the vicarage. He pored over the mysterious maps that crudely outlined some of these new frontiers that were being visited by these adventurers somewhere in the vast unknown. He dreamed long dreams of these places that lay beyond the solitude of Sturton le Steeple. This hamlet in the hills along the border of Lincolnshire and Nottinghamshire looked out over the meadowlands to the giant towers of Lincoln Cathedral. The village lay west of the River Trent, along which boats crept past the fields of grazing sheep and cattle. Near the ancient Roman road that led from Lincoln to Doncaster it had grown up on the watershed between the Trent and the Idle valleys. Years later the parish church of St. Peter and St. Paul was built. Its high tower formed a landmark for the countryside and the village was given its present name, Sturton le Steeple.

Freeholder John Robinson was born here around 1550. A son was born to him and his wife, Ann, about 1576 and he also was called John. The will of Ann Robinson, dated 16 October 1616 was discovered in 1911. It definitely places the home and birthplace of John and indicates the type of family of which he was a part—that of a substantial farmer of the period. There were other children in the family: William, Mary, and a daughter whose name has been lost. A virulent epidemic swept Sturton le Steeple in 1583. Many neighbors died but the Robinson family survived.[1]

The parish church was more than a worship center. Weddings, christenings, and funerals were held there along with lectures, classes conducted by the vicar, and gatherings of the vestry and town officials, including coroner's inquests and hearings by the justice of peace. Business deals were transacted on the church porch. Weapons and powder were sometimes stored there along with tithe payments of wool and grain. Proclamations from the bishop and king were read from the pulpit and notices were posted on the doors. Socials and festivals centered in the church-yard.[2]

John, no doubt, received his early education from the vicars of the Church of St. Peter and St. Paul. It is probable that he was then sent to nearby Lincoln, Gainsborough, or Retford to prepare for Cambridge. Later years indicate that he must have been a scholarly lad and that his parents were concerned that he should receive university training.

John's father was a yeoman, a husbandman who owned a home and land and rented pasture for the grazing of his flocks and fields for planting. The patches of wheat, rye, oats and barley, the vegetable and herb gardens, and the fruit orchard produced most of the family food, which consisted largely of "bread, beer, and beef."

Although the class system was rigid, the yeomen who owned land were the backbone of English agriculture and held an honorable place in society. Yeomen fraternized with country gentlemen, and, as Mildred Campbell points out, "Gentlemen were sureties for yeomen, and yeomen for gentlemen as executors of their wills; gentlemen did likewise with yeomen."[3] There was considerable mobility in the class structure during the era of Elizabeth and the early Stuarts, as the yeomen climbed upward in status. Bishop Hugh Latimer was a yeoman's son from Lancaster. Richard Baxter, another eminent churchman, came from a Shropshire farm. John Robinson himself was an example of the yeoman who through the disciplines of Cambridge developed into a leader of his time.[4]

Barnabie Rich explained the process of upward mobility when he wrote in 1609:

Gentlemen . . . do take their beginning in England, after this manner in our times. Whosoever studieth the lawes of the realme, who so abideth in the universities (giving his mind to his books) or professeth physicke and the liberall sciences, or beside his service in the roome of a capteine in the warres (or good Counsell given at home, whereby his commonwealth is benefitted) can live without manuell labour, and thereto is able and will beare the port, charge and countenance of a gentleman, he shall (for monie have a cote and armes bestowed upon him by heralds who in the charter of the same doo of custome pretend antiquitie and service . . .) and thereunto being made so good cheape, be called master, which is the title that men give to esquires and gentlemen.[5]

Yeomen like John Robinson, Senior and Junior, formed a vital part of the British life that nourished Puritan religion. "They also made the most significant and enduring contribution to the settling of the colonies in America."[6]

Farm houses of the time were usually constructed of timber and plaster and had thatch roofs. With the coming of the Elizabethan era the more prosperous people built brick and stone houses with tile roofs. The main room, often called the hall or

Lincoln Cathedral (begun c. 1074)—as it looked in the seventeenth century

keeping room, was the living and dining area. Its large fireplace for heating and cooking was equipped with crane, pot-hooks, spits, andirons, tongs, iron and copper pots and kettles. Here the family ate with the hired help, held their Bible readings, and enjoyed sociability with their neighbors. There was usually a long trestle table with joint stools and benches, and a cupboard where the pewter and silver mugs, trenchers, and bowls were displayed.

Chimneyed fireplaces were among Elizabethan innovations that helped carry smoke outside dwellings and provide more comfort. Window glass was another improvement that helped lighten the dark confines of damp, cool homes. People were required by law to provide their own firewood, and John had to perform his stint with the axe in the woods and at the chopping block. In nearby Scrooby Manor, a short distance from Sturton le Steeple, all farmers were required by a court order to "prepare fuel for the winter" during the summer season. In 1622 two husbandmen failed in this responsibility and were fined 6s 8d payable to the lord of the manor.[7]

Bread was the basic food, with meat the second staple. The popular meats were beef, mutton, pork, poultry, rabbit, and fish. For dessert there were sweets and cheeses. The chief meal of the day was at noon, with a light supper at night.

The parlor held the best bed and was also used as a living room. The other bedrooms had two or three beds each, along with chests for storage of clothing, bedding, and valuables. There were straw beds and feather beds, bolsters and pillows, blankets and quilts. Some homes boasted a kitchen and the better farms had an aggregation of out buildings: barns for animals, crops, and farming equipment; dairy house for churning butter and making cheese; malthouse for the preparation of beer and cider; and bakehouse where the flour, dough box, and baking equipment were kept.[8]

John Robinson, Senior read daily to his assembled family from the Geneva, or Breeches Bible, so called because the translators put pants rather than fig leaves on Adam in the creation account in the book of Genesis. The use of the Bible strengthened family ties as the household listened to the moving words of adventure, beauty, and uplift in their own daily vernacular. The head of the family was expected to play the role of teacher to his children and his servants. The youthful listeners heard and drew into their subconscious the ethics of the Great Book which formed the basis for their moral judgment, while providing them with a fund of common knowledge and tutelage in literary style. We understand why Puritan William Gouge called the family "a little church and a little commonwealth."[9]

The Geneva Bible appealed to the people because it could be held in the hands of the reader; it was small and portable. It was printed in two columns, divided into verses, and provided illustrations, maps, and pithy and provocative marginal notes from the Calvinist translators. It reached England soon after the publication of Henry VIII's Great Bible and was adopted by many Puritans and by the vanguard who led the way to the New World. It was a new and revealing experience to read in their own tongue

SKETCH MAP OF
THE DISTRICT ROUND
ROBINSON'S ENGLISH HOME

profound and eternal truths that they could appropriate into their own daily lives. This direct experience with God provided new motivation for them.

Open Bibles were spread out on the counters of shops and their words discussed in the market place and on the street. Groups assembled in countless cottages to listen to readings from the newly opened treasure house of inspiration by the light of betty lamps, reed lamps, and the flicker of hearth fires. These Bible gatherings inspired thousands of people in the quest for the meaning of life. These meetings were comparable in a way with the integrating influence of television in twentieth-century life, forming a new cohesiveness in Britain.

The yeoman was a businessman who journeyed to country fairs and town markets to buy and sell cattle, oxen, horses, sheep, and pigs, and to dispose of his grain, hay, and vegetables. John Robinson must have joined his father on some of these expeditions and perhaps he visited the ancient Lincolnshire seaport of Boston on the River Witham to the south. St. Botolph founded a monastery there in 654. It was destroyed by the Danes, rebuilt and named St. Botolph's Town, and later Boston. Markets were held here frequently and the May pleasure fair brought visitors from all over East Anglia. As they rattled along in their carts over dirt roads they spied the high tower of Stump Church, the landmark which had long guided travelers across the fens and sailing ships up the Wash. The lad from Sturton le Steeple no doubt peered into the stone prison cells in the ancient Guildhall, where he was in later years to be locked up by the soldiers of James I.

Travel was primarily by horseback and wagon. Stagecoaches had not yet been developed. There were a few four-wheel, lumbering carriages. The roads were hazardous, and the ancient Roman ways were still the best. The others were full of ruts and potholes, dusty in dry weather and boggy when the rains came. Sloughs often conquered the carriage or wagon and a farmer would have to be called with his oxen to get the equipage on the road again.

Lincoln was some ten miles away, the dignified old city with its cathedral, majestic in its golden oolite stone from Lincoln heath. If John studied here as a boy, which is probable, he grew attached to the booming voice of Great Tom, the five-ton giant bell in the Great Tower, which had been erected in 1307. He strolled in the Close, watching the dignitaries in their sable cloaks and gaiters come and go about the chapter houses, the library, and the episcopal palace, and passed reverently under the Great Central Tower into the dim splendor of the cathedral.

There was fabulous York some sixty miles to the north. The old Roman city at the junction of the Ouse and the Foss was fortified by high walls. It was an adventure to pass through one of the four great "bars," to climb up a stone stairway and to walk the wall, gazing down on the palaces and halls below, and to watch sun and shadow play upon the mighty Minster. Once an inland port of the wool industry, there were countless ancient houses and shops along its narrow and crooked streets.

It was a rich and romantic part of the homeland, the low-lying fens and venerable wolds, a historic spot in which to live and grow into appreciation of the English heritage. The country fairs were highlights in John's boyhood. They boasted puppet shows, performing animals, and jugglers. Nicholas Breton wrote in 1618 of the country dances:

> At our meetings on the holidays between our lads and the wenches, such true mirth at honest meetings, such dancing on the green, in the market-house or about the maypole, where the young folks smiling kiss at every turning and the old folks checking (choking, closing breath) with laughing at their children when dancing for the garland, playing at stoolball for a tansy and a banquet of curds and cream, with a cup of old nappy ale.[10]

Movable stages and pageant carts were used by craft guilds for performance of miracle plays at Whitsuntide and the feast of Corpus Christi.

The Elizabethan age led the world in music as in poetry. Among the creators of song were Morley, Byrd, Giles Farnaby,

Church of St. Peter and St. Paul, Sturton le Steeple—John Robinson's childhood church

10

Orlando Gibbons, Weelkes, and Wilbye. Tudor and Elizabethan England were rich in folk songs.[11]

> Tinkers sang catches; milkmaids sang ballads; carters whistled; each trade, and even beggars had their special songs; the bass-viol hung in the drawing-room for the amusement of waiting visitors; and the lute, the cittern, and virginals, for the amusement of waiting customers, were the necessary furniture of the barber's shop. They had music at dinner, music at supper; music at weddings, music at funerals; music at night, music at dawn; music at work, music at play.[12]

The Industrial Revolution was bringing changes even in this early era. Some yeomen families worked in the cloth industries, bringing wool to their homes where they spun and wove it. The "putting out system" supplied wool for the simpler processes of making textiles, such as sorting, carding, and spinning.[13] Fulling mills sprang up by the streams. East England was a sheep growing center. For years wool had been shipped to Flanders for manufacture into cloth. As Low Country immigrants crossed over, a native cloth-making industry started up. It is estimated that in 1550 there were 150,000 sheep in East Anglia alone. During Elizabeth's reign farmers enjoyed a slightly higher level of prosperity. The villages expanded and homes improved.

The manufacture of wool and clothing flourished along with trade in grain, butter and eggs, the making of sugar, soap, and paper, the mining of coal, salt, and the production of iron, copper, and brass. The population was swelling in nearby York. Norwich, also close at hand, was growing. It had become the major center of the cloth trade with the influx of refugees from the Low Countries who sought escape from the tyranny of Spain on the continent.

Thomas Fuller wrote that

> the yeomanry is an estate of people almost peculiar to England. France and Italy are like a die which hath no points between sink and ace, nobility and peasantry. . . . The yeoman wears russet clothes, but makes golden payment, having tin in his buttons and silver in his pocket. . . . In his own country he is a main man in Juries. He seldom goes far abroad, and his credit stretches further than his travels. He goes not to London, but *se-defendendo*, to save himself a fine, being returned of a Jury, where seeing the King once, he prays for him ever afterwards.[14]

New vistas of economic opportunity offered higher income to yeomen households, the possibility of better education for their children, and the enjoyment of new comforts. The country parson, William Harrison, wrote in 1577 about the improvements in daily living that had taken place since his father's time "not only among the nobility and gentry but likewise of the lowest sort in the places of our south country." He said that old men in his village "noted three things to be maruellouslie altered in England within their sound remembrance."[15]

One was the introduction of household chimneys which afforded release from the former smoke-haunted status of the English cottage. Second, there were better sleeping accommodations. In place of the flock-bed stuffed with coarse wool with a sack of chaff for a bolster, the farmer now enjoyed feather beds, sheets, and pillows.

The third area of progress was in table furnishings. Where the fathers had eaten with spoons from wooden chargers, the sons used pewter plates, poringers, and tankards, and even pieces of silver.

The wills of John Robinson's father and mother reveal a substantial yeoman estate. His mother, Ann, left to John

> all the pailes, toupes, gates and all fences round about the messuage (dwelling and out houses) or Toftstead (homestead) wherein I now dwell with all and singular rackes and maingers beastes, houses and plowhows with all the glasse about the said messuage to remain and be to him and his heirs forever.[16]

Mention of "the glasse about the messuage" is noteworthy. It indicates that the Robinsons had window glass in their house around 1600. This is significant because we know that glass was expensive and highly valued.

Judging from the will of her mother, Eleanor White, Bridget Robinson (the wife of John), came from a prosperous home. This meticulously drawn will, dated April 7, 1599 (transcribed into modern English), is pertinent to our story. It affords insight into the furnishings of a 1600 village home and the implements of farming and animal husbandry as well as the cultural standards of this family. Linen tablecloths and napkins were plentiful. Silk curtains, decorative valances, needlepoint, pewter, silver, and books indicate education and refinement.

> I give to my daughter, Janie White, over and besides the portion given her by her father, 32 pounds, 5 shillings, 7 pence, and a like amount in like terms to my daughter, Frances White.
>
> To my son, Charles White, four standing bedsteads, four covered stools of one sort, four cushions suitable, one cupboard in the best chamber and another cupboard in the great chamber, two tables with their frames and two joined chairs there; one great chest in my own chamber. All the tables, cupboards, stools and forms in the Hall, a valence of needlework, five silk curtains, two of my best feather beds, two bolsters, two pair of fustian pillows, two good mattresses, two pair of my best blankets, my best counterpoint with three of my best coverlets, six pair of linen sheets and six pair of pillow cases marked with a C, two dozen of table napkins, two broad table cloths, two cupboard cloths, my marriage ring, my silver salt, one bowl, one gilt pepper cellar, and six silver spoons, all his father's books, all my brass and my pewter with earthenware, all boards and cupboards in the kitchen and buttery, all my

household implements of husbandry, implements belonging to the stable, to the brewhouse, to the backhouse, kilnehouse, oxhouse and cowhouse.

Item: all the rest of the benefit and yearly profit of my lease at Muskham not given by my husband I give and bequeath to my three sons, Thomas, Roger and Edward, whereof my will is that as every of my said sons shall accomplish the age of 13 years 20 pounds shall be bestowed toward the binding of them as apprentices at London in sure good places . . . if my Executors and Supervisors shall think them fit to be put for apprentices and if not then the said money to be bestowed for their best advantage . . . till they come to 20 years of age.

Item: I give to my said three sons, Thomas, Roger and Edward, besides all the benefit of my lease of Muskham every one of them 20 pounds to be put forth by my executors to their best profit and advantage as they shall accomplish their several ages of fifteen years.

Item: I give to my son, Legatt, and his wife (Catherine) 10 pounds between them and to their daughter, Marie Legatt, 10 pounds which I will shall be put forth for her best advantage when she shall come to her age of 10 years . . . to my five youngest children, Thomas, Roger, Edward, Janie and Francis, 11 pounds, 10 shillings a year out of my lease at Beauvale for 7 years after my death.

Item: To my daughter, Legatt, two pair of linen sheets, one long needlework cushion and two pair of pillow cases in full satisfaction of her child's portion.

Item: I give to my daughter, Bridget, 50 pounds in money, 1 pair of linen sheets, 1 pair pillow cases, 2 tablecloths, 1 long needlework cushion, a dozen napkins, 2 linen towels, and my new silver bowl . . . to my daughter, Janie, one silver spoon, 2 pair of linen sheets, and 2 pair of pillow cases . . . to my daughter, Francis, one silver spoon gilt, 1 pair linen sheets and 2 pair pillow cases.

Item: I will that portion given to my daughter, Janie, by her father's will and mine shall be paid within one year after my death and put forth to her best profit and advantage till her marriage or full age of 21 years . . . of the profit I do allot 5 pounds yearly for her maintenance and the rest to go forward to the increase of her portion.

Francis her full portion shall be paid within one year next after my death to my son, Legatt, to her use if his wife be then living unto whom I commit the bringing up of said daughter. (I allot) 5 pounds yearly for her bringing up and maintenance (the balance was to go forward).

I bequeath to my brother, William Smith, 5 pounds, 12 shillings, 3 pence to be paid within one year after my death. If he depart this life before receipt thereof, then I will it shall be equally divided among his children.

Item: I give to my sister (Elizabeth) Saltmarshe one hooped gold ring . . . to my nephew, Thomas Disney 20 shillings in money . . . to every one of my sister Mounson's children 5 shillings a piece . . . at their several ages of 21 years . . . to my servant, Anthony, 11 shillings in money . . . every one of my other servants 1 shilling 5 pence a piece, to the poor of Sturton 10 shillings . . . every one of my god children 1 shilling 5 pence . . . to my cousin, Robert Poole, my best gelding or else in money 5 pounds 12 shillings 3 pence . . . my cousin, Thomas Leacock 10 shillings.[17]

Some of these possessions came to Bridget and John after their marriage. A few years later they invested part of their inheritance in the purchase of the Green Gate house in Leyden which was to become the center of the Pilgrim community there.

The Pilgrims have often been presented as simple, humble, and ignorant people who were divorced from the culture of their time. In contradiction, the records indicate that the nucleus of the Pilgrim community came from an enlightened area of England, where they were part of the intellectual and cultural ferment of the Elizabethan period. They were close to the amenities of Lincoln, Boston, York, and within the arc of influence that emanated from Cambridge. They were exposed to the resurgence of religious inquiry, the flowering of music and letters, and the "intense and electric experience of a young people (the British nation) coming to maturity, with a new world opening out before them, not only across the seas, but in the mind."[18]

John and Bridget Robinson grew up in Nottinghamshire where they had considerable security and comfort. This background, combined with John's attractive personality and university training, led to the gathering around them of men of comparable social and intellectual outlook like John Carver, William Brewster, William Bradford, Edward Winslow, and Samuel Fuller, who were to develop into the leaders of the Leyden-Plimoth community.

The average yeoman and his household still battled economic hardship but improvement was underway. Thomas Wilson recorded in 1601:

I know many yeomen in divers places of England which are able yearly to spend betwixt three or five hundred pounds yearly by the Lands and Leases and some twice and some thrice as much; but my young masters the sons of such, not content with their states of their fathers to be counted yeoman and called John or Robert (such an one), but must skip into his velvet breeches and silken doublet and, getting to be admitted into some Inn of Court or Chancery, must ever after think scorn to be called any other than gentleman.[19]

John Robinson was nurtured in a healthy environment. He shared with his father and the hired help in the plowing, fertilizing, harrowing, and planting, in the care of the orchard, vegetable garden, meadows, and stables, and in the feeding of their cattle, sheep, and pigs. He worked in the brewhouse and the dairy house just off the kitchen, at the woodpile and the fireplace, at the well, and on the wagons and the plows in the sheds. He helped his mother and sisters make butter, cheese, and beer, and weed the knot garden where intricate patterns of flowers were nurtured. (William Harrison listed in 1577 three hundred different varieties of blossoms in his village plot.)

John must have joined in the rogation week tradition, following the village dignitaries in their annual walk around the boundaries of Sturton. In later years he mentioned these "parishional assemblies gathered by their parish perambulation."[20] In the autumn there was the excitement of harvest. "From June to October every hand was occupied and every back was bent. These were the decisive months for the whole populations in the damp northern climate, with its one harvest."[21]

When the patchwork fields were transformed by the golden brown of barley and wheat and the orchards were heavy with fruit, the ingathering of the crops enlivened the countryside. A German visitor wrote of the harvest festivals he observed in England in 1598:

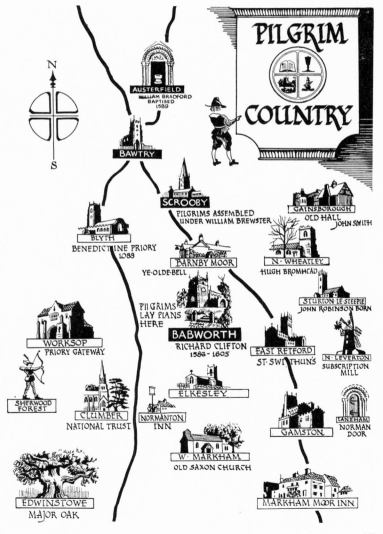

15

As we were returning to our inn we happened to meet some country people celebrating their Harvest-Home; their last load of corn they crown with flowers . . . . They keep moving about, while men and women, men and maidservants, riding through the streets in the cart, shout as loud as they can till they arrive at the barn.[22]

Sturton le Steeple was a small, self-contained and self-sustaining community, an island in Nottinghamshire,

and the countryside was still the great universal provider which came almost to one's door. Its fields supplied food; its forest and trees, firewood and the raw material for furniture; its clay or stone provided houses. Village men were not farmers or carpenters or builders, they were more often than not all three rolled into one. A man could turn a hand at almost anything, just as his wife could cook, bake, doctor; brew home beer, wine, medicine; sew, spin and embroider; look after hens and the dairy; launder; raise vegetables and flowers, and make her own beauty aids.[23]

This "Pilgrim country" was a good training ground for the men and women who were to shift for themselves on the rugged shores of New England where they would be forced to fell and hew trees, frame cottages, thatch roofs, dig, plant and harvest, spin flax and wool, dye yarn, and concoct medical recipes from their herb gardens.

There were daily walks for John along country lanes to visit his tutor at the vicarage; and on Sundays contemplative moments inside the cool of the great stone Church of St. Peter and St. Paul. There were games to be played like stool ball, skittles, shuttlecock, tossing the bar, throwing the hammer, putting the weight, wrestling, and practice at archery.

During the reign of Henry VIII laws were enacted to promote the practice of shooting with the long bow. Every male subject was obliged to exercise himself with this weapon and to keep a bow and arrows in his home at all times. Only the handicapped and aged were exempt from this requirement. Fathers and guardians were ordered to teach their boys this ancient art and to train them from the age of seven years.[24]

Football was played by groups of varying size without rules or referees, but due to its roughness it was forbidden by law. Sir Thomas Elyet wrote in 1531 that it "is nothyng but beastely fury and extreme violence, whereof procedeth hurte, and consequently rancour and malice do remayne with them that be wounded."[25]

John's farmhouse was near the banks of the Trent. He fished its waters from his dory. He sailed on expeditions north toward the Humber and the great North Sea. He followed the meandering streams to the Witham and possibly on to Boston and the Wash, where he watched wave-beaten ships from foreign ports unload their cargo. He was within walking distance of Scrooby, Austerfield, and Babworth, the "Pilgrim towns," where later he was to help shape the future of two communities in the Netherlands and in the New World.

The vale of the Trent was rich in corn and cattle and the fenland was like an English Holland, abounding in geese and duck, pheasant, partridge, quail, and woodcock. As John explored on horseback the nearby areas of Lincolnshire, Nottinghamshire, and Yorkshire, he learned the pleasant sounds of the countryside: the creak of wagon wheels on narrow dirt roads set between hawthorne hedges, the whipping canvas of windmill sails, the shrill of water fowl, and the baying of hounds which ranged the fields and woods.

His boyhood was a time of resurgent faith in England. The fears which had brooded so long over the country that the Spanish invasion would come any day, that a Roman Catholic rebellion would break out, or that Elizabeth I, who came to the throne in 1558, would be assassinated, were shattered. The tension was broken with the defeat of the Armada. The queen now gave her attention to the unification of the country.

Seventeenth-century English sports—archery, fowling and fishing, and tennis

The new philosophy calls all in doubt,
The element of fire is quite put out;
The sun is lost and the earth, and no man's wit
Can well direct him where to look for it.
And freely men confess that this world's spent,
When in the planets and the firmament
They seek so many new; they see that this
Is crumbled out again to his atomies.
—John Donne

2 "THE NEW PHILOSOPHY CALLS ALL IN DOUBT"

A number of young men from the Sturton le Steeple area had turned their faces toward the citadel of learning at Cambridge: John Smith, a neighbor, the Nevilles from North Leverton, Anthony Hickman of Gainsborough, and Roger and Francis Manners, sons of the late Earl of Rutland, were enrolled at Corpus Christi College there. John Robinson set out for Cambridge at the age of sixteen and matriculated April 9, 1592 at Corpus Christi. The admissions book records: "*Johannes Robinson Eboracensis Admissus est. Tutore Mro Jegon.*" He was listed under "*Sizatores.*" A sizar was a student who worked for his college expenses. His tutor was Thomas Jegon, a brother of John Jegon, who was the master of Corpus Christi College.[1]

The new student from Sturton le Steeple considered the university a buzzing confusion. There were some 1,500 students in a city of 6,500 residents. For the first weeks he was lost amid the new surroundings and the sophistication of the famous intellectual center. His college had been founded in 1352 by funds contributed by two Cambridge guilds: the Guild of Corpus Christi and the Guild of the Blessed Virgin. During the evil days when the Black Death was claiming many lives, guild members established a college where masses would be sung by the students for their departed souls and so expedite their speedy departure from purgatory. Corpus Christi was fifth in age among fifteen colleges. It was also called Benet or Benedict because of the Church of St. Benedict which adjoined it and served as the chapel.

In 1573 there were 91 members in Corpus Christi, and in 1621 there were 140. Among the eminent graduates were Nicholas Bacon, father of Francis Bacon; Matthew Parker, Archbishop of Canterbury; Dr. John Copcot; and Thomas Cavendish, who returned in 1588 from a voyage around the world with his crew clad in silk and his top mast gleaming with cloth of gold. Christopher Marlowe went up to Corpus Christi where he took his M.A. in 1587. John Fletcher, the poet, son of the Bishop of London, entered Corpus Christi in 1591.

The master of each college was surrounded by senior and junior fellows who administered property, budget, and curriculum and shared in the teaching. Any fellow who married was required to resign his fellowship. Each fellow was assigned a small group of pupils, and in many cases he took charge of the finances of his pupils and paid their bills to the college and the tradesmen. The

COLLEGIUM CORPORIS CHRISTI & BEATÆ MARIÆ apud CANTA

Viro Venerabili, Pietate
& Morum Candore & omni
Eruditionis genere Spectati
ssimo D. THOMÆ TENISON
S.T.P. Sereniss. Regiæ Ma:tis
Sacris, Parochiæ S. Martini
juxta agros Pastori Vigilan
tissimo, hujus Collegij non
ita pridem Socio, hanc
delineationem D.D.C.Q.
Tho: Logan.

A. *Capella.*
B. *Bibliotheca.*
C. *Refectorium.*
D. *Culina.*
E. *Magistri Hospitium.*

R. Loggan delin: sculp: Oxonij S.R.M.

Domus hæc perantiqua à duabus (uti vocant) Gildis, et nomen et Originem duxit. Ædem condiderunt, utriusq; Gildæ Fratres Anno 1351; proprijs quidem sumptibus, auspicijs
instituta, Latitudine et Tenementis aliquammultis, in Vico et Agro Cantab: sitis, dotarunt. Inter hosce Fundatores maxime claruerunt Ioh. de Cantabrigia Miles, unus è Regij Iusticiarij, et Hen.
tores, quosq; pia gratia; quâ decet, Memoria recolit; Scil. Eliz: de Bello Campo, Thomæ de Brotherton, Edwardi 1:mi filij natu min: et Norf. Ducis, Conjug: et Matt: Parker Cant: Arch: Qui præter 2 Societ: et 4 Schu
mag: sui: Aud: et Fran: Perulamij, magni Scientiaru Instauratoris, Patr: Egregij; Rog: Mannors Reginæ Eliz: à Cubic: et prænob: Rutlandiæ Comiti prosapiâ Oriundum, Ioan: Bowright S.T.P. Ioan: Mees Leonar: Cuns.
bor: Archiepiscopum. Qui fere omnes, aut Soc: aut Alumnorum nominibus hujus Coll: Album ornavere Viros, insuper, tulit egregios, præter memoratos Præmles, Tho: Goetherick Elicnsem, Angl: Cancellar.
Episc: Norvic: Pet: Gunning Eliens: Episcopos, præterea, inter Lumina et ornamenta hujus Collegij numerandi sunt viri in civil: Reip: Negot: aquud: celebres, dicti Cancellarij: Rog: Manne
vrinelli: conscripti, Dux, Gills: Gerard Baro de Bromley, Tho: Howard de Escrick, D. Guil: Paston, Rob: Com: Yrimuthæ Pater, Hinc deniq; prodiere, viri scriptis histus, Rob: Dallington Miles Hospitij Suttoniani ma:
sæculi ingeniorum adeo feracis; Qui, quod vulgò noti sint, et uberiores fructus indies orbi Literario spondeant, hoc Ære non inciduntur: quod superest, sunt in dicto Coll: 1. Mag: 12 Soc:

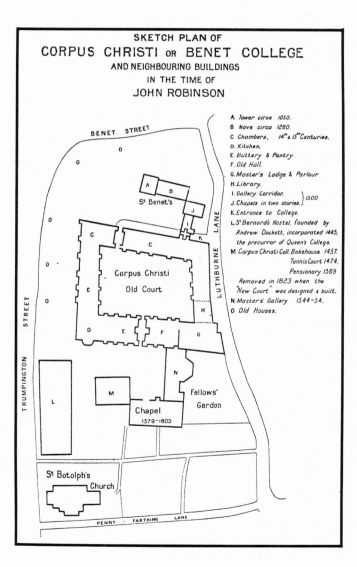

five or six of his satellites made up his company. He slept in the large room, now used as the students' sitting room, with his protégés on trundle beds underneath and around him. The small rooms that are now the bedrooms were then used for study. In this manner some 150 could be housed in one small quad. The fellows and undergraduates dined in the great hall, the fellows at the high table on a dais, and the others at tables below.

In Robinson's time the student composition was changing. More sons of the gentry and nobility appeared in the quads. They had become more numerous than any group except sons of the clergy. Students from the families of tradesmen and yeomen became "gentlemen" automatically on taking a degree.

Books at Cambridge were rare and costly. Many volumes were chained to library lecterns or bookstands for protection. Those that could be taken to private rooms were kept in chests with two locks—one key usually held by the master and the other by the senior dean.

Curriculum emphasis was on logic and rhetoric. The course in logic consisted of expositions by Aristotle and his school as developed in the universities of the Middle Ages. Rhetoric was based largely on the Latin of Quintilian and the Greek of Hermogenes of Tarsus. Scholars analyzed the orations of Cicero as models of style and the proper background for the statesman. The colleges were deeply concerned with theology, which was basic in all fields of learning.

Examinations were public declamations. Two candidates called sophisters debated each other in Latin before a critical audience who voted on their qualifications. Of one such disputation that took place between Samuel Collins and John Williams it was stated that "no greyhound did ever give hare more turn upon Newmarket heath than the replier with his subtleties gave to the respondent."[2]

At this period the Cambridge colleges were the chief center in England for creative thinking and liberal teaching. They were the breeding ground for the Puritan movement. A fellow Cantabrigian, William Ames, who in later years became a close associate of Robinson and the chief theologian of this group of Puritan scholars, wrote of their alma mater: "Cambridge is or should be, as an eye to all our land: for that the alterations that fall out there cannot but be felt in all parts."[3]

It is true that Oxford led Cambridge in the Middle Ages, but the Reformation bypassed Oxford while it brought fortune to Cambridge. The university to the east "lay open to the new winds blowing from Europe." Erasmus referred to three foundations of the New Learning there: Queen's, Christ's, and St. John's. Thomas More commented on the greater enthusiasm for the study of Greek at Cambridge.[4] Erasmus was invited to Queen's College and did what he could to win Cambridge to Renaissance scholarship. In 1540 Henry VIII founded professorships of divinity, Hebrew, Greek, medicine, and civil law. Cambridge suffered

(pages 20-21)
Corpus Christi College, Cambridge—a seventeenth-century print

a serious setback under Mary Tudor, but revived with the accession of Elizabeth and entered a new period of development.

The break with the church in Rome reinforced the interest of scholars in religious discussion. The divorce from papal authority demanded fresh thinking, reexamination of tradition, and a careful study of the continental scholars who were formulating Protestant thought.

Cambridge students were routed out of their beds at five A M for morning prayers. Breakfast at six consisted of a ha'penny loaf, butter, and beer. Tutors then struggled to guide their neophytes in the intricacies of Latin, Greek, and Hebrew. Latin was still the language of the scholar, and lectures were in Latin and apt to be dull.

Hebrew and Greek were relatively new subjects. They had been introduced into English education by Erasmus and Paulus Fagius who brought them over from the continent. Thus, John Robinson was initiated into study of the Old and New Testaments in their original tongues. The old books began to live with fresh

William Perkins (1558-1602)—Cambridge University Puritan scholar

meaning and significance. This new method of scholarly biblical research formed the core of the Puritan awakening and gave a unique academic quality to Puritan writings and teaching.

Following the tutorials there were general lectures. Dinner was at eleven A.M. with beef or mutton sometimes, and often "a few porage made of the brothe of the same byfe, wyth salte and otemell, nothynge els." Sizar Robinson served his tutor first and then ate his meals. In the afternoon there were declamations and disputes on set subjects and other lectures on rhetoric and philosophy. Then the gownsmen enjoyed free time for games like quoits or tennis. Corpus Christi was celebrated for its bowling green. The existence of a tennis court is shown in Loggan's view of the campus about 1688.

Supper at five in the evening was a frugal repast with tansy or pudding followed by evening prayers. The monastic diet was supplemented by "bevers" and other snacks during the course of the day. The formal routine of pedagogy was eased during the evening hours by uninhibited discussions in the tongue of Mother England. At other times students were expected to speak in Latin. College bedtime was nine P.M. from Michelmas to Easter and ten P.M. from Easter to Michelmas. Discipline was strict. Special permission was required for a student to leave the premises of his college unless he was a B.A. of a year's standing, and then he could go only in the company of a tutor or master of arts.

There were no fires in the rooms except in the college halls. Master Thomas Lever of St. Johns proposed a half hour's walk or run as the only remedy against the shivering chill that permeated the stone buildings. Martin Bucer, who came to Cambridge as Regius Professor of Divinity under Edward VI, testified that the town was the coldest spot in all England. So the king presented him with a German stove to alleviate his hardships and make his sojourn more bearable.

Considerable moral fiber was demanded of the sizar if he was to stand up under his menial tasks. Sizar John must awaken his tutor for morning chapel, serve his meals, polish his boots, and clean his lodgings. Fetching water, sweeping, scrubbing, and bed-making left him little time for leisure. John also accompanied his tutor to the playing fields to attend him at a game of quoits or field out for him at tennis. During his rare free moments he strolled along the "backs," watching students punt on the "Cam," and was reminded of his quiet haunts beside the Trent. No doubt when lonely he sought refuge here as he endeavored to set in order his reactions to this complex new world.

There were no organized athletics at Cambridge. Exercise such as walking in the fields, jumping, running, bowls, pitching the bar, and archery were deemed an aid to health amid the "beastly air of Cambridge." Football was considered unscholarly and swimming was forbidden. In 1571 Dr. Whitgift, the vice chancellor and head of colleges, ruled that if any scholar should go into any river, pool, or other water in the county of Cambridge, by day or by night, to swim or wash, he should, if an undergraduate, be twice publicly whipped, and if a bachelor of arts, he should be put in the stocks in his college hall for a whole day and fined.[5]

Visits to bear-baitings, boxing matches, and cockfights were not permitted. Students were not allowed dogs or "fierce birds" or cards and dice except in moderation at Christmastime. Nevertheless, in the midst of the humdrum pursuit of learning there were interludes of levity. On one occasion Master Jegon punished the undergraduates for some minor offense. He made use of the fines collected to whitewash the refectory hall. One student pinned this verse on the bulletin board:

Dr. Jegon, Benet College Master
Brooke the Scholars' heads and gave the wall a plaister.
Whereupon Master Jegon wrote:
Knew I the wag that wrote these lines in Bravery,
I would commend him for his Wit, and beat him for his
　　Knavery.[6]

One Henry Pepper took part on May 28, 1600 in an open-air performance in the courtyard at the Black Bear Inn. He was charged with injudicious conduct. It is possible that John Robinson, who by that date had become dean of Corpus Christi, may have been involved in issuing this disciplinary statement:

Dominus Pepper was seen in an improper habit, having deformed locks of unseemly sight and great breeches undecent for a graduate scholar of orderly carriage. Therefore the said Pepper was commanded to appear presently and procure his hair to be cut and powled, and was suspended *ab omni gradu suscepto et suscipiendo.*[7]

University legislation required that the quad chambermaids must not be under fifty years of age. Another rule decreed that when royal visits took place there was to be no humming, hawking, whistling, hissing, laughing, stamping, or knocking on the part of the student body.

London was some fifty miles away. Thomas Hobson, the jobber, made his weekly trips over the road, his cart loaded with parcels and messages. Riders on horses rented from his stable often rode beside him on their way to the metropolis, and Robinson must have traveled south to see some of the sights of the great gray mother of the Thames.

From the day John Robinson reached college he was exposed to Puritan influences. It is doubtful if they proved radical departures to him since he was familiar with ideas of revolt in his home and in the church life of the Basset-Lawe Country. However, for eleven years he was to be an observer and contender on this battlefield where advanced ideas of Protestantism and Puritanism were debated and forged.

Under the pressure to reform, traditional religious discipline had been relaxing. The old rules regarding participation in communion and public prayers were not as strictly enforced. There were rumblings of rebellion against the wearing of vestments which for decades had been the approved academic costume. As early as 1565, when Dr. Longworth, the master of St. John's, was not in residence, some 300 of his students came to chapel without their hoods and surplices. He did not reprimand them and for a time the faculty permitted them to attend classes unsurpliced.

About this same period Thomas Cartwright led Trinity in a revolt against vestments. One report on his college stated that "they lean or sit or kneel at prayers, every man in a several position as he pleases: at the name of Jesus very few will bow: and when the Creed is repeated, many of the boys, by some men's directions, turn to the west door."[8] The controversy inspired a petition to Queen Elizabeth I which prayed that "they might not be forced to receive a Popish ceremony which they had laid aside." But the queen did not like the tone of Cambridge and sent back a sharp negative. Bolder members of the faculty stated that they were in danger of losing students if this obnoxious custom was emphasized: "They feared religion and learning would suffer very much by rigour and imposition."[9] But her royal highness ordered that vestments must be preserved.

There was also objection to the stained-glass windows in the chapels that contained requests for prayers for the souls of the dead. The offending windows were condemned as remnants of superstition and in some colleges they were removed.

Thomas Cartwright was forced to retire from Cambridge for a time due to the hostility of the queen over his opposition to vestments and other outgrown symbols. He returned, after a brief exile, in 1569 as Lady Margaret Professor of Divinity. He advocated reform of the Established Church based upon conformity to the scriptures. Students were enthusiastic over his lectures, and his ideas spread to other colleges and disturbed their masters. John Whitgift, master of Trinity and soon to become archbishop, found his college "distempered with many opinions, which Mr. Cartwright lately returned from beyond the seas, had raised therein."[10]

During Master Whitgift's absence, Thomas Cartwright and two of his followers gave three sermons in one day in the chapel "so vehemently inveighing against the ceremonies of the church." The result was that at evening prayers all the scholars except three cast off their surplices "as an abominable relic of superstition." The lectures and sermons of Whitgift were not well attended because the students flocked after Cartwright. When he preached at St. Mary's "the clerk thereof was fain to take down the windows in the church." Consequently Whitgift forbade Cartwright to read public lectures and expelled him from the university in 1571.

The tradition of revolt was well established by Robinson's time. The rebel Robert Browne had matriculated at Corpus Christi during the eventful years of the Cartwright controversy. Browne was an outspoken advocate of the right of private judgment and carried the teachings of Cartwright to a logical conclusion. He could not go along with the moderate Puritans who hoped to bring the church up to their views and were therefore willing to accept the union of church and state. Browne was a Separatist who broke with the Established Church because he felt that it was not a true church. The Church of England at that time included all baptized people however irreligious they might be. The true church, he argued, should be composed only of good Christian people.

Parliament passed a severe law in 1582 making it treason to worship in any way except in accord with the Church of England. The penalty was death. Anyone who attended his own religious gathering was a traitor to the queen because he rejected her supremacy in the church. As a result Robert Browne, along with numerous others, was arrested.

"Trouble-Church" Browne was a fellow alumnus of Robinson's. The young student heard stories of this predecessor at Corpus Christi, about his writings, imprisonment (he was jailed thirty-two times), and exile in Holland. He read *A True Confession of Faith of the Brownists*, published in 1596, which recorded the persecution waged against these rebels:

> We have been further miserably entreated by the Prelates and chief of the Clergy: some of us cast into most vile and noisome prisons and dungeons, laden with irons, and there, without all pity, detained many years, no man remembering our affliction: until our God releases some of us out of their cruel hands by death, as the Cities of London, Norwich, Gloucester, Bury, and many other places of the land can testify. Yet here the malice of Satan stayed not itself, but raised up against us a more grievous persecution, even unto the violent death of some, and lamentable exile of us all . . . . So that through their barbarous cruelty 24 souls have perished in their prisons, within the City of London only (besides other places of the land). . . . For all this, yet were not these savage men satisfied, though blood in abundance ran out of their wide mouths, but they procured certain of us (after many years imprisonment) to be indicted, arraigned, condemned, and hanged as felons. Henry Barrowe, John Greenwood and John Penry, whose particular examinations arraignments and manner of execution . . . would make thy heart to bleed, considering their unchristian and unnatural usage.[11]

Heated disputation and fiery sermons fomented controversy in the college halls. When Queen Elizabeth received word of continued dissent at the university she notified Archbishop Whitgift that she held the final authority in the church. She "misliked much that any allowance had been given by his Grace and the rest of any such points to be disputed, being a matter tender and dangerous to weak, ignorant minds."[12]

The "weak, ignorant minds" did not, however, retreat before royal authority. Cambridge continued to write, discuss, and argue. Robinson and his contemporaries were concerned with weighty questions, with thorny theological issues like election, justification, and the differences between Roman Catholic and Protestant doctrine. John read the writings of the famous alumni, Henry

CANTEBRIGIA, o:
pulentiſſimi Angliæ Reg:
ni, vrbs celeberrimi nomi:
nis, ab Academiæ condi:
tore Cantabro, cognomi:
nata: A Granta, fluuio
vicino, Cairgrant; Sax:
onib. Graunteceſtre, et
Grantebrige, iam olim
nuncupata.

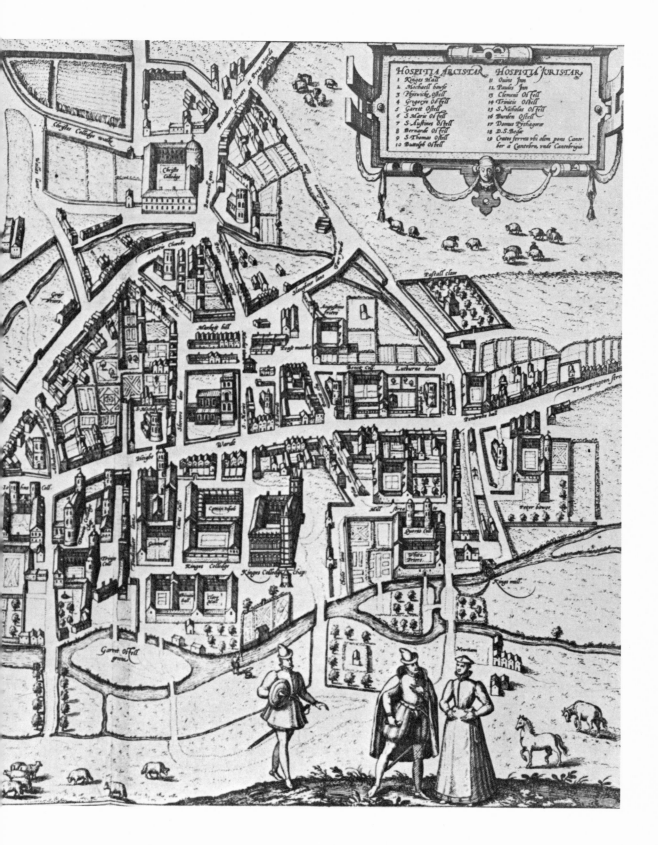

Barrowe and John Greenwood, who had been held as prisoners of Queen Elizabeth in the London Clink. Barrowe, a graduate of Clare College, a man of means and social standing, was a member of Gray's Inn. Although a worldly sort of fellow, he had been drawn to the Puritan position. When John Greenwood, about ten years his junior at Corpus Christi, was arrested in 1586 while holding a private conventicle in London, the lawyer decided to pay him a visit in the Clink. The jailer admitted Barrowe and then held him there on the orders of Archbishop Whitgift.

Henry Barrowe was one of the "hot brains." When he was summoned before the Privy Council in 1588 he was asked if he knew the Bishop of London. He replied, "I know him not as a bishop, but as a wolf, a bloody persecutor, and an apostate." He stated that the Archbishop of Canterbury "was a monster, a miserable compound . . . neither ecclesiastical nor civil—even the second Beast that is spoken of in the Revelations."

Why should our adversaries wish to persuade the civil magistrates to deal with us by the *sword* and not by the *Word*, by prisons and not by persuasions? As for dungeons, irons, close prison, torment, hunger, cold, want of means to maintain families—these *may* cause some to make shipwreck of a good conscience, or to lose their life, but they are not fit ways to persuade honest men to any truth or dissuade them from errours.[13]

Barrowe and Greenwood were confined in various London prisons for years. Together they wrote and laid down their demands for democracy and self-government. Barrowe penned scathing criticisms of the church and its clergy. The Church of England, he said, was a false church, which he felt it was his duty to desert. Hence, he became one of the most radical of the Separatists.[14]

Barrowe and Greenwood were summoned before the prelates of the church. As Barrowe was being questioned by a group of high churchmen, Whitgift shouted at him: "Where is his keeper? You shall not prattle here. Away with him. Clap him up close. Let not man go to him. I will make him tell another tale ere I have done with him." Barrowe and Greenwood were sentenced to death only to have their execution date postponed that they might endure more persecution by Canterbury.

These two prisoners worked with John Penry, the fiery Welshman, who wrote tracts against the established order. Penry was a classmate of William Brewster, who was to become Robinson's close friend, at Peterhouse College. Under the influence of the Geneva reformers at Cambridge he was converted from Roman Catholicism. While laboring with the Welsh church he was depressed over the condition of his people, and addressed an appeal to Parliament asking for aid in carrying religion to Wales: "The livings are nearly all impropriate, with no preachers but ignorant and unlearned ministers. Seldom or never is there evening

(pages 28-29)
Cambridge University—a 1599 print

30

prayer." He proposed that the numerous Church of England clergy who were idling at their posts be sent to Wales to do a little genuine work.

Archbishop Whitgift accused him of heresy: "I tell thee, it is a heresy, and thou shalt recant it as a heresy."

"Never, God willing, so long as I live!" Penry replied.

Haunted and imprisoned because of his bold pamphlets on reform he wrote: "Truth, being found, hold it we must, defend it we must! . . . No truth can be traitorous unto that state or any prince or potentate."

He was in prison when Barrowe and Greenwood were hanged April 6, 1593. Within the shadow of death he recorded: "Imprisonment, yea death itself, are no meet weapons to convince the conscience grounded upon the word of the Lord."[15] He was hanged, drawn, and quartered at St. Thomas-a-Watering on May 29 of that same year.

Barrowe had written some time before his execution: "Ever for our parts our lives are not dear to us; so we may finish up our testimony with joy. We are always ready through God's grace to be offered up upon that testimony of our faith which we have made."[16]

During this rising tide of persecution the reformers already sensed that they would have to seek haven as exiles in some other country to escape from tyranny. It might be the continent or even some more distant land. One wonders if young Robinson, who was to emerge as the leader of the most famous band of exile-seekers, realized that Henry Barrowe left a sum of money to the company of exile Francis Johnson in Holland for a stock or trust fund. Before this time money had been "sent from London for the poor" of the congregation of English refugees in Amsterdam.[17]

After the martyrdom of John Penry, at his dying request, his friends conferred in London about the measures they should adopt to provide for their departure to some foreign country. A petition was presented to the Privy Council setting forth this plan, but no action was taken.[18]

John Smyth, a Cambridge graduate from Christ's College, was for a time imprisoned in the Marshalsea because of his teachings on reform. He managed to move north to Lincoln and then to Gainsborough, to Robinson's country, and to become minister of the church there. These two men were soon to meet, become friends and fellow exiles in the Netherlands.

Richard Clyfton, still another Cambridge scholar, had returned from his university training to serve as vicar of the thirteenth-century Church of All Saints in Babworth, Nottingham, just seven miles from Scrooby. Here his liberalism was discovered by William Brewster and a number of other future Pilgrims who visited his church and were inspired by his preaching.

At this point one must not lose the main actor amid a melee of minor characters in this sixteenth- and seventeenth-century drama. These numerous contemporaries mentioned earlier all play a role in the unfolding of the Pilgrim story. John Robinson was to become one of a company of scholars who plunged vigorously into the Protestant revolution, engaging in research, lecturing, and writing. From their fertile minds there poured forth millions of spoken and written words. To understand Robinson and the Pilgrims one must appreciate the ideas presented by this cohort of Puritan authors. They were substantial thinkers, and their contribution was not only religious and intellectual but of literary significance as well. The men already spoken of are only part of this company. Others will be considered later. Together they form one of the most unique groups in Western literature, noteworthy because of the intellectual caliber of their books. These Puritans marshalled a mighty brain trust. Their movement was one of the intellectually best equipped in history; and they prevailed in their reformation through the force of their logic expressed in dynamic Elizabethan English.

Robinson was awakening under the tutelage of his elders who moved in the vanguard of revolt against church and crown. His mind was in turmoil as he struggled to decide where he was to take his stand. In the course of a few tumultuous years he was to cast his lot with the "holie army" who were despised and trampled by the seemingly invincible powers of the mighty. He developed an affinity for certain Cambridge men who were to help determine his course. He admired three professors from whom he sought counsel even after he had completed his formal studies.

William Perkins, catechist at Christ's College and preacher at St. Andrews, was one of the distinguished Puritan scholars. He was expected to "read a lecture every Thursday in the term on some useful subject of Divinity." Robinson heard him lecture and preach because he indicated in later writings how much he owed to Perkins. Robinson published in Leyden, before 1624 for the use of his parish there, a catechism which his professor had developed, giving along with it his own ideas on the church and the Christian life. In the preface he spoke of Perkins' work as "fully containing what every Christian is to believe touching God and himself." Perkins emphasized conscience as the center of his theology:

> By study of the scriptures the individual can test his conscience and correct it if it is in conflict with the Word. God has endowed man with reason and conscience is a function of reason. The examination of scripture with reason sheds light on the open mind. Man's conscience is known to none, beside himself, but to God.[19]

The forthrightness of John Robinson's thinking was due in part to the teaching of the dynamic Perkins, who listed in a plainspoken and humorous manner some of the false notions about religion in the 1590s that revealed the shocking ignorance of the people:

> That God is served by the rehearsing of the ten commandments, the Lord's Prayer and the Creeds.

That none can tell whether he shall be saved or no certainly.

That it is safest to do in Religion as most do.

That merry ballads and books are good to drive away the time, and to remove heart-qualms.

That ye know all the Preacher can tell you.

That drinking and bezeling in the ale-house or tavern is good fellowship, and shows a good kind nature, and maintains neighborhood.

That it was a good world, when the old Religion was, because all things were cheap.[20]

Perkins continued:

Religion hath been amongst us this thirty-five years; but the more it is published, the more it is condemned and reproached of many. Thus not profaneness nor wickedness but religion itself is a byword, a mockingstock, and a matter of reproach; so that in England at this day the man or woman that begins to profess religion and to serve God, must resolve with himself to sustain mocks and injuries even as though he lived amongst the enemies of religion.[21]

Robinson learned from William Perkins that

every man must join the practice of his personal calling, with the practice of the general calling of Christianity. More plainly: Every particular calling must be practiced in and with the general calling of a Christian. It is not sufficient for a man in the congregation, and in common conversation, to be a Christian, but in his very personal calling, he must show himself to be so.[22]

Robinson also referred to his admiration for Laurence Chaderton, who served as the first master of Emmanuel College. He was one of the few Puritan representatives at the Hampton Court Conference called by James I in 1604. Years later, in 1618, the Pilgrim Press in Leyden, operated by William Brewster with Robinson as a consultant, published an edition of Chaderton's sermons. Robinson mentioned this project in his *Works*.

Paul Baynes was a third university figure who won the admiration of the student from Sturton le Steeple. He found guidance and inspiration in the "golden words" of "Holy" Baynes who succeeded Perkins as lecturer at Great St. Andrews. Silenced by the archbishop, Baynes continued to preach widely throughout England as the guest of Puritan sympathizers. With his income cut off by the hierarchy, he was forced to live in poverty, yet his letters reveal warm and friendly interest in the struggles of fellow reformers.

Other Cambridge Puritans influenced Robinson. William Haller wrote of "the Spiritual Brotherhood" there which included Arthur Hildersham, who entered Christ's College in 1576; John

Dod, who was at Jesus College in 1585; William Gouge, at Kings in 1595; and John Preston, Kings, 1604.[23] Also there was Richard Sibbes, at St. Johns in 1595 and John Cotton, who entered Trinity in 1596.

During his twentieth year Robinson was drawn into a theological controversy such as he was to face later in Holland. A graduate of the University of Bourges, Peter Baro from Geneva, had been brought over as Lady Margaret Professor of Divinity at Cambridge. After a number of years he was accused of heresy. His criticisms of Calvinism were somewhat similar to those advanced later by Arminius in the Netherlands. A heated debate took place in 1595 and 1596 between Dr. Baro, Dr. Goad, and Mr. Chaderton, who opposed his views. This raised for Robinson the personal question of how much Calvinism he could accept.

In the midst of the intricacies of theological disputation the central figure of the Pilgrim story was groping to evolve his beliefs. He was to become a leading figure in an intertwining complex of men of letters who were struggling to reinterpret the basic realities in religion.[24]

The thoughts of men had been stirred by the forward-reaching concepts of Copernicus, Erasmus, Luther, Calvin, and scores of others in volcanic outpourings. "Tradition and innovation jostled each other." Interest in religion led to theological speculation and discovery. These controversies spilled over into secular thought. Compared with the Italian Renaissance, which was primarily secular, this age "tried to justify even its historical, scientific and linguistic studies by reference to the Christian religion."[25]

At Cambridge the events of history were measured and evaluated through study of the Bible in its original tongues. These new insights dramatized the shortcomings of institutional religion and aroused the sensitive to demand reform. John Robinson was one of the earnest students who was researching continental theology, church history, and scriptural antecedents. He followed the outlook of his English Puritan mentors who had developed an affinity with reformers like Bucer, Martyr, Calvin, Zwingli, Beza, and Pareus. The English scholars of this period "had great ability for restating in forceful idiomatic English the theology of the continent."[26]

More significant for Englishmen than the authority of Calvin and his school was their scrutiny of the scriptures. "Scrutamini Scripturas (search the scriptures). These two words have undone the world," wrote John Selden.[27] Robinson passed many hours bent over his Hebrew Old Testament and his Greek New Testament, striving to capture the truths that were foundation stones in the building of Christendom. His devotion to Greek was to win for him the distinction of serving as Praelector Graecus so that he continued his research in the mother tongue of Christianity and passed on to his students his enthusiasm for the Greek New Testament that had come to his desk because of this vision of Erasmus.

The Dutch scholar had visited England in 1499. During this period he met John Colet, William Grecyn, and Thomas More, who encouraged him to perfect his Greek. On his return in 1505,

Erasmus helped quicken interest in study of the New Testament in the original. He made a significant contribution by publishing its twenty-seven books in Greek in 1516. There were five printed editions before he died and their circulation moved this classic out of the confines of libraries and made it readily available to scholars. In his *Paraphrases* he made a plea that the Bible should be given to all the people in their native tongues: "I wish that the husbandman may sing portions of them as he follows the plough, that the weaver may chant them at his shuttle, that the traveler may with their narrative while away the weariness of the way."[28]

The dream of Erasmus had become a reality in Robinson's time as the Geneva Bible was circulated widely among the English people. He pored over the Geneva New Testament of 1557 and the complete Geneva Bible of 1560 which had been smuggled into England from the press of the Marian exiles (who fled under "Bloody" Mary Tudor) who had engineered this revealing translation. He was moved by the reports of the labors of the English scholars—William Whittingham, Anthony Gilby, and Thomas Sampson—whose scholarship and dedication had placed this book in his hands. These translators had used Greek, Latin, French, and English versions in preparing their New Testament. The Old Testament was a revision of the Great Bible compared with the Hebrew text. The marginal annotations opened up countless new avenues of interpretation and thus stimulated Robinson's critical posture toward institutional religion. The Geneva scholars also quickened his resolution to explore for himself the original Greek and Hebrew of the biblical books.[29]

The Geneva Bible proved to be a landmark. It was "rivaled in importance only by the Tyndale and 1611 Bibles. It quickly became the cheap, popular version of the Scriptures; for well over half a century this was the Bible most read by Englishmen and most often reprinted."[30] The widespread reading of this newly-opened treasure exerted extensive influence upon the British mind. As Thomas Hobbes put it: "After the Bible was translated . . . every man, nay, every boy and wench, that could read English, thought they spoke with God Almighty and understood what he said."[31]

The young Corpus Christi student sensed that a new day might dawn with the advent of the Geneva Bible, if only he could carry its message in all its directness and power to the people!

Give me liberty to know, to utter,
and to argue freely according to conscience
above all liberties.
—John Milton

3 "GIVE ME LIBERTY TO KNOW"

In order to understand the background of Robinson's time and the battle that scholars waged for freedom one must deal briefly with the historical setting.

Henry VIII (1509-47) has been regarded as the founder of the English Reformation, but he was never a true Protestant. He was called "Defender of the faith" because of the book he wrote against Luther. After his quarrel with the pope he persuaded his vassal Parliament to vote him Supreme Lord of the Church of England through the Act of Supremacy of 1534. He capitalized on the rising sense of nationalism among his people and the urge toward unification of English interests against continental controls.

In the Act of Restraint of Appeals of 1533 the preamble stated that "this realm of England is an empire." Henry asserted that his country was to be a self-governing nation, free from the interference of the kings in Europe and the pope in Rome.[1] He was interested in a religious revolution because he wanted to oust the accepted head of the church and step into that post himself. He assumed that the doctrines and ceremonies of Rome would continue, but in this he was mistaken. Critical minds pushed ahead toward purification of long-accumulated abuses and corruptions.

The king did not wish a social revolution such as developed on the continent as a result of religious reform. His motive was to gain political sovereignty over the influential church and the economic profit that would come through confiscation of the monasteries. He raided these Roman Catholic properties in order to secure funds; one bishopric was kept empty during the entire reign of Elizabeth in order that its income could be devoted to the support of the court. Hilaire Belloc stated that the one fixed principle behind the religious revolution was the loot of religious endowments. Kings and queens, courtiers, magistrates, and ambitious laymen were ever alert to get their hands on the possessions of the church.[2]

The king's anticlerical revolt not only threw off religious domination by a foreign power but also subjected the clergy to the influence of the laity. Laymen took over some of the wealth and influence of the monasteries. These developments helped initiate a social revolution. "Better the king than the pope" was the adage employed to placate those who demanded more reform. There were a few independent minds who insisted, however, that the king should not be head of the church. The state was his business. The church had but one head, its founder, Jesus; and the primary source of its authority was the Bible.

Anne Boleyn, wife of Henry and mother of Elizabeth, read Tyndale's New Testament and introduced it to her husband. Due in part to her influence, the forbidden book gained a few readers and she helped convince the king that a Bible in English for the use of the people was sorely needed.

In 1538 Henry VIII ordered that a copy of the Great Bible in English should be placed in every church. This was the translation of Tyndale's associates, Myles Coverdale and John Rogers. The fateful step made the scriptures available, and as citizens learned to read they were initiated into the adventure of discovering the facts of Christianity for themselves.

Henry had unknowingly struck a blow for freedom. "England became the people of a book, and that book was the Bible. It was read at churches and read at home, and everywhere its words as they fell on ears which custom had not deadened to their force and beauty, kindled a startling enthusiasm," wrote J. R. Green.[3]

Henry endorsed only changes that he considered safe, such as the abolition of the grosser forms of idolatry and relic-mongering, the diffusion of the English Bible among the people, and the introduction of Renaissance learning at Oxford and Cambridge. "He continued to abhor and persecute Protestants, and if he had not done so he might have lost his throne in the then state of opinion."[4]

Reformers and reactionaries were equally confused in the melee of transition. "Papists were beheaded for accepting the Pope's decrees and Protestants were hanged for rejection of the Pope's doctrines."[5] Henry admired Erasmus and shared the Dutch scholar's mistrust of monks and priests. He accomplished more than he expected when he brought Erasmus to Cambridge. The Rotterdam liberal introduced the study of the New Testament in Greek. His new and revolutionary approach was destined to initiate a renaissance of scholarship and religious insight. It was Erasmus who opened the fountainhead of biblical exploration which was destined to overthrow the absolute monarchy in which Henry VIII gloried.

The innovations introduced by the king slowly created a new ecclesiastical and social order which could harmonize only with a Protestant outlook. The revolution which he inaugurated in his Reformation Parliament, between 1529 and 1536, moved forward with inexorable momentum through an entire century until it erupted in civil war and the execution of King Charles I in 1649.

Edward VI (1547-53), "that blessed ympe," the ten-year-old son of Henry VIII and Jane Seymour, became "the boy king whose unscrupulous advisers did their worst to make Protestantism hateful to the people." The frail lad was manipulated by advisers who exploited his regency as they struggled for power among themselves.

Under the leadership of Archbishop Cranmer a modest effort was made to correct the abysmal illiteracy and incompetence of the clergy through educational reform. Many dignitaries of the church were known to be incapable of teaching the principles of religion to their people, so an act was passed that compelled all bishops to preach four times a year. This shock treatment required them to undertake a little reading and study. The revision of the *Book of Common Prayer* was also accomplished during this period.

Edward's court invited Martin Bucer of Strasbourg to become professor of theology at Cambridge and Paulus Fagius to teach Hebrew there. Both of the continental reformers fell ill due to the chill of their damp, unheated quarters, and Fagius died. Bucer recovered only to die in 1551, a short time before Bloody Mary came to the throne to initiate her persecution of Protestants. Later under her orders the bones of these scholars were exhumed and burned along with their books, various Protestant writings, and all copies of the Bible that could be collected.

After the ten-day reign of Lady Jane Grey, Mary Tudor (1553-58), the child of Henry VIII and Catherine of Aragon, came to the throne. In her zeal to restore the Roman Catholic faith she turned to Spain to find a husband and thus unwittingly assured that England would become a Protestant country. She married Philip on July 25, 1554, restored Roman Catholicism, and pressured Reginald Cardinal Pole to absolve the kingdom from the sin of its past disobedience to the Holy See. Her subsequent persecution of the Puritans drove her people away from Rome. Their rising national pride inspired them to strive for freedom from the ecclesiastical and political domination of the continent.

Mary set out to exterminate the reformers. Only Roman Catholics were safe. Starting with John Rogers on February 4, and Bishop John Hooper on February 9, 1555, she executed nearly 300 people, many of them the best minds of the land. Their deaths created revulsion toward Rome and all followers of the pope and earned her the title "Bloody Mary." Many reformers fled to the continent to establish congregations in Frankfort, Aarau, Strasbourg, Zurich, Densbrugh, Emden, Basel, Wesel, Marburg, Wittenberg, and Geneva. Most of the leaders of reform in England who had not escaped to Europe were in the Tower, the Fleet, the King's Bench, Newgate, and the Marshalsea prisons.

Elizabeth (1558–1603) and the Elizabethans were born in the turmoil of Reformation and revolution. Elizabeth, as a Protestant, was welcomed by her people after the excesses of Mary, but she was no follower of the reforms of Geneva. This daughter of Henry VIII and Anne Boleyn loved pomp, luxury, and power, and she shared her father's political outlook on religion. "The church should be a department of state, organized by Parliament and ruled by the national tribunals. There should be no conventicles and no chapels, to be nurseries of sedition."[6]

The Duke of Norfolk reminded her: "Let your Highness assure yourself that England can bear no more changes in religion, it hath been bowed so oft that if it should be bent again it would break."[7]

The new queen was largely lacking in religious feeling. She

was a Henrican Catholic under Henry VIII, a Protestant under Edward VI, a conforming Roman Catholic under Mary I. She disliked the Roman Catholics because they called her a bastard. She disliked Calvin and the Puritans because of their harping on the independent church. As a shrewd politician she sought balance between the factions and insisted that she be recognized as the supreme sovereign in the religious realm. She sensed that her people wanted a national church, independent from foreign control. This was in accord with her own nationalistic feeling.

Elizabeth's church settlement was a compromise. She was named Supreme Governor of the church in the Act of Supremacy. An Act of Uniformity, passed in 1559, was intended to regulate the worship and government of the church throughout the kingdom. *A Common Prayer Book* was introduced and thirty-nine articles were drawn up, which the clergy were required to accept. The compromise was achieved with the help of churchmen who had lived as exiles on the continent under Mary, where they had imbibed Reformation principles. From this time forward Calvinism began to influence English thought. Fox, in his *Book of Martyrs*, struck a propaganda blow for the cause of the hitherto persecuted reformers.

Elizabeth broke with Rome in 1570 and was excommunicated. The Puritans sought to introduce bills in the House of Commons that expressed their political views challenging royal supremacy. They insisted on free speech in Parliament, but the queen limited their freedom of expression to government bills.

Archbishop Edmund Grindal tried to check her attempts to suppress local gatherings of the clergy. She suspended him and appointed John Whitgift in 1583, who was willing to follow her orders. Attempts to express contrary opinions or to organize worship in violation of the legal forms, whether by Roman Catholics or by Puritans, were rigorously put down. The Separatists were to be banished from the realm. The reformers sought redress in Parliament but the queen forbade Parliament to meddle in religion, and she set up royal commissions to handle ecclesiastical affairs. In politics she was restrained in some ways by Parliament, but in ecclesiastical affairs she was the dictator. The High Commission handled all prosecutions and she made the appointments. In 1565 the licenses of all preachers were called in by the archbishop. New licenses were to be given only to the men who proved conformable and amenable.[8]

Under Elizabeth regulations on church attendance were issued. In Lincolnshire in 1584 it was ordered that Mr. Jermyns was to preach on Sunday afternoons and Wednesday mornings, to teach the people their duties toward God and the queen. One half of all the people in every house above the age of twelve, who were not ill or lawfully hindered, were to be at the sermon every Sunday in the morning and one from every house at the sermon in the afternoon on Sunday and on Wednesday. A Feckenham parishioner protested that "he would go down to the meadows and hear as good a sermon under a hedge as any made by that parson."[9]

Queen Elizabeth I (1533-1603)

Events on the continent helped further the Protestant cause in England. Elizabeth and her statesmen were frightened by the growing threat of Spain. Philip II in his outreach for power was at war with the Netherlands. Many Netherlanders in the south were Roman Catholics and loyal to Spain. The provinces of the north were united in rebellion against Spanish rule, which brought the threat of heavier taxation and suppression of freedom under the Inquisition. Resistance was strongest among these northern Calvinists who were led by William the Silent.

Elizabeth cautiously offered aid to the Dutch because Spain also threatened the security of England. With the assistance of the papacy and her armies of occupation Spain had gained extensive holdings in the New World. Portugal, annexed by Philip II in 1580, also controlled vast areas of the globe. The English refused to recognize these claims, and when war broke out with Spain in 1585 the British were united in defense of their own country and in resistance to Spain in Holland and France.

The war was fought on the seas, in the channel, in Spanish ports in the Old World and the New; it was fought in France and in the Netherlands; it was fought in Ireland. In the summer of 1588 it was fought against the concentrated power of the Spanish Armada near the south coast of England. The defeat of the Armada did not mean that the enemy was destroyed. It did show that the enemy was not invincible.[10]

However, in spite of the slow alteration of outward forms during these years, the Protestants in Parliament were propelling the government toward change. There was a nucleus who held strong sympathy for reform. "The whole development of the age bears the impress of an irresistible impetus."[11]

The state of the ministry in the Established Church in the sixteenth century and early seventeenth century was distressing. There is an account in the British Museum of parishes near Doncaster, ten miles from Scrooby, written about 1612 by Thomas Toller and Richard Clark, vicars at Sheffield and Braythwell. They mention sixty parishes and found in them preachers "sufficient and painful, 12; non-preachers, 42; negligent and insufficient, 26; scandalous ministers, 10."[12]

A document dated November 1590 recommended erection of a college at Ripon, and goes on to state that the people in the area were all ignorant of religion having been untaught for over thirty years. The majority of the clergy were spoken of as "dumb dogs." Manuscripts in Dr. Williams' Library, London, present observations from Staffordshire in this period: "There be 118 congregations which have no preacher, neither have had (for the most part) now more than 40 years; there be 18 congregations served by laymen, by scandalous, 40." "Lewd," "a bad liver," "of scandalous life," "very ignorant," "drunkard," "a common drunkard," "a grievous swearer," "of loose life," "a mere worldling," "a gamester," are entries continually repeated after the clerical names are recorded. One minister was "a weaver," having been "a gentleman's household servant many years." One is "very famous for his skill in gaming, and especially in bowling."

The report from Cornwall, which bears the date 1586, carries descriptions such as these: "a man careless of his calling," "a very lewd man," "a dicer," "a very lewd fellow," "a pot-companion," "a food dicer and carder both night and day," "a common alehouse-haunter and gamester," "his conversation is most in hounds," "he was lately a serving man."[13]

One Puritan listed some ninety-three faults and errors in the Church of England. Among them were fixed liturgies and set prayers, baptismal rituals, forms for celebrating the Lord's Supper, popish vestments, the canon laws, courts of the bishops, the prevalence of unworthy members in the church, and the incompetence of ministers and bishops.

In spite of protests, Queen Elizabeth continued to silence able Puritan ministers and appoint unworthy and even disreputable men to benifices. In petitions to Parliament, the Puritans protested against "Dumme Dogs, Unskilful sacrificing priests, Destroying Drones, or rather Caterpillars of the Word."[14] Mention was made of the affectations of the clergy who spoke "in fonde fables to make their hearers laughe, or in ostentation of learning of their Latin, their Greke, their Hebrue tongue, and of their great reasing of antiquities."[15]

In *Seconde Parte of a Register* (1586), it is noted that in Essex County "Mr. Levit, parson of Leden Roding, a notorious swearer, a dicer, a carder, a hawker and hunter, a verie careless person, he had a childe by a maid since he was instituted and inducted."[16] James Allen, a vicar of Shopland, who had been a serving man, was unable to preach because he could not render an account of his faith in Latin or in English. Mr. Mason, a parson of Rawrey, had a child by his maid and was brought before the justice.

These church appointments, made by crown and bishops, were called "livings." It is clear that they were distributed with little regard for the spiritual and intellectual qualifications of the recipients.

Puritans spoke out against the abuses that riddled the Established Church and demanded reformation: "What a pitifull thing it is, to come into a congregation of one or two thousand soules," so reads *A Parte of a Register*, "and not to finde aboue foure or fiue that are able to giue an account of their faith in any tollerable manner, whereby it may be said probably: *This is a Christian man, or hee is a childe of the Church.*"[17]

Less than one half of the clergy were educated. In 1603 only 454 out of 1,065 ministers in the province of York were licensed preachers and only 3,352 out of 8,179 in the province of Canterbury. Ministers seldom preached because they were untrained, unwilling, or indolent. They were poorly paid, and many vicars farmed to eke out an existence; some grazed cattle in the churchyard. There was widespread corruption in administering the parish tithes. Laymen often seized the tax money that should have gone to the church, and from it paid the vicars a pittance. The bishops were pluralists and held more than one living. The Bishop of St. Asaph's held sixteen livings. When Richard Bancroft was made Bishop of London he resigned eight rectories and prebends.[18]

A satire on the manner in which church livings were granted for bribes or as political plums is presented in the play *Return from Parnassus* (1602):

> *One actor*: Fain would I have a "living," if I could tell how to come by it.
> *Echo*: Buy it!
> Buy it, fond echo? Why, thou dost greatly mistake it.
> *Echo*: Stake it.
> Stake it? What should I stake at this game of simony?
> *Echo*: Money.
> What, is the world a game? Are livings gotten by playing?
> *Echo*: Paying.
> Paying? But say, what's the nearest way to come to a living?
> *Echo*: Giving.
> Must his worship's fists be needs then oiled with angels?
> *Echo*: Angels.[19]

The queen and the archbishop were harsh in inflicting punishment for the most trivial offenses. George Cotton, for hearing a portion of scripture read by Greenwood in a friend's house, was thrown into prison without trial for twenty-seven months. Quentyn Smith was put in irons at Newgate for a similar offense.

A law was passed in 1593 which stated that if any person attempted by speech or pen to persuade any other from attending church he should be committed to prison until he submitted. If during three months he refused, he was to be banished from the realm. If he returned without permission, he must be hanged.[20]

> With a refinement of cruelty it was made a penal offence to give shelter to a Separatist. For a man to receive into his house his dearest friend, if that friend refused to attend the services of the Queen's Church, made him liable to the ruinous fine of ten pounds a month. His friend might be dangerously ill, and might have no other home; but the law was inexorable; to give him shelter from rain, snow, fog and frost was a crime. For a man to keep in his house his own wife, child, mother, father, sister, brother, if they refused to attend the Queen's churches, made him liable to the same penalty unless he could show they had no other home.[21]

Such was the state of the church in England when John Robinson arrived in Cambridge. Nevertheless, in spite of this dismal picture, there were hopeful stirrings in other areas. Queen Elizabeth was sixty years old and was entering the thirty-fifth year of her reign. Spain had been vanquished and England was established as a great Protestant power. In her court were Cecil, Leicester, Gresham, Walsingham, Frobisher, and Drake.[22] The early volumes of the poets Samuel Daniel, Michael Drayton, and Henry Constable were in the bookshops. The plays of John Lyly,

Robert Greene, Christopher Marlowe, and William Shakespeare, now in his late twenties, were being staged in London.

Richard Hakluyt was writing his history of the seas. George Chapman was preparing to introduce Homer to English readers. Sir Walter Raleigh, then forty, was in the Tower of London, where he was to write his *History of the World*. Francis Bacon, age thirty-one, was just entering Parliament and planning his *Temporis partus masculus*. Bacon was the chief exponent of experimental science. He published his *Advancement of Learning* in 1605, and later developed these ideas in his Latin work *Novum organum*. Bacon revolted against the tyranny of traditionalists who still quoted Aristotle, insisting that the truths of science should be determined through experiment. In the midst of the fog of superstition he flung open the windows of English minds to the bracing winds of skepticism and reason.

Sir Thomas More's *Utopia*, written in Latin in 1516 and translated into English in 1551, proved immensely popular. It stimulated British minds to think about and seek a better social order.[23]

During Robinson's years at the university there was movement and questioning. The critical examination of the past was sharpened by probing of the present. Scholasticism was dying. The new learning was evolving, creating tension in politics as well as in theology and revolution in social patterns.

The Renaissance and Reformation were mingled in Elizabethan England. "Shakespeare's England had a charm and a lightness of heart, a free aspiring of mind and spirit not to be found elsewhere in the harsh Jesuit-Calvinist Europe of that day."[24] The madrigals and lyric poems reflected the spirit of a people who were freed from medieval controls. A new burst of vitality was displayed. Villagers sang in the streets and travelers along the roadways. Minstrels wandered with their fiddles and pipes from pubs to humble cottages and sprawling manor houses. The village church boasted its bell ringers who played on festive days.[25] Liberated from the peril of foreign invasion and the threat of dire poverty, there was an upsurge of spirit that was expressed in books, songs, exploration, quickening of conscience, and assertion of individual freedoms.

During the last days of Elizabeth's rule John Robinson had been studying and teaching at Cambridge. After four years as a sizar he received his B.A. and was elected to the rank of scholar. The Order Book contains this item: "*Johannes Robinson Nottingh. electus in Scholarem, Jan. 23, admissus Febr. 16, 1595.*" As a scholar he received free quarters in the university and an allowance to help cover his expenses. He was approved for his bachelor's degree February 25, 1595.[26]

He was now permitted to attend lectures in various colleges and to follow any line of study that he wished. He was ambitious and decided to continue at the university for at least another three years. He was chosen fellow of his college March 27, 1597, and was elected to a vacant fellowship. Two years later, March 28, 1599, he won his master's degree. The "Great Commencement" ceremonies were conducted in St. Mary's Church; members of his family came up from Sturton le Steeple. Possibly Miss Bridget White, daughter of a Puritan neighbor in nearby Greasley, made the journey with them.

Candidates engaged in disputations and then were awarded their degrees. They crossed over to the Regent House where they knelt before the vice chancellor and were graduated. At this time the young master of arts was required to take an oath that he would remain at the university and participate in its life for two more years.[27]

John Robinson became a regent master, teaching subjects in which he had majored. In 1599 he was elected *Praelector Graecus*, reader in Greek. In 1600 he was made *Deanus*. As dean he was an overseer of students. The February 5, 1602 entry in the College Register reads: "*Johannes Robinson Nottinghamiensis Artium Mag Sacerdos*." This indicates that he had taken orders in the Church of England, and that he participated in the services in Corpus Christi Chapel, and spoke in the pulpit of Benet Church and in other Cambridge churches.[28]

In 1602 John Jegon, the master of Corpus Christi, was appointed dean of Norwich. For ten years the young Robinson had been associated with this scholar. Now that Master Jegon was departing he considered whether or not the time had come for him to leave the halls of learning and take his place in the outside world. There is a letter signed by Robinson and a group of colleagues which they sent to Sir Robert Cecil expressing their regret over Master Jegon's move and urging the election of a worthy successor. John's former tutor, Thomas Jegon, was chosen to follow his brother as master of Corpus Christi.

Robinson's evolving religious views were due in large measure to his critical studies of the Old Testament in Hebrew and the New Testament in Greek. He discovered what other Puritans had come to realize—that reference to the Bible was the standard method for evaluating the doctrines of the church. The new practice of consulting the New Testament in its original tongue stimulated scholars to probe after and strive to recapture the true factual essence of the Christian faith.

To their simple and direct ideas Puritan scholars added a vital testimony that was lacking in the religion of many bishops and parish ministers. This was their deep personal experience of the truths which they believed. The populace had listened wearily to the professional proponents of Christianity. It was refreshing to hear the appeal of the Puritans to their own individual experience. Samuel Eaton sneered, "These are they that prate, not preach, like men raptured with their own spiritual nonsense."[29] It was this message of the heart that reached the common people and won them.

The resolute and scholarly position of the Puritans provided dignity for their cause. Henry Hallam testified that after many reforming ministers had been silenced by Elizabeth's restrictive orders "the Puritans formed so much the more learned and diligent part of the clergy, that a great scarcity of preachers was experienced throughout this reign (Elizabeth's), in consequence of the silencing of so many of the former."[30]

Lord Treasurer Burghley stated that it was the clear and scholarly interpretation of the Bible by the Puritans that turned the mind of England permanently Protestant. He wrote to Queen Elizabeth:

Though they were over-squeamish and nice in their opinions, and more scrupulous than they need, yet with their careful catechising, and diligent preaching, they bring forth that fruit which your most excellent Majesty is to desire and wish, namely, the lessening and diminishing of the papistical numbers.[31]

During university holidays John Robinson made his way back east to his home village. He could see now with new understanding that the Basset-Lawe Country was permeated with the reforms of Cambridge, spearheaded by Cambridge men who had studied there before him. The vicars and rectors of the area who had imbibed the wine of liberalism were now preaching their disturbing precepts. Among his immediate neighbors were Richard Clyfton of Babworth, John Smyth of Gainsborough, Richard Bernard of Worksop, Thomas Toller, whose local parish is obscure, Robert Gifford of Laughton-en-le-Morthen, Hugh Bromhead of North Wheatley. William Brewster of Scrooby, the prominent and well-to-do layman who was a friend of these reforming dominies, was also a neighbor.

These men were rebellious against the meaningless ceremonies of the church and were striving for the reform of abuses. Some went as far as separation, like Hugh Bromhead, who wrote that the Mother Church was "Babylon, the mother of all abominations, the habitation of devils, and the hold of all foul spirits, and a cage of every unclean and hateful bird."[32]

Basset-Lawe was a seed bed of ferment. It was part of East England which lay open to the winds of Europe. Cambridge was the gateway to this flat country which was like the Dutch and Flemish lowlands and close to Europe. During the fifteenth and sixteenth centuries thousands of refugees sought haven from Spanish tyranny, settling in the fens and sea towns that were like their continental homes. They brought to their adopted land the tradition of freedom. They worked in the textile mills and this wool district became a stronghold of Puritanism. The rising yeoman and merchant class challenged the control of the feudal lords. "Gothic England died first in East Anglia."[33]

On his visits from college to the Basset-Lawe Country, John had been spending more and more time with his old neighbors, the Whites, and their daughter, Bridget. The Whites had settled in Sturton le Steeple before the Robinsons and were one of the leading families in the village. Thomas White had served as bailiff of Sturton. His will had been written in 1579 and his grave was in the churchyard of St. Peter and St. Paul. Alexander, his son, married Eleanor Smith, the daughter of William and Katherine

Smith of Honington, Lincolnshire. Their children were Catherine (who married Deacon John Carver of Robinson's Leyden flock, who was to be the first governor of Plimoth Plantation), Charles, Bridget, Thomas, Roger (who became prominent in the Leyden community), Edward, Jane, and Frances. The last two were also to move to Leyden.

Alexander White was a prosperous farmer who leased lands in Beauvale, including Beauvale Abbey in Greasley parish. The abbey was a fourteenth-century Carthusian monastery, and the Whites may have been living in the ancient priory at this time.

The journeys back to Sturton le Steeple were welcome interludes during Robinson's eleven years at the university. He turned from the conflicts and tensions to the benison of the home land; the lush beauty of patchwork fields, majestic trees, ancient cottages, and the sweet songs of the countryside.

One may be sure that John took Bridget to visit the parish church in nearby Gainsborough to hear John Smyth; and to Babworth to listen to Richard Clyfton. These ministers were independent thinkers and he liked them. By horse cart they explored the dirt roadways round about and walked footpaths along the hedgerows through fields of cows and sheep. It was a gracious country through all seasons of the year; spring with daffodils and hawthorne, summer with hayricks and strawberries, autumn with the harvests of the good earth, and winter with hoarfrost on the meadows and chimney pots spiraling their smoke against a gray sky. They punted along the Trent or sat in the sun on its banks, watching the boats as they passed. They talked about their families, the university, and most often of their hopes, dreamily picturing the future they longed to spend together.

Deeply influenced by the long succession of Cambridge pioneers and by contemporaries like Perkins, Chaderton, and Baynes, the young dean of Corpus Christi was moving steadily toward a dramatic break with the Establishment. He rebelled against the pricks of authoritarianism. He was weary of the haggling and the harassments which hounded all liberals. He knew that he must resign his post at the university if he married. The struggle to make this decision tormented him at the time he was battling to formulate his beliefs. This pressure toward conformity strengthened his romantic impulse to marry Bridget White, surrender his deanship, and pursue his quest for truth in the outside world.

The same year that Thomas Jegon was chosen master of Corpus Christi was the eventful year of Robinson's resignation and marriage. The new master was not to prove as successful as his brother. Under his leadership bickering took place among the fellows and students and the financial resources were at low ebb. Thomas Jegon spent much of his time in the calm of his rectory at Sible Hedingham. These changes at Corpus Christi may have hastened Robinson's departure from the university.

The Corpus Christi Register lists his resignation: February 10, 1603. Soon he was back in the Basset-Lawe Country and in five days he stood in the chancel of the Church of St. Mary, Greasley, Nottinghamshire while Bridget's vicar pronounced them man and wife. It is possible that their friend, Richard Clyfton of Babworth,

participated in the service. The entry in the register reads: "Feb. 15, 1603 Mr. John Robynson to Mistress Bridget White." The prefixes Mr. and Mistress are significant since they were used in these old registers in special cases only.[34]

Weddings in seventeenth-century England were festive affairs when villagers joined in the merrymaking. Ancient custom regulated courtship, betrothal, and parental arrangements regarding dowry, church, and social formalities. One does not know how the Cambridge dean and his bride looked on these traditions, but it is certain that a large and cheery conclave of Whites, Robinsons, relatives, and friends from Nottinghamshire, Lincolnshire, and Yorkshire gathered in the Greasley church and for the feasting and rejoicing that followed their vows in the chancel.

Some thirty days after the marriage ceremony the queen passed away. It was the end of the Elizabethan era and the beginning of the Stuart and the Pilgrim era.

St. Mary's Church, Greasley—John Robinson and Bridget White were married here

49

I will make them conform, or I will
harry them out of the land, or else do worse.
—King James I

4 "I WILL MAKE THEM CONFORM"

"This morning about three o'clock Her Majesty (Queen Elizabeth) departed this life, mildly like a lamb, easily like a ripe apple from the tree,"[1] so wrote John Manningham in his diary. Archbishop Whitgift dispatched the Dean of Canterbury to wait upon King James VI of Scotland and to commend the nation and the church to his care, as he became James I of England (1603–25). The Anglicans and the Puritans both hoped for the favor of the young king who came out of "the Scotch mist," tutored by the Presbyterian dominies of the north country.

The clumsy and ambling Scot proved to be argumentative, garrulous, and proud of his learning. He had published his first book in 1584; *Essays of a Prentice in the Divine Art of Poesy*. Although he was reputed to be a poet and a Latin scholar, he dribbled at the mouth and shocked those who were accustomed to a little Tudor dignity. In *Conterblaste to Tobacco* he condemned the weed and its users. He later blasted the liberal theologians in Holland and defended his divine rights in *A Remonstrance for the Right of Kings*. About all that James had in common with Elizabeth was that both of their mothers had been beheaded.

The April journey from Edinburgh to London roused the emotions of Elizabeth's thirty-seven-year-old cousin. He was greeted by crowds who acclaimed him; and, flattered by adulation, he passed out pardons and peerages freely. But he and his wife, Anne, were shocked to learn that a plague was raging in London. It looked as if there would be no coronation on the day of James the Apostle, July 25. On the doorways of those doomed by the plague red crosses were painted. When darkness crept over the terrified city, wagons creaked out to gather up the dead and bury them in common graves. During 1603 some 30,000 Londoners died. James took up temporary residence at Windsor to escape exposure.

Under the intoxication of realizing his long-cherished dream of taking over the glory of Queen Elizabeth, he could not foresee the stormy events of the twenty-two years that lay ahead or conceive that his son Charles would be executed forty-six years later by the rebels who were to torment his father interminably. It was an incredible coincidence that his son and successor to the crown should meet the same tragic fate as his mother, Mary Queen of Scots.

Hopeful that King James would prove more friendly to their cause, the Puritans presented their Millenary Petition. They had intended to have it signed by 1,000 ministers, but succeeded in obtaining only about 800 from twenty-five counties. (John Robinson was one of the advocates of reform.) The requests in the petition were moderate. They sought relaxation of the laws that enforced ceremonies that had long been criticized, such as the use of surplice and cap. They asked that men who were neither educated nor devout should be kept out of the ministry. They sought some reforms in the ecclesiastical courts and a more equitable and efficient administration of church revenues. They prayed the king not to permit popish doctrines to be taught in Protestant pulpits, but they did not request the abolition of bishops or the establishment of a Presbyterian policy.

James announced that a conference would be held at Hampton Court in January 1604. The Established Church assembled their battery: the Archbishop of Canterbury, eight bishops, six deans, and two prominent divines. The Puritans were allowed only four spokesmen: Dr. John Reynolds of Lincoln, Laurence Chaderton of Cambridge, Dr. Thomas Sparkes of Oxford, and John Knewstubs of Cambridge.[2]

Dr. Reynolds criticized the twenty-fifth of the thirty-nine articles. Bishop Bancroft angrily repeated the ancient canon, *Schismatici Contra episcopos non sunt audiendi*—schismatics are not to be heard when they speak against bishops.[3]

The king spoke out for the Church of England and, puffed up by the flattery of its churchmen, he badgered the Puritans. When Reynolds protested against the line in the marriage service, "With my body I thee worship," the king said, "As for you, Dr. Reynolds, many men speak of Robin Hood, who never shot in his bow. If you had a good wife yourself, you would think all worship and honour you could do her were well bestowed upon her."[4]

Reynolds had the temerity to say to the king: "May your Majesty be pleased to direct that the Bible be now translated, such versions as are extant not answering the original."[5] This request was rebuffed by the Bishop of London and by the monarch, but it led to the appointment of a commission of fifty-four scholars who gave the King James version to England in 1611.

Mr. Knewstubs took exception to "the wearing of the surplice, a kind of garment used by the priests of Isis." Whereupon James, pleased to parade his erudition, said that since England did not border on Egypt there was little danger of surpliced Anglican clergymen being mistaken for priests of Isis.

This bantering was rudely displaced by anger when Reynolds spoke of the way theological conflicts might be settled by the local padres in their assemblies. He used the word presbytery which was an inflammatory word to the new king who had faced encounters with the Presbyterians in Scotland. He retorted,

If you aim at the Scottish presbytery, it agreeth as well with monarchy as God and the Devil. I will none of that. Then

King James I (1566-1625)

52

IACOBUS. D.G. MAGNÆ. BRITANNIÆ. FRANCI.
SCOTIÆ. ET. HYBERNIÆ. REX. ANNO. M.DC.XXI.

Jack, and Tom, and Will, and Dick, shall meet and censure me and my council . . . . I will have one doctrine and one discipline, one religion in substance and in ceremony.

He addressed his jubilant bishops: "My lords, if once you were out, and they (the nonconformists) in, I know what would become of my supremacy; for *no bishop, no king.*"

Turning to the Puritans, he snapped: "If this be all your party hath to say, I will make them conform themselves, or else I will harry them out of the land, or else do worse!"[6]

Some constructive results, however, were achieved at Hampton Court: it was agreed that certain changes should be made in the Prayer Book, and a new translation of the Bible was initiated.

James I was proud of the manner in which he had subdued the Puritans. He boasted to the bishops, "I peppered them soundly. They fled me from argument like scoolboys." The Archbishop of Canterbury, Whitgift, flattered his new master: "Undoubtedly your majesty speaks by the special assistance of God's Spirit." Bishop Bancroft of London added: "I protest my heart melteth with joy, that Almighty God, of his singular mercy, hath given us such a king, as since Christ's time, the like hath not been."[7]

After Hampton Court, James failed to sense that the Puritanism he had derided represented the religion of the gentry, a movement that was bound to grow. He was content to lecture Parliament on

Puritans and Novelists (innovators) which I call a sect rather than a religion—ever discontented with the present government and impatient to suffer any superiority, which maketh their sect unable to be suffered in any well-governed commonwealth.[8]

These persecuted clergy found friends in the House of Commons. A committee was created to confer on matters of religion. The committee took the Puritan side, stating their regret over "Pressing the Use of certain Rites and Ceremonies in this Church: as the Cross in Baptism, the Wearing of the Surplice in ordinary Parish Churches, and the Subscription required of the Ministers, further than is commanded by the Laws of the Realm."[9]

These protests, however, did not check Bancroft who continued to suppress Puritanism with merciless severity. It was decreed in 1604 that all persons separating themselves from the communion of the English Church and forming new religious societies were to be excommunicated. All persons maintaining that such "meetings, assemblies, or congregations of the King's born subjects" were true churches, were to be excommunicated. Such a person "could not serve on juries, could not be a witness in any court and what was worst of all, could not bring an action, either real or personal, to recover lands or money due him."[10]

James I, called "the wisest fool in Christendom," published a book in 1597, *Daemonologie*, and with his blessing Parliament passed legislation in 1604 stepping up punishment for those who were guilty of witchcraft. As a result many accused of witchcraft were burned during the early years of his reign. He enjoyed disputing with Parliament, the bishops, and the Puritans. He liked to argue in Latin and to be called *Rex Platonicus*. Ambassadors and scholars replied in Latin, and the tactful ones made deliberate mistakes so that his highness could show his superior wisdom by correcting them.[11]

James was exhilarated over the doctrine that he proclaimed to Parliament: the divine right of the king. Before his first Parliament he propounded his thesis, intoxicated by the new wine of his absolutist theory of government. "The state of the monarchy," he stated, "is the supremest thing upon earth; for Kings are not only God's lieutenants upon earth and sit upon God's throne, but even by God Himself they are called gods!"[12]

By the time James dissolved his first Parliament he had successfully launched the three perilous feuds of Stuart England: the constitutional, the Roman Catholic, and the Puritan conflicts. Members of Parliament harbored resentment against James as its members watched "the Scots creeping into English lordships and English ladies' beds, in both of which already they began to be active."[13]

Morality was at low ebb in the royal court. The king liked to stage masques. One was presented at Theobalds in 1606 in honor of King Christian IV of Denmark. The streets were strewn with gold leaves that bore the word welcome. Sir John Harrington wrote an account, reporting that the festivities reminded him of "Mohamet's paradise." Each day the women abandoned their sobriety and rolled about intoxicated. On one occasion the performers were supposed to represent the visit of the Queen of Sheba to King Solomon. The woman who played the part of Sheba carried precious gifts to both of their majesties, but she tripped over the steps and spilled her casket of gifts upon the Danish king. Confusion ensued, but his highness was wiped clean with napkins and he arose to dance with the tipsy Sheba but "fell down and humbled himself before her and was dragged to a couch in an inner room."[14]

James' controversial *Book of Sports*, published in 1604, aroused John Robinson and many other churchmen. They were already disturbed over the secularization of the sabbath and the corruption of religious festivals like Whitsuntide. It had become the custom at this season in many churches for lay officers to brew and sell ale to raise funds for the parish. "Wild heads" turned out for the fun, "decked out in bright scarves and ribbons, their legs gartered with bells, riding hobb-horses and dragons, to dance into church and up the aisle, piping and playing, as the congregation climbed upon the pews to cheer and laugh at their antics."[15]

James outlined for his subjects the pastimes they could legitimately enjoy after going to church on Sunday.[16] He declared that Englishmen were not to be "disturbed or discouraged from dancing, archery, leaping, vaulting, having May games, Whitsun-ales, Morrice dances, setting up May Poles, and other sports therewith used, or any other harmless recreations on Sundays after divine service." He also ordered all clergy to read his new ordinances from their pulpits. The Puritans realized that this was a trick to catch them, because those who refused were brought before the High Commission Court for punishment.

Robinson was one of scores of Cambridge students and fellows who had followed the proceedings of Hampton Court and the stubborn reaction of King James' thinking. He was close to three of the Puritan representatives at this conclave. Laurance Chaderton was his professor. John Knewstubs had taken his B.D. at St. John in 1576 and was prominent in the Cambridge circle of scholarship. He was familiar with Dr. John Reynolds, the influential preacher in Lincoln, next door to his home town. He knew these three major contenders for the Puritan cause. Robinson was more than an onlooker; he, too, was a participant. He was vitally affected by the pronouncements of King James. Most of his years of preparation and decision had been passed under Elizabeth's reign. During this period an oppressive rigidity existed that incited passion for freedom.

Already impatient and critical, he was prodded into growing revolt against autocracy by the proclamations of James. He had hoped vainly for a relaxation of tension during the last years of the queen but this hope was not realized. Her successor was a bitter disappointment. During his years at Cambridge he had become familiar with the harassed pioneers who paid for their advanced views with suffering. He could envisage something of the dismal future that lay ahead for the younger generation under the king.

Soon after his marriage he secured a church post at St. Andrews in Norwich. He may have gone there because of his friendship for Bishop Jegon, who had been master of his college; or because it was a strongly independent town due to the Dutch influence and the tradition of Thomas Bilney and Robert Browne; or Thomas Newhouse, a Cambridge-trained minister, may have invited him to become one of his associates there. While at work in the parish he was contemplating the role he was to assume in the conflict that was consuming England.

The Reformation was accepted by certain of the leading citizens of Norwich due to the labors of Thomas Robert, rector of St. Clements, who died in 1576, and Thomas More, vicar of St. Andrews, who passed away in 1592. These men had objected to the "imposition of ceremonies and everything savouring of Popery."

More important than Robinson's ministerial duties was his determination to find a way to liberate the church that he loved. He pored over the writings of Perkins, Chaderton, and Baynes, his Cambridge mentors. He heard once again the tragic account of how the Mother Church had burned Thomas Bilney, the Cambridge luminary, in 1531 at Lollard's Pit near Norwich. He talked with people who had known Robert Browne when he had launched his reform in a Norwich church and laid down the principles of the Separatist position, and he reread the books of Francis Johnson, William Bradshaw, Henry Jacob, William Ames, and Robert Parker.

Norwich was the second largest city in the kingdom. As the capital of East Anglia it boasted a castle, a cathedral, and a fifteenth-century Guild Hall. It was known for its strong-willed people. East Anglia stretched out into the German Sea, set apart from other sections by fens and marshes. It had been invaded many times by Teutonic peoples and its ports visited by traders from the Netherlands and Germany. Citizens from the lowlands had flocked in to escape Spanish tyranny. In 1587 there were 4,679 Dutch and Walloons in Norwich.

An anonymous manuscript in 1609 shows that Robinson lived in Norwich in 1604 for about a year and was a minister in St. Andrews Church. It states that two of his children were baptized there.[17] Although he served as a Puritan in the Church of England, he held strong scruples against ceremonies and vestments, and because he practiced omissions or made modifications in the services that he conducted he was soon in difficulty with his bishop. Bishop Jegon stuck by the articles of his church more loyally than he did to his own college dean, for Jegon was at heart an Establishment man.

The 1609 manuscript gives citations from otherwise unknown writings of Robinson and it records his statement that his withdrawal from the Church of England was not entirely voluntary, but was forced upon him.

> My forsaking the church of England was no rupture (as you speak) but an inforced departure. Upon the most advised deliberations I could possibly take, either with the Lord, by humblying myself before Him or with men, for whose advice I spared neither cost nor pains, but sought out in every place the most sincere and judicious in the land for resolution to the contrary, as both God and men can witness with me.[18]

Robinson criticized the stifling formalism of the *Book of Common Prayer*: "The service book quencheth the spirit of prayer. Ergo, it is a devised worship."[19] He advocated choice of ministers by the people: "And good reason why the Church should both well know and freely approve her ministers to whom she is to commit herself, souls and bodies."[20]

He pointed out some shortcomings of the Norwich church:

> St. Andrews is not a people separated and sanctified from the world into holy covenant with God, but a confused assembly, and so in that confusion hath her self received no power from Christ, and so can give none to any other. Secondly, St. Andrews hath not the liberty either to engage any minister though never so holy, or to remove any though never so profane, but at the will of the Bishop, their and their minister's spiritual lord.[21]

A proclamation was issued by James I in 1604 which required all ministers to accept and follow the new *Book of Canons*. The bishops were compelled to tighten up on their men. Bishop Jegon

57

of Norwich sought to bring the clergy of his diocese into line. Reports had been coming to him about the liberties John Robinson was taking with the rubrics and the statements he was propounding from the pulpit. The young cleric had questioned the authority of the bishops since he found no justification for their deeds in the New Testament. He set conscience above obedience to his bishop, so he was suspended from his position at St. Andrews and denied the privilege of preaching. He then assembled a few friends for conversations and prayer, but their names were reported and they were excommunicated.

Henry Ainsworth refers in later years to persecutions that were inflicted on his young friend:

> If any among you not meddling with the public estate of your Church, but feeling or fearing his own particular soul-sickness, do resort to a physician (whose receipts are not after the common sort) for advice about his health, or of friendship and acquaintance to see him, he is subject to the censure and thunderbolt of your Church. Witness the late practice in Norwich, where certain citizens were excommunicated for resorting unto and praying with Mr. Robinson, a man worthily reverenced of all the city for the graces of God in him. Would any unmerciful man have dealt so with his bond-slave in a case of bodily sickness? But hereby all may see what small hope there is of curing the canker of your church.[22] (Written to Richard Bernard, a critic of Robinson's views.)

Although suspended, Robinson still loved the church and wished to retain some connection with it. He hoped that the severity of the bishop might be mitigated and that he would be allowed to carry on his work in some private chapel or public hall where he could expound his views on a simplified and revitalized religion. He applied to the corporation of Norwich for mastership of the Great Hospital and for a building that he might lease, but he failed in both these efforts.

He felt that canon law and the facts in the New Testament could not be reconciled, that reformation of his church was almost hopeless, that the bishops and lords formed a dominating hierarchy that was contrary to the original spirit and intent of the Christian Church. So he reluctantly resolved "on most sound and unresistable convictions" to follow his Puritan principles to their logical consequences and to separate from his beloved church. The circumstances of his intense inner struggle answer the sarcastic insinuations of Bishop Joseph Hall, who claimed that he was a victim of disappointment and bitterness and so suddenly abandoned his profession to become a Separatist.

In June 1605 Francis Mason gave a sermon in the "Greene Yard" in Norwich. It was a plea for the reformers to move with moderation. He argued that such internal disputes afforded points of attack for the Roman Catholics on one hand and for the Separatists on the other. Peace was the basic need and submission was necessary. They could not afford more Brownists (the extremists who were followers of Robert Browne of Norwich).

Robinson was not convinced by this appeal. Sometimes it was necessary to refuse submission to authoritarianism that had no basis in reason, to ceremonies that were riddled with superstition, to dogmas that had been foisted upon men by the wiles of popes and priests.

It is evident that the young cleric did well in Norwich, made friends, and achieved some good. His booklet *People's Plea for the Exercise of Prophecy* (1618) was dedicated to "his Christian friends in Norwich and thereabouts . . . even as when I lived with you." He expressed opposition to the Rev. Mr. Yates of Norwich who had written a treatise denouncing lay preaching in the church. Robinson answered, defending the right of laymen to speak.

During his stay in Norwich he suffered disillusion with the church and intense agitation and perplexity about his future. If he were to take the course of the rebel how could he care for Bridget and the children? In a passage that he wrote to Richard Bernard he explained the mental struggles through which he was passing. He said he found "some taste of the truth" as he studied the literature of the reformers. He was impressed by "the learning and holiness" of these men, "blushing in myself to have a thought of pressing one hair-breadth before them in this thing, behind whom I knew myself to come so many miles."

He would never have broken his bonds "had not the truth been in his heart as a burning fire shut up in his bones." If he had suffered the light of God to have been put out in his heart by the darkness of other men he would have remained "straitly tied."[23] He was no willing deserter from his old church. He was not rabid or contumacious; but he was without a job, with no income, and with a family on his hands. He packed their few belongings and journeyed to Sturton le Steeple to the Robinson-White haven of refuge where he and Bridget poured out their tribulations.

It was disillusioning to realize that his own college master had set fidelity to the Archbishop of Canterbury above devotion to a pupil, associate, and friend for over a decade. When put to the test the pontiffs of the church stood together against any challenge to their hyperorthodoxy. They formed a mighty citadel of entrenched power, the Church almighty, a kingdom of the world, not of the spirit, a syndicate of Pharisees and Sadducees such as the one that struck down the founder of Christianity. They were sticklers for protocol, for the rubrics, for sacerdotal theological doctrine, for priestcraft. Their strength was consumed with trivial and extraneous concerns. There was no time to search for the realities that must lie somewhere beneath this subterfuge of legend. They were enslaved by devotion to their long, broad-sleeved surplices of fine linen and lace which they wore over their silk cassocks. They treasured richly embroidered stoles, fine silken copes and dalmatics.

Most of the religious leaders he knew were looking backward, enslaved by conformity with tradition. Their churchmanship was a docile adherence to ancient forms and practices. Membership in the church held no meaning. All baptized in childhood were automatically members as long as they lived. Most of those "in the fold" were untrained in the Christian faith. This was wrong Church members should be enlightened, educated, and in the church because it was a society of those who were pledged to live in accord with Christian ethics and as examples of the Christian way.

There were magistrates and primates who compromised with conscience by bending before royal mandates, however tyrannical. But this was not true of Robinson. He was willing to risk peril and make a stand for right even though the move formed a direct challenge to his sovereign, who proclaimed that he was the voice of God in the world.

The bucolic peace of the countryside only set his mind throbbing with more doubts and questions. Leaving Bridget and the children, he set out for his old university "where I hoped most to finde satisfaction to my troubled heart." He admits that he "made questions" of "separation" and in his conversations he "disputed for it" but as yet he had not "otherwise professed it." The talks he had there and the addresses he heard tended to strengthen his resolution.

He saw and heard Laurence Chaderton:

Coming to Cambridge, I went the forenoon to Mr. Cha: (Laurence Chaderton) his exercise, who . . . delivered in effect this doctrine; that the things which concerned the whole Church were to be declared publicly to the whole Church and not to some part only; bringing for instance and proof the words of Christ, Matt. 18:17: "Tell it to the Church" confirming therein one main ground of our difference from the Church of England, which is, that Christ hath given his power for excommunication to the *whole church* gathered together in his name, as I Cor. 5, the officers as the governors, and the people as the governed in the use thereof: unto which Church his servants are commanded to bring their necessary complaints.[24]

He shared Chaderton's ideas regarding the tyrannical practice of excommunication by the bishops, a right which belonged to the people. The authority of the church should rest with its members.

In the afternoon he went to hear "Holy" Baynes, successor to William Perkins, who spoke on Ephesians 5:7-11. "Do not associate with them, for once you were darkness, but now you are light in the Lord; walk as children of the light. . . . Take no part in the unfruitful works of darkness, but instead expose them (Eph. 5:8, 11)." This suggested that servants of the Lord should separate themselves from the unworthy and wicked in the church, and break away from the conglomerate admixture of good, indifferent, and evil who make up the church.[25]

Robinson's sojourn at the university stiffened his resolution to carry on along the path of resistance, trusting that he could find some spot of freedom where he might continue to think and teach. He made his way back to the country. We do not know how close he was to the vicar of his boyhood church, St. Peter and St. Paul, or the vicar at St. Marys in Greasley, where he and

Bridget were married. It may be that these men were out of sympathy with the trends at Cambridge and with the native son who had been deprived.

There were fellow ministers he could visit; Hugh Bromhead, curate at North Wheatley; Richard Bernard of Worksop, who backed away later and turned against the Separatist cause; Richard Clyfton of Babworth, whose teaching drew the liberals of the area; and John Smyth of Gainsborough, who was the leader of quite a following of those who were dissatisfied with the state of religion. John's suspension created a stir in the neighborhood and his minister friends were concerned and upset, realizing that the same fate might await them.

It is probable that he gathered a small company of friends around him in Sturton le Steeple, counselled with members of his family, the Whites, who later played a prominent role in his Holland community, John Carver, who became his co-worker, and others who developed into loyal supporters.

As the Lord's free people joined themselves
(by a covenant of the Lord) into a church estate,
in the fellowship of the gospel, to walk in all
His ways made known, or to be known unto them,
according to their best endeavors, whatever it
should cost them, the Lord assisting them.
—William Bradford

5 "AS THE LORD'S FREE PEOPLE"

Four East Anglia towns in Robinson's homeland, where Lincolnshire, Nottinghamshire, and Yorkshire join—Gainsborough, Scrooby, Babworth, and Austerfield—form the setting for the next stage in the Cambridge don's development as the Pilgrim leader.

The jobless young man journeyed to Gainsborough, on the east side of the River Trent, which ran some 200 miles from the highlands of Staffordshire to join the Humber, connecting by canal navigation with all the principal rivers in the southern part of the kingdom. Gainsborough was a principal market for wheat, barley, oats, rye, and beans; sailboats kept up a busy trade on the river. He was familiar with the great chimneys of the Old Hall, the tower of the parish church, the sloops that sailed to Grimsby and Hull, the wagons and mills and the grammar school founded by the reformers who demanded education for their youth.

Robinson visited the grammar school as a boy. He might have studied here since his village was only some nine miles away. He could recall with pleasure the marts and fairs of the bustling little city. But now he was searching for guidance from his friend, John Smyth, who for several months had gathered around him those who were discontented with the Established Church. He met with them in the Old Hall that had been built on the site of the palace where King Alfred had been married and where Canute had been proclaimed king of England by the captains of his navy. Henry VIII had held his court here in 1541. The lord of the manor, William Hickman, who had purchased the Manor of Gainsborough in 1596, was in sympathy with the Puritans. He and his wife, Rose, daughter of Sir William Locke, had suffered exile for their religious beliefs during the reign of Mary I. They returned from Antwerp when the crown passed to Elizabeth. The Hickmans were friendly toward John Smyth and his followers and invited them to meet in the Old Hall, which was described by George Eliot in *The Mill on the Floss*.

It was the Normans who began to build that fine old hall, which is like the town, telling of the thoughts and hands of widely sundered generations; but it is all so old that we look with loving pardon at its inconsistencies, and are well content that they who built the stone oriel, and they who built the Gothic facade and towers of finest brickwork with the trefoil

63

ornament, did not sacrilegiously pull down the ancient half-timbered body with its oak-roofed banqueting hall.[1]

John Smyth was an alumnus of Christ's College, Cambridge, and had been chosen preacher of the city of Lincoln in 1600. He was deposed in 1602 "for having approved himself a factious man in this city by personal preachings and that untruly against divers men of good place."[2] He was in Gainsborough in a state of doubt that lasted nine months. Here, under threats and illness, he became a Separatist and the leader of the Gainsborough independent fellowship. He was "a man of able gifts and a good preacher," William Bradford records.

Robinson met with Smyth and the Gainsborough company, discussing what they believed and what they should do. The little circle welcomed the Cambridge scholar to their secret gatherings, eager to hear the story of his encounter with the bishops and reports from the outside world. In this company of friends probably were Thomas Helwys, John Murton, Hugh and Ann Bromhead, the "fatherly" Richard Clyfton, Richard Jackson and Robert Rochester from Scrooby, Francis Jessop of Worksop with his wife, Frances, youngest sister of Bridget Robinson, William Brewster of Scrooby, and possibly young William Bradford from Austerfield.

Robinson also met with a similar small group in Scrooby, gathered there around William Brewster, who was about ten years his elder. They were both Cambridge men and they struck up a deep and enduring friendship. They shared a passion for spiritual freedom and a broad religious outlook.

William Brewster, born about 1566, spent his boyhood in comfort and plenty on the vast acres of Scrooby Manor, which his father managed for the Archbishop of York. He studied at Peterhouse, Cambridge's oldest college. In 1584 or 1585 he was invited to join Sir William Davison, who was to become secretary of state under Queen Elizabeth, as his youthful secretary. In their struggle to throw off the yoke of Spain, the United Provinces of the Netherlands sought help from England. Queen Elizabeth dispatched Davison to Holland with financial aid. Brewster lived with him in The Hague, Leyden, and other Dutch cities. Bradford states that "the secretary found him so discreet and faithful that he trusted him above all others that were about him. He only employed him in all matters of greatest trust and secrecy."[3]

When Elizabeth resolved to execute Mary Queen of Scots in 1587, Davison was assigned the burden of the legal process, and the queen made him the scapegoat. He was tried before the Star Chamber Court and committed to the Tower. Brewster "remained with Mr. Davison some good time after he was put from his place, doing him many faithful offices of service in the time of his troubles."[4]

Broadened by his residence in Holland, and disillusioned by the intrigues of the court, Brewster made his way back to Scrooby around the year 1590. Through Davison's efforts he received the court appointment as postmaster and took over his father's position at the ancient manor. Sandys, Archbishop of York, had

Scrooby Manor, Scrooby, Nottinghamshire

64

Louis J Holman

appointed William Brewster's father as his steward and bailiff retainer at Scrooby in 1576. William, Junior, had met Sir Edwin Sandys, one of the six sons of the archbishop, while he was in London. Sir Edwin had traveled widely in Europe where he wrote his book *Europae Speculum*, reporting on the state of religion and ecclesiastical affairs. His views on religious tolerance were ahead of his time. (John Robinson owned a copy of this book which bears his own signature on the title page, and it may be seen in Pilgrim Hall, Plymouth.) In his treatise Sir Edwin stated that he found in every country men who believed in and hoped for the lessening of controversy and the increase of unity among Christians. Sandys was later to prove a friend to the Pilgrims. As a member of Parliament and a promoter of the Virginia Company he helped them plan their crossing to America.

Scrooby was a quiet village on the Great North Road about half way between London and Scotland on the Ryton near the point where it joins the gentle Idle. These pokey streams flow into the Humber watershed that drains the moors of East Anglia.

In addition to a small cluster of houses, there was a parish church, St. Wilfrid's, "well builded" of stone and a great "tymber" manor house set on the Ryton and surrounded by a moat. *Domesday Book* recorded in 1086 that it was a manor of some forty rooms, a chapel with a great hall where the Archbishop of York held court. In Brewster's time there was the manor house, the chapel, bake house, brewhouse, the gallery, the house that stood at the east end of the orchard, and other buildings in the little court, the house at the east of the great court, which had been the archbishop's office, along with the barns and stables.

William Brewster was the genial host at Scrooby Manor, the village squire who was manager of the estate, bailiff, postmaster, and magistrate. He was respected for his university training, knowledge of the world, ample income, and friendly nature. He provided bed, food, and drink for travelers, and feed and shelter for their animals. As postmaster he was required to keep ready for instant use three "good and sufficient horses" with "furniture fit and belonging," such as saddles, bridles, dispatch bags, and three horns "to blow by the way." Wayfarers usually arrived armed with pistol, sword, or dagger for defense against highwaymen.

Weary guests enjoyed the welcome of Scrooby Manor—oak logs glowing in its huge fireplaces, a mug of hot toddy or buttered ale to flavor their roast beef and Yorkshire pudding. Fynes Moryson wrote in 1617:

> There is no place in the world where passengers may so freely command as in the English inns, and are attended for themselves and their horses as well as if they were at home, and perhaps better, each servant being ready at call in hope of a small reward in the morning.[5]

Bradford wrote of Brewster:

> He lived . . . in good esteem among his friends, and the good gentlemen of those parts especially the godly and religious. He did much good in the country where he lived, in promoting and furthering religion; and not only by his practice and example,

and provoking and encouraging of others, but by procuring of good preachers to all places thereabouts, and drawing on of others to assist and help forward in such a work; he himself most commonly deepest in the charge, and some times above his ability.[6]

The secret groups "ordinarily met at his (Brewster's) house on ye Lord's Day, ... and with great love he entertained them when they came, making provision for them to his great charge."[7]

In addition to Scrooby and Gainsborough, a third neighboring village, Babworth, played a role in developing the Pilgrim Church. Babworth lies in Nottinghamshire midway between the Idle and the Ryton, the rivers that form part of the Valley of the Trent. All

St. Wilfrid's Church, Scrooby (rebuilt in 1380)

Saints Church was built there in 1290. Richard Clyfton, a graduate of Christ's College, Cambridge, was appointed minister in 1586. William Brewster on his home visits from the queen's court had heard Clyfton preach. He liked his ideas and often journeyed the seven miles from Scrooby to hear him on Sundays, taking with him others who were dissatisfied with the state of the national church.

Clyfton was soon in trouble because of his Separatist teachings. Reprimanded by his bishop, he was at length deprived of his living in 1605. He then moved to Scrooby at the invitation of his friend Brewster. He and Robinson had met at some of the secret gatherings at Gainsborough and Scrooby and may have visited together in the Old Rectory at Babworth.[8]

Brewster also welcomed John Robinson after he was deprived of his post in Norwich, and no doubt took the lead in securing him a salary from friends in the area. Without this financial support Robinson might have been forced to continue in some Church of England post until he entangled further with the bishops and was shipped away to prison.

One may be reasonably sure that John and Bridget and their children lived in Brewster's compound for a year or so. This so-

Sturton le Steeple countryside

journ is important in the development of the Pilgrim leader. He and Brewster spent time over their books (because both owned good libraries) and in discussion of Cambridge ties, religion, and politics. They must have strolled through the hamlet of red-brick homes and barns with their tile roofs and prosperous gardens, along the sleepy Ryton to the old Monks Mill, which had graced the village for over 700 years. Ducks and geese haunted the marshes about the placid stream. Cuckoos called from hedges along the lanes and sleek cattle grazed in the pasture lands.

The association of these two minds was of prime importance in the Pilgrim story. Brewster stood out in this era of fanaticism as a man of sound judgment and common sense. As the lay leader of the Scrooby-Leyden-Plimoth enterprise he complemented Robinson and helped implement his ideas.

Two groups soon developed: one in Gainsborough and one in Scrooby. It was more convenient for those in the Scrooby area to meet there in the manor house of William Brewster. It was difficult to conceal their journeying back and forth from the spies who checked their movements. Bradford records:

> These people became two distinct bodies or churches, and in regard to distance of place did congregate severally; for they were of sundry towns and villages, some in Nottinghamshire, some in Lincolnshire, and some of Yorkshire where they border nearest together.[9]

Robinson, Brewster, Clyfton, and their associates endured persecution for a time and then decided as the "Lord's free people" that they possessed a God-given right to withdraw from the Church of England and form their own congregation.

It has not been determined exactly at what point they developed the famous covenant. It was probably at Scrooby in 1606, as Bradford recalls:

> So many, therefore, of these professors as saw the evil of those in these parts, and whose hearts the Lord had touched with heavenly zeal for His truth, they shook off this yoke of antichristian bondage, and as the Lord's free people joined themselves (by a covenant of the Lord) into a church estate, in the fellowship of the gospel, to walk in all His ways made known, or to be made known unto them, according to their best endeavors, whatsoever it should cost them, the Lord assisting them. And that it cost them something this ensuing history will declare.[10]

So in secrecy in 1606 the Scrooby church was formed. After consenting to the covenant, the members chose Richard Clyfton as minister, John Robinson as teacher, and William Brewster as elder.

Providence brought another kindred spirit, young William Bradford of Austerfield, who by mind, character, and tempera-

ment was close to Robinson and Brewster. Bradford's parents had died and he was being raised by uncles. His home still stands today, not far from the quaint little St. Helen's Church, consecrated in 1086, where he was baptized in 1590, about the time that William Brewster returned from the court to take up his duties in Scrooby.

The lad was bright, attractive, and interested in learning. Brewster grew fond of him, became his foster father and tutored him. Robinson developed the same affinity. Bradford's relatives objected, pointing out that if he affiliated with "fanatasticall schismatics" he would lose his friends. his property, and his reputation. But he was drawn to Robinson and Brewster, his engaging tutors from the great university, and determined to cast his lot with them. The wrath of his uncles and the scoffing of his neighbors could not divert him.

Robinson and Brewster spent many hours with him, teaching him Hebrew, Greek, and Latin. In the first great American book, *Of Plimoth Plantation*, Bradford's journal covering a period of some forty years, he registers his grasp of these languages as well as of history, literature, the Bible, and theology. His Elizabethan English possesses the same moving eloquence as the King James Bible. Although he never visited the halls of a university, unless it was in Leyden, William developed the cosmopolitan and cultivated outlook of a Cambridge man.

Home of William Bradford, Austerfield, Yorkshire

70

Robinson's association with Bradford is significant because this youth was to become his most famous disciple and lead the Pilgrim movement in the New World for three decades after Robinson's passing. His political leadership and religious outlook reflected the tolerant views of his Cambridge tutors. Bradford wrote later of this period of tutelage under Robinson and Brewster: "To keep a good conscience and walk in such a way as God had prescribed in His word, is a thing which I shall prefer above you all, and above life itself."

In 1606 Bishop Tobias Matthews of Durham was made Archbishop of York. He was an avid censor of Puritan and Separatist literature and possessed a bloodhound's nose for detection of heresy. At his instigation a wave of terror swept the area. In March 1607, a messenger was sent to apprehend Gervase Neville, a grandson of the High Sheriff of Nottinghamshire, who was "one of the sect of Baroists or Brownists holding and maintaining erroneous opinions and doctrines." For such schismatical obstinacy he was to be delivered "to the hands, ward and safe custody of the Keeper of his Majesty's Castle of York." Neville was jailed as a "very dangerous" Brownist, charged with making "contemptuous and scandalous" speeches and "frequenting of conventicles and the companie of others of his profession." This was a reference to the Scrooby and Gainsborough meetings.[11]

Warrants were also issued for Richard Jackson and Robert Rochester of Scrooby and Francis Jessop of Worksop (a brother-in-law of Robinson). Brewster was ordered to appear "upon lawful summons at the Collegiate Church of Southwell" but he refused to go. Warrants for his arrest were dated September 15 and December 1, 1607, describing him as a "very dangerous schismatical Separatist, Brownist and irreligious subject." A fine of twenty pounds apiece was imposed April 22, 1608 upon these three Scrooby citizens for not appearing upon lawful summons. This was a substantial fine. William Brewster, the most affluent in the company, probably paid the entire sum which would be close to $3,000 in current value. Robinson and Brewster recognized that Archbishop Matthews in York and King James in London might soon lock them up and they could languish the rest of their years in the dank obscurity of some foul dungeon.

Under Mary I many English intellectuals had fled to the continent, although some returned during the more tolerable days of Elizabeth. However, the stream of emigration continued and under James it was increasing once again.

On the first day of March 1607 Brewster resigned his postmastership under pressure from higher authorities. A short time after, he was commanded to appear before the dread Court of High Commission for being "disobedient in matters of religion." He considered himself fortunate to escape with only a heavy fine.

The inventory of Brewster's property at the time of his death listed 397 books. Robinson likewise had a significant library. The two men discussed the Puritan writers, most of whom they knew personally. We assume that they read and talked before the fireplace, with a mug of ale or cider, enjoying the aroma from their long-stemmed clay pipes. The new custom of using tobacco had been brought to England by Sir John Hawkins about 1565. Sir Walter Raleigh made "drinking tobacco" a popular pastime.[12]

They reviewed the hostile record of crown and church. They both had encountered ample repression and had come to sense the futility of expecting to win their foes to their views. Robinson narrated his experiences at Cambridge, Norwich, and in the neighborhood around Sturton le Steeple.

Brewster brought a firsthand story about his contemporaries at Cambridge, the martyred Greenwood, Barrowe, and Penry. They were locked up in London prisons while he was in the queen's court. Since Secretary of State Davison, a Puritan sympathizer, was for a time clerk of the Privy Council, Brewster was able to glean some knowledge from his superior on the treatment of these pioneers. He had also seen Archbishop John Whitgift, one of the severest foes of the Puritans, "the old Beelzebub of Canterbury," a fellow alumnus of Peterhouse College who served the queen as her "little black husband." Whitgift had boasted of his contempt for the "common sort of persons, particularly those that read the Bible."

Warnings had been flashing for years. The forces of constriction and oppression were growing more powerful and threatening. The Scrooby fellowship was merely existing now, marking time under the continual suspicion of the king's spies. There had been veiled and open warnings, threats, and fines. It was only a matter of time and they would be jailed. James I appeared to have developed a peculiar dislike for their small company. He was fearful that if they applied a rule-by-the-people precept in the church they would likewise introduce the same troublesome practice in government.

Robinson and Brewster had gone so far that they could never conform to the old regime. They had fought their way through the entanglements of the hierarchy and their breath of freedom was like a fine wine, stimulating the mind to probe further after larger unfoldings of the truth. Robinson inquired about the state of religious liberty in the Netherlands. Brewster reported that he was impressed with Dutch tolerance and democratic practices. Again and again their conversation turned to the shores of Holland.

A letter of warning had been written to the Separatists by John Penry from his cell in King's Bench Prison before his execution, urging them to make plans to leave the tyranny of England and seek some more hospitable soil:

And, my good brethren, seeing banishment, with loss of goods, is likely to betide you all, prepare yourselves for this hard entreaty, and rejoice that you are made worthy for Christ's cause to suffer and bear all things. And I beseech you that none of you, in this case, look upon his particular estate; but regard the general state of the church of God, that the same may go, and be kept together, whithersoever it shall please God to send you.

Let not those of you, that either have stocks in your hands, or some likely trades to live by, dispose of yourselves where it may be most commodious for your outward estate, and, in the

mean time, suffer the poor ones, that have no such means, either to bear the whole work upon their weak shoulders, or to end their days in sorrow and mourning, for want of outward and inward comforts, in the land of strangers. But consult with the whole church, yea, with the brethren of other places, how the church may be kept together and built, whithersoever they go . . .

Yea, I wish you and them to be together if you may, whithersoever you shall be banished, and to this purpose, to bethink you beforehand where to be; yea, to send some who may be meet to prepare you some resting-place. And, be all of you assured, that He who is your God in England, will be your God in any land under the whole heaven.[13]

Robinson had been reluctant to sever ties with the Mother Church. The radical step had cut him off from his profession, income, and friends. He would become an outcast as far as a future benefice or teaching post was concerned. Unlike Brewster, he had no other income. He was trained for service in an institution in which he could not now serve and keep his integrity.

Joseph Hall, three years Robinson's senior at Cambridge, later Bishop of Exeter and Norwich, published a letter to Robinson and John Smyth in 1608 in which he censured and advised them in a tone of righteous condemnation:

St. Helen's Church. Austerfield (consecrated in 1086)—William Bradford was baptized here.

The God of heaven open your eyes, that you may see the injustice of that zeal which hath transported you; and turn your heart to an endeavour of all Christian satisfaction; otherwise, your souls shall find too late that it had been a thousand times better to swallow a ceremony, than to rend a church; yea, that even whoredoms and murders shall abide in easier answer than Separation.[14]

Robinson replied in *An Answer to a Censorious Epistle*:

To the Title of Ring-leader, wherewith it pleaseth this epistler to style me, I answer, that if the thing I have done be good, it is good and commendable to have been forward in it; if it be evil, let it be reproved by the light of God's word, and that God to whom I have done that I have done, will (I doubt not) give me both to see, and to heal mine error by speedy repentance: if I have fled away on foot, I shall return on Horsebacke. But as I durst never set foot into this way, but upon a most sound and unresistable conviction of conscience by the word of God (as I was persuaded) so must my returning be wrought by more solid reasons from the same word, than are to be found in a thousand such pretty pamphlets and formal flourishes as this is.[15]

Norman-built Old Hall, Gainsborough, Lincolnshire—Pilgrims held early secret meetings here
All Saints Church, Babworth, Nottinghamshire (built in 1290)

He now sensed day after day the peril of those who dared to challenge the power of the Establishment. He realized as he thought of Bridget and the children the price they were paying for freedom. Some of his Cambridge associates were in prominent parishes with generous stipends and handsome rectories for their families. In contrast, he was isolated in an obscure village, eking out an existence, working with a small company of humble people who faced harassment and danger of imprisonment.

In his *Dialogue* Bradford wrote about sixty English citizens he knew who had been arrested for their religious beliefs: "Allowing them neither meat, drink, fire or lodging, nor suffering any whose hearts the Lord would stir up for their relief, to have any access to them, so as they complained that no felons, traitors, nor murderers in the land were thus dealt with." Spies were hired by the crown and bishops to visit prisoners, engage them in conversation, and try to lure them into saying something that could be used as evidence against them.[16]

But after these things they could not long continue in any peaceable condition, but were hunted and persecuted on every side, so as their former afflictions were but as flea-bitings in comparison of these which now came upon them. For some were taken and clapped up in prison, others had their houses beset and watched day and night, and hardly escaped their hands; and the most were fain to flee and leave their houses and habitations, and the means of their livelihood.[17]

The Vicarage, Scrooby (period of Henry VII)

Though they should be but stepping
stones unto others for the performing of so
great a work.
—William Bradford

6 "STEPPING STONES UNTO OTHERS"

During the early months of 1607 John Robinson was deeply involved in the plan to remove to Holland. With his copastor, Richard Clyfton, he conducted Sunday services, weekday lectures, and Bible study. Clyfton, the elder of the two deprived clergymen, was called pastor and the younger Robinson, teacher. As the weeks passed, more and more of the labor of the arrangements fell upon the shoulders of the teacher. The fellowship continued to grow as residents of neighboring communities came to the manor house for secret gatherings to discuss their present and future lot in England.

Teacher Robinson visited the homes of his parishioners scattered throughout the area. He made his way on horseback to their cottages where he shared their sicknesses and sorrows and heard reports of the indignities which they continued to suffer at the hands of the Establishment. In every home they spoke of their efforts to negotiate quietly and secretly to dispose of farm, stock, home, and furnishings—transactions that were difficult to keep hidden from the magistrates. They endeavored to prevent representatives of the bishops and the king from learning of their plans to illegally flee the country. It was necessary to obtain a license to leave the shores of England and these permits were not granted to dissenters.

Under compulsion to seek freedom in Holland, they must break their ties with "their native soil and country, their lands and livings, and their friends and familiar acquaintances" and set out for a strange land. It was "an adventure almost desperate," and as a group of country husbandmen they must find new ways to support themselves.

> Yet this was not all, for though they could not stay, yet were they not suffered to go; but the ports and havens were shut against them, so they were fain to seek secret means of conveyance, and to bribe and fee the mariners, and give extraordinary rates for their passage. And yet were they often times betrayed, many of them; and both they and their goods intercepted and surprised, and thereby put to great trouble and charge.[1]

In 1600 Thomas Wilson reported: "There is no person neither stranger nor subject that may depart out of the realme without

79

licence of the Queene or the Privy Counsell or the Warden of the Cinque ports."[2]

A multitude of problems developed as these hard-working, proud people parted with the possessions they cherished. It was a bold sacrifice for conscience sake to surrender one's holdings because of principles and to venture privation in a foreign country. Week after week decisions were made, property transferred, and plans developed for the escape to the free air of Holland. Robinson made countless journeys back and forth to Sturton le Steeple with Bridget and the children to visit with the Robinsons and the Whites, to decide what should be done with their furnishings, clothing, books, and other possessions. What should they try to carry with them and what should they leave in Sturton le Steeple?

At length in the fall of 1607 the equipage set forth. On foot, in horse carts, and by small boats the Scrooby company moved secretly in little units from their villages southward toward Boston. On the journey they passed through the beauty of autumn fields and peaceful hamlets with their church spires. They moved cautiously to conceal their plans, sleeping in rural inns, in homes of villagers, and in the fields. Soon the high towers of the Stump Church came to view and they made their way into the streets of Boston. In the thirteenth century the Lincolnshire city had been a buzzing seaport, second only to London. The Hanseatic League established a guild and merchants who made their homes here helped build the majestic Stump Church.

Some of the Pilgrims found shelter with friends as they tried inconspicuously to hide away and await the arrival of the Dutch ship they had hired to carry them across the channel. The ship and her captain did not appear. Bundled into crowded dwellings and local inns, the migrants had to dole out their precious shillings for food. Impatiently they scanned the harbor for a sight of their Netherlands vessel. At length she crept into the Wash. John Robinson and his leaders rounded up the scattered flock and assembled them after dusk on the wharf, where dinghies carried them out to the small ship. They crept up the ship's side with their treasured goods and whispered together in little groups upon the deck. As they were about to give thanks for their embarkation, King James' spies rushed out from behind the storage sheds, clambered into dories and up the ship's ladders, crying, "In the king's name we arrest you!"

The ship's captain had betrayed them to the search officers with whom he had made an agreement. In an uproar of protestation, the passengers were lowered once more into open boats and rowed ashore. The officers ransacked their goods, searched them, and rifled their persons for money, even to their innermost garments and the women "beyond the bounds of modesty." They watched helplessly while their luggage, books, and cash were plundered. The officers marched them back into town and made them a spectacle to the crowds who flocked curiously about them. In their sorry plight they were presented before the magistrates.

Pilgrim Memorial, Scotia Creek, Boston—scene of Pilgrims' thwarted effort to leave England in 1607

Messengers were then dispatched to the lords of the council for advice on how to deal with these defiers of the law.

The magistrates treated them courteously but could not release them without orders from the council board. So the male leaders, including Robinson, Brewster, and Clyfton, were locked up in the grim stone cells of the Boston Guildhall. For a month or so they remained in this prison while their wives and children were left with the other passengers to wander off and seek shelter anywhere they could. Several of the men were released, but seven leaders were held, including Robinson and Brewster, in durance and were "bound over to the assizes."[3]

By the time they were liberated and had made their journey back to their towns to the north, it was late autumn. Robinson found Bridget and their children safe with his family and her relatives in Sturton le Steeple. He and Clyfton endeavored to keep the dispersed fellowship together, meeting secretly in obscure places since they were now openly branded as dissenters who had defied the king's edicts and attempted to flee the homeland illegally.

He rode over to Scrooby and must have spent part of the winter of 1607-08 there with William Brewster, striving to keep up the faith of a people who were uprooted and homeless, without property or employment, suspected by their neighbors, and spied upon by hirelings of the bishop and the king. Through the support of friends and the labor of those who could work on the farms they managed to keep body and soul together, gathering in tiny companies to speculate on what their next move was to be. Should they surrender their dream about Holland? Would it not now be wise to relocate on English soil where they could make a living rather than risk jail once more? The next time might mean life imprisonment or execution such as had been meted out to many of their predecessors.

Would they be double-crossed again by some Dutch sailor who would respond to a bribe and betray a promise? How could their small band cope with the omnipresent furies of their monarch? There was much to discuss and much to fear. But somehow their hardship bred heroism rather than hopelessness. John Robinson was heartened by the resolution of his associates. It was determined that they would make another effort—this time not from Boston in the south but from the Humber in the north.

They negotiated with contacts in Holland and by the spring of 1608 they had made a contract with another Dutchman at the port of Hull for the employment of his ship from Zeeland. This time they used the utmost caution and secrecy. Convinced of the captain's dependability, they signed an agreement and made a payment. He was to meet them on a large common that bordered the Humber River between Hull and Grimsby. The women and children with their goods were placed aboard a hired barque which went upstream. To avoid suspicion the men set out by land as inconspicuously as possible. They were all to assemble on the common.

Pilgrim Memorial, Immingham, Grimsby—Pilgrims made their successful escape to Holland in 1608 from here

The barque arrived first with neither the men nor the ship in sight. The water of the broad Humber was very rough and the seasick women persuaded the boatmen to put into the shelter of a creek. But the tide ebbed quickly and left them stuck fast on the sands.

The Dutch ship sailed into the Humber the next morning. The master was disturbed when he found the barque grounded until the return of the tide. Then he spied the men tramping nervously up and down the shore, ready and waiting. So he dispatched a long boat to bring them aboard. A number were soon on deck, and as he ordered the long boat to return and pick up the balance he saw a "great company on both horse and foot, with bills and guns and other weapons, for the country was raised to take them. Whereupon the sea captain swore his country's oath *sacremente*, and having the wind fair, weighed his anchor, hoisted sails, and away."[4]

The men on board pleaded with him to delay. They were terrified as to what would happen to their wives and children stranded in the barque and their comrades huddled on the banks of the Humber. As they swept out to sea under a spanking breeze they took inventory of their own lot. They were destitute, without money and supplies, with only the clothes on their backs. However, they were not permitted to muse long in commiseration since a heavy gale caught them in its course and for seven days a fearful storm raged. The tempest swept them north off the coast of Norway, and even the mariners despaired of the foundering ship.

But when man's hope and help wholly failed, the Lord's power and mercy appeared in their recovery; for the ship rose again and gave the mariners courage again to manage her. And if modesty would suffer me, I might declare with what fervent prayers they cried unto the Lord in this great distraction. When the water ran into their mouths and ears and the mariners cried out, "We sink, we sink!" they cried [if not with miraculous, yet with a great height or degree of divine faith], "Yet Lord Thou canst save!" Upon which the ship did recover, but shortly after the violence of the storm began to abate, and the Lord filled their afflicted minds with such comforts as everyone cannot understand, and in the end brought them to their desired haven[5]—[after the passage of a fortnight].

Meanwhile on the shores of the Humber the men who had been left behind eluded the soldiery, hid for a time, and then rejoined the women and children who came ashore from the barque, "crying for fear and quaking with cold." They were finally rounded up by the troops of James and marched to the nearest magistrate who was hesitant to condemn the helpless band, so they were hurried from one place to another. No one knew what to do with them. They could not send them home because they had sold their property. To imprison so many women and children might cause the populace to be aroused in their favor. The justices were

Old Guildhall, Boston—Pilgrim leaders were imprisoned here

in a quandary. In the end "they were glad to be rid of them upon any terms, for all were wearied and tired with them."[6]

So the wanderers were set free to travel back to their old haunts, to seek refuge once again with friends in the south. Their trials, tribulations, and mistreatment were known to many in Boston, Grimsby, Hull, and other areas where good-hearted citizens rose up to defend them. Some of the remnant in England shrank disheartened from these conflicts, but others came forth with fresh courage.

Robinson stayed with them to the end, considering that it was his duty to advise and protect and hold them together until he could find some way to get them across to Holland.

After these hazards and handicaps "they all gat over at length, some at one time and some at another, and some in one place and some in another, and met together again according to their desires, with no small rejoicing."[7] By the summer of 1608 about 125 members of the Scrooby congregation had made the journey to Amsterdam. Robinson came in the last contingent, along with Clyfton and Brewster. The first arrivals were on hand in the port of Amsterdam to greet the ship that brought the last of their company. They probably met for a celebration when their minister, teacher, and elder disembarked, gathering in the Church of the Ancient Brethren which had been established by an earlier band of refugees.

It was a hectic beginning due to their separation, the protracted delays, the loss by robbery of many of their funds, clothing, and supplies. Robinson must have prayed long and eloquently to illumine the dark path that lay ahead. He was frantically busy with practical affairs. Where would his family and the large company find shelter? Some of the Dutch opened their homes to them. The Reformed pastors were friendly and other English refugees did what they could to house and feed the new exiles. The magistrates tried to cooperate. But beyond temporary hearth and bread, jobs had to be found to make these people self-supporting. Fortunately Amsterdam was prospering. The wharfs and mills offered employment to those who had to start at the bottom of the ladder since they were largely farmers and unskilled in shipping and industry.

The pastor located a temporary home for his family. He walked with them along the great canals, exploring Amsterdam. The city had been built on piles over salt marshes. The population of the United Provinces was about 2,000,000 at this time. Between 200,000 and 250,000 people lived in Amsterdam. Only London and Paris were larger. In less than thirty years, from 1595 to 1612, the city had enlarged threefold.

The English villagers were soon caught up in the strange, bustling confusion of a vital port where vessels docked from every section of the then-known world and the streets were alive with natives from all parts of Europe. Because of its port and stock

Prison cells in Guildhall, Boston—Pilgrims were confined here

83

market, Amsterdam had developed into a world center for merchandise, securities, and banking. A unique bank was established at the outset of the seventeenth century. A merchant who deposited currency of his country could draw checks against this bank in bank florins and these checks could be exchanged for value. Currency manipulation abounded and traders were glad to be able to deal in something that was stable. Dutch credit rated high and foreign governments came here to arrange loans.

The stately buildings and gabled houses along the canals were proof of the wealth of Holland in her golden age. Summer flowers bloomed everywhere in window boxes, house gardens, and in cascades trailing from the cobblestones into the waterways. The streets were refreshingly clean, the Dutch industrious and friendly, and the atmosphere free from the threat of spies.

Robinson knew, however, that there were hazards to be met. They were foreigners who spoke a strange language and it was well nigh impossible for them to find worthy employment until they learned Dutch; even then time was required to acquire skills in an industrial community to compete for the lowliest

Place where Pilgrims landed on their arrival in Amsterdam in 1608

labor. It was a chilling thought to realize that they had cut themselves off from their country, language, and culture, to become exiles in a strange land—dependent upon the kindness of the Dutch and the opportunities that providence might provide. Moreover, they were separated, perhaps forever, from relatives in England. In a mood of loneliness and homesickness Robinson wrote: "And no place upon the face of the earth should be free for us, poor creatures; we have lost assured hope that heaven itself is open for us . . . in which we shall, at the length, be fully free from this, and all other incumbrances."[8]

At this time he learned that Francis Johnson, the controversial Separatist, was in Amsterdam, serving as the storm petrel of the Ancient Brethren Church. He paid his fellow Cantabrigian a visit and found him to be a stimulating though erratic individual. He was distressed to learn about the argumentation and scandal that had been going on among the Ancient Brethren. It was a traumatic experience after the intellectual freedoms of the university and the harmony of the Scrooby fellowship to sense that fellow exiles could degenerate into petty disputation.

It is necessary at this point to turn back a few years to review the

background of the Ancient Brethren Church into which the Scrooby people expected to find a welcome.

Francis Johnson had received his M.A. at Christ's College in 1585, shortly before John Robinson matriculated at Cambridge. His nonconforming ideas forced him to desert his teaching there and flee to Holland. While in the Low Countries Johnson opposed the Separatist positions of Barrowe and Greenwood, but he was intrigued by their banned writings and stole back to London in 1592 to interview these reformers in prison. His conversations with them won him to their views. He returned soon after to become minister of the English church in Middelburg, Holland. However, on a later trip to England in 1597, he was arrested, reprieved, and condemned to join an expedition to Rainea in the Gulf of St. Lawrence. His brother, George, was banished with him. But due to delays and storms the expedition proved a fiasco. On their return to port, the two managed to escape to Holland, where Francis was made minister of the Ancient Brethren Church, which was a branch of the church formed in London under the leadership of Barrowe, Greenwood, and Penry.

When released from the Clink Prison in London, Johnson married Thomasine Boys, widow of a prosperous haberdasher. This union initiated the infamous "Milliner's War," which with other intrigues caused the eventual collapse of the Ancient Brethren Church. Thomasine brought her new husband a generous dowry, but her love of finery aroused jealousy among the members of his flock and plunged them into controversy. Francis' brother, George, headed the opposition, while Henry Ainsworth endeavored to patch up the quarrel.

George Johnson did an in-depth study of his sister-in-law's misconduct. He declared that she and the wife of the Bishop of London "for pride and vaine apparel were & joyned together, that she wore 3, 4, or 5 golde rings at once, moreover her busks and her whalebones in her brest were greeved."[9] George's accusations against Thomasine were listed in detail:

First the waring of a long busk [corset] after the fashion of the world. . . . 2. Wearing of the long white brest after the fashion of yong dames, and so low she wore it, as the world call them kodpeece brests. . . . 3. Whalebones in the bodies of petivotrd . . . against nature, being as the Phisitians affirme hinderers of conceiving or procreating children. . . . 4. Great sleeves sett out with whalebones, which the world call . . . . . [This was so shocking a word that George Johnson could not bring himself to write it.] 5. Excesse of lace upon them after the fashion of yong Marchants wives Contrary to the rules of modesty. 6. Foure or five golde rings on at once. . . . 7. Acopple crowned hatt with a twined band, as yong Marchants wives, and yong Dames use. Immodest and toyish in a Pastors wife. . . . 8. Tucked aprons, like round hose. . . . 9. Excesse in rufs, laune coives, muske, and such like things. 10. The painted Hipocritical brest, shewing as if there were some special workes, and in truth nothing but a shadow. Contrary to modesty, and sobriety. 11. Bodies tied to the peticote with points, as men do their dublets to their hose. . . . 12. Some also reporte that she laid forth her heare also.[10]

The Ancient Brethren were provided with racy reading as long as the war of George versus Thomasine continued:

First she strode gazing, bracing or vainting in shop doores. Contrary to the rules of modest behaviour in the daughters of Zion. . . . 2. She so quaffed wine, that a papist in their company said to another woman: You leave some, and shew modesty, but Mrs. Johnson, shee etc. shee doth not . . . . 3. She laide in bedd on the Lordes day till 9 a clock, and hindered the exercise of the worde, she being not sick, nor having any just cause to lie so long. [11]

This gossip column affords us a light break in the midst of heavy, otherworldly paper warfare and verbal skirmishing. Theological dogma changes faster than human nature, as any modern dominie can attest.

George continued his attacks until Francis brought charges against him that he was a nourisher of talebearers, a slanderer, and a teller of untruths against his brother. He told the church meeting that unless George was excommunicated he would not continue as pastor. George was finally expelled in 1602.

Then there was the Daniel Studley scandal. This elder became a liability because he was involved in numerous immoral relationships which aggravated the schismatic factions. The carryings-on of the Ancient Brethren impelled some members to withdraw. Christopher Lawne and three colleagues published a blistering expose: *The Prophane Schisme of the Brownists or Separatists*, etc.

Although some of these denunciations were deserved, Robinson expressed regret that the cause of freedom of conscience had been injured by this small, hard core of controversialists. It was a shock to Robinson and Brewster to find themselves isolated from their own countrymen and forced by circumstances to associate with scandalmongers. Their predecessor-exiles had gotten off on the wrong foot in Amsterdam. Their bungling had set a harmful precedent, since in the eyes of the Dutch they were busy-bodies. And in the eyes of the Church of England they were proof of the folly of separation. The Puritan leaders and the Separatist leaders considered them a liability and a tragic experiment. So Robinson and Brewster met separately with their Pilgrims after attending a few gatherings of the Ancient Brethren. They were determined that this was not the way they would go.

It was disappointing to see Richard Clyfton remain with the Ancient Brethren, but they respected his right to choose. No doubt he wanted to drop anchor and adventure no further. He was an older man in a youthful group. Bradford wrote:

He was a grave and fatherly old man when he came first to Holland, having a white beard: and pity it was that such a reverend old man should be forced to leave his country, at those years to go into exile. But it was his lot, and he bore it patiently. Much good had he done in the country where he lived, and converted many to God by his faithful and painful ministry, both in preaching and catechising. Sound and orthodox he always was and so continued to his end.[12]

Years later, Timothy Clyfton, grandson of Richard Clyfton, served as a deacon in the English Reformed Church, the Begijnhof in Amsterdam, which was founded in 1607, the year before his grandfather arrived with Robinson and the Pilgrim company. Its first minister, John Paget, preached and wrote against the ideas of Clyfton and Robinson. But as time passed the distinction between the fine points of their doctrinal disputes dimmed. Members of the fragmented Ancient Brethren Church found a home in the Begijnhof, which still stands today surrounded by a colony of charming sixteenth- and seventeenth-century houses, including the oldest frame house in Amsterdam. The chancel window in the church is a Robinson memorial which represents in stained glass the pastor aboard the *Speedwell* in Delfshaven, offering his farewell to the first contingency to leave Leyden for the New World. So, at length, the prophet who was censured by John Paget found a place of honor in the peace and solitude of this beautiful church.

In losing Clyfton they were drawn closer to Robinson, who during the year of adjustment in Amsterdam emerged as the man who was able to hold them together.

Robinson discovered that John Smyth, his former colleague from Gainsborough, also felt at home in the Ancient Brethren Church.

Smyth further disturbed the turbulent fellowship with his controversial ideas, and soon he and his company "were already involved in contention" which "no means that Robinson and Brewster could use would allay."

Joseph Hall, later Bishop of Norwich, published a letter in 1608 addressed to "Mr. Smyth and Mr. Rob[inson], Ringleaders of the late Separation to Amsterdam." It was a "loving monitory letter" in which he condemned their separation. Robinson replied:

> Separation from whatsoever is contrary to God is the first step to our communion with God.[13]
>
> It is the Church of England, or State-Ecclesiastical, which we account Babylon; and from which we withdraw in spiritual communion. But for the commonwealth and kingdom, as we honour it above all the states in the world, so would we thankfully embrace the meanest corner of it.[14]

Clyfton engaged in controversy with John Smyth over his views of baptism by immersion and self-baptism and wrote *Plea for Infants and Elder People concerning their Baptism* (1610). Clyfton was also caught up in Francis Johnson's quarrel over the source of authority in the local church. He agreed with the Franciscans who held that authority rested with the elders rather than the people. Henry Ainsworth headed the other faction, the Ainsworthians, who shared Robinson's more democratic belief that the congregation made the decisions. Robinson and the Pilgrims liked Ainsworth. He was one of the brilliant scholars produced by

Pieterskerk, Leyden, 1670—fourteenth-century Roman Catholic cathedral converted into a Protestant church during the Reformation

Cambridge, with a flare for Hebrew. Arriving in Amsterdam without a job, he supported himself as a porter in a bookshop. It was discovered in due time that he was adept in Hebrew, and he translated the Psalms, the Song of Solomon, published his notes on the Pentateuch, and his famous collection of psalms.

Robinson disliked the emphasis on the power of the elders which prevailed in the Ancient Brethren Church. He believed that authority rested with the people of the congregation. The Ancient Brethren finally split over this matter: how to interpret the words from Matthew 18:17, "Tell it unto the Church." If one of the church fellowship was wronged, the problem should be brought before the church for discussion and decision. And what was the church? Robinson said the church was the congregation. Ainsworth agreed with this principle which had been advanced by Barrowe and Greenwood. But Francis Johnson contended that authority lay with the elders and Johnson's trouble-making elders agreed. As these two factions battled and found themselves at loggerheads, Ainsworth suggested that Robinson and Brewster be brought in to mediate the dispute. The Pilgrim leaders then proposed a compromise. Johnson repudiated the agreement when it was suggested that Ainsworth and his followers migrate to Leyden with Robinson and his deserters. But Ainsworth and company decided to hang on in Amsterdam.

In the dispute that shattered the Ancient Brethren Church, Clyfton lined up with the Franciscans (followers of Francis Johnson), took over Ainsworth's post, and served as their teacher until his death in 1616.

This rash of disputation did not erupt fully while Robinson remained in Amsterdam. He was not at home among them after his long residence in the atmosphere of Cambridge. As he took inventory of their situation he registered disappointment with the spirit of the Ancient Brethren Church and other English exiles, and his thoughts turned to nearby Leyden with its distinguished university. He discussed with William Brewster the possibilities of a move to Leyden. Brewster had visited the city during his previous travels throughout the Netherlands while he was secretary to Lord Davison, and Robinson had contacts with the university due to his Cambridge associations.

The Scrooby fellowship gathered for frequent discussion. They heard reports of hardship from the unemployed job-hunters and the difficulties of adjustment to Dutch life. There was a perilous drain on the ever-shrinking common treasury. When Robinson mentioned what Leyden might offer, there were lamentations at the prospect of another uprooting and objections were voiced.

Some were ready to settle in Amsterdam in spite of their hazardous beginning. They were exhausted after more than a year of rootless existence in England, their two traumatic efforts at escape, and the privations they were enduring in their Dutch environment. What were the opportunities of employment in the new city? Amsterdam was larger, a seaport and trading center where local industry and world trade prospered. Leyden, on the other hand, could not offer as many opportunities. A few had made friendly contacts in Amsterdam and some had found tolerable, though humble, dwellings. Another move was hazardous. It involved loss of jobs, reduction of income, the travail of being uprooted once again, and the danger of a journey into the unknown. Would the town fathers permit them to enter in their penurious state? Who would help them find shelter there if they decided to make another move?

One can sense why Robinson was desirous of moving from the wrangling of the brethren to a university atmosphere. Saddened by this display of English fanaticism, he announced, after careful group deliberation, that they were going to Leyden.

Johnson resented the exodus of the Scroobyites, which meant a reduction in the size of his parish and hence in his income. He reviewed Robinson's book *A Justification of Separation*, and "before the Congregation, made a solemn testification against the manifold errors contained in it; and not only so but wrote to Master Robinson to rebuke him for the same."[15] Elder Studley issued an "Alphabet of Slander" against the departing company, calling them "ignorant idiots, noddy Nabalites, dogged Doegs, fairfaced Pharisees, shamless Shemites, malicious Macchiavellians."[16]

In late 1610 the Franciscans excommunicated the Ainsworthians and seized the meeting house in the Bruinistengange. The Ainsworthians, who won the majority, took refuge in a former Jewish synagogue. Amid bitter recrimination the court awarded the meeting house to the Ainsworthians and another shift was made in the quarrel. The Franciscans packed themselves off to Emden.

On the death of Francis Johnson, leadership passed to elder Francis Blackwell. He and his contingency decided to move to Virginia. Stealing back to England to make final preparations, they were arrested. When he was accused, Blackwell "slipped his own neck out of the collar" by betraying other Separatists. During his trial he denied that he was a Separatist and so "won the bishops' favor [but lost the Lord's]." Following in the footsteps of the chameleon, Elder Studley, he contended that his dissembling was for the good of the cause, "yea, for the best." The archbishop in court whereupon blessed the voyage of Blackwell and company as their chief announced that a way was now open for the Separatists to set out for a better world.

They sailed in the fall of 1618, "packed together like herrings." Soon they ran into high winds and were driven off their course. The water supply gave out, and an epidemic of "ye fluxe" developed. The captain and a number of ship's officers died, depriving them of competent navigators. Six months out from the port of Gravesend, "after long seeking & beating aboute," they crept into the Chesapeake River and anchored off Jamestown. Out of some 200 passengers only fifty were alive. These scattered and their colony never took root. Blackwell had been buried at sea along with his Elder Bowman, called "Judas, the Purse Bearer."[17] So, at length, the Franciscan element of the quarrelsome Ancient Brethren was swallowed up in the vast unknown of the New World.

Reason, which is the adversary of all
tyrants, teaches us that truth can be as little
restrained as light.
—The Leyden Magistrates, 1581

7 "TRUTH CAN BE AS LITTLE RESTRAINED AS LIGHT"

Robinson drew up a formal petition to the magistrates of Leyden, requesting permission to settle there. This document may be seen today in the Archives of Leyden:

To the Honorable the Burgomasters and Court of the city of Leyden: With due submission and respect, Jan Robarthse, minister of the Divine Word, and some of the members of the Christian Reformed Religion, born in the kingdom of Great Britain, to the number of one hundred persons, or thereabouts, men and woman, represent that they are desirous of coming to live in this city, by the first of May next, and to have the freedom thereof in carrying on their trades, without being a burden in the least, to any one. They, therefore, address themselves to your Honors, humbly praying that Your Honors will be pleased to grant them free consent to betake themselves as aforesaid.[1]

No date or signature is given, but the action of the magistrates, written in the margin, bears a date, and is as follows:

The Court, in making a disposition of this present memorial, declare that they refuse no honest persons free ingress to come and have their residence in this city, provided that such persons behave themselves, and submit to the laws and ordinances; and therefore the coming of the memorialists will be agreeable and welcome.

Thus done in their session at the Council House, 12 February, 1609.

Signed, J. van Hout[2]

When King James' ambassador at The Hague, Sir Ralph Winwood, learned that the "bourgomaster and court of the city" had granted consent to the Pilgrims, he entered a protest in the king's name. This pressure from England was embarrassing to the Leyden officials, but they stood their ground with dignity. The Dutch were struggling to emerge from their long and devastating war with Spain and did not wish to offend friends in England. Yet they dared to uphold freedom of religion when they gave permission to James' troublesome rebels to enter their city. Their reply to the king forms a document of worldwide significance because they here affirmed a new concept of religious and civil liberty which at that period only Holland was sufficiently advanced to practice.

We reckon to be unjustly charged by Sir (Ralph) Winwood, the Ambassador to His Britannic Majesty, to the effect that we had entered into agreement with certain Brownists. It is, however, true that in February last a petition was presented to us in the name of Ian Roberts, minister of the divine word, together with some of the community of the Christian Reformed Religion, born in England, requesting that, as they had the intention of taking up their abode in the city of Leyden, there might be granted to them a free consent thereto. To this we made reply by an official document, that we did not refuse free entrance to honest people provided they behaved themselves here to all the Statutes and Ordinances, and, for that reason, the entrance of the petitioners would be welcome and agreeable to us—as may be seen by the Petition and the attached reply of which we send your Excellency a copy, promising that nothing has been done by us further in the matter; and that we have not been aware, nor do we at present know, that the petitioners have been banished from England, nor that they belong to the sect of the Brownists.

We therefore beg your Excellency to communicate these presents and the attached document to the Lord Advocate, to the end that no misunderstanding may arise between ourselves and his Majesty's Ambassadors, and that we may be held excused by their Excellencies and consequently by His Majesty. Herewith, etc. April, 1609.[3]

This document makes it clear that the English Establishment regarded the Pilgrims as citizens who had been "banished from England," and that James I was keeping an eagle eye on them, spying on their conduct in Europe, and recording their misbehavior for future punishment.

Assured of a kindly reception by the Leyden dignitaries, and conscious of the rumblings among the Ancient Brethren, "which things Robinson and Brewster foreseeing, prudently resolved to remove thence, before they became involved in them," they hesitated no longer.[4] Their local plans and arrangements were scrapped and their chances of self-support hazarded, but "valuing peace and spiritual comfort above all earthly riches," they pressed ahead in their quest of freedom.[5]

So for the third time Robinson and his company gathered up their meager belongings and loaded them aboard the barges that were to carry them by canal, river, and lake to their new home. The little Dutch vessels bore them along the Haarlem Canal to the Haarlemmer Meer to open waters, to the canals that led into the Rhine and then on the canals between the green, flower-decked banks along which stood the public buildings, shops, and dwellings where they were to find shelter in a second adopted city.

Jan van Hout, Secretary of Leyden—a friend to the Pilgrims

Leyden was at this time a metropolis of about 70,000 inhabitants—prosperous, attractive, and abounding in cultural advantages. A French visitor wrote:

> The city of Leiden is, without contradiction, one of the grandest, the comliest, and the most charming cities of the world. The cleanness and breadth of its streets; the number of its canals provided with bridges, bordered on either side by lindens, which during the summer heats cast delightful shadows, where the people make their promenade; the tidiness and elegance of its buildings, and its great number of public places embellished likewise with lindens or elms; and the extreme neatness of the bricks with which the streets are paved—all this in former times caused Polyander, a celebrated professor who was housed on the Rapenburg, to boast that he lived in the most beautiful spot in the world. Which he was wont to prove familiarly, thus: "Of the four quarters of the world Europe is the noblest and the nicest: the Low Countries are the best part of Europe; of the seventeen provinces of the Low Countries, Holland is the richest, and the most flourishing and the finest; the most beautiful and altogether charming city of Holland is Leyden; while the handsomest canal and the loveliest street in Leyden is the Rapenburg"; wherefore concluded he, "I am lodged in the most beautiful spot in the world."[6]

William Bradford called it "fair and beautiful, and of a sweet situation."[7]

As the Pilgrim company sailed into the busy canals in the summer of 1609 they were impressed by the ancient city in the midst of the Rhineland with its lush meadows among the most fertile in the world, dotted with villages surrounded by flocks and herds, presenting a panorama that led off to the distant spires of Delft and The Hague. Leyden was built on thirty islands created by rivers and canals and joined by many bridges. The Old Rhine and the New Rhine flowed through the city with its public and commercial buildings and its gabled dwellings of red brick and inlaid stone. About the city was a walled fortification with towers and battlements, and beyond the canals, the skillfully farmed polders with their windmills and hamlets.

Robinson found that a large number of Protestants had fled to Leyden—artisans, merchants, men of science and industry, seeking refuge from the Spaniards. Religiously the city was cosmopolitan. There were Roman Catholics, Lutherans, French and English Protestants, Anabaptists, and others all living under the tolerant policy which granted them haven.

Around them were "goodly cities, strongly armed" and "abounding in all kinds of wealth," but the Pilgrims were poor and in need of the humblest of jobs to ward off starvation. The sacrifice sale of their property in the homeland, their detention there without holdings or support, their imprisonment and looting, the high price of crossing, and the costly experiment in Amsterdam had all but exhausted their means. They were still strangers

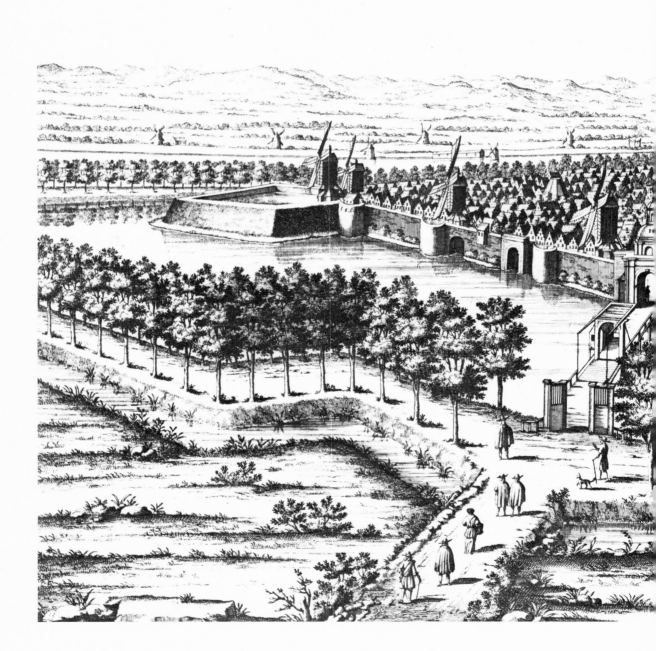

in a foreign land, struggling to be at home in the language and to acquire some knowledge of the crafts.

They put their hands to "such trade & improvements as best they could." That they were willing to tackle almost any honorable job is evidenced by the list of their occupations: baai-worker, saai-worker, wool-comber, wool-carder, stocking-weaver, twine-spinner, hat-maker, block-maker, cabinet maker, tailor, tobacco-pipe maker, brewer, baker, mason, and carpenter. Due to their dependable qualities "they came to raise a competent & comfortable living, but with hard and continual labor," and with sore "conflicts and misgivings in some." A few became shopkeepers and merchants.[8]

William Brewster taught English to the continental students at the university. His knowledge of Latin was an aid in tutoring the German, Danish, Belgian, French, and Dutch pupils. He developed an English grammar "to learn it by, after the Latin manner" and "many gentlemen, both Danes and Germans, resorted to him, some of them being great men's sons." So it was noted that "his outward condition was mended, and he lived well and plentifully." He soon established the Pilgrim Press, encouraged by Robinson and others who were eager to publish books that were forbidden in England and were needed to carry on reform there. Young Edward Winslow served as his editor and Robinson his advisor in the perilous enterprise.

Robinson visited the halls and library of the university, which had been founded at the request of the citizens in one of the gloomiest periods of Dutch history, during the war with Spain. As a reward for their courage they were offered freedom from taxation or a university. They chose "to erect a free public school and university." It was endowed with substantial revenue, derived in large measure from the old abbey at Edmont and "was provided with a number of professors, selected for their genius, learning and piety, from among the most distinguished scholars." The new institution was consecrated in 1575.[9]

The Cambridge professor was impressed by the conclave of minds assembled at the university. Lambert Danaeus and Francis Junius had held the chair of theology, Justus Lipsius the chair of history, and John Drusius, sought after by both Cambridge and Oxford, oriental studies. Philip Marnix St. Aldegond had been famous as a diplomat and a writer on religion; Scaliger had served as professor of belles-lettres. Peter Molinaeus taught natural philosophy; Francis Gomar, the Calvinist, and Jacob Arminius, the liberal, had expounded theology. Arminius died some three months before Robinson's arrival; Simon Episcopius took his post.

Erpenius was the orientalist; Cluverius, who spoke ten languages, the geographer; Gerhard Johannes Vossius lectured in belles-lettres and chronology; Peter Paauw was the founder of the university botanical gardens; Daniel Heinsius was an editor and translator; Cornelius de Groot, father of Hugo Grotius, was the outstanding scholar of law. Festus Hommius was a regent and pastor in Leyden. Anthony Walaeus, Flemish translator of the Bi-

(pages 96-97)
View of Leyden (seventeenth century)

ble and an authority on Aristotle, developed into a close friend of Robinson. Anthony Thysius taught poetry and eloquence and edited the Greek and Latin classics.

The Cambridge historian Mullinger called Leyden "the most famous Protestant seat of learning in the seventeenth century." The university drew students from all parts of the Low Countries and also from England, France, Germany, Hungary, Poland, and Russia. The streets were enlivened by the colorful presence of these young people. Robinson felt at home with the cosmopolitan outlook.[10]

A college of theology had been established in 1592 to train competent leaders for the Dutch Church. The head of this school, which was closely related to the university, Peter Bertius, had studied in England. The Walloon Church had also opened a college for French students in May 1606. These centers of learning provided Leyden with an influential corps of intellectual leadership and a company of well-educated ministers and laymen.

The school of Dutch painters, who were to portray ordinary people, their houses, farms, food, and pleasures, presenting the solid qualities of Dutch life, was coming into being. The artist Esaias van de Velde was working in Leyden. Adrien van der

View of the port of Leyden (eighteenth century)

Venne was studying at the university. Jan van Goyen and Jan Lievensz were teenagers in the city along with Rembrandt van Rijn.

Robinson was soon at home with the Dutch scholars and accepted in their academic circle. His English language was no barrier because he was well trained in Latin and accustomed to lecture in this more or less universal language of academia which prevailed in the Netherlands. He also progressed in his mastery of the Dutch language. There is no record in the university register of his membership there until this statement appears:

Sept. 5, 1615   *Joannes Robintsonus*   *Anglus*
Coss. permissu.   *Ann. xxxlx*
  Stud. Theol. alit Familiam. [11]

We learn from this record that he was thirty-nine years old in 1615, that he had a family, and that his field was theology.

It is likely that he established contact with some of the men at the university soon after he reached Leyden. There were numerous practical matters to which he had to attend during his first weeks. One immediate objective was to locate a place where he and his people could meet for worship and discussion. Separated from one another and facing hardship, they needed fellowship. They did not appeal to the municipal court for aid but made out the best they could on their own until Robinson bought, on January 11, 1611, from Heer Van Poelgeest, a "spacious" old house which stood facing the south transept of the Pieterskerk Cathedral. It was known as the Groenepoort or Green Gate. The estate was across a narrow street from the cathedral, under its very eaves, on the Kloksteeg, where the Pesyns Hof now stands. It was within a thousand yards of the university with its dignified halls and valuable library. Behind the Green Gate House was a garden and beyond this an open square where some twenty-one small houses were erected by William Jepson, the carpenter, to form a compact community.

The Green Gate estate was purchased jointly with William Jepson, Henry Wood, and Randall Thickins, who soon married a sister of Bridget Robinson. They paid 8,000 guilders (some $10,500). One fourth was handed over as a down-payment and the remainder was paid off at 500 guilders a year. This was a stiff obligation for the congregation. But they managed heroically as they did in later years at Plimoth Plantation in handling and paying off their huge debt with the London Merchant Adventurers. From the outset they were an independent body with a high sense of honor and financial responsibility.

John and Bridget moved into the Green Gate with their children: John, Bridget, and Isaac, and their ward, Mary Hardy.

There is a document in the records of the Notary J. van Tethrode of Leyden dated January 2, 1621 where the signature of John Robinson appears on a bond in recognition of indebtedness given by Thomas Brewer, John Robinson, minister of the Word of God, and William Jepson for the behoof of Seigneur

Johan de Lalaing to the sum of 744 guilders, 13 stivers and 3 pence on account of several years' accumulated interest, the last due on May day, 1621. The three subscribers promised to pay this interest on May day, 1621 without any further delay, which promise they confirmed in the document.[12]

The Cambridge professor, whose youth and student days had been lived in the so-called Golden Age of England, was now a resident of the Netherlands and was enjoying its Golden Age which had come into being following the truce with Spain.

Robinson and his newcomers heard on all hands the story of Leyden's heroism during the perilous days of the city's siege which lasted from October 1573 to March 1574. The Spanish commander, the Duke of Alba, was enraged by the determination of these stubborn Dutchmen to defend their religious liberty and announced that he would reduce them to obedience. He built a line of forts to encircle the city walls. No supplies of any kind could reach the besieged. The defenders were reduced to eating horses, dogs, weeds, and roots.

A band of desperate citizens appeared at the house of the burgomaster, Peter van der Werff, begging for food. He replied, "Dear fellow townsmen, I can offer you but my own flesh; I know that death awaits me at the hands of the enemy; and were I less assured of this, I should still prefer it to an act of perjury. To die would be sweet—if by dying I could save yourselves and your fellow-citizens."

The valiant words of the burgomaster so aroused the citizenry that they rushed to the city walls and cried to the Spaniards: "We will eat our left hand, and fight you with our right. We will burn down the city rather than surrender to you!"[13]

Relief boats were unable to bring in food since the Spaniards controlled the canals. The Dutch opened the dykes and the country around Leyden was converted into a huge lake. With the approach of a fleet of hardy Zeelanders the besiegers abandoned their forts and fled. Many were drowned in the flood. Others were pursued by the Zeelanders who killed about 1,000 of the retreating invaders. The fleet moved to the gates of the city and into the canals as the starved inhabitants rushed out to seize food. Over 6,000 citizens had perished from starvation and disease.

On the third of October Leydenites celebrated their liberation from the Spaniards. The cry of deliverance—"Leyden relieved! Holland reprieved!"—echoed through the city streets. The festival developed in later years to major proportions and all citizens ate herring and white bread, presented in a public ceremony by the burgomaster; and then in their homes they enjoyed a meal of the traditional hotchpotch, a stew made of meat and vegetables.[14]

The long conflict continued sporadically in other areas until the war-weary Spaniards agreed in 1609 to a cessation of hostilities and signed a twelve-year truce with the Dutch. The youthful republic of the United Provinces entered an era of peace and prosperity. The people set to work with vim to rebuild their country. There was a sudden upsurge in manufacturing and commerce.

Ships carried exports and imports from all parts of the world. A new supply of workers was a by-product of the influx of refugees who sought freedom of worship and safety from coercion: the Flemish and Walloons from the Southern Netherlands, Jews from Spain and Portugal, German Protestants who found life intolerable under Roman Catholic princes, Huguenots from France, and Separatists from England who fled to the Dutch Republic where they were granted protection from tyranny.

By the time the Pilgrims arrived the city had recovered from its disasters and was enjoying unparalleled prosperity. Industrious citizens from the southern provinces, driven out by the Spaniards, had moved into Leyden bringing new business. The manufacture of cloth developed into the major trade and the city became the Manchester of Holland.

The Netherlands cities formed the chief market for English wool and the cloth trade was one of the sources of Dutch wealth. Leyden was famous for its manufacture of woolen goods. Industry was on the upgrade and the boundaries of the city had been extended for the fourth time in 1610 due to the expansion of the population.

Emergence from their war with Spain had sparked a new confidence in the Dutch. When Philip closed the ports of Spain and Portugal to them, their sea captains set out for the Indies to secure the precious spices for themselves and the first squadron of Dutch vessels reached Java in 1596. They also sought a sea route to the Indies that was not infested by Spanish men-of-war and endeavored to make a northeast passage across the arctic ice. The first effort in 1596 failed. In the year 1609 Henry Hudson, on a similar voyage, turned his ship from the impenetrable ice pack to the New World, to the Hudson River, and the founding of New Amsterdam.

Dutch ships ventured forth into the Mediterranean, the Western hemisphere, the East Indies, China, Japan, South Africa, Ceylon, and the coast of Malabar. In time the East Indian commerce brought a golden harvest of profit. The herring trade had long formed a bulwark of Holland's income. The historian, Emanuel van Meteren, estimated in the early seventeenth century that 1,600 ships were employed in the herring industry which produced 300,000 tons of salt fish each year and supported nearly a fifth of the population. A merchant marine of some 10,000 vessels, manned by 168,000 seamen, supplemented the fishing fleet. The country's produce was carried in these bottoms to many ports of the globe to bring back timber, ore, grain, wool, and spices.[15]

John and Bridget Robinson liked their surroundings. The children were happy in their Green Gate home. Educational opportunities appeared to be good. There were Dutch and French schools, and Latin schools which prepared students for the university, emphasizing Latin and Greek with some mathematics, history, and geography. The Latin schools strove to follow the ideas of Erasmus. Towns were ambitious to see that their academic institutions excelled. "In Holland the general level of education was probably higher than in most parts of France and the British Isles," G. N. Clark wrote in *The Seventeenth Century*.[16]

The Robinsons were impressed with the civil liberty of Holland. A unique tradition prevailed regarding the sovereign. He was not entitled to wield absolute power. His control ceased to be legal when he encroached upon the rights that were guaranteed to citizens in the local communities. William of Orange had formulated this principle in a proclamation which he issued when he assumed the field against the Spaniards in 1568: "The privileges are not free grants of the sovereign to his subjects, but form contracts binding both prince and people."[17]

During the war with Spain, Holland had sought assistance from the English government. Queen Elizabeth agreed to a treaty by which England furnished money and troops to check Philip's aggression. Certain "cautionary towns" were held by the British as security for their aid. A number of British subjects came over to live in Holland. One article of the treaty drawn up in 1585 stipulated that the Dutch "will permit to the governor and garrison the free exercise of religion as in England and to this end a church will be provided for them in each town."

These centers of worship for the British troops were open to other English-speaking residents who wished to visit them. If these settlers needed financial help the Dutch treasury stood ready to appropriate funds. Seventeen English centers of worship were provided in Amsterdam, The Hague, Leyden, Middelburg, Arnhem, Rotterdam, Bruges, and other towns.

Freedom of religion was upheld by law and quite generally practiced. The Prince of Orange had declared in 1564 before the Council of State: "Although attached to the Roman Catholic faith, I cannot possibly approve that princes should wish to rule the consciences of their subjects and deprive them of their liberty of faith and worship of God." This statement is a marked contrast to King James' pronouncements on his divine rights.

The Leyden magistracy admonished the Dutch Reformed Synod in 1581 when dogmatism was in evidence:

Liberty has always consisted in uttering our sentiments freely; and the contrary has always been considered the characteristic of tyranny. Reason, which is the adversary of all tyrants, teaches us that truth can be as little restrained as light.[18]

When called upon to coerce those who differed from the majority on religious faith, Leyden officials stated:

The design of the States undoubtedly is, that none should be persecuted on account of their religion.

There are no better means to blot out heresy than temper and moderation for we have often seen that certain books were little minded at first, but afterwards, when condemned as heretical, they came into repute and credit.

Force will not make Christians, but only fill the world with vile hypocrites under the name of Christians.[19]

The democratic process functioned quite effectively. Among its states was Friesland, where republicanism was fairly advanced.

Stadts Ververlingh floot

44

Stadts Ververlingh floot

K

I

AENWYSINGEN
Op dese Kaart

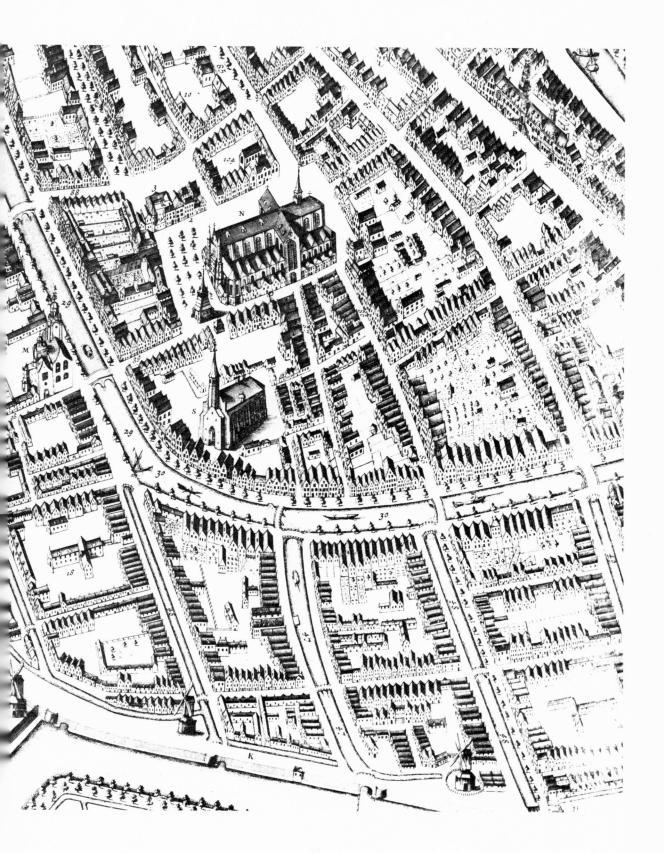

Local governments held considerable authority. The rights of pasture, woodland, and water were preserved in each town. The Pilgrims observed these working traditions and were influenced by them.

Leyden was bathed with an atmosphere of wholesome skepticism which blew like a freshening sea breeze through Master Robinson's wearied mind, long-harassed by repression. The thinking of his fellow seekers was also stimulated by this tonic air. He observed the tolerant practices that permitted amplitude of thought and worship. He rubbed elbows with Roman Catholics, Lutherans, Calvinists, Remonstrants, French Huguenots, Swiss and Dutch Reformed, Anabaptists, and Jews. It was evident from the variety of views he had met in Amsterdam and Leyden that the Dutch were ahead of his own England in religious tolerance.

Holland led the world in publishing during the seventeenth century and probably produced more books than all the rest of Europe put together. The Elzevir Press in Leyden was one of the foremost publishing houses. Relative freedom permitted publications here that provoked protest from other nations. But these objections were defended by the Dutch on the grounds that criticism was countenanced in Holland and foreign countries would have to accept the fact.

Their residence in Holland contributed profoundly to the Pilgrims' philosophy of life. They discovered that there was much to learn from the Dutch. George M. Trevelyan has pictured the Netherlands as the teacher of England. His words apply in particular to the Pilgrims who lived in close contact with Dutch culture:

> By taking to the seas the English fell under the influence of the Dutch. As friends or as enemies, as partners or as rivals, men of the two nations were now in perpetual contact. Holland affected every department of English life, more, perhaps, than any other nation has ever done by the mere force of example. The little republic, which from 1600 to 1650 maintained its territory as a safe and prosperous oasis in the midst of the wilderness of fire and destruction around, was during these years the leader of mankind in most of the sciences and arts. She was the school of scientific war, agriculture, gardening, finance and trade, and of numberless arts and crafts; the academy of painting, the home of theology whence Calvinist and Arminian alike drew their theories; the asylum for philosophy and free speculation; and last but not least the example to our merchants and our politicians of a community which had attained prosperity, enlightenment, and power by rebellion against a legitimate Prince.[20]

Public education was fairly widespread. By 1609 the schools were the common property of the citizens and were supported by

(pages 104-5)
Map of Leyden in the seventeenth century

taxes. The Protestants sensed the significance of popular education because of their emphasis on study of the Bible. They promoted schools and use of the Bible which tended to popularize the Reformation.[21]

Certain democratic practices were discussed by Robinson and the Pilgrims. In the Dutch family a father's estate was usually left to all the children equally. Moryson, the English traveler, who was a younger son, admired the Dutch plan of equal inheritance and condemned the English law of primogeniture which gave preference to the eldest son. This was taken over by the Pilgrims.[22] Isaac de Rasieres, the Dutch representative from the New Amsterdam colony, who made a visit to Plimoth Plantation in 1627, wrote that "in the inheritance they place all the children in one degree, only the eldest son has an acknowledgment for his seniority of birth."[23]

The Pilgrims also followed the gavelkind practice established in the county of Kent, England which left land to all sons together, not merely to the eldest or to any one son alone.[24]

The Dutch were careful in the keeping of town records: deeds, mortgages, and wills. The law respecting the transfer of land stated that no land in Holland could be bought or sold but by writing before one of the Eschevins (municipal officers) and one secretary of the town, who enrolled it in the public registers. After fifteen or sixteen months the title could not be disputed. A law to this general effect was passed at Plimoth Plantation in 1636 and was later adopted by the Massachusetts Court.

The records of the Plimoth colony are as complete as they are due to the training that the English received in the Netherlands. As it developed every Pilgrim was required to prepare an inventory of his possessions and to make a will. These records, many of which are still extant, indicate what kind of clothes they wore, what their furniture and equipment were like, what books they owned and read, and thus provide an invaluable treasury about home life.

The Dutch considered marriage a civil ceremony outside the authority of the church: Robinson concurred and his company adopted this practice. The Leyden city records testify to this separation of religious authority over marriage in the statute of 1590. William Bradford describes the first marriage held in Plimoth, that of widower Edward Winslow to widow Susannah White, May 12, 1621: "According to the laudable custom of the Low Countries." It was thought proper to have it performed by the magistrate "as being a civil thing, upon which many questions about inheritance depend."[25]

The Puritan in Holland by Douglas Campbell presents an array of material on the Dutch influence upon the Pilgrims.[26] He asserts that from 50,000 to 75,000 heads of families moved from Holland to England as refugees from Spanish domination, carrying with them their artisan crafts and agricultural skills, their Bibles, and their Protestantism. Like missionaries scattered about the countryside they made an enduring impression on English life.

Several thousand English troops were stationed in the Netherlands from 1585 for a period of many years. John Motley estimates that after the truce of 1609 some 5,000 English and Scottish troops were serving in the Dutch army. Captains Myles Standish and John Smith had been employed by the Holland military. In addition to military personnel, a large number of English merchants and religious refugees lived in Holland. These people were exposed to the more advanced Dutch practices in government, education, and religion, and this cultural exchange proved beneficial to the British.

Campbell minimizes the English heritage as he emphasizes the contributions of the Dutch to the Pilgrims. The Netherlands exposure was certainly noteworthy, but both cultures shared in shaping the Scrooby-Leyden-Plimoth community.

Request of one hundred Pilgrims in Amsterdam to be permitted to dwell in Leyden (request granted February 12, 1609)

Substantial interrelations existed between England and Holland by the time the Pilgrims arrived. For example, Thomas Basson, an English Protestant, moved to Leyden as a refugee from Cologne. He was English tutor to Jan van Hout, leader of the city council, who urged fellow Dutchmen to study the English tongue. A number of other tutors served in Leyden, as William Brewster did, teaching citizens and students at the university.

Basson published English poetry, pointing out that knowledge of English was necessary since England was sending so many of her young men to Holland. He liked controversial subjects and printed titles by Arminius, Vorstius, and two by Ainsworth. He may have known Robinson and Brewster since his house was near them on the Kloksteeg. Basson published 180 books, and the records show his shop was sold in 1630 after some forty-seven years of activity.[27]

The Thomas Browne Institute of Leyden University was recently established in honor of Sir Thomas Browne, the English physician, who received his M.D. at Leyden in 1633 and wrote *Religio Medici*. A. G. H. Bachrach, the director, has edited a series of books which explore the cultural relations between England and Holland during the seventeenth century. His own work, *Sir Constantine Huygens and Britain*, presents this Dutch diplomat and poet who spent many years in England and said, "England made me." The British influence upon the Dutch is explored fully in this study.[28]

A number of the Leyden Pilgrims became naturalized Dutch citizens for business purposes because only a citizen could gain admittance to the trade guilds. Among those who took out citizenship was William Bradford, in 1612, at age twenty-three, soon after he married Dorothy May, daughter of Elder Henry May of the Ancient Brethren Church in Amsterdam. The young groom sold lands that he had inherited in Austerfield and bought a house on the Achtergracht, the Back Canal. He set up his own business as a fustian (corduroy) manufacturer. When their son was born they named him John in honor of John Robinson.

In 1617 Jonathan Brewster applied for his Dutch citizenship papers. He had on arrival in Holland served as an apprentice to a ribbon-maker. Others of the Green Gate fellowship who became citizens of Leyden were Isaac Allerton, a tailor from London; Degory Priest, a hatter from London; Richard Masterson, a wool-comber from Sandwich; Thomas Rogers, a dealer in camlet (waterproof cloth); John Turner, a merchant; Roger White, Francis Jessop, and William Jackson, all from the Scrooby area.

Robinson had been drawn to Leyden because of its reputation for freedom of speech. He was familiar with the commonplace reproaches of those who berated the university city as "a common harbor of all opinions, of all heresies," as "a cage of unclean birds," "all strange religions flock thither," "the great mingle mangle of religion."[29]

Along with their civil liberties and general religious tolerance the States had their internally established Protestant Church of the Netherlands, constituted under the Presbyterian form. Its church buildings and pastors were chiefly supported by the state.

Congregations of foreigners were usually provided for in the same manner. But Robinson did not make such requests for a church building, for aid in his support, or for any financial help from the Dutch government. He and his people were determined to take care of themselves.

He may not have fully realized at the outset how the Dutch Reformed Church differed from the Church of England. It did aid churches and their leaders, but it did not superimpose controls, and it permitted autonomy in the local congregations. As time passed Robinson found himself drawn closer to its traditions.

Robinson, Brewster, Brewer, John Bastwick, and a few other

Englishmen close to the Green Gate congregation registered as members of the university, thus gaining mental stimulus and social standing. The university brought them in touch with a creative center of Protestant thought. Here were men of stature who shared the views they endorsed. It was good to be part of this learned company. Robinson's contact with continental Christianity stimulated his natural bent for the ecumenical. He was introduced to a faith that was more inclusive than the mother church in Britain. These encounters inspired him to move forward along the frontiers of a world view.

The Pesyns Hof, Leyden—Walloon home for the aged built c. 1683 on the site of John Robinson's home

That which is commonly called schism
ariseth from the conceit of faith
or want of love.
—John Robinson

8 "CONCEIT OF FAITH OR WANT OF LOVE"

One salutary result of the move to Leyden was the increasing unity of purpose that brought the Scrooby people into closer fellowship. Their trials in England and their experiences in Amsterdam developed their sense of oneness. Since they were isolated as a foreign refugee company in Holland, they now realized that with Robinson as their leader they were also set apart as members of an intellectual vanguard who were unwilling to travel the path of spiritual mediocrity.

After the removal to Leyden they completed the organization of their church, appreciating more fully the necessity of union and an effective program of faith and action. They were satisfied to follow Robinson and do without a "teacher." Bradford testified, "Mr. Robinson was duly recognized as sole pastor, and Mr. William Brewster chosen as their ruling elder." The pastor was called and ordained by his church people. It is evident that he wanted to be reordained. He believed that the ministry of the Church of England was a "false ministry" since it was derived from the Church of Rome. This "false ministry" was to be repudiated by those who believed that Christ was the supreme head of the church. This made reordination indispensable and the church itself performed this rite, without any bishop.

He wrote: "And for me, do they not know in their consciences that I was ordained publicly upon the solemn calling of the church in which I serve, both in respect to the ordainers and the ordained?"[1]

John Murton reported on the organization of the Leyden fellowship: "Do we not know the beginning of his church, that there was first one stood up and made a covenant and then another, and these two joined together and so a third, and these became a Church say they?"[2]

The Leyden Pilgrims gathered early on the sabbath. They stood for a "long prayer" because they ruled out kneeling as an outmoded superstition. The pastor then read from the Geneva Bible, offering his explanation to make it intelligible, thus replacing the "dumb reading" practiced in the Established Church. The congregation sang a psalm without any musical accompaniment. The sermon was long and built around the scripture. But judging from the tone of Robinson's *Essays* his sermons tended to be practical and fairly cosmopolitan in their references. He once wrote:

113

Next, to the memorable sayings of wise and learned men which I have read or heard and carefully stored up as a precious treasure for mine own and others' benefit; and lastly, to the great volume of men's manners which I have diligently observed and from them gathered no small part thereof, having also had in the days of my pilgrimage special opportunities of conversing with persons of divers nations, estates and dispositions, in great variety.[3]

Following the sermon another psalm was sung. On certain Sundays the sacrament of communion was celebrated. Then the congregation went forward to place their offerings in the box and the benediction was given.

They met again in the afternoon to engage in discussion. Following a prayer, the pastor or elder read from the Geneva Bible, chose a text and expounded it, and then opened the gathering to "prophesying." The male members were given a chance to speak. This practice was ridiculed by critics, and Separatist leaders were called "rude mechanick fellowes." But Robinson defended the activity of the laymen in the church. He referred

to that which is written, Acts XIII:14 where Paul and Barnabas coming into the synagogue, the rulers, after the work of the ordinary ministry was ended (considering them not as apostles, which they acknowledged not, but only as men having gifts) sent unto them that if they had any word of exhortation to the people, they should say on.[4]

He continued:

There are they, whose names I forbear for their credit's sake, who have not spared, and that in their public writings, to lay to our charge, that we will needs have all and every member of the church, a prophet, and to prophesy publicly. With what minds they let loose their tongues to utter these, and many more most false and absurd vituperies against us, we leave it to God to judge, who knoweth: with what conscience and desert of credit therein, unto thee, Christian reader, into whose hands this our apology shall come.[5]

Here Robinson makes clear that the service was one of order and dignity. "Prophesying" was in no way to be identified with the emotional mumblings and outbursts of the revivalists and Pentecostal groups. It meant rather an intelligent and discriminating comment on the scriptures and relevant Christian doctrine. Moreover, this practice prevailed only in the afternoon meetings, not in the more formal morning service where only the minister, elder, and invited dignitaries participated.

This sharing by lay members stimulated them to think about the meaning of the scripture, to react to its truths and to stand on their own feet and put their thoughts into words. This dialogue method proved a valuable teaching technique; it also trained the people to share responsibility and to develop leadership in the church service and in the business gatherings which were a fore-runner of the New England town meetings that were to spring up later in settlements across the seas.

John Yates, who had been a fellow at Emmanuel College, Cambridge and then minister of St. Andrews, Norwich, was a scholarly Puritan, whom Robinson knew and respected. He wrote a treatise against lay preaching, *Persons Prophesying out of Office*. His arguments were copied and sent to Robinson at Leyden by W E (who was probably William Euring). As the Leyden pastor studied this criticism he wrote a defense, *The People's Plea for the Exercise of Prophecy*, defending the participation of laymen in the services of the church.

To counteract this aspersion that all the members of a church were to prophesy publicly, Robinson wrote:

It comes within the compass but of a few of the multitudes, haply two or three in a church, so to do; and touching prophecy, we think the very same that the Synod held at Emden, 1571, hath decreed in these words: "First, in all churches whether by springing up, or grown to some expense, let the order of prophecy be observed, according to Paul's institution. Secondly, into the fellowship of this work are to be admitted not only the ministers, but the teachers too, as also of the elders and deacons, yea, even of the multitude, which are willing to confer their gift received of God to the common utility of the church; but so as they first be allowed by the judgment of the minister and others." So we believe and practice with the Belgic and Dutch churches.[6]

Richard Clyfton described in his *Advertisement* (1612) the form of worship that he used in the Ancient Brethren Church in Amsterdam. We can assume that the Scrooby and Leyden congregations followed about the same pattern.

1. Prayer and giving thanks by the pastor or teacher.
2. Reading of two or three chapters of the Bible, with brief explanation of the same, as the time may serve.
3. The singing of some of the psalms of David.
4. A sermon—that is, the pastor or teacher expounds and enforces some passage of the scripture.
5. The singing again of some of the psalms of David.
6. The sacraments are administered—that is, the Lord's Supper on stated Lord's Days, and baptism wherever there might be a candidate.
7. Collection is then made, as each one is able, for the support of the officers, and the poor.[7]

Ainsworth's *Psalter* was a book of 342 pages. It gave a complete new translation in prose by an able Hebrew scholar, and was printed at the same time that the King James Bible appeared in 1611. The psalms were presented by Ainsworth with numerous pithy notes and comments as a commonsense biblical critic. Side by side with these prose translations were metrical arrangements

adapting the translation in "singing notes" for use as a common song. This friend of the Pilgrims who had suffered many hardships in Amsterdam, presented nearly forty tunes set forth in melody done after the fashion of the time. Ainsworth's *Psalter* differs from the traditional English usage because it was created in Holland for a group of English refugees. He reflected the song usages that had been current in Elizabethan England and also among the French and Dutch.

He explained the sources of his tunes:

> Tunes for the Psalms I find none set of God; so that each people is to use the most grave, decent and comfortable manner of singing that they know . . . . The singing-notes, therefore, I have most taken from our former Englished Psalms, when they will fit the measure of the verse. And for the other long verses I have also taken the gravest and easiest tunes of the French and Dutch Psalms.[8]

The Ainsworth *Psalter* was cherished by the Pilgrims in Leyden and Plimoth. A copy was found in Brewster's library. They preferred it to the new *Bay Psalm Book*, published in 1640, and continued to use it in New England until after the Pilgrim settlement merged with the Massachusetts Bay colony in 1692.

Psalm 23 was one of their favorites:

> Jehovah feedeth me, I shal not lack;
> In grassy folds He down dooth make me lye;
> He gently leads me quiet waters by.
> He dooth return my soul; for His name sake
> In paths of justice leads me quietly.

Edward Winslow reflected the happy hours at church meetings when he spoke of the Leyden psalm-singing as "the sweetest melody that ever mine eares heard."[9]

The people of the Green Gate loved to sing. They had come from a land that was at the forefront in music. They looked forward to their gatherings and crowded into the friendly house for their psalm sings. The tunes they sang were not as doleful as many suppose. The congregation mingled their voices with fervor, and were lifted out of their anxiety and loneliness. They also used madrigals that were popular in England. Some 125 editions of songbooks had been printed between 1560 and 1600.

It was a pleasure for the people to sit in the quiet of their church meeting place and listen to the reading of Bible messages, and then to hear their interpretation. Many carried their Geneva Bibles with them and followed as the pastor or elder read. They were comforted to hear the prayers spoken in understandable words, beseeching direction upon the little colony in their precarious adventure. There was always uplift in the eloquence of the pastor, who radiated courage. His winged words bore them far away in time to Abraham in Mesopotamia, Moses in Egypt, Amos in his vineyard, Ezekiel in his valley of dry bones, Daniel in the

(pages 116-17)
Pilgrims at worship—from an 1859 painting by Dutch artist George Johan Schwartze

Persian court, and the Prince of Peace along the Galilean shores. He always brought them back to the canals of Leyden with replenished faith to face another day.

After the benediction the chatter of conversation exploded. They talked of their struggles with jobs, house-hunting, tussles with the Dutch language, where to shop, and the price of potatoes and cheese.

When there was business that required action by the congregation it was taken care of at the close of worship. This was considered appropriate by Ainsworth, who wrote: "The Church judgments are the Lord's works, nor ours, and therefore fittest to be done on the Lord's day." Robinson also advocated such Sunday practices: "This whole proceeding we make, and use ordinarily on the Lord's day, as being properly the Lord's work, a work of religion."[10]

Robinson sought to emphasize the essentials and to eliminate the superfluous. All Christian ritual was subject to the test: Was it justified by the teaching of Jesus and the facts of the New Testament? If not, it should be eliminated. There were numerous superstitions that had attached themselves to Christian worship through the changing centuries such as the adulation of the cross, the magic in communion, holy water, crossing oneself, the use of candles, incense, the pagan rites that had accumulated around festivals of the Christian year. He sought to simplify, to disengage from the extraneous. This demanded much more of the worshiper. He could no longer lean on devices developed by the priesthood. He had to seek and find God in his own mind. Separating himself from all tangential secondaries, he had to reach out for the primary—the personal encounter of his soul with the divine.

Pastor Robinson probably conducted his church services without wearing vestments, in a direct and dignified manner. He appeared in a costume of wool, corduroy, or cotton with baggy knee breeches, a jacket with belt and buckle, white cotton cuffs, and a white cotton ruff or collar around his neck.

The Green Gate, and later the Fort Meeting House in Plimoth, were stark and barren of all symbolism. The Pilgrim tradition eliminated much beauty such as the use of the organ, vestments, the altar, cross, and candles. This stripping was due to their effort to free themselves from all forms and objects that had become an end in themselves and all practices that held no biblical authority. It was not that they disliked symbolism, beauty, or music. They rejected these rites because of the abuses that had grown up around them. They had been part of a hierarchy of restraint and control that choked their freedom of expression and negated their basic intelligence. It was an unbearable situation, and it is easy to understand why they registered a reaction of such vigor and totality.

In this rigorous housecleaning some values were lost or shelved for generations. In our era the churches of the Congregational Way have witnessed a renaissance of interest in liturgy and a restoration of beauty in the church. But these changes have come about through the will of the people, not by order of the bishops; and with the clear understanding and teaching that they are only aids to worship and have none other than symbolic meaning. The marriage service has been brought back into the church, although records are still under civil control. Prayers of reassurance and comfort are used in funeral services, but the emphasis on the rational interpretation of faith continues.

Robinson was a conscientious and active pastor, watching over his flock, praying with them, counseling them in their problems, finding jobs for the unemployed, caring for the sick, teaching the Christian precepts, while never neglecting his study and writing. "He taught (lectured to his congregation) thrice a week himself," Bradford records, "and wrote sundry books besides his manifold pains other wise."

It was some time before he obtained the privilege of becoming a member of the university, although he had attended lectures, used the facilities of the library, and mingled informally with certain of the faculty. This incorporation with the university, which took place officially in 1615, carried honor and prestige. It placed him beyond the control of the city police and entitled him to receive half a tun of beer every month and about ten gallons of wine every three months free of city and state duties. The impost tax on wine was almost as high as the purchase price. Water was not safe to use for drinking so beer and wine were important in daily diet. Other benefits to members of the university were freedom from obligation to contribute to public works and fortifications, freedom from serving in the night watch, and freedom from billeting soldiers in their homes in time of war.

About a year before the Pilgrim band came to Leyden an English church had been formed with Robert Durie as minister. It was an English-speaking congregation of the Dutch Reformed Church, Calvinistic in theology and Presbyterian in government. The state gave them a house of worship called St. Catherine Gasthuis. It was located near the Green Gate home of the Pilgrims. Because of Robinson's outlook there was a harmonious relationship with this body.

The Pilgrims did not, however, accept any such gift from the state because Robinson did not wish to ally himself and his followers with any system that might endanger their freedom.

Although he started out as an enforced Separatist, he could not draw lines of demarcation between Christians. He practiced intercommunion with the Dutch Reformed, Walloon, Huguenot, and Scottish churches, and the Protestant bodies with whom he came in contact on the continent.

He brought to the Green Gate Dutch professors whom he met at the university and theologians who came from England to visit him. They spoke, no doubt, at the informal lectures which were part of the weekly schedule, and such encounters tended to lift the intellectual level of the parish and to develop tolerance.

Robinson encouraged his people to visit other churches, as John Jenny, a brewer from Norwich, did in his travels. Jenny attended Dutch services "without any offence to the Church." In return, many of the Dutch and French-speaking Walloons paid visits to the Green Gate to hear Robinson speak and to mingle with his congregation. Several of these continentals later cast their lot with him and journeyed to the New World. Among them were Philippe de la Noye (called Delano), Godbert Godbertson (Cuthbert Cuthertson), Moses Symonson (Simmons), Hester Mayhieu (Mrs. Francis Cooke), and Bridget van der Velde, who married John Tilly, and Edward Bumpus.

His close neighbor, the Pieterskerk, became a symbol to him of the fraternity he felt for the Dutch Reformed Church. Its high spires and buttresses were surrounded by open cobblestone courtyards, and his own house stood with other old dwellings in the square around the ancient cathedral. It was only a few paces down the Kloksteeg to the canal and the Nuns Bridge on the Rapenburg, and to the clock tower of the university that graced the fifteenth-century abbey of the White Nuns. When he turned in the other direction it was only a block to the home of William Brewster on Choir Alley.

Living for eleven years across the street from the Pieterskerk, he often wandered through the great doors into the vast structure with its red-brick interior. The choir was built of yellow-gray stone, matching the huge sandstone pillars that towered above the large, clear-glass mullioned windows and above the arches to a second level of smaller windows in the same style, to the wooden ceiling.

On Sunday afternoons and festival days citizens could stroll through the church or sit and enjoy the concerts played by the organist who was employed by the city. The instrument was not used in the services but was available for the enjoyment of citizens at other times.

The nave and choir were immense as in an English cathedral. Formerly a Roman Catholic shrine, all statues and relics had been removed by the reformers so that its walls were bare. The leaded glass windows were thus devoid of all distracting imagery. Andrew Fairservice pictures the interior "as crouse as a cat with a' the fleas kaimed off her." But to Robinson its plainness was a challenge to the discipline of the mind.

The Scrooby unit in Leyden was small but influential. At least twenty-one members can be identified: in addition to the Robinsons, Brewsters, and Bradford there were Roger White, Bridget Robinson's brother; Jane White, her youngest sister (who married Ralph Tickens, looking-glass maker from London, in 1611). There were Elizabeth Neal, "maid of Scrooby," who married William Buckrum, a block-maker from Ipswich; George and Thomas Morton, sons of a prosperous Roman Catholic family from Harworth, up the Ryton River from Scrooby; Francis Cooke, a woolcomber from Blyth, a hamlet close to Scrooby (his wife, Hester Mayhieu, was a Walloon); and George Morton, a merchant from York, who married Juliana Carpenter, a sister of Deacon Samuel Fuller's wife.

Samuel Fuller, a serge-maker of Redenhall, a deacon in the Leyden church, took the lead in helping Robinson break away from the Ancient Brethren Church in Amsterdam and move to Leyden. He was to be famous as the "physition & chirugeon" of the Pilgrims. He married Agnes Carpenter in Leyden in 1613.

There was Edward Southworth, a silk worker, who married Alice Carpenter (one of the daughters of Alexander Carpenter who came from Wrington near Bath to join the Ancient Brethren in Amsterdam). Thomas Southworth was a brother of Edward. William Pontus, a fustian-maker from Dover, married Wybra Hanson in 1610. She may have been from Austerfield since her name was the same as Bradford's mother. Two young people lived with William Brewster, Robert and Ann Peck, who were probably from Sutton-cum-Lound.

The influence of the Scrooby group was not due to numerical strength, but rather to the fact that they furnished the natural leadership. Of course, Robinson and Brewster were the dominant figures. Their earlier guidance of the Scrooby fellowship made them the acknowledged nucleus in the growing Leyden community. Due to these two pilots a peace-loving settlement was created in Leyden. Their residence there was free of the quarrels which seemed to characterize many of the English refugee groups on the continent. It could be said fairly of Robinson's group,

> to the honor of God, and without prejudice to any, that such was the true piety, the humble zeal, and the fervent love of this people . . . toward God and his ways, and the single heartedness and sincere affection one toward another, that they came as near the primitive pattern of the first churches as any of these later times has done.[11]

With the harmonious teamwork of Elder William Brewster, Deacons Samuel Fuller, John Carver, Robert Cushman, and substantial citizens like William Bradford, Edward Winslow, George Morton, Francis Cooke, Jonathan Brewster, Isaac Allerton, Robinson was building a strong and enlightened community. Newcomers of good character were welcomed. There were no class distinctions that disbarred the humble, nor were there Pharisaic doctrinal requirements. The Green Gate company was quite a family at its peak, numbering 300 or more.

Soon after his arrival Robinson was invited by the saints in Amsterdam to serve as arbiter in another of their unhappy disagreements. (It should be explained here that the word saint was taken from the New Testament and referred to the faithful in the early church. It had no relation to canonization and sainthood in the Roman Catholic concept. Nonchurch members were called strangers.)

Before Ainsworth's withdrawal from Francis Johnson's congregation he forwarded a letter to Robinson signed by thirty members, entreating him to send some delegates to hear the statements of the two sides and to advise them. Leyden dispatched messengers, who offered these suggestions: (1) that they should continue to worship together, having aired their oppositions; (2) that the protestors should affiliate with the Leyden church; (3) that a middle course be adopted: that all business of the church should first be considered and resolved by the pastors and elders privately and then submitted to the church for confirmation only.

Francis Johnson's party could accept no one of these proposals. So the Ainsworthians withdrew December 15, 1610, but continued their appeals to Robinson since their quibbling did not end. Robinson had written to them on November 14, 1610 that their "desire to continue together," would "nourish," and

> even beget endless contentions. If therefore it would please the Lord so far to enlarge your hearts on both sides, brethren, as that this middle way be held . . . it would surely make much to the glory of God and the stopping of their mouths, and should be to us matter of great rejoicing, whose souls do long after peace and abhor the contrary; and that thus, walking in peace and holiness, we might all beg at God's hands the healing and pardon of all our infirmities, and so be ready to heal and forgive the infirmities of one another in love.
> Leyden, November 14, 1610[12]

The recalcitrants in Amsterdam, however, held to their course of argumentation.

Certain of the Amsterdam church asked Robinson to send the names of the thirty members who had written asking for his mediation, but he refused because he knew they were bent on making trouble for these peacemakers. He grew weary of their controversies:

> And so we came unto them; first of ourselves, and afterwards at the request of Mr. Ainsworth, and them with him, being sent by the church, and so enforcing ourselves upon them, for the delivering of the church's message, did reprove what we judged evil in them, and that, we confess, with some vehemency.

Impatient with this endless backbiting, Robinson and Brewster sent the saints a long epistle which concluded: "How much better it would have been if they had admitted their faults rather than to blame their brethren, and this would have saved them, 'yea, and us all,' from being a 'by-word to the whole world.' "[13]

He was conscious that the freedom generated by separation could, if misdirected, lead people into disputation and contention. He warned that their revolt should "be tempered with much wisdom, moderation, and brotherly forbearance." More than once he was sought out as arbiter between the theological wranglers of Amsterdam. During one visit to a meeting of Ainsworth's parish he found the company "so disorderly and clamorous" that he reproved them, only to increase the tumult. Then "amazed and aghast, he did then openly testify that he would rather walk in peace with five godly persons, than to live with five hundred or five thousand such unquiet persons as these were."[14]

He and his friends quickly realized the wisdom of their removal to Leyden. Their congregation formed a refreshing contrast to the factious Ancient Brethren. For this reason they were accepted by the leaders of the Dutch Church and by the citizens of their newly-adopted home.

The pastor expressed their unity with the Dutch community in these words:

> We do profess before God & men, that such is our accord, in the case of religion, with the Dutch Reformed Churches, as that we are ready to subscribe to all and every article of faith in the same Church, as they are laid down in the *Harmony of Confessions of Faith,* published in their name.
>
> What more shall I say? We account them the true churches of Jesus Christ, and both profess and practice communion with them in the holy things of God, what in us lieth. Their sermons such as ours frequent, as understand the Dutch tongue; the sacraments we do administer to their known members, if by occasion any of them be present with us; their distractions and other evils we do seriously bewail; and do desire from the Lord their holy and firm peace.[15]

Richard Bernard had been a contemporary of Robinson at Cambridge. He was a minister in Worksop near Scrooby in 1601 and no doubt had visited with him. At one time he sent Robinson a list of his reasons "to prove the bishops antichristian." However, as he sensed the increasing number of reformers in his area, gathering in Gainsborough and Scrooby, he was afraid of being labeled a Separatist. He admitted that some of the people he knew were drawn toward the "despised Separatists because of the love and care they displayed for one another." However, he felt compelled to try to argue Robinson and his Scrooby group back into the fold in his *The Separation Schisme and Christian Advertisements and Counsels of Peace.*

In 1610, which was a busy year crowded with responsibilities for settling his company and family in Leyden and establishing his church there, Robinson completed and printed *A Justification of Separation,* one of the most significant books from his pen. Briefly, he maintained that the authority and nature of the true church was to be found in the Bible. The Church of England was not framed after the New Testament model. Therefore, it was a duty to separate from it. The church was made up of those who made a voluntary profession of faith and separated themselves from the world "into the fellowship of the gospel and the covenant of Abraham."

He ridiculed the legal residence basis which automatically brought into the Established Church everyone who was either born in or moved into a parish without demanding adherence to Christian faith and conduct. In his view, only those who made a voluntary confession and undertook to follow the principles of the Christian life should be members. Therefore, any small group who felt this Christian commitment had the right to form a church, and the election of officers and the exercise of discipline rested with this corporate body of members and not with bishops, presbyters, and elders.

Robinson attacked Bernard's positions one by one and with logic and candor defended the claims of the Separatists. How-

ever, he displayed a degree of tolerance uncommon for this contentious period:

> I am verily persuaded there are in many congregations [of the English Church] many that truly fear God: (and the Lord encrease their number, and graces) and if they were separated from the rest into visible communion, I should not doubt to account them such congregations, as unto which God had given his sacraments. . . .
>
> I doubt not but the truths taught in Rome have been effectual to the saving of many.[16]

Defending his own church against the charge of divisiveness, he said,

> If ever I saw the beauty of Sion, & the glory of the Lord filling his tabernacle, it hath been in the manifestation of the divers graces of God in the Church, in that heavenly harmony, and comely order, wherein by the grace of God we are set and walk: wherein, if your eyes had but seen the brethrens sober, and modest carriage one toward one another, their humble, and willing submission unto their guides, in the Lord, their tender compassion towards the weak, their fervent zeal against scandalous offenders, and their long suffering towards all, you would (I am persuaded) change your mind.[17]

Robinson's moderation in comparison with some of the other zealous leaders in the way of separation was recognized. Bernard admitted that Robinson was "one yet nearest the truth unto us, as I heare, and not so Schismaticall as the rest."

At the time of this writing Robinson agreed in general with prevailing Separatist ideas even to the point of reluctance to hear preaching from the pulpits of the Establishment. This was a natural shrinking from the propaganda of the hierarchy. And as one who had recently, painfully, and at marked cost severed his ties, he was sensitive and skeptical and prone to keep his distance from the institution that had hurt him.

The Pieterskerk, Leyden, 1670

We seek enlightenment from others who see further into the matter, for we are always prepared to give way modestly to those who teach better things.
—John Robinson

9 "WE SEEK ENLIGHTENMENT FROM OTHERS"

About this time William Ames, Robert Parker, and Henry Jacob turned up in Leyden. They entered into discussions with Robinson about his provocative book. They pooled their convictions on the platform for Puritanism they were endeavoring to set up. Ames was against separation. Parker, also, urged Robinson to keep ties with the Mother Church. Jacob wanted reform without withdrawal. The Leyden pastor, who became the center for these seminars, was wise enough to listen to these thinkers, weighing their points with an open mind. His innate affinity for brotherhood was stimulated by these meetings and he publicly admitted that his former firmness on fellowship with the Anglicans was now more temperate and that he was for exchange and intercommunication in every possible way.

It is curious how these three men gravitated toward Leyden. It may have been a desire to be near the university or they may have wished to visit Robinson. They were familiar with his work and could talk with him about certain controversial aspects of Puritanism. Bradford records that some of the Leyden congregation

> knew Mr. Parker, Doctor Ames and Mr. Jacob in Holland, when they sojourned for a time in Leyden; and all three boarded together and had the victuals dressed by some of our acquaintances, and then they lived comfortable, and there they were provided for as became their persons.[1]

This implies that the three were welcomed by Robinson and the parish, that they visited and participated in public meetings where they exposed the people to scholarly preaching. There must have been many congenial and exciting encounters as these men got together for discussions and arguments on church and state.

At the heart of Robinson's struggle was the principle of personal religion as contrasted with traditionalism and formalism. He was compelled by conscience to search out and define for himself the Christian precepts. He was willing to stand alone before ecclesiastical and imperial power. He separated from his Mother Church when it became impossible for him to remain in its fellowship. Only when subscription was rigidly enforced upon its clergy did he admit that he had to sever ties with an institution that repudiated the truth that was revealed by God in his word.

John Bastwick, who was an English member at Leyden Uni-

127

versity, and also part of the Green Gate congregation, records what Robinson said to him:

> I can speake thus much in the presence of God, that Master Robinson of Leiden, the pastor of the Brownist Church (Brownist was a term often misapplied to Separatists), there told me and others, that if he might in England have enjoyed but the liberty of his Ministry there, with an immunity but from the very Ceremonies, and that they had not forced him to a subscription to them, and impressed upon him the observation of them, that he had never separated from it, or left that Church.[2]

The removal to Leyden not only brought Robinson and his followers into a more liberal intellectual atmosphere, but it also removed them from the extremists and directed them into contact with a nobler school of English Puritanism represented by the fellow exiles who became their neighbors, fellow dialoguers, and conversationalists.

William Ames was the leading Puritan theologian. His *Medulla Theologiae, The Marrow of Sacred Divinity,* was widely used on the continent, in England, and in America for 150 years. This famous text was dedicated to the poor youth of Amsterdam and Leyden, who wished to prepare for the ministry, and under the subsidy of "pious and benevolent merchants." The lectures were given in 1620 and 1621. Born in the same year as Robinson, 1576, Ames received his M.A. at Christ's College in 1607. While a student there he refused to wear a surplice in chapel and, as a fellow, championed reform precepts. He was close to a number of key men in the circle of Puritan leadership: William Bradshaw, Robert Parker, Henry Jacob, Paul Baynes, and Richard Sibbes.

Ames had protected William Bradshaw whose book *English Puritanism* brought down upon him the wrath of king and archbishop. It was Ames who had written a preface for this work and translated it into Latin.

Bradshaw, who was at Emmanuel College during Robinson's time, was a follower of Cartwright. His ideas were similar to those of Jacob, Parker, and Ames. Dr. Ames helped publicize *English Puritanism.* Bradshaw was no Separatist. He wanted the church purified and advocated the autonomy of local congregations. After publication of his book his home was searched by spies, who were ordered to confiscate his writings and arrest him. His wife concealed his manuscripts and books in the fireplace, and Ames hid Bradshaw in his home.[3]

Ames also extended help to Robert Parker, who had launched an attack on the status quo by publishing his book, *A Scholasticall Discourse*, etc. Hunted by the police, Parker was smuggled out of England "at the expense of some opulent English merchants with Ames to Leyden."[4]

They did not manage to get Bradshaw out of the country, but his writings crossed over to Holland and influenced fellow reformers there, and were discussed by Ames, Parker, Jacob, and Robinson.

William Ames (1576-1633)—Puritan theologian who visited John Robinson in Leyden

In 1607 Parker published his book, *The Signe of the Cross,* in Holland. His criticism of the superstitious use of the cross and other symbols in the church created a stir. Archbishop Bancroft of Canterbury ordered his arrest, but Parker managed to escape with Dr. Ames. While in Leyden he was engaged for several months in writing a book against the teaching of the bodily descent of Jesus into hell. As an intellectual Puritan he denied this dogma in *De Descensu Domini Christi ad infernos.* Later, he became chaplain of the British troops in Doesburg and died there in 1614.

Robinson took over Parker's unfinished work written in Latin, *The Ecclesiastical Polity of Christ and the opposed Hierarchial Polity,* and wrote a foreword in the name of the Leyden church. It was published at Frankfort in 1616. In it Robinson stated that Parker had spoken too harshly against the Separatists and denied that their separation was as complete as he insisted, and he acknowledged many excellent doctrines and persons in the churches of England:

> In short we do not separate ourselves in the proper sense or especially because "the discipline of Christ is rejected or corrupted in the Anglican Church" but because the discipline and rule of Antichrist is received and sanctioned by royal statutes and ecclesiastical canons. And it is a matter of conscience with us not to submit ourselves in any way to him. And seeing that Parker himself [like others in other books] in that most learned treatise of his asserts in many words and argues that this Hierarchical Government obtaining in these Churches is unlawful, papal and Antichristian, how can our submission to the same be lawful and Christian, or how can there be any communion in ecclesiastical ordinances. We seek enlightenment on the point from others who, as is quite possible, see further into the matter, for we are always prepared [by the grace of God] to give way modestly to those who teach better things. Farewell.[5]

It was important for Robinson that Dr. Ames settled for a time in Leyden where he could meet with him, and so become familiar with his ideas. They both profited by these chats over their manuscripts. Robinson shared Ames' emphasis on the ethical in religion, agreeing with him that divinity was not a speculative discipline, but rather a practical one. Ames also urged ministers to avoid the "naked finding out and explication of the truth" and to concentrate on "use."

Robinson was inclined to think of the human equation in religion. He upbraided those who "highly advancing a kind of private goodness and religion, and who bend their force rather to the weakening of other men in their courses than to the building up of themselves in their own . . . half imagining that they draw near enough to God, if they can withdraw far enough from other men."[6] And also those who "so soured with moodings and discontentment as that they become unsociable . . . if they see nothing lamentable, they are ready to lament."[7]

He was an advocate of the good life as the essence of religion: "Religion is the best thing, and the corruption of it the worst: neither hath greater mischief and villainy ever been found amongst men, Jews, Gentiles, or Christians, than that which hath marched under the flag of religion." God dislikes "church and chamber religion," he said, "which is not accompanied in the house and streets with loving kindness, and mercy and all goodness toward men."[8]

He was not an advocate of an otherworldly religion. He was an exponent of the Puritan code which "was much more than a table of prohibitions," says William Haller. "It was the program of an active, not a monastic or contemplative life."[9]

In the midst of biblical quotations and theological terms one is apt to forget that the Pilgrims were practical people, spirited and enterprising. They exemplified the definition given by Charles and Katherine George:

The Protestant saint must demonstrate his quality while living in the world and busying himself with its tasks; he is a social and total being; the high road to salvation which he travels advertises these positive aspects of the world, which the Catholic tradition denies.[10]

Like Ames, Robinson stressed the role of reason. Ames wrote, "The *will* . . . cannot will or nill anything unless *reason has first judged* it to be willed or *nilled*; neither can it *choose* to *follow* the *last practical judgment* and do that which *reason* doth dictate to be done."[11] Robinson found his authority in the scriptures interpreted by reason and agreed with Ames, who stated that God had given all men reason, and conscience was a function of reason.[12]

He added: "God who made two great lights for the bodily eye, hath made two lights for the eye of the mind: the one, the Scriptures, for her supernatural light; and the other reason, for her natural light."[13]

Robinson endeavored to keep pace with new knowledge and upbraided those "who think it bold heresy to call in question."[14] He said that he who "strives for truth against error, helps the Lord against his enemy, Satan." He added: "A man shows most knowledge and understanding in the matter of truth: but most grace in the manner of handling it, with reverence, holiness and modesty."[15]

Robinson and Ames agreed on many points, but not on the organization of the church. The former felt that no honest man could remain in the Church of England, which automatically included everybody in a parish irrespective of his belief or behavior. Ames wanted a reformation of the church and refused to take part in some of its rites, but he could not break off relations with it.

The two engaged in a lively correspondence. And when Ames made public use of Robinson's confidential letters the Leyden pastor was offended.

This communication between them before 1612 is found in

The Prophane Schisme. Robinson in his preface to his *Of Religious Communion* of 1614 wrote:

> Now as I neither am, nor would be thought, insensible of this unchristian enmity, [in publishing] certain private letters passing between him and me, about private communion [joining in private worship, as in prayer meetings] betwixt the members of the true visible Church and others.
>
> Doctor [William] Ames was estranged from, and opposed Master Robinson; and yet afterwards there was loving compliance and near agreement between them.[16]

Three letters have been preserved, two by Ames and one by Robinson. Ames argued that it was the duty of Christians to commune with anyone who is in communion with Christ. Robinson denied that external communion necessarily followed the discerning of inward communion with Christ.

Dr. Ames wrote a criticism of Robinson's position and dispatched it to his correspondent with a letter that ended:

> Wishing to M. R[obinson] from the God of all grace, the same light and enlargement of heart for *this,* which hee hath received for the *other* part of communion, I commend my epistle to your friendly censure and myself to your accustomed love. November 23, 1614[17]

Robinson stated that "this manuducent" or "hand-leader" would have done better

> to guide men by the plain and open way of the Scriptures . . . beaten by the feet of the apostolical churches and not by subtle *quaeries* and doubtful suppositions and such underhand conveyances as may lead the unwary into a maze and there lose him.[18]

So Robinson published *A Manvmission to a Manvdvction* in 1615, arguing that to remain in fellowship with the Anglican Church or to carry on one's ministry by virtue of the prelate's license was upholding a system of church government that was not sanctioned by the New Testament.

One feels, however, that both shared a little secret pleasure in this theological sparring, knowing that they were never as far apart as they made appear.

During this dispute with Ames, Robinson handled himself with dignity, grasping the scope of Ames' position, and agreeing that he was correct. He recognized other Christian bodies to be true churches, and he encouraged his people to attend their services of worship. He invited and permitted members of other churches to celebrate communion in his church, although he felt he could not share in the Lord's Supper in the Church of England.

In his *Treatise of the Lawfulness of Hearing of the Ministers in the Church of England,* published after his death, he stated that he was a companion and guide of such as "seek how and

131

where they may find any lawful door of entry into accord and agreement with others."

William Ames bade farewell to Leyden and to Robinson to teach at the University of Franeker in Friesland. He planned to go to America, but died in Rotterdam when his home was flooded in 1633. After his passing, his wife journeyed to Salem in 1637 and his library made its way to Harvard College.[19]

Ames and Robinson, two scholars who exerted profound influence on New England, were not destined to reach Massachusetts. Robinson was fated like Ames to remain on the far side of the Atlantic. Cotton Mather wrote that Ames "was upon the wing for this American desert, but God then took him to the Heavenly Canaan." Nevertheless, both left an indelible impress on the New World: Ames through his books and Robinson through the community he helped establish.[20]

The third member of the Puritan triumvirate who sought out Robinson in Leyden was Henry Jacob. Born in Kent and educated at Oxford, he was one of the early Independent Puritans who emphasized the congregational aspect of the church in his efforts at reform, but he did not advocate separation from the Church of England. As early as 1596 he engaged in "some speech with certen of the separation," that is the Barrowists, "concerning their preemptory and utter separation from the Churches of England" and was "requested of them" to state the reasons why he defended the state church.

Jacob wrote out his thoughts which were passed on to Francis Johnson, who was then locked up in the Clink in Southwark. Johnson wrote a reply and Jacob answered. This correspondence, *A Defense of the Churches and Ministry of Englande,* was published at Middelburg in 1599.

He had been one of the most active promoters of the Millenary Petition, sending out circulars, urging citizens to appeal to the king for reform of the low spiritual state of parishes and the oppression of ecclesiastical authorities. In the summer of 1604, Jacob published *Reasons taken ovt of Gods Word and the best hvmane Testimonies proving a necessitie of reforming ovr Chvrches in England.*[21]

The Bishop of London arrested the author and he was imprisoned. His wife and four children fell into dire need. He appealed for a release. After an interview with the Archbishop of Canterbury he was freed on bail in April 1605. He outlined his ideas in *Principles & Foundations of Christian Religion* before he escaped to Holland later in 1605.

Jacob had arrived in his own way at ideas similar to those of Robinson. He believed that

> a true Visible or Ministeriall Church of Christ is a particular Congregation being a spirituall perfect Corporation of Believers, & having power in its selfe immediately from Christ to administer all Religious meanes of faith to the members thereof.[22]

He also believed that the congregation should have a pastor, elder, and deacons. They should be willing to take the Oath of Supremacy, to remain in "brotherly communion" with the Church of England, to pay all due ecclesiastical and civil dues, and in case of any offense being committed by any of them, to be tried before any civil magistrate and also by the governing body of the congregation to which they belonged.

In 1605, while in Middelburg, Jacob issued a pamphlet, *A Christian and Modest Offer of a most Indifferent Conference,* in which he tried to secure a peaceful solution of the difficulties that afflicted the church. He stated that through proper presentation the Puritan cause would appeal and the reformation of the church would be possible. He said that the congregations in England which were willing to accept him and other Puritans as ministers were true churches even though they were imperfect in their makeup. If the bishops would permit those who shared his beliefs to remain in the Church of England "without personal communion with these corruptions" to which they objected, they could hold to their convictions with a clear conscience; but if they were forced to conform, then they must become Separatists.

In 1609 he published *To the right High and Mightie Prince, James,* which contained "an humble Supplication for Tolerance and libertie to enjoy and observe the ordinances of Christ Jesus in the administration of His Churches in lieu of human constitutions, etc." The tolerance for which he pleaded was not to be realized in England for many decades.

It is believed that Jacob was in correspondence with Robinson before he issued his supplication and that he joined him about this time in Leyden. Although thirteen years older and an Oxford man, Jacob was drawn to the Pilgrim leader. He affiliated with the congregation and remained in Leyden for six or seven years. As a writer and preacher he must have spoken often to the people and helped to shape their religious thinking.

In 1610 he printed in Leyden his treatise, *The Divine Beginning and Institution of Christs True Visible or Ministerial Church,* and also the *Unchangeableness of the same by men, viz.* In these writings Jacob stated his acceptance of the Congregational polity. He defined a church as "an entire & independent body politic" and approved the restriction of church membership to the "proved elect" and the autonomy of each congregation.[23]

The generally-accepted thesis for years was that Robinson converted Jacob to the position of independency, but as Champlin Burrage points out, Robinson was not an Independent in 1610, but a Separatist. Since 1605 Jacob had been a leader in defining the ideas of the Independents. Instead of Robinson converting Jacob, it is now believed that Jacob and those who shared his views, like Ames and Parker, turned Robinson from rigid separatism toward independency.

Jacob, Ames, and Parker did not share exactly the same views, but no one of them believed in separation. Robinson in 1610 stated in his *Justification* why he felt that separation was necessary; and Jacob in his *The Divine Beginning* presented the non-separating Puritan position. When Ames and Parker joined them, the four examined all angles of their differences and agreements. Robinson sensed that these three men were better balanced than the reformers of Amsterdam. He appreciated their position which sought reform without separation. In some measure Robinson moved from Separatist convictions a little closer to their views, although he had never been an absolute Separatist like Browne, Barrowe, and Greenwood.

We know that Robinson also influenced Jacob, Ames, and Parker, who respected his scholarship and his gentlemanly behavior. Some believe that Robinson became an Independent Puritan before his death and others that he remained a Separatist. He was the most moderate of Separatists, stressing respect for all Christian bodies.

Jacob's idea of a non-Separatist church within the Established Church, working for its regeneration, was a noble one, but it had no chance of success in such an entrenched and all-powerful hierarchy. Jacob's heart was set on bringing the Establishment to embrace his reforms and to permit him and his people to worship according to their convictions, but he failed, as Robinson had tried and failed, to win over the vast inertia of a monolithic institution. So ultimately it was a matter of conform or separate.

F. J. Powicke does not agree with Champlin Burrage's thesis that Jacob won Robinson away from separation. He points out that Jacob left Holland in 1616 to return to London to found a church like Robinson's. Thus he may have been driven by conscience to end his life as an exile and go back to face the music at home.[24] At any rate, he did cross over secretly to London to organize a Congregational church. He consulted with a number of men who were confined in the Clink, and gathered a group to discuss the constitution of a church, as the record reads:

> He having had much conference about these things here: after yet in the Low Countries he had converse & discoursed much with Mr. Jn. O Robinson, late pastor of the Church in Leyden & with others about them: & returning to England in London he held several meetings with the most famous Men of Godliness and Learning, . . . these with others having weighed all things & Circumstances Mr. Jacob & Some others sought the Lord about them in fasting and Prayer together: at last it was concluded by the Most of them, that it were a very warrantable & commendable way to set upon that Course here as well as in Holland or elsewhere, whatsoever Troubles should ensue. H. Jacob was willing to adventure himself for this Kingdom of Christ's sake, the rest encouraged him. The Church Anno 1616 gathered.[25]

After a day of fasting and prayer it was decided to institute a church. Those who wished to share in the enterprise

> joyning togeather joyned both hands each with other Brother and stood in a Ringwise: their intent being declared, Henry Jacob and each of the Rest made some confession or Profession of their Faith & Repentance, some were longer and some

were briefer. Then they Covenanted togeather to walk in Gods Ways as he had revealed or should make known to them.[26]

Jacob and his people used some of the words of the Scrooby covenant of 1606.

Each of the brethren made open confession of his faith, in our Lord Jesus Christ; and then, standing together, they joined hands and solemnly covenanted with each other in the presence of Almighty God, to walk together in all God's ways and ordinances, according as He had revealed, or should further make known to them. Mr. Jacob was then chosen pastor by the suffrage of the brotherhood and others were appointed to the office of deacons with fasting and prayer and imposition of hands.[27]

This was the procedure that Robinson advocated and practiced: "The people first separating themselves from idolatry, and so joining together in the fellowship of the Gospel, were afterwards, when they had fit men, to call them into the office of ministry."[28]

Thus Jacob moved toward the type of church that Robinson and his associates had evolved in Scrooby and Leyden. They appeared to meet on a common ground in an Independent Congregational society.

Jacob had possibly heard some discussion at the Green Gate while he was in Leyden about possibilities of a move to the New World. He likewise thought of going over with some of his friends. Four years after the landing in Plimoth he asked for dismissal as minister of the London church, "to go thither (Virginia), wherein after (blank) years he ended his Dayes." There is a tradition that Jacob reached Virginia, but the record of his days in America has been lost.

He said before his crossing, "The Lord, I doubt not, will raise up others that shall effectually bear witness unto this truth in due time."[29]

A group of Henry Jacob's friends from London reached the colony of New Plimoth in 1634 under the leadership of John Lathrop, who brought over thirty-four members of his congregation. John Robinson's son, Isaac, journeyed with him from the Plimoth area to Cape Cod where they established the transplanted church which was rooted in the dreams and sacrifices of Barrowe, Greenwood, Penry, Jacob, and others who had helped found and sustain the Prison Church in Southwark. This noble old meeting house stands today in West Barnstable.

In 1624 Robinson published his significant book, *Of Religious Communion, Private and Public,* in which he explained the changes that had taken place in his thinking after he had written his *Justification of Separation.* He made clear that he never intended to question the goodness of many in the Church of England who were worthy of communion with Christian brothers. He felt that the order of the true church would be violated if its

135

members should commune formally with the Anglican fellowship.

He was for intercommunion in the personal realm, but not in the area of church canon law. Personal actions included private prayer, thanksgiving, singing of psalms, profession of faith, confession of sins, reading and explaining the scriptures, or hearing this done in a family or elsewhere. On the other hand, church actions consisted of the reception and excommunication of members, electing and deposing of officers, all employment of public ministry, and communion under the sanction of the church order.

So he wrote:

That we who profess a Separation from the English national, provincial, diocesan and parochial church and churches, in the

View of Leyden from the Polders—Pieterskerk and other public buildings can be distinguished

whole formal state and order thereof, may, notwithstanding, lawfully communicate in private prayer, and other the like holy exercises (not performed in their church communion, nor by their church power and ministry) with the godly amongst them.[30]

John Cotton was familiar with Robinson's determination to repudiate what was bad in the Church of England and to hold to what was good. He stated in 1648:

When some Englishmen that offered themselves to become Members of his Church, would sometimes in their confessions profess their Separation from the Church of England, Mr. Robinson would bear witness against such profession, avouching they required no such professions of Separation from this or that or any Church but only from the world.[31]

He [John Robinson] was never
satisfied in himself.
—William Bradford

10 "HE WAS NEVER SATISFIED IN HIMSELF"

One is apt to become impatient with the reading of these polemics and embroilments, but they were, as Bradford put it, "the first breaking out of the light of the gospel in England." It was as if the conscience of man was suddenly unloosed. Everyone was trying to prove the scriptures.

It is understandable that people who had never been permitted to even read the Bible, much less to speak their minds on the meaning of its message, might run rampant in the sudden freedom to exercise their opinions.

A bedlam of argumentation was created by these religious confrontations as Englishmen of various backgrounds and stages of scholarship were faced by the overwhelming task of interpreting the Bible for themselves, out of their own vernacular version, of probing the traditions of the church, and of struggling to define and clarify them.

No wonder that "the cooper, the tinker, the shoemaker, exhilarated, . . . mounted improvised rostrums, became hot gospellers, and made ignorance into a theological virtue," as Perry Miller put it.[1]

One critic derided:

Even *How* the Cobbler dares the Pulpit climb.
Belike he thinks the difference is but small
Between the sword o' the Spirit and the Awle.
And that he can as dexterously divide
The word of truth, as he can cut an Hide.[2]

These tensions resulted in a confused outpouring of spoken and written words, of laborious and tiring expositions, of heated and bellicose contentions.

It was amazing that amid this battle of tongue and pen there existed as much forbearance and chivalry as was actually exhibited among these reformers and their opponents. It was through such dialogue, however, that a more charismatic churchmanship evolved. Robinson and his flock stand out in the midst of these exchanges like a beacon that points the way toward "more truth and light."

In the previous chapter Robinson's relation with the Puritan non-Separatists was discussed. Now the arguments held by the extreme Separatists will be reviewed such as Robert Browne, who was one of the significant early defenders of this position, and who preceded Robinson by some years at Corpus Christi College. John Robinson has often been considered a "Brownist" although he openly denied this affiliation.

Browne was a relative of Queen Elizabeth's lord treasurer, Lord Burghley, who helped to bail him out of jail several times when he was locked up for heresy. He worked for a time in Norwich with a Corpus Christi friend, Robert Harrison, and formed a Congregational church there in 1581.

Browne took up the cudgel against the tyranny of the bishops. He was censored and threatened. He thought of fleeing with his parish to Scotland, to Jersey or Guernsey, but was arrested in London and imprisoned in August 1581 in Bury St. Edmunds by the Bishop of Norwich. He and Harrison escaped to Holland with part of their congregation, where they settled in Middelburg and the next year Browne published his outspoken book, *A Treatise of reformation without tarying for anie*. He advocated separation, not as an end in itself, but as a means of reawakening and reforming the Church of England.[3]

The purpose of the book was fourfold: (1) to refute the false accusations that were made against the Brownists; (2) to clarify the role of church and state; (3) to urge the immediate reformation of the church; (4) to condemn those preachers who evaded their responsibility for reform by pleading dependence on the secular authority.

Browne insisted that neither Queen Elizabeth nor Parliament had jurisdiction over the church. Its spiritual kingdom was not subservient to earthly laws. Jesus was superior to civil rulers, and the pastor to the magistrate. The sheep do not lead the shepherd. The clergy should realize that it was their obligation to reform the church without tarrying for the leadership of magistrates. In all this Robinson would have acquiesced.

Browne expressed disgust for the unworthy ministers who were untrained and undedicated and suggested that "all the dumb ministers" be "hanged up in the churches and public assemblies for a warning and terror to the rest."[4]

In revolt against the liturgy of the Established Church, he said:

> Their stinted service is a popish beadrow [a catalog of persons for whose souls one prays] of vain repetitions as if seven paternosters did please the Lord better than six; and as if the chattering of a pie or a parrot were much more the better, because it is much more than enough. Their tossings to and fro of psalms and sentences, is like tennis play whereto God is called judge who can do best and be most gallant in his worship: as be organs, solfaing [to sing the notes of a scale], chanting, bussing and mumbling very roundly. Thus they have a show of religion. For the minister and people are bridled like horses and every thing appointed unto them like puppies: as to hear, read, answer, kneel, sit, stand, begin, break off, and that by number, measure, and course, and only after the order of antichrist. Their whole service is broken, disordered, patched, taken out of the mass book, and a dumb and idle ministry maintained thereby, yea a vain worship without knowledge and feeling.[5]

Because of the many corruptions in the state church it was necessary for those who wished to become true followers of Christ to withdraw and form their own true church, however small and insignificant that church fellowship might be. Browne believed that the kingdom of God was not to be built up by entire parishes, but rather by small groups of the worthiest even though they were insignificant in numbers.[6] He was brilliant in his analysis of the poverty of the church and courageous in speaking for reform. He was convinced that the parish church must be plowed under and rooted up in order to initiate its reform. The way to start was to abolish the governing and guiding figureheads who were the blind leaders of the blind.

Unfortunately, the intrepid reformer faced dissension in his own exile church when Harrison turned against him. Like the Marian exile church in Frankfort and the Ancient Brethren Church in Amsterdam, the Middelburg church developed into a veritable hornets' nest.

Browne returned to Scotland, but was arrested there, finding the Presbyterians as well as the bishops against him. In 1585 he made his subscription to the Archbishop of Canterbury and signed a document repudiating many of his Separatist ideas. In 1586 he obtained the post of schoolmaster at St. Olave's in Southwark and served there about three years. He was presented to the rectory of Achurch-cum-Thorpe in 1591 and spent forty-two years there. He died during his thirty-second term in prison in 1633, having been arrested for striking a constable with a cane.

His final writing was addressed to Lord Burghley: "For I am poor enough and broken to be [sic] much with former troubles, and therefore had no need of further affliction." So ended the tempestuous life of "Trouble Church" Browne, a pioneer whose frankness was to encourage John Robinson to speak out against the malaise that afflicted the Church of England.

Browne had advocated withdrawal from all false churches. He even proposed separation from the corrupted country of England. Robinson never went to these extremes. Browne considered it "apostacy and idolatrous" for one to visit a service of the Church of England or any of the Reformed churches, while Robinson looked favorably on such interchange.

Browne emphasized excommunication as necessary and good because it weeded out the unworthy, while Robinson was adverse to censoriousness. Browne was a rigid sectarian, but Robinson, although a Separatist, was wary of divisiveness and schism. Browne's symbols of the church were "a sheepfold which is watched and defended . . . a garden shut up, a well spring enclosed, an orchard and vineyeard walled."[7] These concepts were unacceptable to Robinson who encouraged communication and cooperation.

Historians for some years considered Browne to be the founder of Congregationalism. He played a significant role in its development, but today they believe that credit should go to men like John Robinson, William Bradshaw, Richard Sibbes, William Ames, Robert Parker, and Henry Jacob. These scholars helped move Robinson to the moderate Congregational position.

Former writers such ad Daniel Neal, Benjamin Hansbury, and

John Waddington conveyed a confused interpretation of the inter-changes between Robinson and Henry Jacob. They stated that Robinson converted Jacob to separatism, failing to sense that the Leyden pastor's conversations with Jacob (and also with Ames and Parker) stimulated him to move from separation to independency. This is evidenced in the writings of Robinson, Bradford, Winslow, and Cotton.

One feels that his thinking was shaped in part by this intercourse, and is also convinced that he would have arrived at the broader concepts of religion because his mind was receptive to new truth and because of his natural affinity for fellowship. His nature revolted against restraints and limitations. He was far more a Congregationalist in the contemporary meaning of the term, independent and honest enough to make the break with a bad system, yet strong on brotherhood and unity.

Robinson could see that the withdrawal of the Brownists created a dead end of isolationism. He could not embrace the conceit of such a sectarian position. Exclusivism violated his desire for fraternity. While paying tribute to Robert Browne it should be pointed out that Brownism disappeared, but the Robinson philosophy of religion continued to unfold and develop; and it lives today as an irenic sector of the world church, emphasizing cooperation and harmony.

Robinson was certainly one of the foremost founders of the Congregational Way. Some of the Puritans were Congregationalists like the Pilgrims, with emphasis on the autonomy of the church; others were Presbyterians, who expected more supervision and authority from their presbyteries. These systems of polity were not clearly defined in Robinson's time, but evolved later in the 1640's as further experiments were carried out in the New World and in England.

Robinson drew a distinction between the faith and order of the Church of England. He could accept its faith, but not its order. Experience convinced him that the order of the Church of England could not realize the ideal of the church as the communion of saints or approximate the order prescribed by the Bible, so he was impelled to separate. Nor could he uphold the apostolic nature of the Anglican Church. He wrote that when Jesus and his followers gathered the New Testament church, "they did not by the co-active laws of men shuffle together good and bad, as intending a new monster or chimera, but admitted of such, and none other, as confessed their sin and justified God, as were not of the world, but chosen out of it."[8]

The church of New Testament days was supposedly made up of saints. Robinson's opponents countered this argument by pointing out that there were wicked members in the early church, but that this did not make them into false churches. He agreed that there were unworthy members; however, it was not necessary then for the good to separate from them because the apostolic churches possessed the capacity to reform themselves. This was not true in the Church of England. Its power had been

usurped by the bishops and the church so robbed of that which should make it a true church, that is, the capacity to reform itself.

Robinson's point of view was ethical. The true church had to be built on righteousness. It was not just the intermingling of the good and the bad in the national church, but the fact that under the bishops the power of self-purification which God had placed in the people had been lost. The separation was not just from certain offensive ceremonies, but from the church itself which was corrupt because of the evil within it which it was incapable of reforming.

When he was asked why he could not stay in the church and strive for its purification, Robinson replied that separation was necessary to avoid personal sin:

> But this I hold, that if iniquity be committed in the church, and complaint and proof accordingly made, and that the church will not reform or reject the party offending, but will on the contrary maintain presumptuously and abet such impiety, that

City Hall, Leyden—as it looked in the seventeenth century

then, by abetting that party and his sin, she makes it her own by imputation and enwraps herself in the same guilt with the sinner. And remaining irreformable either by such members of the said church as are faithful, or by other sister churches, wipeth herself out of the Lord's Churchroll, and now ceaseth to be any longer the true church of Christ.[9]

This condition existed in the Church of England. Separation was not only a protest against the ceremonies and the Prayer Book or government by the bishops. It was a necessary step in order to avoid personal sin.

Robinson believed that church polity was an essential part of church doctrine. The order of the church was of basic importance. Its principles had been instituted by Jesus and his early followers, and there was no place in this system for an ecclesiastical hierarchy.

"Your grand metropolitans, your archbishops, bishops, suffragans, deans, archdeacons, chancellors, officials and the residue of that lordly clergy" have no justification in the New Testament.

The English parish system, which included people without regard to character, was also alien to a communion of saints. "With what conscience can any man plead the saintship of all that godless crew in the English assemblies?"[10]

The church should be composed of those who had separated themselves from the world, that is, those who were dedicated Christians. They were "gathered" into organized companies for communion and mutual service. They were bound through a covenant with God and as a consequence the power which Jesus gave to the church was lodged in them. The congregation had the power to choose and ordain its own minister, to choose its own officers, to receive and dismiss members.

"The Lord Jesus is the King of His Church alone, upon whose shoulders the government is, and unto whom all power is given in heaven and earth," but he had communicated this power to church members, making each member a prophet to teach, a priest to offer praise and sacrifice, and a king to guide himself and others in godly living. So the power of Christ is given to members of the church. They are to respect their officers, but the power of the officers is given them "mediately by Christ from the church," and the officers are not the church.[11]

Robinson was forced to reject the statement of William Bradshaw: "A patient suffering, when we cannot in conscience obey, is the best obedience." This was the voice of moderation addressed to those who were unhappy with the condition of their church, but unwilling to separate. Was there no other alternative to "a patient suffering"? Robinson questioned. How were evils long entrenched in the religious life of the nation to be altered except through outspoken condemnation? Someone must first give truth to the people and try to shock them into change.

Only bold words and actions could alter the tyranny of the hierarchy, the indolence of the clergy, and the lethargy of the laity. The martyr John Udall was right to accuse all of them: "You are in league with hell, and have made a covenant with death!"[12]

Robinson pondered the words of Paul: "Come out from among

them and be ye separate, and touch not the unclean thing, and I will receive you." He was propelled to make such a radical move into overt resistance. How could he act otherwise in dealing with the traditional English church which was a jumble of the pious and impious? It was a "confused heap" and "every subject of the kingdom dwelling in this or that parish, is bound, will he, nill he, fit or unfit, as with iron bonds, to participate in all holy things, and some unholy also, in that same parish church."[13]

In the face of these shortcomings a new church, a true church, could be formed as good people, the "visible saints" met together, professed their faith, and took a covenant of allegiance to God and the Christian way. "To make a reformed church," he wrote, "there must be a reformed people."[14] The church should be a special fellowship of godly men and women, and not a list of all local citizens, many of whom were indifferent and unworthy.

He explained:

The word *kahal* in Hebrew, in Greek *ecclesia,* in English church signifieth a company of people called out: and that in respect both of the voice or will of the caller, and obedience of the called: and so, restrained to religious use, signifieth a company of people called, and come out of the state of nature, into the state of grace; out of the world, into the kingdom of Christ. Who are therefore entitled "saints" by calling, and "sanctified" or separated "in Christ Jesus": the temple, "house," and "household of God."

And to conceive of a church, which is the body of Christ and household of God, not separated from the profane world, which lieth in wickedness, is to confound heaven and earth, and to agree Christ with Belial.[15]

These Christians, who had separated from the world, were obligated to live as disciples of Christ. Every believer was a "Kinge, a Priest, and a Prophet vnder Christ, to vpholde and further the kingdom of God."[16] Each group of these children of God formed a unit in faith that was independent of all external compulsion and was competent to manage its own affairs.

But this we hold and affirm, that a company, constituting though but of two or three, separated from the world, and gathered into the name of Christ, by a covenant made to walk in all the ways of God known unto them, is a church, and so hath the whole power of Christ.[17]

Robinson revolted against the constrictive use of the Prayer Book with its cut-and-dried platitudes and parochial outlook which held the people under the infallible orders of the bishops. He opposed this "solemn and set bookservice" since God had nowhere commanded in the scriptures which form worship should take. He denied that the Lord's Prayer was intended to limit worshipers to its very words. Jesus did not tie his disciples to any one form, so why should the bishops "presume to impose upon men another form of words"? Nothing should be permitted to become an idol such as the service book.[18]

145

Referring to prayer in the worship service, Robinson said:

We cannot but mislike that custom in use by which the Pastor is wont to repeat and read out of a prayer-book certain forms, for his and the Church's prayer. . . . In prayer we do pour out matter, to wit the holy conceptions of the mind, from within to without; that is, from the heart of God: on the contrary, in reading, we do receive and admit matter from without to within; that is, from the book into the heart. Let him that prayeth do that which he doth, not another thing, not a divers thing. Let the whole man, and all that he is, both in soul and body, be bent upon God, with whom he converseth.[19]

He condemned the political racket that prevailed in the English church, the superstitious practices by which priests exploited their parishioners:

Their sale of orders and institutions and . . . of dispensations for pluralities, and non-residences, of licences to preach up and down the country, and to marry at times by their canons prohibited; of pardons and absolutions, when men are excommunicated, and sometimes when they are dead, before they can have Christian burial: with their extorted fees, and purse-penalties, the very sinews of their kingdom, do clearly pronounce against them, that they and their subordinates are merchants of that great city Babylon, trafficking for all manner of ware, and for the souls of men. Rev. xviii. 10-3.[20]

Puritans believed that the power of excommunication and other disciplinary actions should be exercised by the individual church and its minister and should not be monopolized by the bishops. Robinson said that the "bishops' courts played with excommunication like a child with a rattle." Notorious thieves and adulterers went free while honest men were excommunicated for trifles and only by paying exorbitant fines could they secure a lifted sentence.[21]

He held that anyone was capable of qualifying himself for church membership; but also maintained that a true profession of faith could be made only by persons "visibly, and so far as men in charity could judge, justified, sanctified, and entitled to the promises of salvation, and life eternal."[22]

Robinson did not establish a creed or a dogmatic procedure for entrance into his church. One of his opponents wrote in 1609 that in spite of his Separatist claims to a purer membership than the Church of England, "yet you require but a voluntary profession of covenant, which hypocrites may make."[23] It was true that he did not set up any test for admitting candidates into the church beyond the person's assertion made in his confession of faith, his sharing in the covenant, and his good behavior.

Robinson was strong on the preaching role of the church under educated ministers. He wrote regarding the absence of teaching in Anglicanism:

The reading of the service book, in form and manner, the

celebrating of marriage, churching of women, burying the dead, conformity and subscription, are more essential to your ministry, and more necessarily required by the laws of your church both civil and ecclesiastical, than *preaching* the *gospel* is. The wearing of the surplice, and the signing with the cross in baptism, are of absolute necessity, without partial dispensation, yea, I may add violation of oath by the bishops: whereas preaching the Word is no such necessary or essential duty, but a work casual, accessory, and supererogatory, which may be done or undone, as the minister is able, or willing, without any such absolute necessity, as is here pretended.

Hereupon then it followeth, that since the preaching of the gospel is no necessary part or property of the office of ministry, in the Church of England, that that ministry cannot be of Christ.[24]

In his thinking, appointment of ministers by the monarch was fundamentally evil, and more so because those appointments did not require spiritual and intellectual qualifications to preach.

He agreed with William Perkins that the sermon was of utmost importance in Christian worship. Sermons should be delivered in plain, everyday English. They should not be laden with Latin, Greek, and Hebrew phrases or quotations from the church fathers. The preacher should not indulge in metaphysical or theological disputation, but rather apply the Bible to daily living. The Bible was his authority. His basic obligation was to interpret it and relate its truths to daily experience.[25]

Ministers should be teachers, he insisted, who lived with and served their people:

The greatest part of them [ministers in the Church of England] by far, declare not the Lord's word at all unto the people, but are tongue-tied that way, some through ignorance, some through idleness, and many through pride. And of them which preach how many are there mere men-pleasers, flattering the mighty with vain, and plausible words, and strengthening the hands of the wicked; and with profane and malicious spirits reviling, and disgracing all sincerity in all men: adding unto these evils a wicked conversation, by which they further the destruction of many, but the conversion of none.[26]

Ministers should be chosen by their congregations, who were obligated to support them:

All free persons and estates should choose their own servants, and them unto whom they give wages and maintenance for their labours and service. So it is betwixt the people, and ministers: the people a free people, and the church a free estate spiritual, under Christ the king; the ministers the church's, as Christ's servants; and so by the church's provision to live, and of her, as labourers to receive wages.[27]

Puritan preachers dared to speak out in the vacuum of spiritual need. "Neither the gaol nor the scaffold could stop them from talking, writing and printing."[28] They boldly recast in their own words the precepts of the Bible, impressing upon their people the imperative value of Bible study and attention to their teaching sermons. They challenged men with a regimen of discipline that demanded something on their part and so answered their yearning for "a more decent, more self-controlled and self-respecting existence."[29]

Robinson and kindred spirits among the Cambridge reformers sensed the uneasiness that was abroad in the country. The Established Church "had failed to provide spiritual satisfaction for many of its people." The Puritan movement flourished and inspired citizens to take the risk of embracing an unpopular cause even to the extent of sacrificing their property and ancestral ties, and migrating to a new world. "People were cut adrift in life, bobbed up and down mentally on a sea of indecision" now that "the former reliance on aid from established authority in church and state no longer sufficed."[30]

"In his Geneva cloak, unfettered alike by need to wear the surplice or use the Prayer Book, the nonconforming divine preached and prayed as he pleased." This freedom of mind, this cleavage with tradition, gave him a novel approach, a directness and daring that won him an audience.[31]

This is one reason why Puritan sermons were popular. They answered a need. Crowds flocked to hear the preachers. Sermons were published in vast quantities and widely read. Richard Sibbes drew large congregations at Gray's Inn, London, and William Gouge at St. Anne's Blackfriars.[32] "It is hardly possible to exaggerate the importance of the sermon in the seventeenth century world."[33]

The Leyden pastor disliked labels. He did not want to be called a Brownist, a Separatist, an Independent, a Robinsonian, or even a Congregationalist. He did not contend that his church was *the* true church, but only that it was a true church of Christ, one with many true churches scattered throughout Christendom.

William Bradford recorded:

At first for the name, *Independents*, you are to know it is not a name of choice made by any of themselves, but a title imposed by others which are their opposite.[34]

Mr. Cotton saith [also] that it is no fit name for our churches, in that it holdeth us forth as independent from all others. Whereas, indeed, we do profess dependency upon magistrates for civil government and protection, dependency upon Christ and his word for the sovereign government and rule of our administrations, dependency upon the council of other churches and synods when our own variance or ignorance may stand in need of such help from them.[35]

Winslow denied that the Leyden Pilgrims boasted of separation from the Church of England. Robinson and Brewster never required anyone to repudiate that church or any church. He defended his company against "all the injurious and scandalous taunting reports that are passed on us." He testified that "our practice being wholly grounded on the written Word, without any addition or human invention known to us, taking our pattern from the primitive churches."[36]

Although he separated from his church, Robinson was never an exclusivist. While protesting against the abuses of a state church, he was loyal to his ruler, his country, and to its people. He expressed eloquently his wider sense of the kingdom of God:

> I answer, first, that our faith is not negative, as papists used to object to the evangelical churches; nor which consists in the condemning of others, and wiping their names out of the bead-roll of churches, but in the edifying of ourselves, neither require we of any of ours, in the confession of their faith, that they either renounce, or, in one word, contest with the Church of England, whatsoever the world clamours of us this way. Our faith is founded upon the writings of the prophets and apostles, in which no mention of the Church of England is made. We deem it our duty what is found in them to believe, with the heart to righteousness, and to confess with the tongue to salvation. Rom. x. 10.
>
> Secondly, we accord, as far as the Belgic and other reformed churches, with the Church of England, in the Articles of Faith and heads of Christian religion published in the name of that church and to be found in Harmony of the Confessions of Faith.
>
> Thirdly, if by the church be understood the catholic church, dispersed upon the face of the whole earth, we do willingly acknowledge that a singular part thereof, and the same visible and conspicuous, is to be found in the land, and with it do profess and practice, what in us lays, communion in all things, in themselves lawful and done in right order.[37]

Before the Reformation, the medieval mind assumed that the Roman Catholic Church was the true church, but Robinson said that the true church was not necessarily the organized church. The true church was made up of dedicated people who had withdrawn from the world and pledged themselves to follow Jesus' teachings in a fellowship like that of first-century Christianity. He believed that there were many genuine Christians scattered among all kinds of churches of various names which might not meet the test of the true church.

This was a perception that pierced through the traditional concept of a formalistic sanhedrin to a fellowship of kindred spirits who had discovered the meaning of the Christian faith, and who were to be found in all sectors of Christendom.

Disputations in religion are sometimes
necessary, but always dangerous.
—John Robinson

11 "DISPUTATIONS IN RELIGION ARE ALWAYS DANGEROUS"

Like a pack of foxhounds in pursuit of the challenger to their prowess, the contenders of Amsterdam followed Master Robinson. Although he had escaped to Leyden from their disputes, he could not cut himself off from their argumentation. In order to understand his views it is necessary to enter here into another theological controversy.

Thomas Helwys emerged as an innovator in the Ancient Brethren Church of Amsterdam. He was from Basford in Nottinghamshire. He had attended reformist meetings, including John Smyth's group in Gainsborough. He later fled to Holland where he soon stirred up quite a furor among the Ancient Brethren when he raised the question of the propriety of their residence in Holland. He insisted that they had run away from responsibility and were evading reality. He was troubled over their "flight from persecution" and wrote, "How much better for men to give their lives for the truth they profess in their own countries."

Helwys also condemned the "guides" who encouraged them to migrate to the Netherlands. Robinson answered, "The truth is, it was Mr. Helwisse above all either guides or others, furthered this passage into strange countries; and if any brought oars, he brought sails, as I could show in many particulars, and as all that were acquainted with the manner of our coming over can witness with me."[1]

Robinson, "forced by the unreasonable provocation of Mr. Thomas Helwisse, who in great confidence and passion layeth load of reproaches both upon our flight in persecution, and also upon our persons for it," attempted to justify himself and his church. He cited the flight of Jacob, of Moses, of David, of Jeremiah, of Baruch, and of Elijah; and

> the flight of Joseph and Mary, who carried our Lord with them into Egypt; to our Lord's own example during His public ministry—for He Himself kept out of the way of His enemies till the hour for His suffering came; to His direction to His disciples that when they were persecuted in one city they should flee to another; to the example of Peter, Paul and the rest of the apostles.[2]

Helwys was obsessed with the idea that "the days of greatest tribulation spoken of by Christ wherein the abomination of desolation is seen to be set in the holy place" had arrived. He felt there had been "a general departing from the faith and an utter desolation of all true religion."[3] He said the Roman Catholic Church was wrong; the Church of England was wrong; the Puritans were wrong; the Brownists were wrong; all the reformers in Holland, Robinson, Ames, Jacob, Parker, Johnson, Ainsworth, Smyth, Clyfton were wrong; everyone except Helwys was wrong. God had laid the responsibility upon him to set things straight. He said he and others had been "misled by deceitful leaders," who in an effort to save their lives fled into foreign countries to seek their own safety.[4] Robinson countered that they did not forsake their country, "but were forsaken by it and expelled by most extreme laws and violent proscriptions contrived by the prelates." If they had wished to save their skins they would have played it safe and stayed in England and not risked the hardship of exile. This move was not made to seek safety but rather to preserve their spiritual freedom.

Helwys was a layman who had not received the academic training necessary for a minister. He did, however, plant the first Baptist church on English soil, as is noted later. It was led and officered by laymen. Robinson did not object to this emphasis because he had long stressed the role of laymen in the church. That he held the laity in high esteem we know from his harmonious relations with Brewster, Fuller, and Carver, but he did express irritation and impatience with Helwys. He insisted on an educated ministry in the church. Otherwise it would revert to superstition and chaos.

Helwys asserted that baptism as practiced by the exiles was wrong. Only adults should be baptized. Baptism as received in the Church of England was invalid and baptism of infants should cease. Baptism could be performed by any Christian. He argued that Robinson and other Separatists had spoken out strongly against the Church of England, calling her "Babylon" and renouncing her and her works. Yet he said, they retained her baptism as valid. They professed to have separated from the world and joined themselves to Christ, but the New Testament made it clear that there was no way for men to join Christ but to amend their lives and be baptized and through baptism to put on Christ. If they regarded the baptism received in the Anglican Church as true baptism, then they must regard the Anglican Church as a true church. If this were the case they were wrong to separate from it.[5]

In his book, *Of Religious Communion*, Robinson devoted much thought in consideration of this charge. He said there was "an outward baptism by water and an inward baptism by the Spirit." Even an outward baptism administered by an apostate church had a spiritual significance when so interpreted. And so it was assumed in his church and by the people who wanted to enter it; they were never rebaptized.

Another English refugee in Amsterdam, John Murton, had attended the secret meetings of John Smyth in Gainsborough and had come over to Holland with Smyth and Helwys. He participated with these two in controversy over Se-baptism (self-baptism), infant baptism, and criticism of the exiles for taking up residence in the Netherlands. He penned *A Description of what God hath Predestinated concerning man, . . . as also an Answere to John Robinson* in which he introduced readers to a paper by Robinson (since lost) on the subject of baptism. He said he was convinced that christening of infants was a late invention and that Robinson was wrong when he held that only pastors should baptize. He maintained that any disciple of Christ who had received the call of God to preach could baptize people.[6]

Robinson returned a negative. Only a pastor called by a church could baptize. He went on to say that Murton, Helwys, and John Smyth had gotten themselves into a predicament by baptizing themselves and one another and teaching that any one of "their proselytes and supposed converts" could perform this Christian sacrament. He criticized them for making baptism the central factor in the Christian experience "to which they ascribed so great virtue that they would not so much as pray together before they had it."[7]

Helwys repudiated infant baptism. Robinson felt that it was a useful practice, of value to parents and the church. He argued that it had developed in the place of circumcision. He desired that all children were saved "if such were the will of God, and so could gladly believe if the Scriptures taught it."

Robinson appears a bit vulnerable in this baptismal confrontation. His stand is not too clear. We are sure that he did not believe that an infant dying unbaptized was damned. Such a harsh view would be unacceptable to his nature and reason. He was a stickler for scriptural authority in church practices, and Murton insisted that there was no reference in the New Testament to infant baptism, and Robinson could not find one.

He developed a parallel between baptism and circumcision, but that was not too convincing since it applied only to the male of the species. He recognized that infant baptism had been subject to much evil manipulation and exploitation by the church. But it was a long-established rite and it was difficult for him to come out against it. To take this step would place him in the camp of the Anabaptists, who believed only in adult baptism. He was already battling to throw off the derogatory label of Brownism and he did not want to become embroiled in other sectarian squabbles.[8]

Apparently he did not put into words the view of his Congregational followers that this Christian symbol was a means for dedication by the parents of their child to the Christian way of life. It had no magical influence upon the inner state of the little one. It simply brought him into the church family where he was to be nurtured in the Christian life. He did state that it was "absurd" to exclude infants "from the church or state of grace because they cannot themselves make profession of faith and repentance."[9]

Moderns may smile at this speculation over creedal minutiae regarding theories and forms of baptism, but after the passing of over three and a half centuries this thorny issue remains unresolved. At contemporary Christian conclaves the practice of this

sacrament is still warmly debated. The tenet continues in our time as a major roadblock toward Christian unity.

John Smyth got himself involved with Helwys and Murton. Robinson told him he made a mistake in renouncing the baptism he had received in the Church of England, through baptizing himself and permitting the sacraments to be administered by an unordained man. He said of his old friend from Gainsborough, "his instability and wantonness of wit is his sin and our cross." Amid the unhappy divisions of the Amsterdam church, Smyth applied for church fellowship with the Waterlanders, a group of Mennonites. He died in August 1612 from consumption in the bake house of one of these churches where he was granted shelter by a kind-hearted Dutchman.

In the last section of a little book published after his death, John Smyth revealed a humble spirit. He did not recant or return to the Church of England, or repudiate his small group of followers. He repented of the censorious words that he had spoken in controversy, preferring no longer to answer the works that were written against him, because he felt they would only breed further strife.[10]

The sincere, mercurial Smyth developed, along with his strong Baptist convictions, a revolt against certain Calvinist traditions. He accepted the view of the Mennonites who held that the redemptive way of Jesus took care not only of the elect, but could be effective among all people. He won Helwys and Murton over to these Arminian ideas.

As a result of his outreach toward broader concepts, Helwys approached the point where he appealed for tolerance, stating "that no man ought to be persecuted for his religion and that freedom of conscience should prevail." He and Murton were forthright thinkers and they kept tossing hot theological chestnuts at Robinson, who found some of them baffling to answer.

Smyth died in 1612 and Helwys in 1616, but Murton carried on the battle to uphold their position. A book was published in 1620 which Robinson ascribed to John Murton and his associates: *A Description of what God hath Predestinated concerning man, in his creation, transgressions, regeneration*, etc. (another title which indicates the audacity of the laymen in these awakening times to tackle the profound issues of life).[11] The first portion opposed the Calvinist doctrines of predestination, election, and reprobation and upheld the idea of general redemption and "free choice." As a layman, Murton gave his reactions on the Synod of Dort's defense of Calvinism. He looked at these learned deliberations of the scholars in a practical, common-sense manner. In contrast, Robinson considered their pronouncements with the balance and counterbalance of the professional theologian. Although he was drawn to the brotherly precepts of Arminius, he could not tolerate tampering with the basic tenet at the heart of religion—the sovereignty of God. He believed that the doctrine of free will would lead to religious and political chaos while the concept of

Quai in Leyden

the sovereignty of God and his rule over man would preserve the dignity of the individual and a harmonious body politic.

Although Robinson spoke of Helwys and Murton as "double-washers" he nevertheless gave much time and study to answering their arguments. This was done in his weighty production, *A Defense of the Doctrine propounded by the Synod of Dort against John Murton and his associates . . . with the refutation of their answer to a writing touching baptism.* This book indicates that he had known Helwys, Murton, and some of their associates in England. In one place he appeals to these old acquaintances:

> But let all God's people be exhorted, and admonished to serve him in modesty of mind, and meekness of wisdom, with reverence, and fear: avoiding, as the sands of humble hypocricy, in pinning their faith and obedience upon the sleeves of others, so much more the rock of proud presumption: which is so much the worse than the other, as it is more dangerous for any to overvalue himself than another man.[12]

We learn through Robinson's reactions to the views of these men that he was impatient of litigation and feuding. He did not shy away from argument but he was opposed to divisiveness which was all too prevalent in Christendom.

"No family hath so many unskilled ones to meddle in it; as that of disputing in matter of religion," as he put it.

> But we should affect strife with none, but study, as far as we can to accord with all; accounting it a benefit, when we can so do with any.
> We ought to be firmly persuaded in our hearts of the truth, and goodness of the religion, which we embrace in all things; yet as knowing ourselves to be men, whose property it is to err and to be deceived in many things; and accordingly both to converse with men in that modesty of mind, as always to desire to learn something better, or further, by them, if it may be.[13]

Thomas Helwys returned to London with John Murton and a company of friends, and immediately ran into trouble. Murton was in prison in 1613. It is clear from what Robinson says in 1614 that they had suffered persecution: "I would know how he [Helwys] and the people with him have preached to the city of London? Surely not as the apostles did in the synagogues and public places; much less do they flee *being persecuted* (or go, if so they will have it) from city to city."[14]

Robinson pointed out that religious arguments were usually carried on with violence, and that his desire had been to pacify rather than alienate affections.[15] He made frequent use of a favorite phrase, "Advertise us brotherly."

> If in anything we err, advertise us brotherly, with desire of our information, and not, as our countrymen's manner for the most

156

part is, with a mind of reproaching us, or gratifying of others: and whom thou findest in error, thou shalt not leave in obstinacy, nor as having a mind prone to schism. Err we may, alas! too easily: but heretics, by the grace of God, we will not be.[16]

This man who loved "peace and union above all else," and whose nature shrank from conflict, seemed destined to spend his life in theological argumentation, writing, debating, and defending the truth as he saw it. During these encounters with his adversaries he was able to keep cool, to give here and there, but never surrender his high standards of scholarship and ethics. He was caught in the vortex of dispute that swirled about him, but he managed to hold steady with an open mind and keep on growing in liberality, without being diverted into the byways of fanaticism.

I profess myself always one of them
who still desire to learn something better
and further what the good will of God is.
—John Robinson

12 "TO LEARN BETTER AND FURTHER"

Robinson was cosmopolitan in his reading and interests and managed to establish contact with many of the reformed theologians of his time and a number from the Establishment. He was a willing debater and did not hesitate to step into religious "hot spots," hoping that he might grasp some new revelation. He explained:

> I profess myself always one of them, who still desire to learn further, or better, what the good will of God is. And I beseech the Lord from mine heart, that there may be in the men (towards whom I desire in all things lawful to enlarge myself) the like readiness of mind to forsake every evil way, and faithfully embrace and walk in the truth they do, or may see, as by the mercy of God, there is in me; which as I trust it shall be mine, so do I wish it may be their comfort also in the day of the Lord Jesus.[1]

Regarding the conflicts that divided the so-called religious people of the world, these words opened his last work, "according to the copie that was found in his studie after his decease," from his *Treatise of the Lawfulness*, etc., printed in 1634:

> They who desire peace and accord, both interpret things in the best part they reasonably can, and seek how and where they may find any lawful door of entry into accord and agreement with others: of which latter number, I profess myself (by the grace of God) both a companion and a guide; especially in regard of my Christian countrymen, to whom God hath tied me in so many inviolable bonds; accounting it a cross that I am, in any particular, compelled to dissent from them; but a benefit, and matter of rejoicing, when I can in anything with good conscience unite with them in matter, if not in manner, or, where it may be, in both.[2]

Amid all this academic and ecclesiastical hubbub he watched his children grow, helped with their tutoring, and shared with Bridget plans and hopes for their uncertain future.

There were three "lectures" each week at the Green Gate, congregational ministrations, business meetings, and university functions. In the midst of all this he managed to keep up his

159

study and writing. He also found time to continue the tutoring of William Bradford, who came to the Green Gate after his day's labor of making corduroy. The young man was advancing in his study of Latin and Greek and later developed a desire to study Hebrew that he might "see with his own eyes the ancient oracles of God in all their native beauty." It was rewarding after the turmoil of daylight hours to enjoy the company of this avid pupil.

When Robinson first arrived in Leyden the university circle was agog with vigorous controversy over the precepts of Calvinism. The rebel, Jacob Arminius, had launched his attack on the doctrine of predestination and the Calvinistic views of the Dutch Reformed Church. His new party was called the Remonstrants. The Counter-Remonstrants organized against his criticisms. Arminius promoted a division that had existed from the time that the idea of Calvinism had been introduced from Switzerland and France, that is, the division between the Reformed or strict conservatists and the more humanistic anticonfessionals, representing the majority of the well-to-do burgers.

On July 25, 1609 there was a public disputation at the university on the calling of men to salvation. Arminius denied that men were converted by an invincible divine power. His associate in theology, Professor Gomarus, said to him, "Never did I hear in this University such language, and arguments so effectually opening the door to Popery. . . . I will refute you publicly."[3]

Arminius stated that in no manner did he believe in or favor popery. He said that the theory that God exercises an irresistible force in the salvation of man is contrary to the Bible, to the ancient teachings of the church, and to the concepts of the Reformed Church.

Both these opponents were very eminent scholars. Arminius had studied at Leyden, Geneva, Basle and Padua, while Gomarus had studied at Strasbourg, Heidelberg, Oxford, and Cambridge.

The debate between the two theologians was continued, but Arminius died and was buried in St. Peter's Cathedral a few weeks after John Robinson reached the city. His death in October of 1609 did not ease the controversy that had spread throughout the nation. Conrad Vorstius, who shared the Arminian views, was chosen to assume his chair, but James I registered his objections. It is curious that the king should feel that he had the right to enter into the internal affairs of the Netherlands. He recognized the influence and he was afraid of the power of the University of Leyden.

James wrote to his ambassador, Winwood, at The Hague, calling Vorstius a "viper" and his opinions "monstrous blasphemie and horrible Atheisme," warning the Netherlands States "how infinitely wee shall bee displeased if such a Monster receive advancement in the church." The States weighed this mandate from London. The king sent a second order, threatening to consult other Reformed churches "how to extinguish and remand to hell these abominable Heresies." Meanwhile, he stated his intention "to forbid all the youth of our subjects to frequent a university that is so infected a place as is the Universitie of Leyden."[4]

Ambassador Winwood transmitted a third protest. King James

Acadenua Lugdunenfis

ordered the books of Vorstius which had reached England burned
in St. Paul's churchyard in London, at Cambridge and Oxford.
When the Dutch pointed out that they could not dismiss Vorstius
after bringing him and his family from Germany, James was
furious. He retired to the country where he penned his treatise
against the Arminian upstart, *Declaration du Roy, touchant la
faict de C. Vorstius*, which was published in Latin and English
translations.

To show even more specifically his hatred of heretics James
burned two English Unitarians at the stake: Legate at Smithfield,
March 18, 1612 and Wightman at Litchfield, April 11, 1612. Protests were immediate and widespread over these public burnings.
The populace was growing impatient of religious executions, and
James was forced to commute death sentences for heresy to life
imprisonment. He did allow the old medieval *rite de heretico
comburendo* to be issued for the last time as one more blast
against the radicals.[5]

The appointment of Vorstius was held up, and at length the
curators elected Simon Biscop (whose Latin name was Episcopius), who was also a disciple of Arminius. The young scholar,
then twenty-nine, delivered his inaugural address February 23,
1612 on the subject "How Best the Kingdom of Christ Among
Men May be Built up." He emphasized the practical rather than

Leyden University (1614)—copper engraving of the old college building

161

the theoretical: truth, justice, and peace. Robinson no doubt attended and was sympathetic to his ethical exposition of religion. He did not sense at that date that he would soon be debating with Episcopius before the faculty of the university.

The former opponent of the Arminius-Episcopius platform, Gomarus, had by this time been succeeded by John Polyander, who was called from Dort in 1610. Robinson soon met him and they became close friends. John Polyander was delighted to find a fellow Calvinist from Britain to share his views and support him in his stand at the university. He was curious to hear from the newcomer how he had embraced Calvinistic concepts, traveling a path different from that followed by the continentals.

Since Polyander and Festus Hommius shared Robinson's Calvinist outlook, the two European professors prevailed upon their English guest, who was now a member of the university, to join in the public disputation. These three in their conversations took the orthodox position in opposition to Arminius and Episcopius. If it was in the free will of a man to accept or reject the gospel,

Jacob Arminius (1580-1609), Dutch theologian—leader of the Remonstrants

they reasoned, "What certainty could one ever get of the grace of God, our own will being unstable and changeable?"[6]

Robinson did not gain early prominence at the university because he was reluctant as a newcomer and a foreigner to share in this public forum. He attended the lectures of John Polyander, and also those of Episcopius, making it a point to listen to the arguments of this able man who was critical of prevailing Calvinism. In contrast with what was then customary, he took pains to become familiar with both sides of the conflict.

Bradford wrote:

> By which means he was so well grounded in the controversy, and saw the force of all their arguments, and knew the shifts of the adversary, and being himself very able, none was fitter to buckle with them than himself, as appeared by sundry disputes; so as he began to be terrible to the Arminians.[7]

Gomarus and Arminius had been ardent and outspoken, and went after each other hammer and tongs. Their respective successors at the university, Polyander and Episcopius, were more moderate, and able to exchange views without the bitter antagonism that marked the encounters of their predecessors.[8]

Robinson engaged in several dialogues with Episcopius and established his reputation as a theologian, lecturer, and debater. He was praised by Polyander and Hommius and other members of the faculty and clergy. So his rival Episcopius "put forth his best strength, and set forth sundry theses, which by public dispute he would defend against all men."[9]

The pro-Calvinists prevailed upon Robinson to accept this challenge. "He was loath, being a stranger." But Polyander did some urging as did the "chief preachers of the city," stating that "such was the abilities and nimbleness of the adversary, that the truth would suffer if he did not help them." So the Cambridge dean gained further acclaim from "gown and town" during these interchanges. An account of what was covered in these debates has not been preserved, but we know that the discussions attracted attention and brought recognition to the Green Gate colony and sharpened regard for their leader.[10] However radically Episcopius and Robinson differed in their theology, the debates were conducted with propriety and dignity.

Episcopius developed Arminius' thought in five key areas: (1) tolerance, (2) biblical interpretation, (3) the place of conscience in moral and religious matters, (4) the influence of humanism and rationalism, (5) universal grace. Robinson surely agreed in a large measure on the first three points. He, too, was strong for tolerance, and with his natural affinity for harmony he was influenced by the words of Arminius against the spirit of contention which was then so prominent in theological discussion: "Invective, mutual anathematizing and execration would not excite the minds of people to the love and study of truth, to charity, mercy, long suffering and concord."[11]

Robinson supported Episcopius in a plea for moderation and peace among Christians. He certainly admired the thought of Arminius who said he would inscribe these words over the porch of the assembly of Christians: "Let no one enter this hallowed dome without a desire for the truth and for peace."[12]

The Calvinists limited human conscience through their use of scripture as the ultimate appeal. Episcopius made a challenging statement when he said to them: "If they stood before a king who believed differently, although upon scriptural grounds, would not their individual conscience prove their ultimate defense?"[13] Robinson would agree here that conscience must work with reason to determine truth and right. He wrote: "It is the first duty of man to inform his conscience aright: and then to follow the direction that it gives."[14]

He protected himself by reservations against the deficiencies and limitations of Calvinism with his reliance upon reason and conscience.

> For hidden in the brave heart of English Puritanism was germinating a principle not to be found in the books of continental pedants, the right of individual interpretation, which shattered the Puritan church in the hour of her victory into a hundred sects, and destroyed the whole system of Protestant dogmatics.[15]

Robinson, however, was not able to share Episcopius' emphasis on humanism and rationalism. And he could not surrender the Calvinistic concept of God's grace. To repudiate the sovereign God who ruled the lives of men, to accept freedom of the will would make possible the domination of evil over good, the rule of tyrants and wrongdoers. The view of predestination under a righteous God would preserve the way of self-government, individual enlightenment, and the values for which Protestantism had long sacrificed.

The doctrine of freedom of the will was upheld later by enemies of Puritanism like Charles I and Archbishop Laud because they believed that to undermine predestination would cause the Calvinistic logic to collapse. So it came about that the battle of Arminius against Calvin invaded England and caused a terrific commotion as it had in Holland. As George Trevelyan wrote:

> The excitement produced seems now almost incredible. A generation that was theological as well as religious supposed that all their deepest beliefs and feelings depended on the dispute. The problem which in every age baffles or divides the acutest metaphysicians, supplied the catchwords of the two parties in church and state. Prentices hooted down the street after the Arminian rogues; courtiers damned the Predestinate crew. ... The victory of free will would establish a coercive and despotic government, a sacramental and priestly religion; while Predestination implied privilege of Parliament, liberty of person, Protestant ascendancy, and the agreeable doctrine of exclusive salvation.[16]

164

Arminius had leveled an attack on William Perkins as the great Calvinist defender. This aroused Robinson, Ames, and others of his Cambridge disciples, who rallied to defend his system of thought, which had developed into the foundation of English Puritanism. Similar views were rooted in Dutch life. One noteworthy outcome of the forty years' struggle with Spain was "the emergence of Calvinist orthodoxy as a main spring of power." Its concepts had brought and held the people together and inspired them in their war for freedom. It was not a heritage to be lightly replaced.[17]

The vagaries of Arminianism caused shock and eyebrow-lifting among the sterling citizens of both countries. This antipathy was widespread and was revealed years later when one divine prayed in the Harvard University chapel that the college might be "so tenacious of the truth that it shall be easier to find a wolf in England or a snake in Ireland than a Socinian or Arminian in Cambridge."[18]

But at this time in Holland the controversy between Arminius and Gomarus "spread from the University to the pulpit, and from the pulpit to the street and tavern, convulsing the United Provinces with a veritable fury of contending animosities."[19]

There is a seventeenth-century sketch in the Lakenhal Museum in Leyden which depicts dramatically a street riot that convulsed the city as angry mobs of Remonstrants (the Arminians) and Counter-Remonstrants (the Calvinists) confronted one another with sticks and stones as the constabulary tried in vain to check the violence. One can sense why peace-loving Robinson was shocked by these demonstrations that threatened the security of Leyden and the entire Netherlands and why he reacted against the Remonstrants for creating such spleen among the hitherto pacific Dutchmen. He was a practical man who could see the folly of such internecine strife.

One can picture the Green Gate people in their most dignified apparel filing into some hall of the university to listen respectfully to their learned pastor's profundities spoken in the Latin tongue. His pupil, Bradford, was interested in these academic exercises, and wrote admiringly:

> The Lord did so help him to defend the truth and foil his adversary as he put him to an apparent nonplus, in this great and public audience. And like he did a second or third time, upon such like occasions. The which as it caused many to praise God that the truth had so famous victory, so it procured him much honour and respect from those learned men and others which loved the truth.[20]

Bradford was intrigued by these intellectual exercises. During his free hours he must have haunted the lecture rooms of the university in his quest for knowledge, stimulated by the tutoring of Robinson and Brewster. He and Winslow were the only reporters on this affair in academia and they naturally favored their advocate. However, it does appear that Calvinism got the best of the argument and Robinson won the laurels. Bradford adds: "Were it not for giving offence to the state of England, they would have preferred him otherwise if he would, and [if he would have] allowed them [they would have shown him] some public favour."[21]

Apparently the university people were impressed by Robinson, and they considered offering him a post on their faculty. However, there was King James in England to consider. If he harangued over Vorstius' appointment, what kind of blackmail would be exerted upon the university if they should take on this Pilgrim exile? To recognize a rebel who had renounced the king's church would certainly be asking for trouble. They were forced to make clear their regard in other ways.

When Sir Dudley Carleton succeeded Winwood as English ambassador at The Hague in March 1616, he was issued specific instructions by King James, who pointed out "the violent and sharp contestations" over religion among the Dutch. "If," he wrote, "they should be unhappily revived during your time, you shall not forget that you are the minister of that master whom God hath made the sole protector of his religion."[22]

Dispatches from Carleton soon referred to the differences at Leyden "betwixt the orthodox and Arminian factions." It is clear that the magistrates of Leyden were familiar with this royal snooping from England and were forced to employ caution in extending favors to Robinson and his suspected flock.

The Leyden church was more democratic than the Ancient Brethren Church. It differed from the Amsterdam church regarding the duties and powers of the elders. The elders might deliberate in private, but they were required to take major decisions to the congregation, because their office "being public, requires answerable and public administration."[23] Also there was never more than one ruling elder elected at Leyden. And Brewster, in Leyden and in Plimoth, never tried to dominate his associates. Like the pastor, he was democratic in spirit and practice.

In his insistence upon consideration for the people, Robinson referred action to the congregation. They were the church. The elders and ministers were not to force their will upon them. This deference to public discussion and decision by the people developed the democratic tendency in the church which was carried over into the Plimoth government.

Bradford wrote in his *Dialogue* about the Leyden fellowship:

And for the church at Leyden, they [the members] were sometimes not much fewer in number, nor at all inferior in able men, though they had not so many officers as the other; for they had but one ruling elder with their pastor, a man well approved [Mr. Brewster] and of great integrity; also they had three able men for deacons. And that which was a crown to them, they lived together in love and peace all their days, without any considerable differences in any disturbance, that grew thereby, but such as was easily healed in love; and so they continued until, with mutual consent, they removed into New England.[24]

The Pilgrims succeeded, in spite of their menial jobs, in winning a good reputation in Leyden. The magistrates recognized them as law-abiding, wholesome citizens. The tradesmen found them to be dependable and honest.

And first, though many of them were poor, yet was none so poor but if they were known to be of that congregation the Dutch [either bakers or others] would trust them in any reasonable matter when they wanted money, because they had found by experience how careful they were to keep their word, and saw them so painful and diligent in their callings. Yea, they would strive to get their custom and to employ them above others in their work, for their honesty and diligence.[25]

The Scrooby fellowship was strengthened during the Leyden residence. A goodly number of exiles heard of Robinson and were drawn to Leyden because of him. Some of these additions were to prove sterling leaders in the new colony. Among them were John Carver, Samuel Fuller, Edward Winslow, Robert Cushman, Isaac Allerton, Francis Cooke, George Morton, Jonathan Brewster, Thomas Blossom, Richard Masterson, Phillipe De La Noye, Cuthbert Cuthbertson, Thomas Southworth, Thomas Rogers, John Goodman, Moses Fletcher, Degory Priest, William White, Thomas Tinker, John Tilley, John Turner, John Jenney, Stephen Tracy, William Bassett, Moses Symonson, William Pontus, and Isaac Robinson.

Master Robinson began to shape the outlook of these men who were to establish Plimoth Plantation—a small corps who developed appreciation of his ideals and were to set the pattern for the New England community.

Do not carry things as if the Word
of God either came from you or unto you
alone.
—John Robinson

13 "AS IF THE WORD OF GOD CAME UNTO YOU ALONE"

The controversy between the Arminians (who were called the Remonstrants) on the left and the Dutch Reformed (who were called the Counter-Remonstrants) on the right led to such bitterness among the Dutch that the States General summoned religious leaders to the Synod of Dort on November 13, 1618 to adjudicate the points at issue. The synod continued until May 11, 1619. It was composed of thirty-seven ministers, nineteen lay leaders, five university professors (including Gomarus), and eighteen commissioners of the States General. Theologians from a number of countries were invited by the conveners and twenty-six came from Germany, Switzerland, and England.

The English representatives were Bishop Carlton of Llandaff, later Bishop of Chichester; John Davenant, Bishop of Salisbury; Samuel Ward, professor at Cambridge; Joseph Hall, who was to become Bishop of Norwich; and Walter Balcanquall, Chaplain to King James.

Dort, or Dordrecht, was only a short distance from Leyden. Robinson may have made the journey to the site of the Synod, since he knew a number of the delegates. Two of his close friends attended: William Ames, who served as a paid theological adviser to the Counter-Remonstrants, and Festus Hommius, who was one of the secretaries. The delegates were all Reformed churchmen. After the opening of the synod, Simon Episcopius, leader of the Arminian party, and twelve other Remonstrants were invited to certain assemblies.

The Synod of Dort pronounced its decision in favor of Calvinism. The Remonstrants were expelled from the synod and their views declared to be contrary to scripture. They were accused of being disturbers of their country. Hence, it was assumed that this would mean the end of Arminianism, that they would be silenced, but Episcopius and his adherents stood firm. The States General were forced to urge compliance.

Episcopius made an eloquent defense of his position at Dort. He explained that he took the middle way in his quest for liberty, a course between tyranny and libertarianism. He stated that he had written his own confession of faith; and that it should be used only as a guide and never as a means to force another in the formulation of his faith. As he concluded, Bishop Hall of England murmured, "As I heard him, I bade Calvin goodbye."[1]

He and his colleagues were detained by order of the government at Dort. They were then asked if they would suspend their ministerial labors, cease writing and airing their opinions. They refused to acquiesce. On June 27, 1619 they were summoned to The Hague by the States General and called upon to subscribe to an agreement to abide by the terms which had been drawn up by the commissioners. All except one refused. So a sentence of banishment was then pronounced upon them.[2]

In regard to the Remonstrant preachers generally they were not only forbidden to perform the duties of their office, but their flocks were forbidden to assemble for the purpose of worship. . . . About two hundred Remonstrant ministers were deposed; among the rest, John Gerard Vossius, regent of the Theological College at Leyden, lost his place.[3]

The synod ordered all Remonstrants expelled from their stations in the churches and in the university. Episcopius was driven from the country and his university chair vacated. Peter Bertius, professor of ethics, was dismissed. William Ames was called to Leyden to take the place of Festus Hommius as overseer of the theological education of students for the ministry. Hommius succeeded Vossius as regent of the Theological College. These shake-ups provoked heated conversation at the Green Gate and throughout Leyden.

Seventeenth-century print showing street riot between the Remonstrants and Counter-Remonstrants

The decisive victory of Calvinism over the Arminians at Dort was followed by the trial of Jan van Olden Barneveldt, the head of the Statesright party, who was executed at The Hague, May 23, 1619, a victim of a political conflict. This action was a violent upheaval for the usually tolerant Dutch. Oldenbarneveldt was the Grand Pensionary in charge of all foreign affairs. He believed in strengthening the authority of the individual States, while Prince Maurice, the head of the army, advocated centralization and more power for the union of States. The political factions that developed clashed so violently that civil war was threatened. Prince Maurice, who held the military power, pressured his followers to eliminate Oldenbarneveldt, and so he was condemned and executed after the Synod of Dort. The deliberations there were not responsible for his tragic death.[4]

The aftermath of the Synod of Dort, which started out to be just another assembly of divines and academicians, forms a blot on the escutcheon of Dutch tolerance, as witnessed by the Pilgrims. Its implications in the field of divinity were sad enough, since they reflected an abandonment of the benevolent outlook of William the Silent, of Jan van Hout's hospitality to the straying band of Pilgrims, of the traditional sanctuary granted to Jews, Roman Catholics, and all brands of Protestant rebels. But it is doubly dark due to the underhanded manipulations of politics which afforded legitimacy to the persecution of Oldenbarneveldt, Grotius, and a host of the finest minds of the land. Some of the Pilgrims must have asked: Why were not the followers of the Dutch reformers, Arminius and Grotius, granted the protection that had been extended to them? Robinson was in favor of the Calvinist position on doctrine taken by the Synod of Dort, but he was shocked by the extreme treatment accorded Episcopius and other Remonstrant leaders.

There is no evidence that he allied himself with the bigots who indulged in these excesses. He had in previous years engaged in open forum discussions with Episcopius at the university as a defender of Calvinism. However, these debates were conducted in the spirit of good will. There is every indication that the pastor and the theologian were gentlemen who respected each other and were on friendly terms. Robinson was not a delegate at Dort, and although a most interested follower of its deliberations, he was not implicated in its decisions. We know how he despised intolerance, persecution, and violence, hence he could not have supported the banishment of the Arminian professors and ministers or the execution of the patriot and statesman, Oldenbarneveldt, who was the alleged plotter against the authority of his prince.[5] Robinson did not countenance the aftermath of Dort. The fact that he was an intellectual opponent of the Arminians did not make him a sympathizer with the "persecutors and final butchers of Barneveldt." These tragic events took place some seven years after his public discussions with Episcopius.

Hendrik Riemens wrote:

This *coup d'etat* was necessary in the interest of the country as a whole, but it led to national tragedy. Tried by a special political tribunal, he and the other prisoners were falsely accused and harshly sentenced. Oldenbarneveldt was condemned to death, Grotius and the others to life imprisonment.[6]

Thus the attempt by the Remonstrants to moderate Calvinistic fanaticism was stamped out.

Hugo Grotius, one of the great minds of Europe, was born in Delft, April 10, 1583. He entered Leyden University at age eleven where his father had served as curator. He lived with Francis Junius, a Leyden leader in the Reformation, who advocated tolerance and was highly respected by Robinson. He traveled widely in France, Germany, and England, studied law and became attorney general of the province of Holland, serving as a diplomat in France and Sweden. In 1612 he began his attempts to bring about the reunion of the Christian churches. He tried to persuade James I to take the lead and corresponded with Isaac Casaubon, theological adviser to the king.

The religious dispute between Arminius and Gomarus, the Remonstrant against the Reformed church, developed into a quarrel between church and state, between the provinces of Holland and Utrecht and the Orthodox Calvinist majority in the States General, supported by the head of the army, Prince Maurice. Grotius favored the views of Arminius and after his death Grotius wrote an elegy in honor of the scholar. So he was lined up in opposition to the prince who backed the Calvinists. Grotius had formerly been the spokesman of the States and drafted their peace resolutions and defended the policies of the States. He drew up a carefully prepared compromise solution that might have resolved the Arminian controversy, but it was rejected.

Because of his opposition to the views of Prince Maurice, Grotius was taken to the grim, old castle of Loevestein, which still stands today near Rotterdam. With the aid of his wife he managed to escape in a chest and make his way to Paris. There Louis XIII granted him a pension. He continued his writings, publishing *The Truth of the Christian Religion* in 1621 and his epochal work, *De Jure Belli et Pacis*, in 1625. In his testament of March 17, 1645 he prayed God "to unite the Christians in one church under a holy reformation."

At the forefront of the towering Town Hall of Rotterdam, Holland's leading industrial city and the world's largest port, there are two statues: one of Barneveldt and one of Hugo Grotius. Their place of honor today speaks the repentance of their country for the cruelty inflicted on these two distinguished thinkers, reminding us of one of the great blunders of history.

John Robinson himself held views that were similar in some respects to those of Grotius. He was impatient of division, strong for Christian unity, and an advocate of tolerance. He may have seen or heard Grotius and was certainly familiar with his writings and his influence upon the liberals of the Netherlands.

A Defense of the Doctrine propounded by the Synod of Dort was published by Robinson in 1624. He upheld its theological findings while reminding readers that Dort had not spoken the last and final word. He still held with William Ames and the majority of Puritan scholars to the basic principles of Calvinism. He concluded this work with the phrase, "Glory be to God, and good men!" He recognized the good men of his time and he believed that they were numerous. And he would certainly have included Grotius in this company, along with Episcopius and Arminius.

In his preface he sounded a conciliatory note: "As for men, how uncharitable they are. . . . How injurious in relating their own misinformed collections for their opinions! . . . As if the Word of God came out from them, or to them alone."[7]

His defense of certain Calvinistic doctrines reads today like an outmoded philosophy, but he was upholding a system of thought that appeared to him to be fundamental to the way of life enunciated by the Reformation. The cumbersome terminology with its literalistic interpretation of the Bible, forms heavy reading through which only the historian of dogma might care to plod.

Only the "most sound and unresistible convictions of conscience by the word of God" could satisfy him as he decided what course he should follow as a Christian: "It is unto me a matter of great scruple and conscience, to depart one hair-breadth, from their [the apostles'] practice and institution, in anything ecclesiastical, touching the government of the church."[8]

Like most seventeenth-century Protestants he followed the axiom of limitation to scripture. He referred matters for judgment to the Bible. Such a philosophy is narrow according to our era, but he has to be judged by the thinking of his time. This biblical technique afforded a cozy final court of appeal and made possible a schema that offered security to its adherents. In his Bible study he endeavored to apply reason and common sense to its interpretation. He said, "The words are to be understood according to the subject matter: the words of law and gospel according to the different nature of law and gospel; the words of history (to be weighed) historically; of a sacrament sacramentally and mystically."[9]

With this somewhat modern approach he did about as well with biblical exegesis as most theologians of his time. He and his contemporaries possessed no insight into higher criticism or what historical studies were to reveal to later generations. He was at his best when he permitted his affinity with reason to prevail. In defending his naiveté it might be pointed out that the school of neo-orthodoxy in our own day would accept much of Dort's Calvinism in such pronouncements as the depravity of man, the burden of Adam's sin, the impotence of man to overcome evil save through utter dependence on a transcendent, omnipotent sovereign God.

While advocating fellowship with men of good will, Robinson still clung to a limited view of atonement. He said that the death of Christ was sufficient for all if it had so pleased God to ordain it. He could not believe that this act was for the whole world, but rather for those God had chosen.[10]

He upheld the sovereignty of God as opposed to the complete freedom of the will. As to God he wrote: "God hath not only foreseen and determined the issues and events of His works, but hath also decreed and purposed the works themselves before the foundation of the world."[11]

In his theory of the atonement he accepted the view that man was in a state of sin due to the transgressions of Adam. Adam made this mistake through free choice, God having decreed the conditions under which that choice was made. His sin followed, but not

> as an effect upon a cause working it—God forbid!—but as a consequent upon an antecedent; or as an event necessarily following upon a most holy, wise, and powerful providence, so ordering and disposing, that the same should so come to pass infallibly, though performed by Adam's free, and freely-working will.[12]

The descendants of Adam were born with a disposition to sin for which they were responsible. To change this disposition, the gift of supernatural grace was necessary. Such an atonement from sin was possible through the grace of God in the work of Jesus. But this redemption was not universal. It was limited to the elect (a teaching which does not seem to jibe too well with his broad and brotherly concern for mankind).

Since it was recognized during his debates at the university that he was an important Counter-Remonstrant, he was encouraged to write the *Defense of the Doctrine propounded by the Synod of Dort* for the enlightenment of readers in Holland and England.

It puzzles one to find that Robinson, a liberal of his time, can still be counted in the fold of the Calvinists. How could he be a traditional follower of the iron-handed Genevan when his writings, his nature, and spirit were so much more humane? He certainly was no disciple of the man Calvin, the adamantine brain, the unsportsmanlike and jealous competitor, the regimentalist. But he did embrace the school of thought that emanated from Geneva through Zwingli, Beza, Pareus, Perkins, and other reformers. One should not tag him as a traditional Calvinist, since one knows how he resented being designated as a Brownist or categorized under any existing theological brand.

Winslow claimed that the Leyden-Plimoth church endeavored to follow the teaching of Christ and his apostles, that they did not uphold any one leader like Luther, Calvin, Knox, Ainsworth, Robinson, or Ames.[13]

As Perry Miller put it:

> Men engaged every day in freeing the pure and certain meaning of Christ's gospel from false contradictions would look upon themselves as Christians and not as Calvinists. They supposed themselves in the service of the same universal and eternal truth which Calvin had also served but which existed apart from him and could be studied without reference to anything he had ever written or said.[14]

174

One asks why Robinson and other Puritan scholars developed such an affinity for the ideas promulgated by the dark-robed jurist of Geneva. For one thing, the Calvinists defended the English refugees during the reign of Bloody Mary when some 800 reformers fled to the continent. They were not too warmly welcomed by the Lutherans there. In some cases they were cold-shouldered. In contrast, John Calvin and his associates received them in Switzerland. Today the old Church of St. Gervais there is proud of its stained-glass window which depicts the religious refugees of this period who were granted haven in Geneva.

It has been estimated that at least one quarter of the English Puritans visited Geneva or made it their home. Here they turned out voluminous theological literature, a psalm book, and translated the Geneva Bible which inspired the Pilgrims for decades.

Some of the austerities of Calvin were softened by Ulrich Zwingli, who was calmer and broader in his views and more popular with the Puritans. He was more

a man of affairs. He could ascribe merit to those with whom he disagreed, and could embrace even the pagan world in his scheme of the universe. Zwingli saw the operation of God in all the world and hoped for the outreach of grace beyond the bounds of the church. This freer spirit Zwingli handed down to the Reformed theology.[15]

Zwingli led the Reformation in Zurich. He admired non-Christian saints and hoped that they might share in some manner in salvation:

Hercules, Theseus, Socrates, Aristides, Antigonus, Numa, Camillus, Cato and Scipio. . . . In a word, no good man has ever existed, nor shall there exist a holy mind, a faithful soul, from the very foundation of the world to its consummation, whom you will not see there with God.[16]

Theodore Beza was even more influential with the Puritans. Trained as a lawyer in Paris, he "renewed a vow to serve God openly in his true church" after a severe illness. He journeyed to Geneva to join Calvin, and as rector of the Geneva Academy he became a leading educator. His classical studies and his Greek editions and Latin translations of the New Testament stimulated reform scholarship and the creation of the Geneva and King James Bibles. He trained many ministers of the French and Dutch churches. His *De jure magistratum* (1574) defended the right of revolt against tyranny and played a major role in political reforms. It is due to such scholars as Beza that "the Reformed minister was essentially a preacher, intellectual, exegetical, argumentative, seriously concerned with the subjects that most appealed to the serious minded." And it was these ministers who trained an intelligent laity.[17]

The St. Bartholomew's Day Massacre of 1572 and the Protestant-Roman Catholic wars in France drove many more refugees to Geneva. Beza labored tirelessly to aid them. John Knox of Scotland was serving as one of the preachers in Geneva when he

175

wrote his *The First Blast against the Monstrous Regiment and Empire of Women*. By aiding Knox the Genevans forged another tie of friendship with the English-speaking reformers.

Theodore Beza took an active part in interceding with Church of England dignitaries in an effort to protect the persecuted Puritans. He wrote to Bishop Grindal on June 27, 1566 that the unfair practices followed by the church were provoking schism and causing an irremediable injury to the clergy. When the distinguished Puritan Thomas Cartwright was deprived of his chair as Lady Margaret Professor of Divinity at Cambridge and of his fellowship in Trinity College and forbidden to teach or preach, he slipped across the channel for safety. He, too, was welcomed by Beza at Geneva. Here he was encouraged by conferences with other reformers and in time returned to England to support the *Admonition to Parliament for the Reformation of Church Discipline*.

A second appeal of Calvinism was found in its concise system of thought. Its tenets were well outlined. The legal mind of Calvin provided a convincing theology that could out-argue his competitors. "The essence of the Reformation," says G. F. Elton, "and that which gave it its overwhelming appeal, was not its attack on the abuses but its positive, and of necessity revolutionary, reinterpretation of the Christian religion."[18]

John Robinson, like the best Puritan scholars, was probing in the morass of accumulated dogma and tradition of his national church to rediscover the basic truths. He found help in Calvin, Zwingli, and Beza, who emphasized the quest of the enlightened mind, the study of the Hebrew and Greek biblical sources, and the early church fathers for original concepts upon which the confusions of Christendom had been erected.

Robinson and his co-Puritans, however, looked not so much to Calvin as they did to Israel. The "fascination exercised by the Jewish scriptures," wrote James Moffatt, "on men who sought a model for the moral and civil government of a nation is not difficult to understand and goes far to explain their predilection for the Old Testament."[19]

English Puritans took more to Calvinism than Lutheranism, along with the reformers in France and Holland. Somehow it struck a chord of congeniality in their temperament and background. Although they did not accept it as a system, it offered concepts upon which they could begin to build in their effort to reshape their Christian faith and practice. The idea of self-discipline was especially appealing to them.

Calvin was in many ways a bigot, but he did believe in education. He urged his followers to demand both an educated ministry and laity. He founded a university to train men for religious leadership, and he insisted that children be provided with free, compulsory education. This high regard for learning was warmly supported by the Cambridge Puritans.

It is clear that Robinson was an example of the kindled mind searching for new horizons. He was better able than most

Figure representing John Robinson—from "The Embarkation," attributed to Robert Wier (no portrait exists of Robinson)

Calvinists to keep himself free from the trammels of authoritarianism. He rejected the dogmatic rigidity of Calvin of whom Stefan Zweig wrote: "He never altered an important word in what he had written, he never retraced a footstep, and never made a move in the direction of compromise with an adversary." The dictator of Geneva who boasted, "God has been gracious enough to reveal unto me good and evil," maintained "a petrified imperturbability, an icy and inhuman rigidity."[20]

Calvin died in 1564, twelve years before Robinson was born. His extremes were somewhat mitigated by his successors, but one cannot conceive of the genial Robinson feeling at home in the presence of the gloomy man in sable raiment and black biretta who suffered from migraines, stomach aches, inflamed piles, colic, gallstones, carbuncles, rheumatism, and bladder trouble. It is no wonder that he was far from a hale fellow, well met. At one time he presented a worm's eye view of life: "All our justice is injustice; our service, filth; our glory, shame. Even the best things that rise out of us are always made infect and vicious by the uncleanness of the flesh, and are always mingled with dirt."[21]

This negation and asceticism were alien to Robinson; so was the desire of Calvin to legislate goodness and enforce his superior judgment on frail humanity. He established censorship of clothes, coiffures, jewelry, diet to restrict luxury, and books for sale in the shops. Girls were forbidden to wear silk before they reached the age of fifteen. Tailors were ordered to create no new fashions. No book could be printed without a special permit. Church attendance was enforced under pain of punishment.

Robinson steered clear of such legalism. He believed in enjoying the normal pleasures of living, hence he never advocated legislation restraining food, apparel, or pleasure. Moreover, he was set against arrogance of mind and persecution of those who held alien convictions. Surely he revolted against Calvin's dastardly treatment of the eminent scholar, Miquel Servetus, whom he sentenced to death because he contradicted the Genevan's beliefs. The Calvinism Robinson knew was removed from its harsh beginnings and was represented by his professors at Cambridge. It had traveled a long way since its origin in Geneva. For Robinson it stood for a satisfying doctrinal system, the value of education, self-discipline, independent thinking, individual initiative, and enlightened government.

Out of the teachings of the Calvinist school certain new political ideas evolved. A. G. Dickens states:

> Calvinism was not merely a discipline but a self-discipline. It could build communities capable of self-government, the basis of which lies in disciplined minds, not in political mechanisms. . . . From the stifling parade grounds of presbytery and synod, Beggar and Huguenot, Puritan and Covenanter marched out to battlefields where at least some of the great issues of human freedom lay at stake.[22]

The concepts of the Calvinist way inspired the Huguenots and the Dutch to resist tyranny. The urge to independency invaded the Pilgrim country in East Anglia, the area where parliamentary reform was born and the home base which supplied the bulk of the migration to America.[23]

In dealing with theology, Robinson fortunately held his emphasis on reason and common sense. He once said that reason lifts man before all earthly creatures and makes him second to God:

> For whereas God and nature hath furnished other creatures, some with horns, some with hoofs, others with other instruments, and weapons both defensive and offensive, man is left naked, and destitute of all those, but may comfort himself in that one endowment of reason, and providence, whereby he is enabled to govern them all.[24]

Conjuring with the ultimate mysteries, he fell back upon the unfathomable workings of the infinite mind which lay beyond the realm of the explicable and the bounds of human cognition. His thinking was rooted in the assurance that nothing but the grace of God was man's salvation. He could not accept any doctrine that imperiled this foundation of Christian hope.

Robinson was an intellectual Puritan tutored in the Calvinistic doctrine, but his nature was never hidebound nor straitlaced. He had a warm and magnetic personality. In all his associations he seemed to bear himself with a Christian humility that spoke louder than doctrine. He gave to his group something over and beyond formal piety and Christian dogma. This stamp was evident in Plimoth for many years. One feels more than once in studying his career that he wished to go to New England to be free from some of the Old World patterns and restraints of Calvinism.

Imprisonment, yea death itself, are
no meet weapons to convince the conscience
grounded upon the word of God.
—John Penry, 1593

14 "IMPRISONMENT, YEA DEATH ITSELF, ARE NO MEET WEAPONS"

In the year 1614, when Robinson published *Of Religious Communion*, he was hopeful that a new era of tolerance was dawning. He held long talks with William Brewster about the possibilities that they might be able to go back to their homeland. By that time many petitions for redress of grievances and cessation of persecution had poured into the court. James I was frightened by the attitude toward his policies as voiced by the new House of Commons. He was not adept at dealing with opposition nor gifted in reading the minds of the people. As soon as he found a pretext he dissolved Parliament after it had sat for only two months. Then for seven years he ruled as an absolute monarch, without once summoning Parliament.

The high expectations of the Leyden Pilgrims regarding a return home were dashed to the ground. It was obvious now that they must continue in Holland. A number of new exiles came over to join them, to fill the gaps in their ranks caused by deaths and removals. One of them was Thomas Brewer who arrived in 1615 to assume an active role in Leyden affairs. He belonged to a well-to-do land-owning family in Kent. He matriculated at the university on February 17, 1615 at age thirty-five. Also in the same roll of university members there is entered on January 14, 1617 the names of two additional Englishmen who lived with Thomas Brewer:

> Hugh Goodyear, Englishman, of the county of Lancaster, Master of Arts, aged 27 years, student of theology. Dwelling at Thomas Brewer's.
> Joannes Bastwyck, English gentleman, aged 22 years, student of philosophy and politics, dwelling at the same.[1]

And on September 9, 1617 we read of:

> Alexander Lichton, Englishman from London, aged 40 years, candidate of medicine, dwells at D. Brouwer's (Brewer's) Englishman.[2]

So in the year 1617 Brewer opened his home to at least three nonconformist students from England. These four and other members of Brewer's household talked often with Robinson and mingled with the Green Gate Pilgrims.

Brewer purchased a house on June 17, 1617 from Seigneur Johan de Lalaing in the Kloksteg known as the Groenehuis and located next door to the Groenepoort, the property Robinson had bought from the same De Lalaing. He was described in the census of 1622 as "an English nobleman." He possessed some capital and much courage. As a reformer he liked the writings of Robinson and sensed the potential of the printed page as a tool for the reshaping of England. As Robinson and Brewster talked about printing some of their own books in Leyden, he volunteered to provide financial backing.

Brewer wrote years later that he "walked in communion with Master Robinson," so he must have worshiped with the Pilgrims whom he admired and supported with his money.

As a pamphleteer, Robinson was convinced of the power of the printed word. Although separated from England he realized that he could still work for her freedom through his pen. In an era of printing licenses and book censorship such as prevailed in the homeland, Holland offered a golden opportunity to carry on the Puritan crusade. Before the Reformation press censorship had belonged to the English church; afterward it became a prerogative of the crown. The Stationers Company was granted a monopoly of printing. Presses were permitted only in London, Edinburgh, Dublin, and at the universities. The injunctions of 1559 decreed that all publications were to be licensed either by the queen or by six of the Privy Council, the archbishops, the Bishop of London, the chancellors of the universities, or the bishop or archdeacon of the place where they were printed.

In 1576 the Stationers Company was ordered to conduct a weekly search to prevent the printing of unlicensed books. However, in spite of this system, a number of illegal books were issued and condemned by the queen as "seditious libels." The Star Chamber in 1584 issued an order against unlicensed printing; and in 1586 a decree under Whitgift made such publishers liable to severe penalties. Barrowe, Greenwood, Penry, and Udall were condemned under this ruling.[3]

The bishops and the Star Chamber took over the offensive religious books, which were the most numerous. These restrictions struck a blow at the Separatists who were robbed of the right to defend themselves. Some lodged a complaint with Queen Elizabeth in 1593: "The followers of Reformation lack liberty to answer in their own cause. If they speak they be silenced; if they write, they want printers. They be shut up in close prisons; their hands as it were bound, and then buffeted."

In 1607 Sir T. Wilson wrote to Sir Thomas Lake and asked for the privilege of printing certain books. He begged that the bill should "have reference to none but the King's Counsel, for if I have to do with Bishops or others, I shall never have an end." He offered in return for this favor a gratuity of "40 or 50 angels to buy my lady a velvet gown, and a most devoted and thankful heart."[4]

John Robinson was impressed by the freedom of publication in the Netherlands. There were few restrictions except that private character and public morals were not to be attacked. Printers took on numerous foreign books much to the anger of autocrats overseas. The earliest Separatist writings were printed in Holland.

Robert Browne's chief works were published in Middelburg. Barrowe and Greenwood sent their manuscripts to Dort. Giles Thorpe, a deacon in Ainsworth's church in Amsterdam, set up a press, where he printed a number of important works by Ainsworth, Clyfton, and probably Robinson's *Justification of Separation*.

Leyden was well known for its publishing houses. The Elzevir Press published the writings of the university. It was natural for the Pilgrim company to wish to publish some of the writings of their leader and his associates—Ames, Parker, Jacob—and other scholars who were battling to defend their liberal views against the established order. Elder William Brewster founded the Pilgrim Press for this purpose. He possessed an excellent library and often discussed with the pastor the need to find publishers for books that might be sent back to England to carry on the cause there.

Bradford wrote: "He [Brewster] also had means to set up printing [by the help of some friends], and so had employment enough, and by reason of many books which would not be allowed to be printed in England, they might have had more than they could do."[5]

Thomas Brewer backed Brewster financially. They engaged John Reynolds of London as printer who was assisted by Edward Winslow, also of London. The press was concealed in the home of Brewster on the Pieterskerkkoorsteeg.[6] Hailing from Worcestershire, Winslow had studied in the King's School, and fortunately possessed a flair for the literary. Due to his training at the printer's bench he was equipped to write three books on the New England colony and proved an indispensable recorder, along with his gifted peer, William Bradford. In the record of his marriage at Leyden in 1618 he is described as a printer.

Their first publication was a Dutch book, a translation of Dod and Cleaver's *Tenne Commandements*. Among the titles released in 1616 were Thomas Cartwright's *Commentarii in Proverbia Salomonis* with a preface by John Polyander; and Dr. William Ames' *Rescriptio Contracta*. Both of these authors were close friends of Robinson. The books bore the name of Brewster and the location where they had been printed. This was a dangerous practice because the type used could lead to the identification of other controversial and proscribed books. The Latin imprint gave their place of business as "in Vico Chorali," i.e., in the Koorsteeg or Choir Alley.

Some fifteen to eighteen titles have been attributed to the Pilgrim Press, and it is known that many copies were smuggled into England.

Robinson no doubt served as an adviser of the Pilgrim Press and must have conferred with Brewster and Brewer about their list. Under his direction they published his volume, *The People's Plea for the Exercise of Prophecy*, and works by William Perkins. The perils of the enterprise were recognized, but they determined to take the gamble for their cause. In general, the books they issued upheld their own views, such as the writings of Thomas Cartwright, Robert Harrison, and Laurence Chaderton.

The list that emanated from the Pilgrim Press was fairly substantial, considering the brief period that the clandestine operation was permitted to continue and the small number of hands who were employed. About a dozen other books, in addition to those of Cartwright and Ames, were printed in 1617, 1618, and 1619, all strongly Puritan if not Separatist in outlook.[7]

In 1619 the bold partners brought down a hailstorm upon the Vico Chorali by publishing two books by David Calderwood: *De regimine Ecclesiae Scoticanae Brevis Relatio* and *Perth Assembly*. For some time James I had been trying to force episcopacy down the throats of his subjects in Scotland which they resisted obstinately.

Although the general assembly held at Perth in 1618 had nominally accepted the "Five Articles" that James thrust upon them, articles which endeavored to enforce ceremonies that were distasteful to the Presbyterian mind, the people were unwilling to acquiesce and bow before the rule of the bishops. David Calderwood wrote his version of the Perth assembly "with much scorn and reproach" of his majesty and the bishops, but when he looked around for a printer he discovered that there was no one who dared to publish his views.

He got in touch with Brewster and company in Leyden and they undertook the job. We can imagine the excited discussions between Brewster, Robinson, and Brewer as they read over the provocative words of the irate Scot and discussed how they were to handle this dynamite. They agreed to undertake the venture, and copies of the bombshell were packed into wine vats and shipped over to Scotland. The vats managed to get by the Archbishop of St. Andrews when they were landed at Laith, and once they were opened, the intoxicating aperitif was passed from one Scottish hearthside to another. The king and the bishops were enraged since they suspected that Calderwood was the author. He was hunted from house to house and town to town until the women of Edinburgh raised funds to send him over to Holland.[8]

Calderwood hid for a time in Leyden with the Pilgrims. He attended services at the Green Gate, heard Robinson preach, and conversed with him about the church in Scotland and the restraints which James I was endeavoring to place upon his subjects in the North. He may have stayed secretly with some of the congregation. Winslow records that he was present when they celebrated communion, and that he was invited to share with them in this sacrament. So the Pilgrims proved accessories to another crime against their petulant monarch.

The Edinburgh printer James Cathkin was charged with the responsibility for releasing Calderwood's evil book. He was examined, bullied by the king, but liberated after three weeks in London. He did confess that Calderwood had occasionally slept in his house and that he had talked with him some fifteen days before.

The spies then turned their attention to the Netherlands. Sir

(pages 184-85)
A sixteenth-century printing office similar to the Pilgrim Press, Leyden

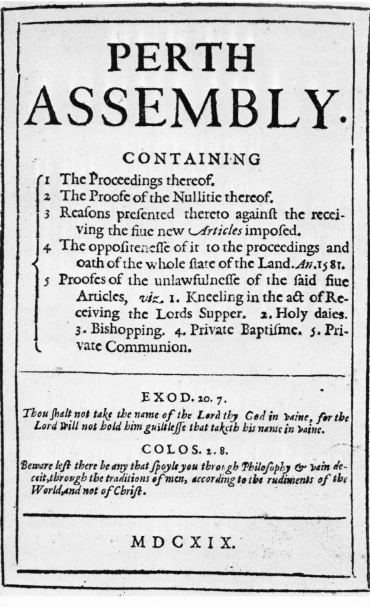

PERTH ASSEMBLY.

CONTAINING

1 The Proceedings thereof.
2 The Proofe of the Nullitie thereof.
3 Reasons presented thereto against the receiving the fiue new *Articles* imposed.
4 The oppositenesse of it to the proceedings and oath of the whole state of the Land. *An.* 1581.
5 Proofes of the unlawfulnesse of the said fiue Articles, *viz.* 1. Kneeling in the act of Receiving the Lords Supper. 2. Holy daies. 3. Bishopping. 4. Private Baptisme. 5. Private Communion.

EXOD. 20. 7.

Thou shalt not take the name of the Lord thy God in vaine, for the Lord will not hold him guiltlesse that taketh his name in vaine.

COLOS. 2. 8.

Beware lest there be any that spoyle you through Philosophy & vain deceit, through the traditions of men, according to the rudiments of the World, and not of Christ.

MDCXIX.

Dudley Carleton, the successor of Sir Ralph Winwood as English ambassador to The Hague, discovered so many copies of the *Perth Assembly* in Leyden that he became suspicious that they were the product of some press there. When he heard of William Brewster, he felt quite certain and on July 17, 1619 he wrote to Sir Robert Naunton, secretary of state, in London:

I have seen at the Hague within these two days, a certain Scottish book, called *Perth Assembly*, written with much scorn and

Title page of Perth Assembly *by David Calderwood printed by the Pilgrim Press in Leyden (1619). This publication aroused James I and led to the closing of the press*

reproach of the proceedings in that Kingdom concerning the Affairs of the Church. It is without name, either of Author or Printer: but I am informed it is printed by a certain English Brownist of Leyden; as are most of the Puritan books sent over, of late days, into England.

Which being directly against an express *Placaat* [edict] of the States General, which was published in December last (1618): I intend when I have more particular knowledge of the Printer, to make complaint thereof; concerning that His Majesty will not dislike I should so do.[9]

Five days later he also reported: "A William Brewster, a Brownist, hath been for some years an inhabitant and printer at Leyden, but is now within three weeks removed from thence, and gone back to dwell in London, where he may be found out and examined." He wrote again on August 20: "I have made good inquiry after William Brewster, at Leyden; and am well assured that he is not returned thither; neither is it likely he will, having removed from thence both his family and goods."

On August 28, 1619 Carleton wrote Naunton that Brewster had been seen in Leyden the day before. He evidently followed through on the suggestion of James I and asked the help of the States in the prosecution of Brewster. Mr. Jacob van Broeckhoven, deputy counsel to the States of Holland, inquired into the matter.

The reply of the Leyden magistrate offers another record of their diplomacy in defense of freedom:

To the Honorable, very learned, wise, prudent, very discreet Sir Master Jacob van Broeckhoven, Deputy Councillor of the High Mightinesses Lords States of Holland at the Hague.

Honorable very learned wise prudent, very discreet Sir and Brother,

We have today summoned into our presence Thomas Brewer, an Englishman; whom being heard, we learn that his business heretofore has been printing, or having printing done: but in consequence of the publication of the *Placaat* regarding the Printers of Books he had stopped it; that the Printing Office was at that time, mostly his business, and that his partner was a certain William Brewster, who was also in town at present, but ill. We have therefore resolved after having consulted on the matter with the Rector Magnificus [Reinerus Bontius], to put in custody the said Thomas Brewer, who is a member of the university, in the place where it is the custom to bring the members thereof: and in regard to William Brewster it has been resolved to bring him, provisionally inasmuch as he is sick, into the Debtors' Chamber, where he went voluntarily. Of which things we have thought proper to inform you, and to await further orders as to what shall be done in the matter.[10]

Naunton reported that Brewster had been "frighted back into the Low Countries by the Bishops pursivants." He wrote on behalf of King James urging that every effort be made to bring the Leyden printers to justice.

On September 12 Sir Dudley Carleton was forced to back water as the elusive Brewster was shielded by Dutch friends. He wrote: "In my last I advertised your honor that Brewster was taken at Leyden; which proved an error, in that the scout who was employed by the magistrates for his apprehension, being a dull drunken fellow, took one man for another."[11]

A determined search was initiated on the continent and in England to capture Brewster. The king commanded Sir Dudley "to deal roundly" with the Dutch authorities "for the apprehension of him, the said Brewster, as they tender His Majesty's friendship." Sir Dudley reported that steps were being taken to search Brewster's and Brewer's property, "to have their books and printing letters seized; as likewise to have them examined of all books, as well Latin as English, they have printed for the space of eighteen months or two years past."

The States felt obligated to protect Brewster and Brewer, but they also wanted to avoid unnecessary antipathy from the British monarch. So there was considerable delay in securing permission from the town and university authorities to make a search of William Brewster's home. A permit was finally granted and authorities appointed to examine his library for unauthorized works.

Brewster had not been captured by the king's spies. He had gone to the debtors' chamber on his own free will and then disappeared according to a secret plan. He was heard of in London, in Leyden, and in London again, much to the frustrations of the king's spies. They searched for him in both places, in Leiderdorp, and in Amsterdam. To what hiding place Brewster escaped and where he remained in hiding until the *Mayflower* sailed in the summer of 1620 is a secret that has been kept to this day. He was no doubt in London part of the time helping arrange for the voyage to America and was tracked there by the Bishop of London, but not found. He may have hidden with old friends in the quiet of Scrooby.

In due time, after the Dutch had done all in their power to delay proceedings and protect Brewster, his house and library were searched and in the attic they found printing materials and certain of the contraband books. John Polyander, the close friend of Robinson at the university, was delegated to search Brewster's home and to take over the banned books and printer's type. Professor Polyander had written a preface recommending one of Brewster's books. He was no doubt acquainted with the elder's excellent library and had browsed there and borrowed from him. Polyander was, of course, in sympathy with the ideas of the Pilgrim company; so it may be that the university officials appointed him to carry out this forced search as a humane representative who would do all in his power to shelter the reformers.

Brewer stepped forward to shoulder responsibility and so try to protect the elder. As a member of the university he could claim some extraterritorial rights that might not have been extended legally to Brewster. Although the elder was a teacher of English among the students, we do not know that he had been made an official member.

The Green Gate people did all they could to help Brewer. They tried to obtain his release on bail, as Sir Dudley complained, writing that the "whole company of Brownists doth offer caution for Brewer, and he being a university man, the scholars are likewise stirred up by the Brownists to plead Privilege in that kind."

When James "requested" that Brewer be shipped over to him in London for questioning he added that he would not punish him "further than with a free Confession of his own misdemeanours and those of his complices," and promised to hand him back unharmed to the Dutch authorities. He also commanded Sir Dudley,

> And for the time to come you are required to move the States [General] to take some strict order through all their Provinces for the preventing of the like abuses and licentiousness in publishing, printing and vending underhand such scandalous and libellous pamphlets.[12]

Brewer was examined and detained in the place assigned to university members. When James I learned that Brewster had escaped him he ordered that Brewer be hastened to England that he might try him and gain some admissions from him. The university insisted on safeguards and obtained from Brewer a statement that he would go of his own free will; and in return Brewer received from Carleton firm promises guaranteeing him good treatment.

Polyander then entered into the negotiations on behalf of Brewer and finally persuaded him to go voluntarily to England after the ambassador had extracted a pledge from King James that he would be treated with all fairness. Thus Brewer set out, not as a prisoner, but escorted by the officers of the university, and then from Rotterdam Sir William Zouche, a member of the Privy Council, became his escort.

In his appearances before the king Brewer was stubborn and cagey and "did all that a silly creature could to increase his dissatisfaction," so Sir Robert Naunton reported as secretary of state. He added in a dispatch to Sir Dudley Carleton:

> But I have beaten him from his asse and have drawn something from him that hath in part contented His Majesty, who bade me tell you that he gives no credit to this fool's confident concern and improbable assertions and that he will be very good friends with you if you can procure Brewster to be taken.[13]

Brewer was questioned fruitlessly for two months until the king grew weary of him. The canny Scot refused to keep his bargain that the crown would pay all of Brewer's expenses. In a parsimonious mood he insisted that he could take care only of expenses in England, and refused to pay his passage back to Holland, so Brewer remained in England for a time, returning to Leyden about three years later.

Shortly after Robinson's death he left Leyden and returned to England where his Separatist beliefs led to further trouble. He

A seventeenth-century printing press

190

was imprisoned in 1626 for denouncing the prelates and confined for over fourteen years. He was released from the King's Bench Prison only after paying a fine of 1,000 pounds, which is approximately $50,000. He lived only a few months to enjoy his freedom.

A Detection of certain dangerous Puritans and Brownists in Kent mentions this intrepid crusader who had not yet learned to keep silent in the face of persecution:

> Thomas Brewer, Gentleman, who writ a book containing about half a quire of paper; wherein he prophesies the destruction of England within three years, by two Kings: one from the North, another from the South.
>
> The said Brewer coming, not long since, from Amsterdam, where he became a perfect Brownist; and being a man of good estate, is the general patron of the Kentish Brownists; who, by his means, daily and dangerously increase.
>
> He, the said Brewer, hath printed a most pestilent book beyond the seas: wherein he affirmith, That King James would be the ruin of Religion. To the like purpose, he published a book or two more: which David Pareus, at Neustadt, shewed to a Knight, who told me of it.[14]

Thomas Brewer is reported to have written many excellent manuscripts. He was an editor who believed to the end in the power of the written word. A posthumous work was published in London in 1656 called *Gospel Public Worship*. In this book he stated that he had published similar works "at Leyden in Holland, where he walked in communion with Master Robinson and also with Master Ainsworth."[15]

This little-known backer of the Pilgrims who spent his fortune and many years in solitude for the cause of freedom, should be pleased to know that the Pilgrim Press continues today in America as an interpreter of liberal religion. The writer of this volume is honored to see it published under this same imprint.

The story of the Pilgrim Press forms one of the most dramatic episodes of the sojourn in Holland. Hidden for some two or three years in a cross lane of the Pieterskerkkoorsteeg, the editors and printers kept up their fight for freedom. They continued this assault upon the bastion of autocracy until the gendarmes of their monarch drove them away, seized their type, and sealed the doors with the royal interdict. The brief cloak-and-dagger contest between the tiny press and the mighty throne gave proof of the courage of the Pilgrims and the loyalty of their Dutch friends.

The press formed an important weapon of protest for the persecuted reformers since they were not permitted to speak out face to face with their enemies in London or Canterbury. They believed in the truths they had discovered and as a small band of exiles they directed their printed words against the hierarchy of the chancel and the court.[16]

If Brewster had been captured he would no doubt have been hanged as many of his Cambridge friends had been. A short time

191

later Alexander Leighton, a minister in Scotland, published in the Netherlands a "libellous" attack upon the Church of England, not as radical as *Perth Assembly*. He was brought before the Star Chamber and sentenced to pay a fine of 100,000 pounds, to be whipped and pilloried in the presence of the court, to have one ear sliced off and his nose split, to have the letters "SS" (stirrer of sedition) branded on his forehead, to be whipped and pilloried again "at some conveniente later time," to have his other ear cut off, and to be imprisoned for life in the Fleet.

Fortunately for the Pilgrim experiment the esteemed Elder Brewster did not meet such a fate. His resourceful exile associates and Dutch friends spirited him away and kept him in safe obscurity until almost a year and a half later when he stole aboard the *Mayflower* to assume his role of leadership on that weighty voyage.

Daniel Plooij of Holland believed that he had solved the mystery of Brewster's disappearance from Holland into England, where he thought Brewster went into hiding, doing what he could undercover to aid the departure to New England. Dr. Plooij pointed out that his name disappeared from the negotiations about the migration. It might have upset the plans of the Pilgrims if it were discovered that one of their prominent leaders was the printer of the pamphlets and books that enraged the king. He stated that Brewster's name did not appear any more until he emerged in Plimoth as the teaching elder.

Rendell Harris suggested that the Master Williamson aboard the *Mayflower* was Brewster traveling incognito. It was the Dutch custom to call people by their patronymics. Jonathan Brewster was called Jonathan Willemsz in the Dutch records, that is, Jonathan, son of William (Brewster). And as Elder Brewster's father was also a William, this made a convenient disguise to book Brewster on the *Mayflower* as Master Williamson.[17]

Historians have been perplexed by a passage in Mourt's *Relation* concerning a certain phantom Williamson. Under the date of March 22, 1621 it reads: "Captain Standish and Master Williamson met the King [i.e., Massasoyt] at the brook, with a half dozen musketeers." Williamson is mentioned again. When William Mullins the shoemaker was dying in February 1620 he made a will in which he appointed as his overseers Governor Carver and Master Williamson.

Plooij and Harris contended that Master Williamson was Master Brewster and he had brought this name Williamson from Holland. The name was employed to avoid arrest and to secure permission to leave the country in peace without intervention on the part of the British government. James I had reluctantly consented to the voyage of the Pilgrims, but he and his advisers did not intend to grant a passport to Brewster or Robinson, the chief agitators. They were searching for Brewster to arrest him, and they were afraid of the religious and political influence of Robinson.[18] However this may be, Brewster did remain undiscovered due to the protective friendship of the Dutch and the ingenious planning of his Pilgrim comrades.

During the period that Robinson and his parish were planning their move to the New World the Walloon community in Leyden was also seeking to migrate to New Amsterdam. Jesse de Forest, a Leyden dyer, a French religious refugee, applied on July 22, 1621 to the English ambassador, Sir Dudley Carleton, at The Hague, in the name of fifty-six Walloon families who wished to go to Virginia, and asked for the assistance of the king of England. They were granted permission but denied financial help. Jesse de Forest persisted and sent a petition to the States General of Holland, and at length in 1624 a ship, the *New Netherlands*, was acquired, and some thirty Walloon families sailed for the Hudson. They reached their destination and hoisted the Dutch flag on the island of Manhattan.[19]

Robinson and his associates had discussed with Dutch officialdom the possibilities of settling on the Hudson River. The Hague knew that the *Speedwell* sailed from Delfshaven in July 1620, and that the *Mayflower* made Plimoth that December. They had no doubt received some reports on how the Plimoth colony established itself and made good. The successful beginning of this settlement, together with records of other crossings to the New World by Pilgrims from Leyden in 1621 to 1623, could have stimulated De Forest and the Walloons to press forward with their preparations. At least it is noteworthy that the first permanent communities in New England and New York were engineered by Leyden religious refugees.

All great and honourable actions are accompanied with great difficulties, and must be both enterprised and overcome with answerable courage. It was granted the dangers were great, but not desperate; the difficulties were many, but not invincible; . . . and all of them, through the help of God, by fortitude and patience, might either be borne or overcome.
—William Bradford

15 "ALL GREAT AND HONOURABLE ACTIONS ARE ACCOMPANIED WITH GREAT DIFFICULTIES"

The Pilgrim group anxiously watched the deterioration of freedom in England. Through correspondents in the motherland and reports from newcomers to Leyden they endeavored to keep in touch with developments there.

In 1616 James I had surrendered three "cautionary towns" in Holland which had been in the hands of England since the reign of Elizabeth. They had been held as pledges for debts contracted by the United Netherlands to the English crown. In hope of improving his shaky finances James hoped to secure a large dowry through the marriage of his oldest surviving son, Prince Charles, with the Spanish Infanta. He had fallen under the spell of Gondomar, the Spanish ambassador, who represented the strongest power in Europe.

To please the Spanish, Sir Walter Raleigh had been released from the Tower in 1617 and permitted to cross the Atlantic in search of a mythical gold mine in Guiana. If he had succeeded in his mission, he might have been liberated from the sentence of treason imposed upon him fourteen years earlier. But he failed and was executed in 1618.[1]

The Thirty Years' War was embroiling all Europe and the English were hostile to James' plans for a Spanish wedding. He was compelled to call Parliament, and its members attacked his policy. Commons urged the king to head a Protestant alliance in an offensive against Spain and condemned his marriage scheme. In a fury the king tore the record of the protestation from the annals of Commons and dissolved Parliament.[2] (It was this Parliament that had resisted the theory that he had advanced in his treatise, *The True Law of Free Monarchies*, which amplified his doctrine that a free monarchy is one in which the monarch is free and above all law.[3])

Robinson had for some months been turning over in his mind the problems that his exile community faced in remaining in Holland. The tide of refugees was ebbing, and he and his people were growing older. Each year death claimed some of their members. The twelve-year truce between the states and Spain would end in 1621. Then what would occur? "Taught by experience (say they) our prudent governors (their pastor and ruling elder) with some of the sagest members, began deeply to apprehend, and wisely to foresee, the dangers, and to think of a timely remedy."

195

If James I were only more humane, they might return to their homeland, but with all other doors closed, they might go to the New World.

Robinson talked with Brewster, Fuller, Carver, and other associates, and they set down the problems that must be resolved:

1. Fewer fellow countrymen were crossing over to join them in facing "the hardness of the place and country. Many that came to them could not endure the great labour and hard fare, with other inconveniences which they underwent and were contented with." Some had weathered the economic struggle and had become self-supporting but a number still lived in meager circumstances. "Yea, some preferred and chose the prisons of England rather than this liberty in Holland with these afflictions."[4]

But it was thought that if a better and easier place of living could be had, it would draw many and take away these discouragements. Yea, their Pastor would often say that many of those who both wrote and preached now against them, if they were in a place where they might have liberty and live comfortably, they would then practice as they did.

[2.] Old age was beginning to steal on many of them; and their great and continual labours, with other crosses and sorrows, hastened it before the time. So that in a few years they would be in danger to scatter, by necessities pressing them, or sink under their burdens, or both. . . . And therefore thought it better to dislodge betimes to some place of better advantage and less danger, if any such could be found.

3. Many of their children

were oftentimes so oppressed with their heavy labours that though their minds were free and willing, yet their bodies bowed under the weight of the same, and became decrepit in their early youth, the vigour of nature being consumed in the very bud. But that which was more lamentable was that many of their children, by these occasions and the great licentiousness of youth in that country, and the manifold temptations of the place, were drawn away by evil examples into extravagant and dangerous courses, getting their reins off their necks and departing from their parents. Some became soldiers, others took upon them far voyages by sea, and others some worse courses tending to dissoluteness and the danger of their souls. . . . So that they saw their posterity would be in danger to degenerate and be corrupted.[5]

One of the religious problems discussed at Dort was the careless, pagan attitude toward the sabbath as manifested by the Dutch people. Padres acknowledged the difficulties they faced in trying to lure the people from sports and from daily occupations on the Lord's Day. The English divines at Dort spoke of the scandalous neglect of sabbath observance. They urged the synod to intervene with the magistrates and to prevent the opening of shops and the practice of business as usual on Sundays.

196

Sir Dudley Carleton wrote from The Hague on July 22, 1619: "It falls out in these towns of Holland, that Sunday, which is elsewhere the day of rest, proves the day of labor, for they never knew how to observe the Sabbath."

[4.] A great hope and inward zeal they had of laying some good foundation, or at least to make some way thereunto, for the propagating and advancing the gospel of the kingdom of Christ in those remote parts of the world; yea, though they should be but even as stepping stones unto others for the performing of so great a work.[6]

Most of the previous expeditions to the New World had been motivated by economic advantage. Certainly the Pilgrim company were eager to improve their material lot, but they were also driven by the spiritual urge to maintain the faith that had already twice uprooted them from their homes and possessions. They were still seekers for freedom of speech and worship, for the building of a Christian community.

5. They had heard much from their Dutch neighbors of the war with Spain. That truce was soon to expire. Bradford spoke of the omnipresent military training and the weapons that were in evidence.[7]

6. Edward Winslow in *Hypocrisie Unmasked* and Nathaniel Morton in *New Englands Memoriall* mention the fear shared by the Pilgrims that their children would lose their nationality and their language. They wanted to preserve their own culture. Thirty-three Leyden Pilgrims had become Dutch citizens before July 1620. After the departure of the first shipload to the New World thirty-two more took out citizenship. They foresaw eventual amalgamation. Soon after their migrations their remnant was absorbed into Dutch life.

So once again Robinson's flock was faced with the old bugaboo of another move. The Scrooby-Babworth-Gainsborough group rehearsed hardships involved in auctioning off their property, diverting hard-earned savings into a common treasury, and secret negotiations designed to outwit the king's magistrates.

And after their betrayal by the Dutch shipmaster and their stormy crossing from Hull, the privations of settling in Amsterdam, followed by that costly uprooting and removal to Leyden, was it not folly to tempt Providence once again and go through all that tension and sacrifice to seek another haven? Nevertheless, others urged them to consider the long-range future and weigh the good and the evil to be faced along both courses, whichever they should vote to take.

John and Bridget Robinson had used funds from their families to buy the Green Gate property. The White family had sent over several new recruits who added their resources. John Carver, a prosperous merchant, had contributed generously for ten years. Brewster had depleted his fortune in the move to Amsterdam and Leyden and had invested much of his reserves in the Pilgrim Press. Bradford had diverted his patrimony into his corduroy manufacturing plant and possibly some had gone into the Pilgrim

Press. So it was with all those who could boast material means. There was little left to set up a common treasury. The impecunious Pilgrims were compelled to seek financial backing in England. They were too proud to beg, so they endeavored to borrow.

The removal to Holland was sufficently radical as a transplant, but it had been but a short journey and to a civilized country. Now they were talking of pulling up stakes and setting forth across a trackless and largely unexplored ocean to an unknown land that was inhabited by savage and hostile people. This would be an uprooting from a great university town to a wilderness.

> The place they had thoughts on was some of those vast and unpeopled countries of America, which are fruitful and fit for habitation, being devoid of all civil inhabitants, where there are only savage and brutish men which range up and down, little otherwise than the wild beasts of the same. This proposition being made public and coming to the scanning of all, it raised many fears and doubts amongst themselves. Some, for their reasons and hopes conceived, laboured to stir up and encourage the rest to undertake and prosecute the same; others again, out of their fears, objected against it and sought to divert from it; alleging many things, and those neither unreasonable nor unprobable; as that it was a great design and subject to many unconceivable perils and dangers; as, besides the casualties of the sea (which none can be freed from), the length of the voyage was such as weak bodies of women and other persons worn out with age and travail (as many of them were) could never be able to endure.[8]

The following is one of the choice passages from Bradford, not only because it shows how logically they were trying to build up their courage to face the dangerous course ahead, but also because of its classical Elizabethan language which flows with a musical cadence:

> It was answered, that all great and honourable actions are accompanied with great difficulties and must be both enterprised and overcome with answerable courages. It was granted the dangers were great, but not desperate. The difficulties were many, but not invincible. For though there were many of them likely, yet they were not certain. It might be sundry of the things feared might never befall; others by provident care and the use of good means might in a great measure be prevented; and all of them, through the help of God, by fortitude and patience, might either be borne or overcome. True it was that such attempts were not to be made and undertaken without good ground and reason, not rashly or lightly as many have done for curiosity or hope of gain, etc. But their condition was not ordinary, their ends were good and honourable, their calling lawful and urgent; and therefore they might expect the blessing of God in their proceeding. Yea, though they should lose their lives in this action, yet might they have comfort in the same and their endeavours would be honourable. They lived here but as men in exile and in a poor condition, and as

198

great miseries might possibly befall them in this place; for the twelve years of truce were now out and there was nothing but beating of drums and preparing for war, the events whereof are always uncertain. The Spaniard might prove as cruel as the savages of America, and the famine and pestilence as sore here as there, and their liberty less to look out for remedy.

After many other particular things answered and alleged on both sides, it was fully concluded by the major part to put this design in execution and to prosecute it by the best means they could.[9]

Robert Cushman and John Carver were appointed to make arrangements for the transoceanic voyage. Cushman, a wool-comber from Canterbury, apparently left the Ancient Brethren Church in rebellion to follow Robinson to Leyden. He possessed some education and financial resources, and was elected deacon. He had bought a small house in Nuns Alley close to the Pieterskerk in 1611, and purchased a larger home the next year in the Nonnensteeg. In 1616 his wife and one child died and he was left with one son, Thomas, who was later to take over the post of William Brewster. Cushman remarried the widow of a shoemaker from Canterbury. He departed soon after for England where he remained for almost three years, struggling to make business provisions for the *Mayflower* expedition.

John Carver, a well-to-do London merchant, affiliated with the Leyden fellowship about 1610. As one of the deacons he was "a pious, faithful, and very beneficial instrument." Born at Doncaster near Scrooby, he had married Catherine White, older sister of Bridget Robinson, Jane Tickens, and Frances Jessop.

The Carvers were reported living in Leydèn along the Dark Canal as early as May 1609. If so, he may have influenced his brother-in-law to bring the Pilgrims from Amsterdam to the university city. Due to his business contacts he may have been cautious about openly affiliating with Robinson's group, but once he joined them, he became a stalwart member. He was considered the richest man in the group and was "of singular piety and rare for humility which appeared (as otherwise) so by his great condesendencye."

At length Deacons John Carver and Robert Cushman were dispatched to England to open negotiations. They visited Sir Edwin Sandys, the friend of Brewster and Robinson, a religious and political liberal, to seek support in securing a charter so they could establish a colony and operate under the sanction of the king, with the understanding that they would be free to worship according to their conscience.

In 1617 Robinson and Brewster drew up their statement of Seven Articles for the Virginia Council in London. Resorting to a little diplomacy they gave a conciliatory statement which tended to gloss over their controversial points.

1. To the confession of faith published in the name of the Church of England & to every article thereof we do with the

reformed churches where we live & also elsewhere assent wholly.

2. As we do acknowledge the doctrine of faith there taught so do we the fruits and effects of the same doctrine to the begetting of saving faith in thousands in the land (conformists & reformists) as they are called with whom also as with our brethren we do desire to keep spiritual communion in peace and will practice in our parts all lawful things.

3. The King's Majesty we acknowledge for Supreme Governor in his Dominion in all causes and over all persons, and yet none may decline or appeal from his authority or judgment in any cause whatsoever, but yet in all things obedience is due unto him, either active, if the thing commanded be not against God's word, or passive if it be, except pardon can be obtained.

4. We judge it lawful for his Majesty to appoint bishops, civil overseers, or officers in authority under him, in ye several provinces, dioceses, congregations or parishes to oversee the Churches and govern them civilly according to the Laws of the Land, unto whom we are in all things to give an account & by them to be ordered according to Godliness.

5. The authority of the present bishops in the Land we do acknowledge so far forth as the same is indeed derived from his Majesty unto them and as they proceed in his name, whom we will also therein honor in all things and him in them.

6. We believe that no synod, classis, convocation or assembly of Ecclesiastical Officers hath any power or authority at all but as the same by the Magistrate given unto them.

7. Lastly, we desire to give unto all Superiors due honor to preserve the unity of the spirit with all that fear God, to have peace with all men what in us lieth & wherein we err to be instructed by any.

Subscribed by
John Robinson
and William Brewster[10]

Article 3 does not mean that the signers were willing to do everything the king commanded. If the action is contrary to the law of God they cannot perform it, and they submit to the penalties for its omission, making no resistance to the ordinary course of the law other than a proper effort to obtain a pardon. In Article 6 one notes the care with which it avoids ascribing any spiritual authority to the clergy of the Establishment.[11]

The articles were to be used as a basis for negotiation toward their permission to move to America. Sandys apparently passed them on to the merchant prince, Sir John Wolstenholme, who could serve as a more acceptable spokesman with the king. He volunteered to talk with Archbishop Abbot of Canterbury, who held some kindly feelings for the Puritans. At length the reaction was favorable enough for Brewster to make a trip to London. Shortly afterward, he disappeared from the scene due to his encounter with James I over the Pilgrim Press.

Thomas Weston, an ironmonger from London, appeared about this time in Leyden to interview Robinson and his associates. He was a promoter who had heard of the Pilgrims' need for funds to finance their journey. He was interested in making a speculative investment. He proved to be one of the most vocal of the London Merchant Adventurers who were to advance capital for their crossing.

Capt. John Smith stated that some seventy men were associated with Weston and his Merchant Adventurers who invested about 7,000 pounds. Based on the debt settlement of 1627 that the Pilgrims made with the Adventurers, when their debt was rewritten, the cost of the *Mayflower* voyage, including the ship lease, equipment, and food could hardly have exceeded 1,800 pounds.[12]

Hubbard says that Thomas Weston disbursed 500 pounds to advance the interest of Plimoth colony. Winslow states in 1622 "he formerly deserved well of us." Bradford adds in 1623, he "became an enemy on occasions."

At this period the outlook appeared to be fairly bright, but the horizon was soon clouded. When Carver and Cushman returned they reported that neither the king nor Archbishop Abbot favored "liberty in religion." The most generous concession that his majesty would grant was mere connivance: "He would connive at them and not molest them, provided they carried themselves peaceably; but to allow, or tolerate, them by his public authority, under his seal" could not be considered.

So "this made a damp in the business. . . . For many were afraid that if they should unsettle themselves, and put off their estates, and go upon these hopes, it might prove dangerous and but a sandy foundation."[13]

The members of the council were suspicious of the beliefs of Robinson and his flock, as were the king and the archbishop, so a statement of defense was called for, and Robinson and Brewster wrote Sir John Wolstenholme and enclosed two declarations regarding the making and the functions of ministers, the two sacraments, and the oath of supremacy. Sir John was one of the important members of the council for Virginia and a friend of Sandys and the Pilgrims. Robinson and Brewster wrote him that they had sent an explanation of their judgments on three points raised by some of "His Majesty's Honourable Privy Council." They intended to clear up the "unjust insinuations made against us." They sent a short and a long form statement, leaving it to his judgment as to which one to present.

The First Brief Note was This.

Touching the ecclesiastical ministry, namely of pastors for teaching, elders for ruling, and deacons for distributing the church's contribution, as also for the two sacraments, baptism and the Lord's Supper, we do wholly and in all points agree with the French Reformed Churches, according to their public confession of faith.

The oath of Supremacy we shall willingly take if it be required of us, and that convenient satisfaction be not given by our taking the oath of Allegiance.

John Robinson
William Brewster

The Second was This.

Touching the ecclesiastical ministry, etc. as in the former, we agree in all things with the French Reformed Churches, according to their public confession of faith; though some small differences to be found in our practices, not at all in the substance of the things, but only in some accidental circumstances.

1. As first, their ministers do pray with their heads covered; ours uncovered.

2. We choose none for Governing Elders but such as are able to teach; which ability they do not require.

3. Their elders and deacons are annual, or at most for two or three years; ours perpetual.

4. Our elders do administer their office in admonitions and excommunications for public scandals, publicly and before the congregation; theirs more privately and in their consistories.

5. We do administer baptism to such infants as whereof the one parent at the least is of some church, which some of their churches do not observe; though in it our practice accords with their public confession and the judgment of the most learned amongst them.

Other differences worthy mentioning we know none in these points. Then about the oath, as in the former.

Subscribed,
John Robinson
William Brewster[14]

The letter to Sir John was delivered by Sabine Staresmore, who had been a member of Henry Jacob's church in London. He now emerged as an emissary of good will in London, writing February 14, 1617:

I asked his Worship what good news he had for me to write tomorrow. He told me very good news, both the King's Majesty and the bishops have consented. He said he would go to Mr. Chancellor, Sir Fulke Grevill, as this day, and next week I should know more. I met Sir Edwin Sandys on Wednesday night. He wished me to be at the Virginia Court the next Wednesday, where I purpose to be.

Sabine Staresmore[15]

Sir John found that the declarations were not necessary. In fact if they had been presented they might "spoil all," so they were held back. "He would not show them at any hand." But there were still "many rubs that fell in their way," and delayed departure for nearly three years.

There were complications in dealing with their agents in England. The destination of their voyage created one problem. Some wanted to go to Guiana. Others insisted on Virginia. Merchants

Sir Edwin Sandys (1561-1629)—Puritan member of Parliament and friend of the Pilgrims

and friends cancelled their pledges. Meanwhile the people in Leyden who had sold their properties were on tenterhooks.

On December 15, 1617 Robinson and Brewster sent a letter to Sir Edwin Sandys stating that the congregation in Leyden had drawn up a statement which Deacon John Carver was bringing to London, trusting that he and Carver would promote their plans to remove to America.

This final plea before the court, as it were, would move the sternest judge. They set forth their qualifications for succeeding. They wanted to assure the councils and financial backers in England that they were worth the risk and would not let them down, that they had the stuff to carry through, despite their poor and humble estate. Rembrandt could not have surpassed this self-portrait in words, one of the gems from the Pilgrim records:

1. We verily believe and trust the Lord is with us, unto whom and whose service we have given ourselves in many trials; and that He will graciously prosper our endeavours according to the simplicity of our hearts therein.

2. We are well weaned from the delicate milk of our mother country, and inured to the difficulties of a strange and hard land, which yet in a great part we have by patience overcome.

3. The people are, for the body of them, industrious and frugal, we think we may safely say, as any company of people in the world.

4. We are knit together as a body in a most strict and sacred bond and covenant of the Lord, of the violation whereof we make great conscience, and by virtue whereof we do hold ourselves straitly tied to all care of each other's goods and of the whole, by every one and so mutually.

5. Lastly, it is not with us as with other men, whom small things can discourage, or small discontentments cause to wish themselves at home again. We know our entertainment in England and in Holland. We shall much prejudice both our arts and means by removal; who, if we should be driven to return, we should not hope to recover our present helps and comforts, neither indeed look ever, for ourselves, to attain unto the like in any other place during our lives, which are drawing towards their periods.

Yours much bounded in all duty
John Robinson
William Brewster[16]

The Leyden church held "a solemn meeting and a day of humiliation to seek the Lord for His direction." Pastor Robinson spoke on the text from 2 Samuel 23:3-4: "And David's men said unto him, see we be afraid here in Judah, how much more if we come to Keilah against the host of the Philistines? Then David asked counsel of the Lord again." Like the people of ancient Israel, he said, they knew that the land of the Philistines lay before them. Some in their midst would draw back before the perils of the unknown. He urged them not to panic before their fears, but rather like David seek the guidance of God, and carry on in the spirit of their biblical forefathers.

They had arrived at a dramatic juncture. Their minds were now set on the larger freedoms that migration promised, yet they were still hounded by apprehensions and misgivings. But the wise pastor "taught them many things very aptly and befitting their present occasion and condition, strengthening them against their fears and perplexities and encouraging them in their resolutions."[17]

Plans for the crossing were fully considered by the people. It was not possible for all to go on the first ship, so certain ones were chosen. Pastor Robinson was to stay with the majority in Leyden and Elder Brewster was to lead the expedition. It was agreed that "those that went should be an absolute church of themselves, as well as those that stayed, seeing in such a dangerous voyage, and a removal to such a distance, it might come to pass they should (for the body of them) never meet again in this world." It was also promised that those who remained would cross over "as soon as they could."

We are well weaned from the delicate
milk of our mother country, and inured to the
difficulties of a strange land, which
yet in a great part we have by patience overcome.
—John Robinson
William Brewster

16 "WE ARE WELL WEANED FROM THE DELICATE MILK OF OUR MOTHER COUNTRY"

Robinson studied the books and maps that he had collected which described the potentials and perils of the vast unknown called America. Consideration was given to settling in Guiana, which at that time included the area between the Orinoco and the Amazon Rivers. This territory had come to the attention of English readers through Sir Walter Raleigh's *Discoverie of the Large Rich and Beautifull Empyre of Guiana* and Lawrence Keymis' *Relation of the Second Voyage to Guiana,* published in 1596. They were followed in 1613 by Robert Harcourt's *Relation of a Voyage to Guiana.* In 1617 there was open for settlement "all the land between the Amazon and the Assequibo" in Guiana. Robert Harcourt of County Oxford had held a patent since 1613 following his voyage to that territory.

A number of books that presented Virginia were read by Robinson and discussed by his co-workers. There was Thomas Hariot's *Briefe and True Report* about the new-found land of Virginia, published in 1588. He was familiar with the writings of his fellow clergyman, Richard Hakluyt, the Oxford scholar, who helped launch the glorious era of English exploration. His *Divers Voyages* was printed in 1582.

In 1606 ten men, including Sir Edwin Sandys and Richard Hakluyt, formed the London Company to colonize Virginia. Francis Bacon, soon to become lord chancellor, criticized the get-rich-quick incentive in colony building. He said that a colony should be a long-range plan. Settlers should be selected for their skills and should include many farmers, and they should expect to spend their lives in the colony.[1]

In the same year a joint stock company was launched for the establishment of two colonies in America. The branch that was to handle the proposed southern colony had its headquarters in London. The management of the northern branch was in Plimoth, Devon. Hence the two branches were spoken of as the London and Plimoth Companies, or the Virginia Company and the Northern Virginia Company, since the name Virginia was then applied to the entire Atlantic coast north of Florida.

The London Company's first expedition set out in February 1607, reached the coast of Virginia, and founded Jamestown. Capt. John Smith, who was in this company, wrote *A True Relation of . . . Virginia Since the First Planting of That Colony.* Of the 500 people in Virginia when Smith left in 1609, only sixty-five were alive six months later.

Ralph Lane, first governor of Virginia, explained that the first settlers there were not of the proper type. Some had come only to search for silver and gold. Others

had little understanding, lesse discretion, and more tongue than was needful or requisite. . . . Some also were of a nice bringing up, only in cities or townes, or such as never (as I may say) had seene the world before. Because there were not to be found any English cities, nor such faire houses, nor at their owne wish any of their own accustomed dainty feed, nor any soft beds of downe or feathers, the countrey was to them miserable, and their reports thereof accordingly.[2]

During his stay in Virginia, John Smith planned an expedition north and wrote in 1616 *A Description of New England.* Smith made a major contribution to the settlement of America through this book, which contained a remarkably accurate map of the area. The Pilgrims had studied his map and read his writings. They carried it on the *Mayflower* and pored over it during their explorations of Cape Cod.

Captain Smith painted a glowing picture of Massachusetts:

The waters are most pure, proceeding from the entrails of the mountains. The herbs and fruits are of many sorts and kinds, as alkerms, currants, mulberries, vines, respices, gooseberries, plums, walnuts, chestnuts, small nuts, etc., pumpkins, gourds, strawberries, beans, peas, and maize, a kind or two of flax, wherewith they make nets, lines, and ropes, both small and great, very strong for the quantities.

Oak is the chief wood, of which there is great difference in regard of the soil where it groweth; fir, pine, walnut, chestnut, burch, ash, elm, cypress, cedar, mulberry, plumtree, hazel, saxifrage, and many other sorts.

Whales, grampus, porpoises, turbot, sturgeon, cod, hake, haddock, cole, cusk (or small ling), shark, mackerel, herring, mullet, base, pinacks, cunners, perch, eels, crabs, lobsters, mussels, wilkes, oysters, and diverse others.

Who can desire more content, that hath small means and plant only his merit to advance his fortune than to tread and plant that ground he hath purchased by the hazard of his life? If he have but the taste of virtue and magnanimity, what to such a mind can be more pleasant than planting and building a foundation for his posterity, got from the rude earth by God's blessing and his own industry, without prejudice to any? If he have any grain of faith or zeal in religion, what can he do less hurtful to any, or more agreeable to God, than to seek to convert those poor savages to know Christ and humanity, whose labors with discretion will triple requite the charge and pains?[3]

The little company pondered the records of these English explorers. A copy of *Good News from Virginia,* was found in Brewster's library, written by a Puritan minister in Jamestown colony, Alexander Whitaker, and also two books on silkworms and their culture. The production of silk in Virginia was under discussion and this trade appealed to the silk workers of Leyden among the Pilgrim circle. They also considered the controls that might exist there under a colony already established and under the authority of a king who held a grudge against them. Would it not be wiser to consider landing further north, in an area as yet unsettled and therefore freer from royal interference?

During this time Capt. Myles Standish, who had served as a soldier with the Dutch forces during their war with Spain, visited with Robinson and Brewster and decided to join the expedition. Descended from an old Roman Catholic Lancashire family, he was about thirty-six years of age, small in stature, and red-headed. "Captain Shrimp" was hot-tempered. As Bradford put it, "a little chimney is quickly fired." Although he was a stranger, he developed into a sterling citizen of Plimoth Plantation. Like most of the other strangers he was drawn to the spirit of the Leyden company, and he soon became a supporter of their principles.

The Leyden group had also explored the possibilities of settling under Dutch auspices in another section of the Netherlands, or in New Amsterdam in the New World. Winslow says that certain merchants and officials of the New Netherlands Company "made them large offers to induce them to go into Zeeland" or "to go under them to Hudson's River," offering them free transportation and the promise of cattle and other conveniences for every family. The New Netherlands Company petitioned the Stadtholders for protection of the Pilgrims if they should head for the Hudson. They wrote:

Now it happens that there is residing at Leyden a certain English preacher, versed in the Dutch language, who is well inclined to proceed thither to live: assuring the Petitioners that he has the means of inducing over four hundred families to accompany him thither, both out of this country and England. Provided they would be guarded and preserved from all violence on the part of other potentates, by the authority and under the protection of your Princely Excellency and the High and Mighty Lords States General, in the propogation of the true [and] pure Christian religion, in the instruction of the Indians in that country in true learning, and in converting them to the Christian faith: and thus, through the mercy of the Lord, to the greater glory of the country's government, to plant there a new Commonwealth; all under the order and command of your Princely Excellency and the High and Mighty Lords States General.[4]

Robinson was familiar with the exploits of Hudson. His Dutch friends at the university talked about a New Amsterdam. Because of the friendly relations and the trustworthy qualities of the Netherlanders, there was much to be said about a settlement in the area. However, they preferred to live under English rule, if this could be achieved. Thomas Weston was a persuasive salesman and his urgings and promises also swung sentiment away from the Hudson. Weston came to Leyden and held conferences with Robinson and finally persuaded them to go on and not to meddle with the Dutch or too much depend on the Virginia Company; he and such merchants as were his friends, together with their own means, would get them forth; and they should make ready and neither fear want of shipping nor money; for what they wanted should be provided.[5]

To this end "they were to draw such articles of agreement." Carver and Cushman

were to receive the moneys and make provision both for shipping and other things for the voyage. . . . So those that were to go prepared themselves with all speed and sold off their estates and (such as were able) put in their moneys into the common crock, which was disposed by those appointed, for the making of general provisions.

William Bradford, indispensable recorder of these events, sold his home in 1619. So once again there was a confusion of sales and auctions carried out in the spirit of sacrifice for a dream of better days that they hoped might lie ahead.[6]

Robert Cushman wrote from London, May 8, 1619 to Master Robinson and the Leyden congregation: "The main hindrance of our proceedings in the Virginia business is the dissensions and factions (as they term in) amongst the Council and Company of Virginia, which are such, as that ever since we came up no business could by them be dispatched."

He explained how Sir Edwin Sandys had been elected as the new treasurer, but a certain faction had divided the company directors. He went on to relate the tragic report of Elder Blackwell and his Amsterdam company, who encountered storm, disease, and almost total extermination on their crossing to Virginia. Then, thinking of his Leyden friends who were preparing for a similar voyage: "Heavy news it is, and I would be glad to hear how far it will discourage. I see none here discouraged much, but rather desire to learn to beware of other men's harms and so amend that wherein they have failed." His letter concluded:

Mr. B. [Elder Brewster who was then hiding in England from the police of James I] is not well at this time, whether he will come back to you or go into the north, I yet know not. For myself, I hope to see an end of this business ere I come, though I am sorry to be thus from you. If things had gone roundly forward, I should have been with you within these fourteen days. I pray God direct us and give us that spirit which is fitting for such a business. Thus having summarily pointed at things which Mr. Brewster, I think, hath more largely writ of to Mr. Robinson, I leave you to the Lord's protection.

London, May 8   Yours in all readiness, etc.
Anno 1619   Robert Cushman[7]

Sir Edwin Sandys interceded for the Pilgrims with Sir Robert Naunton, secretary of state to James I, seeking permission for them "to enjoy their liberty of conscience under his gracious protection in America."

Edward Winslow explains the first glint of interest on the part of the king in their cause:

> This his Majesty said was a good and honest motion, and asking what profits might arise in the part we intended (for our eye was upon the most northern parts of Virginia,) 'twas answered, "Fishing." To which he replied with his ordinary asseveration, "So God have my soul, 'tis an honest trade; 'twas the Apostles' own calling," &c. But afterwards he told Sir Robert Naunton (who took all occasions to further it) that we should confer with the bishops of Canterbury and London, etc. Whereupon we were advised to persist upon his first approbation, and not to entangle ourselves with them; which caused our agents to repair to the Virginia Company, who in their court demanded our ends in going; which being related, they said the thing was of God, and granted a large patent, and one of them lent us £300 gratis for three years, which was repaid.[8]

Brewster's familiarity with the court and officials in the offices of the secretary of state proved valuable in establishing this friendly contact with Sir Robert Naunton.

Some six weeks later the Virginia Company acted favorably on a motion to grant a patent of land to the Pilgrims in the extreme north of the company's territory. This patent was issued to John Wincomb, a Puritan minister in the service of the Countess of Lincoln, and not to the Pilgrims direct. The following February the patent was superseded by a new one issued to John Peirce, a London clothier, an associate of Thomas Weston. The text of this patent has been lost, but it no doubt was more liberal than the Wincomb patent and replaced it as the basic grant to the Pilgrims. On June 1, 1621 a second Peirce patent was issued by the council for New England.

The Virginia Company was divided at this time. King James refused to permit the company to reelect Sandys as treasurer since he was the leader of the opposition in Parliament. It was suggested that the Pilgrims wait until a proper New England Company be formed and sail under their auspices. The Pilgrims were confused, as was their agent, Robert Cushman.

Other difficulties arose with Weston, who altered the conditions that had been agreed on in Leyden. Deacon Cushman had consented, apparently in desperation, to these changes,

> seeing else that all was like to be dashed and the opportunity lost, and that they which had put off their estates and paid in their moneys were in hazard to be undone. They presumed to conclude with the merchants on those terms, in some things contrary to their order and commission and without giving

them notice of the same; yea, it was concealed lest it should make any further delay. Which was the cause afterward of much trouble and contention.[9]

The stiff terms demanded by the Adventurers included ten points:

1. The Adventurers and Planters do agree, that every person that goeth being aged 16 years and upward, be rated at £10, and £10 to be accounted a single share.

2. That he that goeth in person, and furnisheth himself out with £10 either in money or other provisions, be accounted as having £20 in stock, and in the division he shall receive a double share.

3. The persons transported and the Adventurers shall continue their joint stock and partnership together, the space of seven years, during which time all profits and benefits that are got by trade, traffic, trucking, working, fishing, or any other means of any person or persons, remain still in the common stock until the division.

4. That at their coming there, they choose out such a number of fit persons as may furnish their ships and boats for fishing upon the sea, employing the rest in their several faculties upon the land, as building houses, tilling and planting the ground, and making such commodities as shall be most useful for the colony.

5. That at the end of the seven years, the capital and profits, viz., the houses, lands, goods and chattels, be equally divided betwixt the Adventurers and Planters; which done, every man shall be free from other of them of any debt or detriment concerning this adventure.

6. Whosoever cometh to the colony hereafter or putteth any into the stock, shall at the end of the seven years be allowed proportionately to the time of his so doing.

7. He that shall carry his wife and children, or servants, shall be allowed for every person now aged 16 years and upward, a single share in the division; or, if he provided them necessaries, a double share; or if they be between 10 years old and 16, then two of them to be reckoned for a person both in transportation and division.

8. That such children as now go, and are under the age of 10 years, have no other share in the division but 50 acres of unmanured land.

9. That such persons as die before the seven years be expired, their executors to have their part or share at the division, proportionately to the time of their life in the colony.

10. That all such persons as are of this colony are to have their meat, drink, apparel, and all provisions out of the common stock and goods of said colony.[10]

Deacon Cushman had held out for better terms but the Adventurers drove a hard bargain. There were two bitter disagreements: first, "that the houses, and lands improved, especially gardens and home lots, should remain undivided wholly to the planters at the seven years' end. Secondly, that they should have had two days in a week for their own private employment."

Robinson and the Leydenites found it frustrating to spell out satisfactory business arrangements due to the distance that separated them from the Merchant Adventurers and the Leyden emissaries, and he wrote June 14, 1620 to his brother-in-law, John Carver, while the group was waiting in Southampton:

My dear friend and brother:

You do thoroughly understand by our general letters the estate of things here, which indeed is very pitiful, especially by want of shipping and not seeing means likely, much less certain, of having it provided; though withal there be great want of money and means to do needful things. Mr. Pickering [a member of the Leyden congregation] you know before this, will not defray a penny here, though Robert Cushman presumed of I know not how many hundred pounds from him. [Pickering and Brewer were their leading prospective backers in Leyden.] Besides, whereas divers are to pay in some parts of their moneys yet behind, they refuse to do it till they see shipping provided, or a course taken for it. Neither do I think is there a man here would pay anything, if he had again his money in his purse.

You know right well we depended on Mr. Weston alone, and upon such means as he would procure for this common business; and when we had in hand another course with the Dutchmen, broke it off at his motion and upon the conditions by him shortly after propounded. He did this in his love I know, but things appear not answerable from him hitherto. That he should have first have put in his moneys is thought by many to have been but fit. But that I can well excuse, he being a merchant and having use of it to his benefit. But that he should not but have had either shipping ready before this time, or at least certain means and course and the same known to us for it; or have taken other order otherwise, cannot in my conscience be excused.[11]

The pastor said that their faithful Deacon Cushman was not handling things wisely and that they had relied too much "upon generalities" rather than making clear-cut business arrangements. He urged that they fight for the rights of the planters against the Adventurers, holding out on their demands for personal ownership of land and houses after the seven-year period of labor for the common cause. And they should insist on "the two days in a week for private use." What a hardship it would prove to "serve a new apprenticeship of seven years, and not a day's freedom from task."

There were exhausting conferences at the Green Gate between Master Robinson, Elder Brewster, Deacons Fuller, Carver, and Cushman (when they were back from London), and some of the younger members like William Bradford, who was thirty, and Edward Winslow, then twenty-five. Following these long discussions over books and maps concerning that strange New World, correspondence with their contacts abroad, the welfare of their constituency, the state of their treasury and the status of their numerous negotiations regarding ships, supplies, and provisions, John Robinson would sit with Bridget and relate to her the happenings of the day. And they would speculate about how soon they would be departing from the Green Gate to leave behind the friends and pleasant places of their adopted Leyden.

The fact that Robinson did not sail on the *Speedwell* and remained in Leyden has been misinterpreted by one critic who stated that he did not go west because he "had gone sour." There is no evidence whatever to justify such an assumption.

According to the vote of the Green Gate he was to remain in Leyden with the majority of the congregation while Brewster was elected to be in charge of the first expedition. As Bradford relates: "Those who stayed, being the greater number, required the Pastor to stay with them; and indeed for other reasons he could not then well go, and so it was the more easily yielded unto."[12] (This might refer to a health problem of one of his children, because only a few months later, on February 7, 1621, he and Bridget buried a child within the shadowy solitude of the Pieterskerk.)

Then, too, the pastor by necessity stayed behind to wind up financial matters and follow through on the interminable details of such a colossal undertaking, as well as to aid those not able to go with the first group. Some families were divided, leaving behind members who were to come later. The pastor had to shepherd those left without husbands or fathers as well as families who were not ready to make the first crossing, as he had done on the move from England to Holland.

He was to follow as soon as it was possible. The London Merchant Adventurers who took over arrangements for passage, however, kept holding back on his departure. There was the recent furor over the Pilgrim Press which made him suspect at Whitehall. Moreover, he had been a foremost spokesman for the Separatist cause and James I distrusted him. So it developed that his booking on ship after ship was postponed, and he remained marooned in Leyden. All his letters to Plimoth make clear his regret, impatience, and criticism over the frustrating procrastination.

He loved England and also Holland, which had sheltered him. He now loved two countries, and even a third which he sought after and believed could be nobler and better than the first two. One reason that his Pilgrims succeeded in New England was due to the fact that the community they sought to create was their third home. They were adept at adapting. Robinson had taught them to love two countries and to pray for and believe in a third. "He was the soul and spirit of the whole enterprise of the New England migration from England to Holland, from Holland to New Plimoth. He was really the presiding genius and ought to be honored for his far-seeing, eagle-like vision."[13]

His leadership created a strong feeling of comradeship and idealism in the Pilgrim company.

214

There were hundreds and perhaps thousands of English people in Holland at that time, but these people had a special spiritual nexus. They clung together and helped each other in all worldly and ecclesiastical affairs because they believed in God and in John Robinson and in one another.[14]

It had been decided in Leyden that a third person should be added to the committee on arrangements composed of Carver and Cushman, and a stranger from outside the fellowship. This would afford representation to others who desired to join the *Mayflower* expedition. The stranger appointed was Christopher Martin from Billerica in Essex.

The Adventurers wanted to open the expedition to volunteers in order to increase their chances of success and profit. A certain number of planters or strangers were to be accepted and added to the original Pilgrim group. This democratic move was

> not so much for any great need of their help as to avoid all suspicion or jealousy of any partiality. And indeed their care for giving offense, both in this and other things afterward, turned to great inconvenience unto them, as in the sequel will appear; but however it showed their equal and honest minds. The provisions were for the most part made at Southampton, contrary to Mr. Weston's and Robert Cushman's mind whose counsels did most concur in all things.[15]

Cushman wrote to Carver, June 10, 1620 that their provisions were not yet completed, that there were too many fingers in the pie, and that summer would pass before they had anything settled. They were more ready to dispute than "to set forward a voyage."

Deacon Cushman, who appeared to be less astute in business arrangements for the Pilgrims than Deacon Carver, went on to mention his fear that some of the saints from Amsterdam might sign up for the *Mayflower* trip: "I have always feared the event of the Amsterdamers striking in with us. I trow you must excommunicate me or else you must go without their company."

Cushman explained the frustrations they faced. They were reckoning on 150 passengers but only £1,200 had been found beside "some cloth, stockings and shoes." They were short £300 or £400. They were having trouble securing their supply of beer. He deplored the divisions with the other agents, and warned that if there were not other ways and means found soon he feared there would be jangling and insulting.[16] It was another gloomy letter.

In view of the confusion in Leyden and in London, as pictured by Robinson, it is amazing that the *Speedwell* was able to sail from Delfshaven six weeks later on July 22 when the sky was "red and lowering" to join the larger *Mayflower* in Southampton.

So they left that goodly and pleasant
city which had been their resting place near twelve
years; but they knew they were pilgrims, and
looked not much on those things, but lift up
eyes to the heavens, their dearest country,
and quieted their spirits.
—William Bradford

17 "THEY KNEW THEY WERE PILGRIMS"

And now the long-discussed Pilgrim journey from Holland was underway. "At length, after much travel and these debates, all things were got ready and provided. A small ship of some sixty tons (the *Speedwell*) was bought and fitted in Holland." This vessel was to help transport the colony to America and then stay there to be used for fishing. A second ship, the *Mayflower*, was hired in London and was waiting in readiness in Southampton.

In preparation for the sailing of the *Speedwell* from nearby Delfshaven the congregation gathered in Leyden for "a day of solemn humiliation." Master Robinson took as his text Ezra 8:21:

And there at the river, by Ahava, I proclaimed a fast, that we might humble ourselves before our God, and seek of him a right way for us, and for our children, and for all our substance. For I was ashamed to require of the king a band of soldiers and horsemen, to help us against the enemy in the way: because we had spoken to the king saying, the hand of our God is upon all them for good that seek him, but his power and his wrath is against all them that forsake him.[1]

He eloquently presented the hopes of the exiled Jews in Persia in 458 B.C. as they struggled to move forward out of privation and persecution toward a new beginning. He challenged his followers to believe in the future, in the community that they would build with God's guidance, a free church in a free commonwealth. "The rest of the time was spent in pouring out prayers to the Lord with great fervency, mixed with abundance of tears."[2]

The members who were to remain in Leyden then staged a farewell feast in honor of the first contingent that was to lead the vanguard to the New World. Winslow records:

They feasted us who were to go, at our pastor's house, being large: where we refreshed ourselves, after tears, with singing of psalms, making joyful melody in our hearts, as well as with the voice, there being many of the congregation very expert in music.[3]

The embarkees, accompanied by their friends, set forth by *trackchuit,* or canal boat, from the Nuns Bridge on the Rapenburg in Leyden for Delfshaven, some twenty-four miles away. They moved through the waters of the Vliet and the Schie toward Delft. They passed its ancient gates of brick and stone, pock-marked by cannon fire during the days of the Spanish War. Their horse-drawn barges passed quietly through meadows bright with summer flowers, among the cattle, windmills, farmhouses, and church steeples.

They moved on to the haven of Delft or Delfshaven, a pretty town founded in the fourteenth century. The motto on the seal of the old brick church read, "The haven of salvation alone is with God."

The Delfshaven church is on the canal where the *Speedwell* was tied up and where the Pilgrims assembled for their farewells and for embarkation. Built in 1417 as St. Anthony's Chapel, it was converted into a Protestant church in 1574 and called the *Oude Kerk*. After the visit of the *Speedwell* the Dutch began to call it

Seventeenth-century Dellshaven, Holland

the Pilgrim Fathers Church and so it is known today. Delfshaven is now part of the city of Rotterdam and the Pilgrim Fathers Church is at the heart of a vast reclamation program. The numerous fine sixteenth- and seventeenth-century buildings in this area, that fortunately were spared by Nazi bombs, are being skillfully restored to their authentic former state. In the belfry of the church there is a set of bells that was brought from the Hemony Carillon of St. Lawrence Cathedral in Rotterdam after it was gutted by fire during the German bombings of 1940.

There were friends from both Leyden and Amsterdam who came to see them off. Here they "feasted us again." The night was spent on shore "with little sleep by the most." Early the next morning they and their friends climbed the gangway onto the little *Speedwell* for their final farewells. "Truly doleful was the sight of that sad and mournful parting, to see what sighs and sobs and prayers did sound amongst them, what tears did gush from every eye, and pithy speeches pierced each heart."

But the tide, which stays for no man, calling them away that were thus loath to depart, their reverend pastor falling down on

219

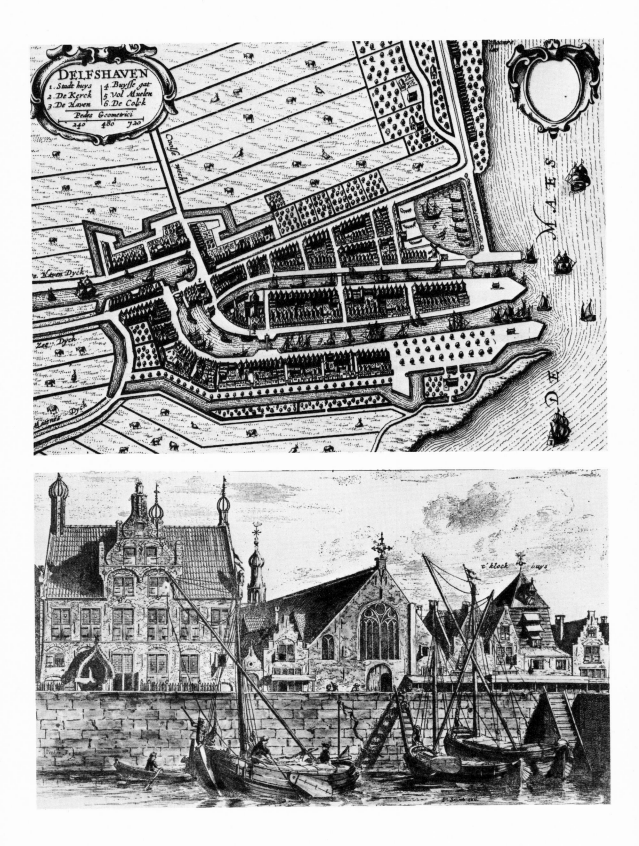

his knees (and they all with him) with watery cheeks commended them with most fervent prayers to the Lord and His blessing. And then with mutual embraces and many tears they took their leaves one of another, which proved to be the last leave to many of them.[4]

The ship lying to the quay and ready to set sail, the wind being fair, we gave them a volley of small shot and three pieces of ordnance, and so, lifting up our hands to each other to the Lord our God, we departed, and found his presence with us in the midst of our manifold straits he carried us through.[5]

So they left that goodly and pleasant city which had been their resting place near twelve years; but they knew they were pilgrims, and looked not much on those things, but lift[ed] up their eyes to the heavens, their dearest country, and quieted their spirits.[6]

From this statement of Bradford, based on Hebrews 11:13-16, the term Pilgrim was applied to the *Speedwell-Mayflower* company and to their immediate followers to the New World.

Hoisting sail on July 22, 1622, the *Speedwell* was carried forward by a "prosperous wind" to join the larger *Mayflower* which had sailed from London and was waiting for them with some of her passengers and equipment on board in Southampton.

As the breeze filled their sails and sped them westward toward the next sojourning place in their unfinished pilgrimage, the faithful company thought sadly of the Green Gate and tested friends there, and of the secure streets and canals of Leyden. Would they reach America safely? Would it be as arduous and formidable as the explorers pictured it? Was it always to be thus with them, to strive, to seek, but never to be at rest like other men?

Even Pastor Robinson's memorable farewell held lingering notes of challenge. There was a haunting summons in his words that followed them as if borne by the summer breeze:

We are now ere long to part asunder, and the Lord knoweth whether ever he should live to see our faces again: but whether the Lord had appointed it or not, he charged us before God and his blessed angels, to follow him no further than he followed Christ. And if God should reveal any thing to us by any other instrument of his, to be as ready to receive it, as ever we were to receive any truth from his ministry: For he was very confident the Lord had more truth and light yet to break forth out of his holy Word.

He took occasion also miserably to bewail the state and condition of the Reformed Churches, who were come to a period in religion, and would go no further than the instruments of their Reformation: As for example, the *Lutherans* they could not be drawn to go beyond what *Luther* saw, for what-

Delfshaven (c. 1650)

Delfshaven—Pilgrim Fathers Church at center (built 1417 as the Oude Kerk)

ever part of God's will he had further imparted and revealed to *Calvin,* they [the Lutherans] will rather die than embrace it. And so also, saith he, you see the *Calvinists,* they stick fast where he left them: A misery much to be lamented; for though they were precious shining lights in their times, yet God had not revealed his whole will to them. And were they now living, saith he, they would be as ready and willing to embrace further light, as that they had received.[7]

Their pastor was always urging them to strive. They had already sacrificed for "truth and light." How much further did he expect them to go? Would that the Lord God would lead them now to "a land flowing with milk and honey" where they could rest in peace.

After a pleasant sail to Southampton, the *Speedwell* anchored alongside the *Mayflower.* The passengers of both ships rejoiced as they greeted one another. But they soon realized that their affairs were in a quagmire of confusion. It was midsummer, and they had "already delayed overlong in regard of the season of the year."

Thomas Weston was on hand to see that they held to their terms with the London Merchant Adventurers. Rebelling against these demands,

they refused and answered him that he knew right well these were not according to the first agreement, neither could they yield to them without the consent of the rest that were behind. And indeed they had special charge when they came away, from the chief of those that were behind, not to do it. At which he was much offended and told them they must then look to stand on their own legs. So he returned (to London) in displeasure.[8]

Christopher Martin had unfortunately been chosen as treasurer, and their accounts were in a muddle. Hot-tempered and high-handed, he had not worked in harmony with Carver and Cushman. Carver had been purchasing supplies in Southampton, Cushman and Weston in London, and Martin in Kent. Weston said the voyage would never get underway with these three agents handling affairs. The Pilgrims needed £100 "to clear them at their going away . . . so they were forced to sell off some of their provisions to stop this gap, which was some three or four-score firkins of butter."[9]

Taking stock of their situation, and after a long discussion, the Pilgrims wrote to the London Merchant Adventurers from Southampton on August 3, 1620 that since they could not confer together they wanted to write and state their objections. Their main differences related to articles five and nine. They had seen nothing in writing before they left Holland. They had not authorized Cushman to sign any articles for them. Here they were in Southampton, having sold their property, and in a dilemma; but it was too late to reject the voyage.

They did not want to appear selfish, and desired success also for those who were investing their money. But they could not accept that their houses, goods, lands, and chattels be equally divided between them and the Adventurers at the end of seven years. However, if sufficient profits had not been realized by the Adventurers in these seven years, they (the settlers) would be willing to continue longer if God preserved them.

We are in such a strait at present, as we are forced to sell away £60 worth of our provisions to clear the haven, and withal to put ourselves upon great extremities, scarce having any butter, no oil, not a sole to mend a shoe, nor every man a sword to his side, wanting many muskets, such armour, etc. And yet we are willing to expose ourselves to such eminent dangers as are like to ensue, and trust to the good providence of God, rather than His name and truth should be evil spoken of, for us.

Aug. 3, 1620   Yours, etc.[10]

"It was subscribed with many names of the chiefest of the company."

Meanwhile, Pastor Robinson and the subdued remnant of Leydeners had made their way back to their homes by canal boat.

"The Embarkation of the Pilgrims at Delfshaven"—a nineteenth-century painting attributed to Robert W. Wier

He was troubled about the mismanagement of business in England and apprehensive that the *Speedwell* and *Mayflower* passengers might encounter more trouble with Weston, Martin, and creditors in London and Southampton. Unable to shake off his anxieties, he penned two letters: one to his brother-in-law, John Carver, written July 27; and the other his famous "Long Letter," to the Pilgrim band. He repeated the strong assurance of his intention to join them very shortly on the other side of the Atlantic, at the very first opportunity to book his passage, and that although he was forced for a time to be physically absent from them, he was with them in spirit. He made it clear that this purpose was foremost in his mind.

> I have a true feeling of your perplexity of mind and toil of body, but I hope that you who . . . are so well furnished for yourself, as that far greater difficulties than you have yet undergone cannot oppress you.
>
> I assure you that my heart is with you, and that I will not forslow my bodily coming at the first opportunity.
>
> I have written a large letter to the whole, and am sorry I shall not rather speak than write to them; and the more, considering the want of a preacher, which I shall also make some spur to my hastening after you. I do ever commend my best affection unto you, which if I thought you made any doubt of, I would express in more and the same more ample and full words.
>
> And the Lord in whom you trust and whom you serve ever in this business and journey, guide you with His hand, protect you with His wing, and show you and us His salvation in the end, and bring us in the meanwhile together in the place desired, if such be His good will, for His Christ's sake. Amen.
>
> Yours, etc.
>
> July 27, 1620   John Robinson[11]

This is his farewell letter to the *Speedwell-Mayflower* company:

> Loving and Christian Friends, I do heartily and in the Lord salute you all as being they with whom I am present in my best affection, and most earnest longings after you. Though I be constrained for a while to be bodily absent from you. I say constrained, God knowing how willingly and much rather than otherwise, I would have borne my part with you in this first brunt, were I not by strong necessity held back for the present.
>
> There are divers motives provoking you above others to great care and conscience this way: As first, you are many of you strangers, as to the persons so to the infirmities one of another, and so stand in need of more watchfulness this way, lest when such things fall out in men and women as you suspected not, you be inordinately affected with them; which doth require at your hands much wisdom and charity for the covering and preventing of incident offenses that way. And, lastly, your intended course of civil community will minister continual occasion of offense, and will be as fuel for that fire, except you diligently quench it with brotherly forbearance.

Let every man repress in himself and the whole body in each person, as so many rebels against the common good, all private respects of men's selves, not sorting with the general conveniency. And as men are careful not to have a new house shaken with any violence before it be well settled and the parts firmly knit, so be you, I beseech you, brethren, much more careful that the house of God, which you are and are to be, be not shaken with unnecessary novelties or other oppositions at the first settling thereof.

Lastly, whereas you are become a body politic, using amongst yourselves civil government, and are not furnished with any persons of special eminency above the rest, to be chosen by you into office of government; let your wisdom and godliness appear, not only in choosing such persons as do entirely love and will promote the common good, but also in yielding unto them all due honour and obedience in their lawful administrations, not beholding in them the ordinariness of their persons, but God's ordinance for your good; not being like the foolish multitude who more honour the gay coat than either the virtuous mind of the man, or glorious ordinance of the lord. But you know better things, and that the image of the Lord's power and authority which the magistrate beareth is honourable, in how mean persons soever. And this duty you both may the more willingly and ought the more conscionably to perform, because you are at least for the present to have only them for your ordinary governors, which yourselves shall make choice of for that work.

An unfeigned wellwisher of your happy success in this hopeful voyage.

John Robinson[12]

At length "all things being now ready, and every business dispatched, the company was called together and this letter read amongst them, which had good acceptation with all, and after fruit with many."

After the bustle and confusion and argument, it was beneficial to hear the words of calm from confident Master Robinson. One may be sure that some one of the company wrote Leyden, reporting the state of their expedition and the plans for their sailing about August 5.

The two laden ships proceeded as far as Dartmouth, where they put in due to leaks in the *Speedwell* to "have her there searched and mended." Soon the *Mayflower* company was saddled with two other thorns in the flesh—Weston and Martin—as poor, frustrated Deacon Cushman makes clear in the bitter letter that he wrote from Dartmouth on August 17 to Edward Southworth, a member of the Leyden congregation:

Our victuals will be half eaten up, I think, before we go from the coast of England, and if our voyage last long, we shall not have a month's victuals when we come in the country.

Near £700 hath been bestowed at Hampton, upon what I

know not; Mr. Martin saith he neither can nor will give any account of it, and if he be called upon for accounts, he crieth out of unthankfulness for his pains and care, that we are suspicious of him, and flings away, and will end nothing. Also he so insulteth over our poor people, with such scorn and contempt as if they were not good enough to wipe his shoes. It would break your heart to see his dealing, and the mourning of our people; they complain to me, and alas! I can do nothing for them. If I speak to him, he flies in my face as mutinous, and saith no complaints shall be heard or received but by himself, and saith they are froward and waspish, discontented people, and I do ill to hear them.

As for Mr. Weston, except grace do greatly sway him, he will hate us ten times more than ever he loved us, for not confirming the conditions. But now, since some pinches have taken them, they begin to revile the truth and say Mr. Robinson was in the fault who charged them never to consent to those conditions, nor choose me into office; but indeed appointed them to choose them they did choose. . . .

Four of five of the chief of them which came from Leyden, came resolved never to go on those conditions. And Mr. Martin, he said he never received money on those conditions; he was not beholden to the merchants for a pin, they were bloodsuckers, and I know not what. . . .

Friend, if ever we make a plantation, God works a miracle, especially considering how scant we shall be of victuals, and most of all ununited amongst ourselves and devoid of good tutors and regiment [discipline]. Violence will break all.

Your loving friend
Robert Cushman[13]

Things were in a sorry plight, even worse than Robinson had foreseen. He worried over the tangle of plans reported by Carver, Cushman, Martin, and Weston. It was a crazy-quilt pattern, what and how they were buying, trying to arrange for a transoceanic voyage, and operating on a shoestring.

After the vessel had been refitted they put to sea again. But when they had "gone again about 100 leagues without the Lands End" the *Speedwell's* Captain Reynolds compelled them to return to Plimoth. He had no stomach for the voyage, so he contrived to eliminate his ship by seeing that she was "overmasted and too much pressed with sails." This opened up her seams and made her leak.[14]

The vessels came about to Plimoth and crept into the Barbican. While the *Speedwell* was being inspected, passengers went ashore to forget their anxieties, see the streets and shops, and visit cautiously with the people. They found friends among the independent men of Devon who were sympathetic to their cause. Some invited them into their homes. The Island House, which still stands in the busy harbor, gave haven to a number of these strangers. They were "friendly entertained" by the Plimothians, who today still make much of this visit and have created numerous memorials in their honor.

Stung by the bitter disappointment over the *Speedwell,* they huddled in Plimoth, devouring their provisions, running up bills, and discussing endlessly what should be done. After these deliberations it was "resolved to dismiss her and part of the company, and proceed with the other ship. The which (though it was grievous and caused great discouragement) was put into execution."[15] Again, there were many sad partings.

Weary Robert Cushman and his family were among those who had to leave the *Mayflower* expedition, "whose heart and courage was gone from them before (as it seems) though his body was with them till now he departed." All this, Bradford continues, may have been God's providence for "after this he continued to be a special instrument for their good, and to do the offices of a loving friend and faithful brother unto them."[16] Of the twenty or so who went back, a number later reached Plimoth, including Deacon Cushman, Deacon Thomas Blossom, and their families.

So provisions were removed from the *Speedwell* and stowed, along with a passenger list of 102 and a crew of thirty or more, aboard the *Mayflower,* an old wine-carrying ship that had plowed the Mediterranean a good many years. Although aged and creaky,

"Departure of the Pilgrim Fathers"—painted by Bernard Gribble

the sturdy vessel was a "sweet ship." Due to her traffic in spirits, her hull was fairly well saturated with alcohol and this might have helped avert an epidemic on the crossing. The seepage from the wine barrels had soaked into the timbers and offered some resistance to bacteria.

The 180-ton *Mayflower,* loaded to the gunwales, crept out of Plimoth, Devon on September 16, 1620. Capt. Christopher Jones of Harwich, a veteran sea captain about fifty years of age and an able navigator faithful to his trust, was master of the ship.

The Pilgrims set sail before final terms could be worked out. On November 3, 1620 a Council of New England was chartered, a few days before the storm-tossed *Mayflower* dropped anchor off Cape Cod. This "Council established at Plimoth in the County of Devon for the planting, ruling, ordering and governing of New England in America" was given jurisdiction over the territory from Philadelphia to the Bay de Chaleur, from ocean to ocean. This term "New England" had first been used by Capt. John Smith in his *Description of New England* in 1616.

Foremost in John Robinson's thoughts as he labored in his study or stood in the pulpit of the Green Gate, was the welfare of the *Mayflower.* Would the Pilgrims perish from sickness as had Elder Francis Blackwell and his Amsterdam company on storm-tossed seas? Would they be massacred on arrival by the savages as many had been in Virginia? Would they simply be swallowed up in the vast void of the unknown as had been the fate of some heroic explorers?

He could only pray and wait, knowing that it might be months before a report could reach Leyden. He could not picture what his brilliant amanuensis, William Bradford, was experiencing and recording for posterity, later to be penned in the first great American book, *Of Plimoth Plantation.*

"The Sailing of the Mayflower from Plymouth"—painted by A. Forestier
Pilgrim Steps

All things stand upon them with a weatherbeaten face,
and the whole country, full of woods and thickets,
represented a wild and savage hue. . . . What could now
sustain them but the Spirit of God and His grace?
—William Bradford

18 "WHAT COULD NOW SUSTAIN THEM BUT THE SPIRIT OF GOD AND HIS GRACE?"

The *Mayflower* was a square-rigger, some ninety feet in length and twenty-six feet in breadth. She carried six elaborate sails and complicated rigging. She was armed with cannon and steered by a whipstaff attached to the tiller. There were high superstructures fore and aft which caused her to toss and roll like a cork. The crew lived forward in the forecastle near the galley, while the captain and mates were quartered at the stern.

The Pilgrims were a youthful company; only four were fifty years and over: William Brewster and his wife, Mary, John Carver, and James Chilton. All the rest were in their twenties and thirties, and thirty-four of the passengers were children.

It staggers the imagination to try to visualize how they all endured the long voyage, huddled into such limited space. Passengers were forced to live below the main deck in a low-ceilinged area called "tween decks." The diet consisted of hardtack, salt horse (salted meat), dried fish, cheese, dried beans and peas. Beer was their drink. The ship's galley cooked only for the crew. The Pilgrims prepared their own food on small braziers set in hearth boxes that were filled with sand to guard against stray sparks. Families cooked on a staggered schedule.[1] Sometimes they had oatmeal sweetened with molasses or a suet pudding. They slept on pallets on the floor.

Fierce storms shook the ship wickedly so that she sprang leaks, and one of her main beams at midship was bowed and cracked. When the crew panicked, the master called the officers together to face the emergency. On investigation they found her sound under water. One of the sailors located a great iron screw that had been brought along from Leyden, which may have come from Brewster's demolished Pilgrim Press. The screw lifted the beam and it was held in place by a post. The decks and upper areas of the hull were caulked and patched up and the vessel plowed slowly along.[2]

There were many days when the winds were so powerful and the seas so high that they were forced to lay to under short sail. During one blow John Howland, a servant of John Carver, was swept overboard, but he managed to catch hold of the topsail halyards and hang on until he was pulled back on deck.

The danger of diseases on the ship matched only the terrors without. Most of the passengers were desperately seasick. Anyone who has known a few days of acute mal de mer recoils at the

231

thought of being crowded for sixty-six days to one's elbows, trying to find a place to sit or lie, with clothing and food supplies piled about, with no refrigeration or sanitary facilities. In addition to these complications, there were children to care for in illness and to amuse when well. That men would take their wives, some pregnant, and their little ones on such a perilous and uncertain journey to a wild and savage country about which they knew nothing—if indeed they ever reached it at all—seems incredible.

The ship boasted a surgeon, Giles Heale, who later became a successful London practitioner. Deacon Samuel Fuller, the Pilgrim physician, was busy passing out lemon juice to prevent scurvy and other of his homemade remedies.

Most of the crew were kind to the pathetic voyagers, but one sailor derided them as "psalm singers." He ridiculed them in their seasickness, cursed them and hoped that he would have the pleasure of tossing half of them into the sea before the end of the journey. This profane chap died of a grievous disease and was the first one buried on the crossing. William Butten, a youthful servant of Samuel Fuller, passed away as they neared the coast of America.

There were times when the seas were calm and the passengers enjoyed some respite from seasickness, when they sang their psalms and ballads, and when the children could play blindman's buff or frolic with the mastiff and spaniel on board.

One moment of excitement was provided when an obstreperous boy threw a lighted squib toward a keg in which gunpowder was stored. If it had not been for the watchful eye of an adult, the ship might have been blown up at sea.

During the voyage a child was born. This may offer an insight into why they survived. With so many young on board there was a future and something to live for. Ill, hungry, miserable, and frightened as they were, this new birth must have sent a tremor of hope through the entire ship. Everyone without doubt, from the children to the roughest seaman, crept down "tween decks" at one time or another for a privileged peak at Oceanus Hopkins.

Their lilliputian bark, tossing in the vast ocean, battled overwhelming odds. Yet the staunch timbers of English oak, the resourcefulness of Capt. Christopher Jones, and the providence of the God in whom they trusted brought them to safe harbor. On November 19 they sighted the highland of Cape Cod.

The pale "prisoners" rushed to topside for a glimpse of the New World. Some knelt in prayer, others wept and embraced one another. They rejoiced that their arduous passage was ending. The land of their hopes lay ahead. On further thought, however, they were dismayed to hear from the crew that it was not Virginia, but some other area far to the north. Uncertainty about their whereabouts and their destination checked their first exuberance.

Master Jones, who had skippered the *Mayflower* for some twelve years, turned her to the south along the arm of Cape Cod that led to Chatham. The rough waters of Tucker's Terror caused him to turn north, where he came into Provincetown Harbor, Cape Cod on November 21, the sixty-sixth day at sea.

In their anger some of the sailors demanded that the captain dump the passengers on shore and turn back to England. Certain of the strangers said that when they got ashore they would do as they pleased because they were outside Virginia and therefore not subject to their charter. The general disorder and the threat of mutiny led the wiser Pilgrim heads to call a council. It was decided that a written document should be prepared in order that every person would know where he stood and that fair treatment would be extended to all, including the hired men, servants, and the humblest on board.[3]

Pastor Robinson's "Long Letter," which he had presented to them as they left Delfshaven, had been read and mulled over during the voyage. Its sound advice was studied and a number of its phrases and ideas concerning "a body politic" were incorporated in the Mayflower Compact. This document was drawn up and signed before any went ashore at Provincetown:

Map prepared by John Smith after his 1614 voyage to New England

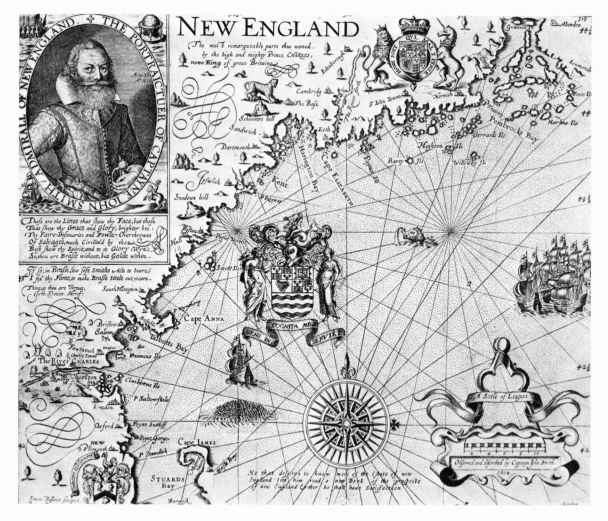

We whose names are underwritten, the loyal subjects of our dread Sovereign Lord King James, by the Grace of God of Great Britain, France and Ireland King, Defender of the Faith, etc.

Having undertaken, for the Glory of God and advancement of the Christian Faith and Honour of our King and Country, a Voyage to plant the First Colony in the Northern Parts of Virginia, do by these present solemnly and mutually in the presence of God and one of another, Covenant and Combine ourselves together into a Civil Body Politic, for our better ordering and preservation and furtherance of the ends aforesaid; and by virtue hereof to enact, constitute and frame such just and equal Laws, Ordinances, Acts, Constitutions and Offices, from time to time, as shall be thought most meet and convenient for the general good of the Colony, unto which we promise all due submission and obedience. In witness whereof we have hereunder subscribed our names at Cape Cod, the 11th of November, in the year of the reign of our Sovereign Lord King James, of England, France and Ireland the eighteenth, and of Scotland the fifty-fourth. Anno Domini 1620.[4]

Forty-one male passengers gathered in the cabin and signed the first political document to be drawn up in the New World. The signers were:

"The Signing of the Mayflower Compact"—painted by Percy Moran (early twentieth century)

John Carver
William Bradford
Edward Winslow
William Brewster
Isaac Allerton
Myles Standish
John Alden
Samuel Fuller
Christopher Martin
William Mullins
William White
Richard Warren
John Howland
Stephen Hopkins
Edward Tilley
John Tilley
Francis Cooke
Thomas Rogers
Thomas Tinker
John Rigdale
Edward Fuller

John Turner
Francis Eaton
James Chilton
John Crackston
John Billington
Moses Fletcher
John Goodman
Degory Priest
Thomas Williams
Gilbert Winslow
Edmund Margeson
Peter Brown
Richard Britteridge
George Soule
Richard Clarke
Richard Gardner
John Allerton
Thomas English
Edward Dotey
Edward Leister

This compact made Plimoth Plantation a self-governing colony under the aegis of faraway Whitehall. It emphasized the covenant concept of Robinson, through which the people pledged to submit themselves under God to the ordinances and offices and seek the good of their associates. The compact bound its signers to promote the common good and to yield obedience to the laws that their community would frame.[6]

This compact was to play a role in the development of American democracy. It repudiated the aristocratic system which exalted the privileges of the few and established a small community based on a signed, mutual agreement. Although loyal in name to their sovereign, they were an independent nucleus 3,000 miles away from the court, living and working together under no magistrate or priest appointed by their monarch. They did not wait for orders from London. In fact, they were afraid of controls and mandates that their highnesses the king and bishops might seek to impose on them. They set up their own plans and made their own decisions.

Brewster and Carver, who had been chosen by the vote of the people to serve as elder and governor, stepped from the ship's dory onto the shore of another continent. The soil beneath their feet was to support the first self-sustaining colony. From the small beginnings of this weary band a new nation was to evolve which would summon pilgrims from a hundred countries around the globe to a land of freedom.

Those who went ashore "fell upon their knees and blessed the God of heaven who had brought them over the vast and furious ocean, and delivered them from all the perils and miseries thereof, again to set their feet on the firm and stable earth, their proper element."[7]

While the shallop, or long boat, that had been carried in sections on the deck of the *Mayflower*, was assembled by the carpenters and sailors, a foot party set out to explore the windblown spit of land. When the shallop was launched they did a more thorough survey, visiting Truro, where they found a cache of Indian corn; Wellfleet, where they discovered black fish on the beach; and Eastham, where the first encounter with the Indians occurred. They considered several spots on the cape, but Robert Coppin, a crew member, mentioned a site across the bay named Plimoth by Capt. John Smith, which he had visited on a previous voyage and suggested that they cross over and investigate. On December 6, with a crew of ten Pilgrims and six seamen, including Robert Coppin and John Clark as pilots, they pushed on through icy winds from the shores of Cape Cod across the bay to Plimoth. Caught in the rain and snow in a rough sea, the rudder of the shallop broke, their mast snapped, and their sail fell into the tossing waves. They managed to make their way in the darkness of Friday evening, December 18, to a spot of land, where they scrambled ashore. They called it Clark's Island in honor of one of their pilots.

They built a fire in the shelter of a great rock where they dried and warmed themselves, spending Saturday and Sunday there. The sabbath dawned fair and sunny. They decided to rest and give thanks to God "for his mercies in their manifold deliverances." Crew members gathered in the lea of this miniature Gibraltar as Deacon Carver, no doubt, led them in prayer.[8] This simple service on an isolated island was a spontaneous reaction that revealed something unique about these men. In the midst of their exposure to hostile nature, cold, hungry, and groping their way anxiously, prodded by enveloping winter and the urgency of an immediate settlement, they took time out in their race with catastrophe to hold the first religious service on the shores of New England. The community of Duxbury has preserved this tradition and each year the event is reenacted.

On Monday they moved into the harbor of Plimoth, sounded the waters, and found them deep enough for shipping. They brought their shallop ashore on December 21. As they explored the land they found open fields that had been cultivated by the Indians, and "little running brooks" which assured them of good water. They decided that it was "a place fit for situation."

Returning to the *Mayflower* in Provincetown, they announced their decision. All arrived safe in Plimoth Harbor on December 26, 1620.

Within a few days they were chopping down the trees with their crude tools to make timbers and boards for the first common house. The village was laid out on rising land that ran from the harbor above the brook up to a high hill. On the hilltop they later erected their Fort Meeting House, on a commanding site where it could serve both as a church and a fortress for defense. Below the hill running down to the sea, along what is called Leyden Street today, they built their small English-style cottages, surrounding them with high cedar posts in the form of a stockade.

On landing they did not find habitation of any sort or see a

human being. It was not until March that they met the first local Indian. They were now on their own, facing a stark New England landscape, compelled to work desperately to initiate the building of their village.

Bradford recorded:

Being thus passed the vast ocean, and a sea of troubles before in their preparation (as may be remembered by that which went before), they had now no friends to welcome them nor inns to entertain or refresh their weatherbeaten bodies; no houses or much less towns to repair to, to seek for succour.

And for the season it was winter, and they that know the winters of that country know them to be sharp and violent, and subject to cruel and fierce storms, dangerous to travel to known places, much more to search an unknown coast. Besides, what could they see but a hideous and desolate wilderness, full of wild beasts and wild men—and what multitudes there might be of them they knew not. Neither could they, as it were, go up to the top of Pisgah to view from this wilderness a more goodly country to feed their hopes; for which way so-

"The Mayflower in Plymouth Harbor"—painted by William Halsall (nineteenth century)

237

ever they turned their eyes (save upward to the heavens) they could have little solace or content in respect of any outward objects. For summer being done, all things stand upon them with a weather-beaten face, and the whole country, full of woods and thickets, represented a wild and savage hue. If they looked behind them, there was a mighty ocean which they had passed and was now as a main bar and gulf to separate them from all the civil parts of the world. . . .

What could now sustain them but the Spirit of God and His grace? May not and ought now the children of these fathers rightly say: "Our fathers were Englishmen which came over this great ocean, and were ready to perish in this wilderness; but they cried unto the Lord, and He heard their voice and looked on their adversity"?[9]

Fortunately the *Mayflower* remained in the harbor all winter. Passengers lived aboard, moving away from the dismal hull as soon as shelters on shore were available. Soon the Great Sickness set in, and one half of their company perished.

"The Landing of the Pilgrims"—painted by Sargent (c. 1820)

But that which was most sad and lamentable was, that in two or three months' time half of their company died, especially in January and February, being the depth of Winter, and wanting houses and other comforts; being infected with the scurvy and other diseases which their inaccommodate condition had brought upon them. So as there died some times two or three of a day in the foresaid time, that of 100 and odd persons, scarce fifty remained.

And of these, in the time of most distress, there was but six or seven persons who to their great commendations, be it spoken, spared no pains night nor day, but with abundance of toil and hazards to their own health, fetched them wood, made them fires, dressed them meat, made their beds, washed their loathsome clothes, clothed and unclothed them. In a word, did all the homely and necessary offices for them which dainty and queasy stomachs cannot endure to hear named; and all this willingly and cheerfully, without any grudging in the least, showing herein their true love unto their friends and brethren; a rare example and worthy to be remembered.[10]

Captain Jones himself was stricken with the Great Sickness and although he had lost almost half of his crew, he dispatched a message to the governor and those who were sick on shore that they should send to him for beer for those who had need of it, even though he had to drink water on the homeward voyage.

The bitter winds swept about the *Mayflower* anchored a mile and a half off shore, and around the frail cottages, whipping their icy breath through the cracks in the single walls. The houses were built out of upright boards around a wattle and daub fireplace and roofed with thatch cut in the nearby marsh. When at last the cold was forced to retreat before the spring sun, only one half of the colony was still alive. Four entire families had been wiped out. Only three married couples were left. Only five out of eighteen wives survived. The record shows that parents sacrificed for their children. Youth were the principal survivors, and the colony, which was a young company on landing, was now even more youthful.

The epidemic had left them depleted, but the survivors rallied quickly. They gathered the orphans into their houses, welcoming them as their own. Widows and widowers remarried. Realistically they closed ranks, tightened their belts, and faced the tasks at hand.

One day in March 1621 an Abnaki Indian appeared in the village announcing, "I am Samoset." He had learned some English from British seamen off Newfoundland. He brought with him Squanto, a local Patuxet Indian, whose people had been wiped out a few years before in a deadly epidemic that swept New England. Squanto became their interpreter and tutor. He taught them where to hunt and fish, where to gather clams, nuts and berries, how to catch the alewives and bury them three to a hill around the maize for fertilizer with their heads turned in about the corn and their tails fanning out. He warned them to stand guard with their matchlock muskets to keep the wolves from digging up the fish and the crows from eating the corn. When he told them about the time for planting corn, he did not say during a certain full moon after the spring solstice. He gave them a time that they would always remember: when the leaves on the oak tree were the size of a squirrel's ears.

Massasoit, grand sachem of the Wampanoag Indians, was brought for a state visit. He became fond of the Pilgrims and agreed to the following treaty which was kept for fifty-five years:

1. That neither he nor any of his should injure or do hurt to any of their people.
2. That if any of his did hurt to any of theirs, he should send the offender, that they might punish him.
3. That if anything were taken away from any of theirs, he should cause it to be restored; and they should do the like to his.
4. If any did unjustly war against him, they would aid him: if any did war against them he should aid them.
5. He should send to his neighbours confederates to certify them of this, that they might not wrong them, but might be likewise comprised in the conditions of peace.
6. That when their men came to them, they should leave their bows and arrows behind them.[11] [They would do likewise.]

Massasoit and his Wampanoags were agricultural Indians and relatively peace loving. In contrast with the hostility of the red men in Virginia, they furnished the Pilgrims with food, visited in their homes, and some came and set up camp outside the village palisade.

The fifty-one survivors took heart as the snowdrifts melted into the landscape, as the buds peeped out on the willows and maples, and the shadbush burst into bloom. They swept and aired their houses, washed their clothes in the brook, pushed ahead with their building program, and prepared the land for their first planting.

They all gathered at the harbor in mid-April to bid farewell to Captain Jones and the *Mayflower* and what remained of his crew. Thankful as they had been to leave her for terra firma, she had been their only home and shelter since they sailed from England. It was a wrench to see their last tangible security departing. Many, no doubt, felt that they would rather risk death in the wilderness than repeat the terrible voyage. Nevertheless, it is something to ponder that not even one chose to return. They watched her until her masts dipped for the last time and vanished from their sight.[12]

Deacon John Carver had been elected governor after the signing of the compact aboard the *Mayflower*. But this able brother-in-law of Robinson died in April 1621, soon after the ship turned back to England. He collapsed in the field while planting corn.

"Massasoit"—a statue by Dallin

240

His wife, Catherine White, sister of Bridget Robinson, died "within five or six weeks after him."

William Bradford was chosen to take Carver's place. Under the direction of the thirty-one-year-old governor the people sowed the seed they had brought with them from England and the corn and beans supplied by the Indians.

In the autumn they gathered in their first harvest. Some twenty acres of corn laid out by Squanto brought a rewarding crop, but their six or seven acres of English barley, wheat, and peas disappointed them. They cut and shocked the maize, tied up their grain, and stored the pumpkins, dried peas, and beans in the Common House. Now they could look about them with a gathering sense of security. Their village included some seven dwellings, with others still in the building. The good earth had blessed them. They set apart a time for thanksgiving. Their Indian friends were invited, and ninety of them arrived with their chief, Massasoit. The Indians brought deer they had killed with their bows and arrows, while the Pilgrims furnished geese, ducks, and turkey brought down by their matchlocks.

They spread rough tables with a tempting array of these meats, along with lobster, clams, fish, eels, beans, pumpkin, salads of leeks and water cress, corn cakes, Indian pudding sweetened with wild honey, grapes, plums, and red and white wine made from wild grapes.

The festivities, which lasted three days and involved sports and contests, cemented the ties of friendship between the Wampanoags and the white men.

The first letter from Master Robinson to the plantation was delivered by Deacon Robert Cushman, who had pulled himself together and crossed over on the *Fortune*, which arrived at Plimoth on November 11, 1621 with thirty-five additional settlers. The pastor expressed his sorrow over the tragic losses of the first winter, and promised that he would come to Plimoth just as soon as he could, and with as many friends as possible.

Thomas Weston of the Adventurers wrote, condemning them for sending the *Mayflower* back without any cargo to serve as payment on their debts.

Bradford sent a spunky retort to Weston and the Adventurers in their comfortable London quarters, pointing out that during the winter so many died that they were scarcely able to keep up with the burials. Those who survived were too weak and exhausted to load the ship before she left in early April 1621. It was utterly false that they spent their time arguing and palavering. It was a calamity that they were tied up with people in England who would abuse them in this manner.[13]

Weston also sent the agreement from the London Adventurers which the Pilgrims had left in England without signing. At length, under pressure from Cushman, who preached them a sermon on "The Danger of Self Love," they reluctantly signed what they felt

"William Bradford"—a statue by Dallin

241

was a grossly unfair contract. However, Weston added one cheerful note, reporting that a new charter for the colony had been secured. This was the Peirce patent which took the place of the first one granted by the Virginia Company. They now felt on firmer ground. This patent is on exhibit in Pilgrim Hall, Plimoth.

The Pilgrims plunged into the job of making the first payment on their debt. They loaded the *Fortune* with beaver and otter skins, clapboards and other timber estimated to be worth £500. It was a good and honorable start. The ship set sail with Cushman and the signed agreement, only to be captured by French privateers and stripped of her cargo. Robbed of clothing and shoes and even their ship's anchor and sails, the *Fortune's* company crept up the Thames in pathetic condition. Cushman had nothing to present to Weston except the sharp letter that Bradford had penned defending the honor of the decimated colony.

Shortly after, Thomas Weston sent over a fishing ship, the *Sparrow*, as his own private business venture. Unexpectedly it put into Plimoth with letters from Leyden and England, "but [with] no victuals, nor any hope of any." There were the usual "tedious and impertinent" missiles from Weston. The settlers now realized that the Adventurers were determined to keep Robinson from coming over. He was considered too critical of the status quo. He had long been under the suspicion of King James as the prime mover in the illegal departure from Holland and as a

"The First Thanksgiving"—painted by Jennie Brownscombe

heretical intellectual. As a group of businessmen they did not want to offend their monarch. It would be wiser to block Robinson's passage and find some safer minister to send to Plimoth.

The first harvests were meager and the settlers were still hounded by hunger, at one time subsisting on five grains of maize a day together with the clams that they picked up on the shore. They longed to have "their hungry bellies filled." Nevertheless, they took Weston's crew into their crowded cottages and fed them for weeks out of their sparse rations until they moved to the north to build the town of Wessagusset, now Weymouth. Deacon Cushman had warned the Pilgrims that this crowd "were no men for us." These improvidents "made havoc with their provisions," sold their blankets and clothing to the Indians in exchange for food, and stole and looted the buried provisions of the Massachusetts tribe. During the resulting crisis Captain Standish was dispatched to Wessagusset.

On this expedition, Standish and his men killed a number of Indians. When Robinson heard of it, he wrote December 19, 1623, condemning their action. He warned that "where blood is once shed, it is seldom staunched a long time after." He suggested that Captain Standish restrain himself and others in time of provocation lest they become militaristic and "affect a kind of ruffling course in the world."[14] He mentioned at the beginning and end of the letter his and Bridget's anxiety about when they were to get over.

The *Anne* and the *Little James* sailed into Plimoth Bay in the summer of 1623 with some ninety new settlers. There were letters from the pastor, but he was not on board. Arrivals on the *Anne* were shocked when they saw the settlers

> for they were in a very low condition; many were ragged in apparel and some little better than half naked. . . . The best dish they could present their friends with was a lobster or a piece of fish without bread or anything else but a cup of fair spring water.[15]

For weeks no rain fell. The crops were drying up in the fields. The governor called for a day of prayer. The settlers gathered in the Fort Meeting House to pour out their petitions. The Indians, who likewise were fearful, congregated outside and lifted their prayers to the Great Spirit. For eight long hours the people called upon the Deity.

As they left the Fort Meeting House, they noticed that there were flecks of clouds in the sky. These soon gathered and a gentle rain started to fall, which "distilled such soft, sweet and moderate showers . . . as it was hard to say whether the corn or our drooping affections were the most quickened and revived."[16] The corn, barley, beans, and pumpkins lifted their wilted leaves, stood straight, and flourished. This dramatic relief stirred the gratitude of the settlers and a second thanksgiving was held in 1623 with a gathering in the new Fort Meeting House.

The plantation economy was built on the labor of its own people, and all were required to work. The basic philosophy of

243

"a calling" stressed the duty of each individual to play his part and work with his own hands. Pastor Robinson had said, "He that without his own labor either of body or mind, eats the labor of other mens' hands only, and lives by their sweat, is but like lice, and such other vermin."[17] These strong words on individual initiative and responsibility impressed William Bradford, and are reflected in the record of his behavior in condemning the loiterers at the plantation in the early days.

> On the day called Christmas Day [he] called them [the planta-tion planters] out to work as was used [usual]. But the most of this new Company excused themselves and said it went against their consciences to work on that day. So the governor told them that if they made it a matter of conscience, he would spare them till they were better informed; so he led away the rest and left them. But when they came home at noon from their work, he found them in the street at play, openly; some pitching the bar, and some at stool-ball and such like sports. So he went to them and took away their implements and told them that was against his conscience, that they should play and others work. If they made the keeping of it a matter of devotion, let them keep to their houses; but there should be no gaming or reveling in the streets. Since which time nothing hast been attempted that way, at least openly.[18]

The sternness of the young governor has often been used as evidence that the Pilgrims frowned on pleasure. Bradford's reac-tion was not due to the Puritan tendency to suppress the revelry and excesses of Christmas, but rather to condemn indolence and indifference to community obligation. Planting and cultivating the soil was a serious business, along with fishing, hunting, felling trees, and house-building. There were so many imperative tasks confronting the colony that there was no time for frivolity. The governor was properly indignant at the dawdling attitude of cer-tain settlers, who, no doubt, had provoked the impatience of the leaders on previous occasions when there were critical enterprises to be performed.

The communal system set up by the Adventurers proved a fiasco. The young men did not want to work for the wives and children of the older men. The good worker received no more than the poor worker. The wife disliked washing clothes and dressing meat for others outside her home. The idea of all to have alike and do alike led to discontent and confusion. So in 1623 Bradford and his assistants decided to assign every family a parcel of land to cultivate on their own. The new system was an immediate success. Even the women and children went into the fields to plant and reap. Thus private enterprise initiated a new era.[19]

The "answerable courage" of the Pilgrims carried them through the first months of plague and famine and at the end of three years of testing they were able to "stand on their own legs," as Weston had challenged.

In March 1624 the *Charity* appeared in Plimoth carrying "three heifers and a bull" and the Rev. John Lyford, who had been brought over as a trial minister. He proved an abysmal failure. He shook the plantation with his intrigues and the libelous letters he was sending back to England. When brought before the court he burst into tears and confessed that he was a reprobate. The court censured him "to be expelled from the place," though his wife and family had liberty to stay until he could make provision to remove them comfortably. Lyford's wife revealed that her husband "had a bastard by another before they were married." After their marriage "she could keep no maids but he would be meddling with them; and some times she had taken him in the manner as they lay at their bed's feet." The "carpet bagger" left for Virginia.

It was now clear to both Leyden and the plantation that a faction among the Adventurers strongly opposed the passage of Robinson. The *Charity* had brought messages from their pastor. He wrote: "Our hopes of coming unto you be small and weaker than ever. The Adventurers deny it to be a part of the covenants betwixt us that they should transport us."[20]

During the long wait for his arrival the sacraments had not been celebrated in the Fort Meeting House at Plimoth Plantation. Elder Brewster, the deacons, and other laymen carried on the life of the church as best they could. The congregation suggested to the elder that he write Robinson and ask if he considered it proper for Brewster to administer the sacraments. So at the close of his letter the pastor answered:

> Now, touching the question propounded by you, I judge it not lawful for you (being a ruling Elder, as Romans XII. 7 and 8, and I Timothy V.17 opposed to the Elders that teach and exhort and labour in the Word and doctrine, to which the sacraments are annexed), to administer them. Whether any learned man will come unto you or not, I know not; if any do, you must *consilium capere in arena.*[21]

> Be you most heartily saluted, and your wife with you, both from me and mine. Your God and ours, and the God of all His, bring us together if it be His will, and keep us in the meanwhile, and always to His glory, and make us serviceable to His Majesty, and faithful to the end. Amen.
>
> Your very loving brother,
John Robinson[22]

Leyden, December 20, 1623

On first thought it appears unreasonable for Robinson to deny the sacramental privileges to his faithful elder who had been his confidant for nearly twenty years. In spite of the high qualifications of Brewster, the exigencies of the situation, the separation of an ocean, he stuck by his principle that only a duly ordained minister could perform these rites. And to be ordained, a man must be qualified not only in character but also education. John Robinson was a stickler for thorough academic preparation. One has to remember here that a prime factor in Robinson's and in the entire Puritan crusade was to rid the Church of England of "dumb dogs," that is, its untrained and unqualified preachers. To surrender this standard would be a dangerous precedent. Cer-

tainly he did not hold back on this sanction of Brewster because he was jealous of his post. He had told the departing company at Delfshaven that they should feel free to choose a pastor because the congregation with two leaders could only be stronger.

The Pilgrims faced a long-time struggle to secure a pastor worthy to follow in Robinson's footsteps. They made the best of their situation without him. He was still their minister although 3,000 miles away, and they were part of his congregation. However, Brewster, Carver (while he lived), and Fuller had taken over, conducting worship, Bible study, and religious discussions, aided by Bradford and other laymen. For over three years the laymen had run the church in Plimoth without an ordained leader, and they were destined to carry the load for six additional years.

Each sabbath morning the settlers heard the beat of a drum that summoned them to the Fort Meeting House on the hill. They hurried into their best garments, gathered their little ones about them, and moved out into the street to join their neighbors. The broad way was alive with voluminous skirts and jackets of bright color, gathered around Captain Standish in his turkey-red cape.

"Pilgrims Going to Church"—painted by George H. Boughton

Some carried Geneva Bibles, others muskets and infants who could not manage the steep climb. Their three leaders—the Elder with his Bible, the governor in a long robe, and the captain with his side arms and a small cane in his hand—followed the drummer and marched ahead three abreast.[23]

It was a moment of uplift, the gathering of the village on this special day set apart from labor in forest and field, a time for remembering their heritage of faith. It was no humdrum chore to make their way to the hilltop each Sunday morning and afternoon, but rather a time of release and anticipation as they journeyed from their world of drudgery to their humble sanctuary in the wilderness.

The *Charity* had also brought over a list of objections from the Adventurers regarding management of the plantation. Bradford and his associates made their defense to the accusations as follows:

1st objection was diversity about religion. *Answer*: We know no such matter, for here was never any controversy or opposi-

247

tion, either public or private (to our knowledge) since we came.

2nd obj.: Neglect of family duties on the Lord's Day. *Ans.*: We allow no such thing. . . . We are conscientious and should not be falsely slandered behind our backs.

3rd obj.: Want of both the sacraments. *Ans.*: The more is our grief, that our pastor is kept from us, by whom we might enjoy them; for we used to have the Lord's Supper every Sabbath, and baptism as often as there was occasion of children to baptize.

4th obj.: Children not catechised nor taught to read. *Ans.*: Neither is true, for divers take pains with their own as they can. Indeed, we have no common school for want of a fit person, or hitherto means to maintain one; though we desire now to begin.

5th obj.: Many of the Particular members of the plantation will not work for the General. *Ans.*: This also is not wholly true, for though some do it not willingly and others not honestly, yet all do it; and he that doth worst gets his food and something besides. [This was the natural resentment against the communal system that the Adventurers set up.]

6th obj.: The water is not wholesome. *Ans.*: If they mean, not so wholesome as the good beer and wine in London (which they so dearly love), we will not dispute with them; but else for water it is as good as any in the world.

7th obj.: The ground is barren and doth bear no grass. *Ans.*: It is here, as in all places, some better and some worse; and if they well consider their woods in England, they shall not find such grass in them as in their fields and meadows. The cattle find grass, for they are as fat as need be. There is enough to support a hundred times as many as we now have.

8th obj.: The fish will not take salt to keep sweet. *Ans.*: This is as true as that which was written, that there is scarce a fowl to be seen or a fish to be taken. Things likely to be true in a country where so many sail of ships come yearly a-fishing? They might as well say there can no ale or beer in London be kept from souring. . . .

12th obj.: The people are much annoyed with mosquitoes. *Ans.*: They are too delicate and unfit to begin new plantations and colonies that cannot endure the biting of a mosquito. We would wish such to keep at home till at least they be mosquito-proof. Yet this place is as free as any, and experience teacheth that the more the land is tilled, and the woods cut down, the fewer there will be, and in the end scarce any at all.[24]

This constant prodding from London would try the patience of Job. This splinter faction of the Adventurers was becoming as inquisitorial as the bishops. They were checking every detail on ecology, home life, religion, and even mosquitoes!

False reports had reached the London Adventurers about the plantation circulated by Lyford and others. They roundly berated the planters, writing:

You are Brownists, condemning all other churches and persons but yourselves and those in your way, and you are contentious, cruel, and hard-hearted among your neighbors and towards such as in all points, both civil and religious, jump not with you.

The planters were reported to be "negligent, careless, wasteful, and unthrifty." They permitted "their affairs to go at sixes and sevens." They passed their time in idleness "and talking and conferring, and care not what be wasted, worn, and torn out."

The Adventurers reveled in their pious admonitions: "Walk close to God." Dwell in love "without secret whisperings and undermining one of another." "Pluck up your spirits and quit yourselves like men."[25]

It was too much even for Bradford's facile pen to pour out a rebuttal. Were they to be tormented forever by these libelous gossipers?

The Adventurers laid down the law—Robinson and the rest of his church could not go over to the plantation unless he and they recanted and reconciled themselves to the Church of England. This harsh mandate did not intimidate Robinson and the Pilgrims. His reply forms one of history's most courageous statements on the folly of religious persecution. In spite of their insecure toehold in Plimoth, their lack of funds and supplies, and their desperate need of passage money to bring over the balance of their company from Leyden, the Pilgrims stood firm and Robinson from Leyden penned his flat refusal which concluded:

> It is too great arrogancy for any man or church to think that he or they have so sounded the Word of God to the bottom, as precisely to set down the church's discipline without errour in substance or circumstance, as that no other without blame may digress or differ in anything from the same.[26]

Deacon Cushman stuck with his job of negotiating with the Adventurers and finally persuaded a handful of them to carry on with the understanding that the planters would ship every valuable they could collect as immediate payment on their debt which then stood at £1,800 or about $90,000. They had no other choice but to continue. They were utterly dependent for supplies even though the interest rates were outrageous.

So the *Charity* was packed with fish and the *Little James* in her tow was loaded with furs. During a gale in the English Channel the captain was forced to cut the *Little James* loose. She was captured by Barbary Coast pirates, her cargo seized, and her crew sold as slaves in Morocco. Capt. Myles Standish was aboard the *Charity*, returning to the homeland to see what he could do to protect the colonists from the Adventurers. He arrived barehanded, without the intended second payment, and therefore was in a poor position to negotiate. The hard-working and honor-motivated Pilgrims were forced to face another blow of fate.

Captain Standish found London ravaged by the plague; the influential people he had hoped to interview had fled to the country. He remained several months, but accomplished little.

249

Nor did he have enough money to pay a visit to Leyden. He managed "with much adoe" to borrow £150 at 50 percent interest and to return to New England by way of Maine.

Not all the visitors to Plimoth Plantation were troublemakers like Lyford and Weston's men.

John Pory, the secretary of the Virginia Colony, stopped by in January 1622 on his way back to England. A Cambridge graduate, author, and member of Parliament, he enjoyed Plimoth and wrote about its possibilities. On his return to London, Pory sent a letter to Bradford and Brewster thanking them for the gift of some books by Robinson and Ainsworth. These "jewels" were enjoyed as light reading on the homeward voyage by an Anglican who was eager to know more about the Separatists' ideas.[27]

Capt. Emmanuel Altham of the *Little James*, who was one of the Adventurers, came in August 1623 and penned a report on the plantation, which then boasted about twenty houses built on both sides of a wide street that led to the fort, all surrounded by a high fence. He spoke of the goats, hogs, pigs, and hens. He gave a lively description of William Bradford's wedding. Having lost his wife, Dorothy, soon after the landing in Provincetown he married Alice, the widow of Edward Southworth. Altham's record makes it clear that there were merry moments at Plimoth and that the Pilgrims knew how to have a good time. Massasoit came to the marriage with his queen, one of his five wives, along with four other chiefs and 120 men with their bows and arrows. They were greeted on arrival with a salute from the matchlock muskets, and then the bows and arrows were safely checked in the governor's house. The red men brought along four bucks and a turkey.

After the civil ceremony, conducted by the governor's assistant, all plunged into the feast of tasty venison, roasted turkey and other delicacies with homemade wine, along with grapes, plums, and nuts.[28] Captain Altham was impressed by the good cheer of the plantation festivity.

Isaac de Rasieres, secretary of the New Amsterdam colony in New York, wrote Governor Bradford on March 9, 1627, congratulating him on the success of the colony. He advocated a covenant of friendship against their common enemy, the Spanish, and suggested that they get together and talk about trade in beaver and otter and in Dutch goods. Bradford replied in Dutch, saying that the people of Plimoth would always be thankful to his people, would never forget them, and they wanted New Amsterdam to prosper. He asked what they would pay for furs and what they had to trade.

When De Rasieres, in his sloop, reached the trading post, Aptucxet on Cape Cod, he crossed the portage on foot and then sent a message to Plimoth that he had not walked that "far this three or four years, wherefore I fear my feet will fail me." Whereupon the governor dispatched the shallop to bring him up from the Scusset River. All of Plimoth was on hand to welcome the distinguished Dutchman. He was greeted in his own tongue and feasted royally. He brought gifts with him: wool, linen, and sugar, which was a scarce luxury item.[29] The portly burgher, while sampling the venison, turkey, and wine, sold the plantation £50 of wampum.

Some settlers felt sure that they had been taken by the jovial salesman. They had never heard of wampum, the shell money made by Indians to the south, which the Dutchman convinced them would work magic in their trading with the Indians. It was made out of the hard-shell clam or quahaug and the shells of sea snails, polished and formed into beads, producing strings of white and purple. Called *wampumpeag*, it proved to be the currency that became popular with the natives in the colony. Plimoth copied the product and for a time maintained a monopoly, so that their Hollander did them a good turn after all.

De Rasieres wrote with Dutch thoroughness a description of the plantation as it appeared in 1627:

The houses were constructed of clapboards with gardens also enclosed behind and at the sides with clapboards, so that their houses and courtyards are arranged in very good order, with a stockade against sudden attack; and at the ends of the streets there are three wooden gates. In the center, on the cross street, stands the Governor's house, before which is a square stockade upon which four patereros [small cannon] are mounted, so as to enfilade the streets. Upon the hill they have a large square house, with a flat roof, built of thick sawn planks stayed with oak beams, upon the top of which they have six cannon, which shoot iron balls of four and five pounds, and command the surrounding country. The lower part they use for their church, where they preach on Sundays and the usual holidays.[30]

But they gathered up their spirits,
and the Lord helped them, whose work they
had in hand.
—William Bradford

19 "THEY GATHERED UP THEIR SPIRITS"

A goodly number of Puritans in England had been following with interest the progress of the Pilgrim colony in America. Some were disturbed over the rumors that circulated. They were the old, hackneyed barkings, initiated by Lyford and others of his stripe, by certain of the Adventurers who were prejudiced against them, and by their chronic enemies in England. Such people repeated the same complaints over and over.

Edward Winslow took it upon himself to write his *Briefe Narration* in an effort to clear up these charges.

First, he denied that the foundation of their plantation had been laid on schism and division.[1] Instead it had been built on love and peace, and the Leyden church was characterized by mutual concern by all its members for one another. Indeed, there had rarely been such a peaceful fellowship. Their objective was to emulate the pattern of the early church, and not to follow any one Christian leader such as Luther, Calvin, Knox, Ainsworth, Robinson, or Ames. They were unifiers who tried to bring people together around the teachings of Jesus and his apostles.[2] Bradford added his support to this view in his *Dialogue*.[3]

Second, Winslow tackled the charge that the Leyden-Plimoth congregation was made up of "schismatics, Brownists and rigid Separatists." He said he had lived in Leyden under Robinson's leadership for three years and knew that he was firm against separation from any of the churches of Christ, professing and holding communion with the French, Dutch, and Scottish churches. He had urged people to be wary in separating and to leave a church only when the spirit of Christ had departed wholly from it, and then not to practice hatred, but rather to seek to improve it.

Winslow could be justifiably proud of his leader's championship of unity. The outreach of Christian fellowship practiced by Robinson is an evidence of brotherhood unusual for the seventeenth century. Those who have attended international assemblies in our own ecumenical era are familiar with the practice of some church bodies who "withdraw" for their own private celebration whenever a universal communion service is planned.

The Leyden fellowship was cosmopolitan in makeup. Seven national groups were represented: Welsh, Anglican, Scottish, Walloon, French, Huguenot, and Dutch. This afforded a broad base for interdenominational and international thinking and created a laboratory where the ecumenical outlook was a reality and not an enterprise of words. Green Gate members were free to worship in the Netherlands churches.

There was intercommunion also with the French churches, with the Walloons and the Huguenots, from whom they heard reports of heroic resistance on the continent against religious tyranny. A number from this Walloon-Huguenot tradition moved on to Plimoth. The Green Gate community even practiced their friendly relationship with the Presbyterians of Scotland. The controversial Scot, the Rev. David Calderwood, visited Leyden in 1619 while the Pilgrim Press was printing his *The Perth Assembly.* He came several times to hear Mr. Robinson. On one sabbath the group was celebrating the Lord's Supper following the sermon. The Scot stood up and asked if he might stay and observe their commemoration. Robinson replied, "You may not only stay to behold us, but partake with us, if you please, for we acknowledge the Churches of Scotland to be the Churches of Christ." Winslow insisted that the Leyden Congregationalists were on friendly terms with the Presbyterians, and he hoped all critics to the contrary would be ignored.[4]

Winslow said of Robinson that "his study was peace and union so far as might agree with faith and a good conscience: and for schism and division, there was nothing in the world more hateful to him."[5]

He clinched his argument with a dramatic portrayal of the farewell at Delfshaven, where the pastor exhorted his departing flock to reach beyond the traditional limitations of Lutheranism and Calvinism, and to seek the expanding revelation of God, ever realizing that there was "more light and truth yet to break forth from God's holy word."[6]

At that time he also told them to avoid and shake off the label of Brownist, which had become a nickname that made religion odious. He said that he would be glad if some good minister would go over to the New World with them or come to them before he made it. He asked them to cooperate with the godly party in the English kingdom, study union rather than division, and strive to draw closer to them.

Third, Winslow contradicted the charge that the Pilgrims would not permit people who differed from them to reside among them. As to the Presbyterians, who "differ so little from us," he said, "our practice witnesseth the contrary." He mentioned the Presbyterians in Newbury, Massachusetts, with whom they "never had the least molestation or disturbance," and who were respected as fully as followers of the Congregational Way. Some of the Presbyterians in Scotland wrote Plimoth, asking if "they might be suffered to exercise their Presbyterial government amongst us. It was answered affirmatively that they might." They sent over a representative to secure a place for a settlement. The plantation welcomed him and the leaders showed him land near Ipswich and Newbury and offered help in establishing the colony.

As to the treatment of Anabaptists at Plimoth, he answered:

'Tis true, we have a severe law, but we never did or will execute the rigour of it upon any, and have men living amongst us, nay some in our Churches of that judgment, and as long as they carry themselves peaceably as hitherto they do, we will leave them to God, ourselves having performed the duty of brethren to them.[7]

Winslow and Bradford were skillful with words and made a creditable defense of the much-maligned Pilgrims. They had other friends also, like John Cotton of the two Bostons, who wielded wide influence among Puritan intellectuals and among the builders of New England. He had watched Robinson's experiment in Leyden from a distance, and conferred with those who had shared in the Leyden fellowship. He also observed firsthand the life of Plimoth Plantation, and agreed with Bradford and Winslow in their account of why the Pilgrims made the move to the New World: "For the church at Leyden was in peace, and free from any division, when they took up thoughts of transporting themselves into America with common consent." To use their own words: "Though they did quietly and sweetly enjoy their Christian and church liberties under the States [Holland], yet they foresaw Holland would be no place for their church, and their posterity to continue there comfortably."[8]

When Capt. Myles Standish returned to Plimoth in 1626 from his voyage to England, he brought disheartening news from the Adventurers and this letter from Roger White, the pastor's brother-in-law in Leyden, announcing Robinson's death:

Loving and kind friends,
    I know not whether this will ever come to your hands or miscarry, as other of my letters have done. Yet in regard of the Lord's dealing with us here, I have had a great desire to write unto you. Knowing your desire to bear a part with us, both in our joys and sorrows, as we do with you. These are therefore to give you to understand that it hath pleased the Lord to take out of this vale of tears, your and our loving and faithful Pastor and my dear and Reverend brother, Mr. John Robinson, who was sick some eight days. He began to be sick on Saturday in the morning, yet the next day, being the Lord's Day, he taught us twice. And so the week after grew weaker, every day more than other; yet he felt no pain, but weakness all the time of his sickness. The physic he took wrought kindly in man's judgment, but he grew weaker every day, feeling little or no pain, and sensible to the very last. He fell sick the 22 of February and departed this life the 1 of March. He had a continual inward ague, but free from infection, so that all his friends came freely to him. And if either prayers, tears or means would have saved his life, he had not gone hence. But he having faithfully finished his course and performed his work which the Lord had appointed him here to do, he now resteth with the Lord in eternal happiness.
    We wanting him and all church governors, yet we still by the mercy of God continue and hold close together in peace and quietness; and so hope we shall do, though we be very

weak. Wishing (if such were the will of God) that you and we were again united together in one, either there or here. But seeing it is the will of the Lord thus to dispose of things, we must labour with patience to rest contented till it please the Lord otherwise to dispose.

For news here is not much, only as in England we have lost our old King James, who departed this life about a month ago; so here they have lost the old prince, Grave Maurice. Who both departed this life since my brother Robinson, and as in England we have a new King, Charles, of whom there is great hope; so here they have made Prince Hendrick general in his brother's place, etc. Thus with my love remembered, I take leave and rest.

Leyden, April 28   Your assured loving friend,
Anno 1625   Roger White[9]

Captain Standish had carried with him, as he went to England, letters to the Leyden fellowship, inquiring when more of them would be migrating to Massachusetts and expressing the desire to welcome Pastor Robinson very soon. Leaders of the Leyden congregation wrote this reply, sending it by way of Standish in London:

Most dear Christian Friends and Brethren, as it is no small grief unto you, so is it no less unto us, that we are constrained to live thus disunited each from other, especially considering our affections each unto other, for the mutual edifying and comfort of both in these evil days wherein we live, if it pleased the Lord to bring us again together. . . . Although we cannot answer your desire and expectation, by reason it hath pleased the Lord to take to himself out of this miserable world our dearly beloved Pastor, yet for ourselves we are minded as formerly to come unto you, when, and as, the Lord affordeth means; though we see little hope thereof at present as being unable of ourselves; and that our friends will help us, we see little hope. . . . In the meantime, we commit you unto him . . . in all his ways according to that his Word, and to bless all our lawful endeavors for the glory of his name and the good of his people.

Your assured and loving friends
And brethren in the Lord,
Francis Jessop
Thomas Nash
Thomas Blossom
Roger White
Richard Maisterson[10]
Leyden, November 30, A.D. 1625

Their pastor died March 1, 1625. King James I passed away March 27 in the same year. Their noblest friend and their implacable enemy "left this world near about one time. Death makes no difference." Standish also brought word of the passing of Deacon Robert Cushman.

Bradford records the epochal loss to Plimoth Plantation in the denial of their five-year hope, sustained through many reverses, that Pastor Robinson would come to Plimoth:

> It is a marvel it did not wholly discourage them and sink them. But they gathered up their spirits, and the Lord so helped them, whose work they had in hand, as now when they were at lowest [ebb] they began to rise again, and being stripped in a manner of all human helps and hopes, He brought things about otherwise, in His divine providence as they were not only upheld and sustained, but their proceedings both honoured and imitated by others. As by the sequel will more appear, if the Lord spare me life and time to declare the same.[11]

John Robinson was laid at rest March 4, 1625 in St. Peter's Church close to the Green Gate complex, in the vast quiet where he had often meditated, the chief church of his Dutch Reformed brethren with whom he had developed a close friendship.

The records of Pieterskerk state: "*4 Maart Jan Roelends Predicant van de Engelsche Gemeente by het Kloekhuijs*—begraven in de Pieters Kerk."[12] In English it reads: "John Reelands [Robinson] Preacher of the English Congregation by the Belfry—buried in Peter's Church."

The Green Gate congregation was present along with friends from the other English church, the leading ministers of the city, and associates from the university.

> The University and ministers of the city accompanied him to his grave with all their accustomed solemnities, bewailing the great loss that not only that particular church has whereof he was pastor, but some of the chief of them sadly affirmed that all the churches of Christ sustained a loss by the death of that worthy instrument of the Gospel.[13]

The Pilgrim congregation paid the fee of nine florins to St. Peter's for the cost of opening and hiring the grave for the interment. This was the accustomed fee for funerals that were held before half-past one. The simplicity and absence of extravagance would have pleased the pastor. It would not have troubled him or his associates that the hired grave in which his body was laid

Burial record of John Robinson

would be used later for other burials. When the distinguished scholar, Arminius, was buried, the fee paid St. Peter's was only six florins.[14]

In the choir of the Pieterskerk, opposite the spot where Robinson was buried and where today the great memorial tablet hangs on the wall, is a large tablet in honor of Jacob Arminius. The defenders of two diverging schools of Christian thought found their resting place within the peaceful confines of the church that they both loved.

The exact location of Robinson's permanent grave is unknown. Tradition places it in the bay or alcove which projects from the cathedral at the point that is closest to his house.

The remnant of the Leyden church held together for a number of years, but they never succeeded in securing another minister. With the increasing departure of members to Massachusetts, the Green Gate was materially weakened. By 1634 the membership roll had been reduced to a fifth of what it had been in Robinson's time.

The manuscript of Robinson's book, *Treatise of the Lawfulness of Hearing of the Ministers in the Church of England,* was found in his study following his death. After his friends published it, a small group of four or five in his parish spoke against his liberal practices and caused the first rent in the fellowship. These men leaned toward the exclusivism practiced by the Separatists in Amsterdam. Ainsworth's successor there defended the Leyden seceders. The Pharisaic omniscience that Robinson rigorously opposed, the wrangling that he berated, now crept into his once harmonious fraternity. Fortunately, however, the majority were not willing to consent to this retrogressive step. Thereupon the minority withdrew and apparently moved to Amsterdam.

The absence of regular pastoral oversight soon loosened the bonds of unity. Moreover, the stream of refugees from England, which brought new recruits during Robinson's time, slackened as the dictatorial powers of Archbishop Laud waned. The flow of seekers for freedom now moved, not in the direction of Holland, but toward America.

Some members of the church affiliated with the English Reformed Church and the Dutch Reformed churches. The records of the church council of St. Peter's show an entry on June 17, 1639 concerning an application for membership from John Masterson, a native of Henley, and his wife, Catherine (Lisle), and Stephen Butterfield from Norwich, who had become a bookseller after making a living for a time as a "say weaver."

> John Meester and his wife and also Steven Butterfield, English, from the congregation of the sainted Robinson, complaining of a lack of appropriate exercises since his death, so that they cannot be edified in the way they might be were they members of some other Church provided with a pastor; request that they may be allowed to become members of our church.
>
> Their request is granted by the brethren.[15]

The saints in Plimoth were bereft. Their hours of hunger and cold had been warmed by the thought that soon their pastor would be with them to gather them round him in the Fort Meeting House, to comfort them in their sorrows, and to kindle their hearts once again with hope. That prayer could never be realized. His lucid teachings had led them on three journeys, but God had destined him to accompany them only on the first two. His eloquent letters could no longer bring them admonition. He was not yet fifty years of age! The Lord must have some better portion prepared for him that he should be snatched away at this critical time.

In his anguished waiting in Leyden for his opportunity to cross over to Plimoth, Master Robinson had been further distressed by the sickness, privation, and ill fortune that dogged his faithful people across the seas. It is unfortunate that he could not have received before he died Bradford's hopeful report that the tide was turning at Plimoth Plantation.

The governor's letter was not penned until June 9, 1625, to Deacon Robert Cushman, who would have passed on the good word to Leyden as soon as he received it. Bradford wrote: "It pleased the Lord to give the Plantation peace and health and contented minds, and so to bless their labours as they had corn sufficient, and some to spare to others, with other food."[16] The planters had believed that this new era of modest prosperity formed the foundation for the new epoch which would be inaugurated with the arrival of their leader from Leyden.

No doubt at the next Sunday gathering in the Fort Meeting House, which they had hopefully erected for him, they mourned his departure. Bradford prepared a thumbnail sketch of this learned man who was

> of solid judgment and of a quick and sharp wit . . . a hater of hypocricy and dissimulation, and would be very plain to his best friends. . . . He was never satisfied in himself until he had searched any cause or argument thoroughly and to the bottom; and we have heard him sometimes say . . . he knew he had sufficiently answered others, but not himself, and was ever desirous of any light, . . . and the more able, learned and holy the persons were, the more he desired to confer and reason with them.[17]

Bradford produced another pen portrait in which he spoke of the pastor's ability in civil affairs, proving helpful to his people in material ways, like a common father to them. He was a builder of a successful community of people whose piety, zeal, and goodwill brought them close to the pattern of the first Christian churches.[18]

When the Rev. Thomas Prince made a journey to Leyden in 1714 he wrote a report on Robinson's enduring influence there:

> The most ancient people from their parents told me, that the city had such value for them, as to let them have one of their churches, in the chancel whereof he lies buried, which the English still enjoy; and that as he was held in high esteem both

by the city and university, for his learning, piety, moderation, and excellent accomplishments; the magistrates, ministers, scholars, and most of the gentry mourned his death as a public loss, and followed him to the grave.[19]

Bridget Robinson continued to live after her husband's death in the Engelsche Poort at the Green Gate. She was mentioned as being in Leyden on April 6, 1640 in the Poll Tax Register. Prof. John Hoornbeek stated that she and her children joined the Dutch Reformed Church. According to the same register of October 15, 1622 the Robinsons had six children: John, Bridget, Isaac, Mercy, Fear, Jacob, and a maid named Mary Hardy.

Ann, the oldest of the children, named in honor of her grandmother in Sturton, married Jan Schetter of Utrecht before 1622, so her name was not listed in the register. She was left a widow by the autumn of 1625.

John matriculated at Leyden University, April 5, 1633.

Bridget, born in 1608, married John Greenwood, who studied theology at Leyden University in 1629. After his death she married William Lee of Amsterdam in 1637.

Isaac, born in 1610, arrived in Plimoth colony on the *Lion* in 1631.

Mercy, born in 1612, was buried in 1623.

Fear, born in 1614, lived her life in Leyden. She married John Jennings, Jr. in 1648. He died in 1664, leaving three children. She died before May 31, 1670.

Jacob died at an early age, in May 1638, and was buried in St. Peter's.

Bridget Robinson's will was drawn up October 28, 1643 at the office of notary J. F. van Merwen on the Breerstraat. It indicates that she was still a widow and at that time had four children: John, a doctor of medicine, who was married and lived in England; Isaac, who was married and lived in New England; Bridget, who had married William Lee; and Fear, who later married John Jennings, Jr.[20]

Prof. Antonius Walaeus stated May 25, 1628, and Prof. Festus Hommius (both friends of Robinson) agreed, that the Leyden pastor would like to educate his son to serve as a minister among the Dutch rather than the English churches. He had sought the help of certain well-to-do men in Middelburg in order that the boy might study there for several years. Professor Walaeus and the Reverend Teellinck supported him in this effort. This plan indicated again his close affinity with the Dutch Reformed Church.[21]

This document was found in 1872 in the archives of the English Reformed Church at Amsterdam:

I, the undersigned, hereby certify that D[omine] Rubbensonus, pastor of the English church here which is called the Brownists, had at divers times conversed with me concerning the separation between their congregation and the other English congregations in this country, and that he has at divers times testified that he was disposed to do his utmost to remove this schism; that he was also averse to educating his son for the work of the ministry in such congregations, but much preferred to have him exercise his ministry in the Dutch churches; that to this end, by the help of Domine Teellinck and myself, he had also begun to move some good people in Middelburg to provide some decent support for his son's studies for a few years; that he, moreover, at divers times assured me that he found in his congregation so many difficulties in connection with this, that he with a good part of his congregation was resolved to re-move to the West Indies [current for America] where he doubted not he should be able to accomplish his desires.

This has passed between us at diverse times.

Given at Leyden, 25, May, 1628

Antonius Walaeus,

Professor of theology in the university

That which is above testified concerning the union of the English churches in this country, I, the undersigned, likewise certify that I have divers times heard from the late D[omine] Robinson.

At Leyden, 26, May, 1628

Festus Hommius, Rector of the Theological College[22]

There is no evidence that Robinson intended to move to the West Indies. His Dutch friend was doubtless thinking of Plimoth colony in the west.

These conversations with Dutch neighbors lead one to feel that he was not only weary of his long waiting for passage to Plimoth, but also of ecclesiastical controversies and would have liked to have breathed the freer air of the New World.

After Robinson's death the Green Gate people found it difficult to carry on. The property was sold in 1637. Bridget Robinson died in 1643. In 1655 the remnant of the fellowship was absorbed into the English-Scot Reformed Church, which had been founded the year that the Pilgrims reached Leyden. Robinson was seeking to arrange a merger with this group just before he passed away. This congregation held together until 1807.[23]

Around 1681 to 1683 the Pilgrim center was demolished and the Pesyns Hof was built, a hostel erected by the Walloons as a home for the aged. It still stands today in the Bell Alley directly across from the Pieterskerk walls which hold the memorial tablet to the Pilgrim leader.

Meanwhile across the seas the Plimoth section of the Leyden church was progressing, increasing in outreach, and carrying on the concepts of Robinson, rooting them in the culture of the New Continent, where they were to exert creative influence for 350 years and more.

It is not by good and dainty fare,
by peace and rest and heart's ease in enjoying
the contentments and good things of this world
only that preserves health and prolongs life.
—William Bradford

20 "IT IS NOT BY GOOD AND DAINTY FARE"

The planters were concerned with the millstone of debt that hung about their necks. They also felt an obligation to fulfill their promises to help bring over the rest of their friends in Leyden. Payments to the Adventurers had been slow due to the Great Sickness and to piracy. The debt with its appalling interest rate kept piling up into frightening figures. Therefore, in 1626 they dispatched Isaac Allerton on the *Marmaduke* to England. The widower had just married Elder Brewster's daughter, Fear. He carried a cargo of furs and returned with a legal document signed by forty-two of the Adventurers who agreed to free the planters of debt for a settlement of £1,800 (approximately $90,000, since a pound was worth about $50). In addition there was the carry-over on an old debt of £600.[1]

Capt. John Smith, the explorer, who was in London at this time, evidently felt that this was a favorable settlement for the Adventurers. He stated that the Virginia Company had invested £200,000 (approximately $10,000,000) in the colony to the south and had not received a shilling in return from the planters there. He reported in 1624 that altogether £7,000 ($35,000) had been spent on Plimoth.[2]

The encounter of the Pilgrims with the London Merchant Adventurers is almost as confusing and tedious as their theological battles in England and Holland. It must have appeared to them that the Almighty had laid upon them an additional yoke, that they were destined to spend another period of testing in the wilderness. The loan led to unbelievable complications and hardships that harassed them for twenty-five years. This liability was an overwhelming load in relation to the number of people in the plantation which was about 180, but the colonists felt bound to live up to their promises. Eight of the Pilgrims signed as guarantors. These eight "undertakers," as they were called, included William Brewster, William Bradford, Myles Standish, Edward Winslow, John Howland, Isaac Allerton, John Alden, and Thomas Prence.[3]

The settlers now owned the plantation subject to a huge mortgage held by the Adventurers. According to the agreement, all freemen were to help carry the load by paying each year three bushels of corn or six pounds of tobacco to the undertakers. In 1627 the land and cattle were divided. Everyone received twenty acres of tillable land to be added to the one acre allotted when

263

the plantation had concluded its common course. Livestock was also distributed to some 156 individuals, every six receiving one cow and two goats.[4]

It may be of interest here to mention some of the later arrivals.

The *Fortune* of 1621 brought Leyden saints like William Bassett; Jonathan Brewster, son of William; Deacon Robert Cushman; Philippe de la Noye, born of French parents; Thomas Morton; Moses Symonson, from Dutch parentage. Among the strangers were Thomas Prence, later a governor, and John Winslow, brother of Edward.

The *Anne* and *Little James* of 1623 carried a group of saints: Patience and Fear Brewster, children of the Elder; Cuthbert Cuthbertson, a Walloon; Mrs. Bridget Fuller, wife of Deacon Fuller; John Jenney, builder of the first mill in Plimoth; George Morton, a wealthy merchant from the Scrooby area; Nathaniel Morton, his son, who served as secretary of the colony. Among the strangers were Barbara (last name unknown), who married Standish; Robert Bartlett, cooper from Sussex who married Mary, oldest daughter of Richard Warren of the *Mayflower*; John Faunce, father of the future Elder Thomas Faunce; Nicholas Snow, who married Constance, daughter of Stephen Hopkins; and Mrs. Elizabeth Warren with her five daughters.

James Sherley, an Adventurer who proved to be a steadfast friend, journeyed to Leyden and rounded up thirty-five from the Green Gate who came over on the *Mayflower* (a second ship by this popular name) in 1629. Included in this company were some of Pastor Robinson's faithfuls: Thomas Blossom, a leader and deacon in Leyden; Richard Masterson, also a Leyden deacon, who had expended his estate for the public good; and the youthful Thomas Willet of Leyden, later the first English governor of New York. Among the strangers was Kenelm Winslow, another brother of Edward. Passage had been arranged for Bridget Robinson on this second *Mayflower*, together with three of her children, but for some unknown reason she changed her mind the last minute and did not sail.

The plantation undertook the cost of bringing their fellow Leydeners across and housed and fed them for some eighteen months until they could plant and harvest their crops. It was, said Bradford, "a rare example of brotherly love, for they never demanded, much less had, any repayment of all these great sums thus disbursed."

The Rev. Francis Higginson of Salem remonstrated over the exorbitant cost of an Atlantic crossing in the year 1629, mentioning that it was "wondrous dear, as £5 a man and £10 a horse and commonly of £3 for every tun of goods."[5]

Straggling saints who came during the next few years included John Bradford, son of the governor; Isaac Robinson, son of the pastor; Constant Southworth, who served as treasurer of the colony; and Thomas Southworth ("rarely Indowed both in Sacred and Civil Respects"). Strangers like William Collier, a Merchant Adventurer who became the richest man in the colony, and Timothy Hatherly, who opposed discrimination against Baptists and Quakers, arrived in the early 1630's.

It has been established that the so-called Pilgrim ships brought over 108 saints and 133 strangers, 5 hired hands, 56 servants, and 60 unidentified settlers, making a total of 362. Plimoth Plantation was a small colony for the first ten years.[6]

The Pilgrims had maintained their record for honesty in America as in Holland. While in Leyden bankers loaned them money freely because they found that they kept their word. Local people were glad to employ them and the magistrates paid them a tribute as they planned to leave the city, stating that "These English have lived among us now these twelve years, and yet we never had any suit or accusation come against any of them."[7]

What motivated these people to labor and persist until it developed into a habit in order to meet a debt of honor? Something singular had been nurtured in the Leyden community that led them to assume their compact and keep their word. Their endurance race is an example of pay-your-own-way philosophy unique in history. The Pilgrims stood alone. Necessity forced them to set up their own system of farming and other industries. Capt. John Smith stated that they did not follow the example of Virginia where settlers depended on controls from London. The New Englanders were overseers of their own lands "and so well bred in labor and good husbandry as any in England."[8]

Plimoth was an agricultural community. Corn was the basic crop and came to be used like currency as a means of exchange. Cattle were as essential to the plantation household as a burro to a Mexican peon. They provided milk, meat, and hides, while oxen pulled stumps and plowed the fields. The small community started to prosper when the Puritans moved into the bay. Plimoth cows brought a good price, and the fur trade helped to pay the English debts.[9]

The settlers continued to farm, fish, and trade in furs in the wrestle with debt. They granted the undertakers a monopoly of the fur trade to help them meet the debt payments. The first trading post was set up in 1627 at Aptucxet on Cape Cod. This was followed in 1630 by another at the mouth of the Penobscot River in Maine and soon after by one on the site of Augusta on the Kennebec in Maine. In 1632 they established a post at Windsor, Connecticut, which the Dorchester Puritans tried to take from them in 1635.[10]

Agricultural pursuits were supplemented in the 1630's and 1640's by industries that were built on Town Brook and the adjoining ponds: a grist mill, a fulling mill, a leather shop, and an iron foundry.

At last in the year 1645, after twenty-five years of battling with epidemics, lack of experience, pirates, turncoat backers, blundering agents, and high interest, they managed to master their chronic liability, "debts hopeful and desperate."[11] The final claim of one Adventurer was not paid until 1648. To settle this last item, Winslow and Prence sold their own houses and other undertakers sold some of their own land.[12]

In this contest they not only revealed a high sense of honor and a stubborn will, but they succeeded in building the basis of a free and self-sustaining economy. "The Pilgrims paid out some £20,000 worth of beaver and other goods to discharge a debt of £1,800 due to the exploitation of the London Adventurers."[13]

Not all the Merchant Adventurers were unfair or avaricious. Some were genuinely sympathetic toward the efforts of the colony and tried to help them, and some lost money due to the complicated delays. Robinson commented in one of his letters that "five or six [of the Adventurers] were lovingly toward us."[14]

The English across the sea were still locked in a struggle for constitutional and religious liberty. There were high hopes that a new king would bring better days, but these were dashed with the accession of Charles I. It was evident that he was as much opposed to parliamentary government as his father, James, had been. The road to reform in church and state was barricaded by his arrogance, and the long-suffered grievances of the people continued. It became clear that Charles I was going to rule in a high-handed manner without consulting Parliament or the people. For eleven years Parliament was not summoned and the concern and uneasiness of his citizens grew deeper. Therefore the reformers increasingly turned their thoughts to the West. Observant Puritan eyes were on the small independent colony at the north rather than on the Anglican colony at the south. They waited to see if Plimoth could make a go of it.

John White of Dorchester was one of the promoters of a great migration plan. His idea was shared by many in Lincolnshire, Suffolk, London, and other strongholds of revolt. A Company of Massachusetts Bay was formed and a stream of immigrants began to flow to the countryside around the pilot colony of Plimoth.

1628 saw the beginning of the great Puritan migration. John Endecott's ship, the *Abigail*, guided a covey of settlers to Salem. Within two years the Massachusetts Bay boasted a population five times that of Plimoth Plantation.

Governor Endecott's Puritan expedition was made up of seven vessels containing 300 men, 80 women and maids, 26 children, 140 head of cattle, and 40 goats. Before they sailed on June 20, 1628, Francis Higginson, a graduate of Emmanuel College, Cambridge, spoke to them: "We do not go to New England as Separatists from the Church of England, though we cannot but separate from the corruptions in it, but we go to practice the positive part of church reformation, and propagate the gospel in America."[15]

Warmly welcomed by the Plimothians, he immediately discovered that they were of one mind. When he disembarked his Puritans from the *Abigail* in Salem many of them were suffering from scurvy and a fever that had broken out on ship. Their company was rapidly decimated, so he dispatched a message to Plimoth and summoned Deacon Samuel Fuller, "physition & chirurgeon," who hurried to the new community. While treating these newcomers there was much talk about the Plimoth experiment, how their Fort Meeting House church worked, how they were orga-

266

nized, and what they believed. The doctor had been close to
Pastor Robinson and was a sort of lay preacher, doing his bit to
carry on during the long period in which they had no resident
leader. He impressed the Puritans with his reports on an independent church that had survived since 1606 in three different
countries.

Endecott wrote a letter of appreciation to Governor Bradford:

God's People are all marked with one and the same mark and
sealed with one and the same seal, and have for the main, one
and the same heart guided by one and the same spirit of truth.
And where this is there can be no discord, nay here must needs
be sweet harmony. And the same request (with you) I make
unto the Lord that we may, as Christian brethren, be united by
a heavenly and unfeigned love, bending all our hearts and

The Peirce Patent

267

forces in furthering a work beyond our strength, with reverence and fear, fastening our eyes always on Him that only is able to direct and prosper all our ways.

I acknowledge myself much bound to you for your kind love and care in sending Mr. Fuller among us, and rejoice much that I am by him satisfied touching your judgments of the outward form of God's worship. It is, as far as I can gather, no other than is warranted by the evidence of truth. And the same which I have professed and maintained ever since the Lord in mercy revealed Himself unto me. Being far from the common report that hath been spread of you touching that particular. But God's children must not look for less here below, and it is the great mercy of God that He strengthens them to go through with it. . . .

Naumkeag, May 11, Anno 1629

Your assured loving friend,
John Endecott[16]

Governor Endecott had heard reports that the Plimoth church was rigidly Separatist. He was pleased to discover that they were not, but were carrying on after the Robinson pattern. The Salem church was Congregational in polity, but its people did not wish to separate from the Church of England. They were influenced by Plimoth, as were other early churches in the Bay. Plimoth was also influenced by her neighbors to the north. It required a number of years of experiment in New England and in England to create what is known today as a Congregational church. Distance from London and Canterbury and the adversities of the frontier tended to mitigate difference and magnify fellowship.

Historians have classified the Puritan schools in respect to their conflicts over tenets of faith into three groups: on the right, the Presbyterians; in the center, the Congregationalists; and on the left, the separating Congregationalists.[17] It was this central company who shaped the pattern of religion in Massachusetts.

Perry Miller explained how Congregationalism developed in the Bay colony among the Puritan settlers of the nonseparating type.[18] They were followers of William Ames, Henry Jacob, Robert Parker, William Bradshaw, Paul Baynes, John Cotton, Thomas Hooker, and John Davenport. They believed in John Robinson's Congregational Way rather than in the Presbyterian Way. In their thinking it was not necessary to separate from the Church of England as Robinson had felt compelled to do in his earlier years. They did separate themselves from the malpractices of that church and from the corruptions of the world. They agreed with Robinson that the true church should be local and not national, and that it should be independent in organization.

The Pilgrims have been misrepresented as zealots who sought to convert new arrivals to New England, as ironbound in their convictions. This misconception exists in spite of the fact that they had demonstrated the opposite qualities in rejecting the pharisaism of the Amsterdam dogmatists, in sharing with their Dutch, Huguenot, and Walloon neighbors, in friendly outreach to the Scots, and in their willingness to worship in the Mother Church which had persecuted them. Robinson shunned proselyting and emphasized humility and mutuality. His followers in

Plimoth did not seek to impose their ideas on their neighbors. Although the senior citizens of Massachusetts, they extended a welcoming hand to the nonseparating Puritans, to the Presbyterians, and even to Anglicans as they came over.

Robinson and his Plimoth congregation never followed the separatism of Browne or other exclusivists. They practiced cooperation. Separatist Roger Williams, with all his leanings toward liberality, could not accept Plimoth's friendly stance toward Anglicanism. Led by Brewster, Bradford, Winslow, and other advocates of Robinson's brotherliness, Plimoth shared in and supported the Congregationalism of her nonseparating neighbors.[19]

Leaders of Plimoth were invited in July 1629 to attend the formation of the church in Salem. Governor Bradford, Brewster, Fuller, and others set out in their shallop, but head winds delayed their arrival, so that they did not hear the brethren repeat the covenant "in the presence of God to walke together in all His ways, accordingly as he pleased to reveal himself unto us in His blessed Word of truth." They made it in time "to give them the Right Hand of Fellowship," and to congratulate Pastor Samuel Skelton from Lincolnshire and Teacher Francis Higginson from Leicester, both Cambridge graduates.

The procedure they followed was similar to the formation of the Leyden church. The Salem church sent a letter describing how they organized, thus seeking the advice of Plimoth and deferring to its traditions.

The governor set apart "a solemn day of humiliation for the choice of a pastor and teacher." On the day of their assembling they spent the morning in prayer and teaching and then proceeded to examine the two candidates "concerning their calling." The two men, Skelton and Higginson, spoke of their inward calling from God and their outward calling from the people, "when a company of believers are joined in covenant to walk together in all the ways of God," and emphasized that all members "are to have a free voice in the choice of their officers." So Mr. Skelton was chosen pastor and Mr. Higginson to be teacher.

And they accepted the choice, and Mr. Higginson with three or four of the gravest members of the church laid their hands on Mr. Skelton, using prayer therewith. This being done, there was imposition of hands on Mr. Higginson also. And since that time, Thursday (being as I take it the 6th of August) is appointed for another day of humiliation for the choice of elders and deacons and the ordaining of them.

The reporter who wrote the letter concluded:

Here was a right foundation laid and that these two blessed servants of the Lord came in at the door and not at the window.
Salem, July 30, 1629   Charles Gott[20]

Robinson and the Leyden congregation would have been pleased if they could have attended the formation of the Salem church along with Bradford, Brewster, and Fuller. It was a classic example of the procedure they had established in Scrooby and Leyden.

In 1630 Governor John Winthrop arrived with a large expedition to found Boston and its first church.

Aboard his flagship, the *Arbella*, Winthrop led a fleet of seventeen ships, carrying nearly 1,000 settlers to New England. His vessels were amply provisioned with food, beer, wine, and fresh water. Compared with the *Mayflower*, they looked like the Spanish Armada.

Before departing England, Winthrop followed Governor Endecott's diplomatic gesture to the Establishment. His proclamation stated:

> We esteem it our honor to call the Church of England our dear mother, . . . ever acknowledging that such hope and part as we have obtained in the common salvation, we have received in her bosom and sucked it from her breasts. We leave it not, therefore, as loathing that milk wherewith we were nourished there; but blessing God for the parentage and education, as members of the same body, shall always rejoice in her good.[21]

Governor Winthrop, however, soon descended from his high horse of flowery rhetoric to the realities of frontier life. There was nothing like the New England wilderness and a severe epidemic to smooth down the separating points of theology and turn his mind to his only neighbors, the Pilgrims in Plimoth.

Due to the reputation of John Robinson, the ecclesiastical achievements at the plantation were respected as the first independent establishment in the New World. It was not surprising that Boston and other congregations used a covenant similar to that developed at Scrooby and Leyden. Winthrop's planters took this pledge: "To walk in all ways according to the Rule of the Gospel, and in all sincere conformity to his Holy Ordinances and in mutual love and respect each to other, so near as God shall give us grace." Salem and Boston realized that the reputed Separatists of Plimoth were pretty sensible people who had learned much during the past decade about the Indians, the fur business, and the church.

The theory that Congregationalism was modeled after Robinson was first advanced by William Rathband in 1644, with the publication of *A Briefe Narration of some Church Courses* in which he wrote:

> Master Robinson did derive his way to his separate congregation at Leyden; a part of them did carry it over to Plimoth in New England where Master Cotton did take it up . . . [and] the most who settled their habitations in that Land [of New England] did agree to model themselves in Churches after Robinson's pattern.[22]

It was not true, Winslow said, that the plantations as they came over "took Plimoth as their precedent as fast as they came."

Some of their leaders did advise with Plimoth "how they should do to fall upon a right platform of worship," deferring to their experience, "since God had honored us to lay the foundation of a Commonweal and settle a church in it."[23]

Winslow went on to say:

We accordingly shewed them the primitive practice for our warrant, taken out of the Acts of the Apostles and the Epistles . . . together with the commandments of Christ, and for every particular we did from the book of God. They set not the Church at Plimoth before them for example, but the Primitive Churches were and are their and our mutual patterns and examples, which are only worthy to be followed.[24]

The minister of Winthrop's Boston church, John Cotton, had been a Lincolnshire neighbor of the Pilgrims. A graduate of Emmanuel College, Cambridge, he had served as dean there as Robinson did at Corpus Christi. As minister of St. Botolph's Church in Boston, he exerted wide influence as a scholar. He preached to the assembled fleet of Governor Winthrop in Southampton on "God's promise to his Plantation," just as Robinson had done ten years before in Delfshaven. When Laud was made archbishop, Cotton was summoned to appear before the Court of High Commission. Realizing that he might be headed for prison, he chose to sail for Boston, Massachusetts.

The non-Separatist followers of Ames were delighted to pull out of the ecclesiastical argumentation of England and move to Massachusetts to try to realize on its shores what they had failed to achieve at home. The era of protest was ending and the era of constructive building was at hand. It was no longer necessary "to strive against ceremonies, or to fight against shadows."

While visiting the Salem church, Samuel Fuller and Edward Winslow wrote to Plimoth Plantation on July 26, 1630, stating that the Salem church had received a letter from Governor John Winthrop about the epidemic raging among his settlement at Charlestown, announcing that they had set apart a day for prayer and the formation of a church, when the

godly persons amongst them could solemnly enter into covenant with the Lord to walk in His ways.

They do earnestly entreat that the Church of Plimoth would set apart the same aay for the same ends, beseeching the Lord as to withdraw His hand of correction from them, so as also to establish and direct them in Hiw ways. And though the time be short, we pray you be provoked to this godly work, seeing the causes are so urgent; wherein God will be honoured and they and we undoubtedly have sweet comfort.

Be you all kindly saluted, etc.

Your brethren in Christ, etc.
Edward Winslow

Salem, July 26, 1630   Samuel Fuller[25]

Dr. Fuller also wrote from Charlestown on August 2, 1630, where he was helping Governor Winthrop and his people fight their epidemic. He mentioned how four men "entered into church covenant," who were joined by five more, "and others it is like will add themselves to them daily." This was the beginning of the First Church in Boston. Fuller also reported that John Cotton of Boston had stated that "they [the people of Boston] should take advice of them at Plimoth, and should do nothing to offend them." Some of these, he explained, want to see us "out of the love which they bear us, and the good persuasion they have of us; others to see whether we be so ill as they have heard of us."[26]

Governor John Winthrop described a visit he paid to Plimoth Plantation on October 25, 1632 and what the Pilgrims did on Sunday in their Fort Meeting House:

> The governor, with Mr. Wilson, pastor of Boston, and the two captains, etc. went aboard the *Lyon* and from thence Mr. Peirce carried them in his shallop to Wessaguscus [now Weymouth]. The next morning Mr. Peirce returned to his ship, and the governor and his company went on foot to Plimoth, and came thither within the evening. The governor of Plimoth, Mr. William Bradford (a very discreet and grave man) with Mr. Brewster, the elder, and some others, came forth and met them without the town, and conducted them to the governor's house, where they were very kindly entertained, and feasted every day at several houses.

> On the Lord's Day there was a sacrament, which they did partake in; and, in the afternoon, Mr. Roger Williams (according to their custom) propounded a question, to which the pastor, Mr. Smith, spake briefly; then Mr. Williams prophesied; and after the governor of Plimoth spoke to the question, after him the elder; then some two or three more of the congregation. Then the elder desired the governor of Massachusetts and Mr. Wilson to speak to it, which they did. When that was ended, the deacon, Mr. Fuller, put the congregation in mind of their duty of contribution; whereupon the governor and all the rest went down to the deacon's seat, and put into the box, and then returned.

> October 31, 1632, about five in the morning, the governor and his company came out of Plimoth; the governor of Plimoth, with the pastor and elder, etc. accompanying them near half a mile out of town in the dark. The Lieutenant Holmes, with two others, and the governor's mare, came along with them to the great swamp, about ten miles.[27]

Doctor-deacon Fuller was the roving salesman for the plantation. Entertained by the dignitaries as he ministered to their sick, he spoke about the Plimoth experiment. Sometimes he met with disagreement as with John Warham of Dorchester with whom he talked "till I was weary," because he believed that "the visible church may consist of a mixed people, godly and openly ungodly."[28] Warham was a reluctant Puritan, clinging to this Church of England tenet.

272

Raising the old bugaboo about rigid separation, the people of the Bay were cautious about Plimoth for a time. Cotton told Samuel Skelton of Salem that he might be listening too much to Plimothians:

> You went hence of another judgment, and I am afraid your change hath sprung from New Plimoth men, who, though I must esteem as godly and loving Christians, yet their grounds which they have received for this tenet (regarding use of a church covenant) from Mr. Robinson, do not justify me, though the man I reverence as godly and learned.[29]

Cotton preached at Salem in an effort to keep that parish from moving too far toward separation. He admitted that Samuel Skelton was right, and that he was in error regarding the nature of a church covenant. So the Boston dignitary approved the Plimoth-Salem practice of requiring members to take the covenant of the particular church which they chose to enter, which helped to make it the common practice.[30]

The difference between Robinson and Ames "as a parent of Congregationalism amounted in practice to no larger a difference than that between a Boston man and a Plimoth man."[31] They followed the Congregational Way, accepted letters of transfer, and joined together in fellowship. About the only point of divergence was that Robinson had declared his separation, while Ames, Cotton, and their company claimed to stay inside, although they repudiated the same evils in the Establishment.

The Bay ministers, in general, however, were more conservative and strait-laced than those in the Fort Meeting House. Doctrine was more rigid there. The Pilgrims were deterred from dogmatism by the teaching of Robinson, whose emphasis on "further light" gave them a forward-looking perspective that checked the growth of self-righteous conceit.

In considering the differences between the Pilgrims and the Bay Puritans, Dr. Edmund S. Morgan pointed out Plimoth's lack of missionary zeal to convert the natives and the newcomers who were not classified as saints.[32] It was true that the Pilgrims were not proselyters. They did not go out into the highways and byways to convert men to their way. They concentrated on their own practice of religion, and this made them easier to live with. Their position appeals because it removes adherents from the age-old concomitant of Christian institutionalism, missionary fanaticism.

There was a second difference. The Pilgrims did not build a theocracy because they had no dominant divines. They had no Cotton Mather or Judge Samuel Sewall who ruled with a Calvinistic scepter. There seemed to be a little more give and take in the Pilgrim nature; perhaps it was because they had come a longer way. Twenty-two years of hard discipline lay behind them. They had not left England escorted by a fleet of ships, amply provisioned, with the backing of many wealthy Puritans. They had straggled on foot and by cart through byways and hidden paths, fleeing persecution and the pursuit of the king's men. They had lived twelve years in Holland and for ten years had gone it alone in the New World. Like the willow, they had learned to bend with the wind. Disciplined searching and long suffering had softened their Calvinism. Governor Bradford agreed with Cotton:

> And whereas Mr. Baylie affirmeth that, however it was, in a few years the most who settled in the land [New England] did agree to model themselves after Mr. Robinson's pattern, we agree with reverend Mr. Cotton, that "there was no agreement by any solemn or common consultation"; but that it is true they did, as if they had agreed by the same spirit of truth and unity, set up, by the help of Christ, the same model of churches, one like to another; and if they of Plimoth have helped any of the first comers in their theory, by hearing and describing their practices, therein the Scripture is fulfilled that the kingdom of heaven is like unto leaven which a woman took.[33]

The congregation that was organized at Charlestown on July 30, 1630 divided into three churches: Charlestown, Watertown, and Dorchester. They asked for the interest and the prayers of Plimoth and for the advice of Fuller, Allerton, and Winslow regarding church government.[34] The Pilgrims rejoiced to have some neighbors. They were very glad to be invited to these congregational parties. They did not journey about trying to sell the Plimoth Fort Meeting House, but rather to enjoy fellowship with compatriots and share in the excitement of the Bay.

Some Puritans had been hopeful that they could "transport both the English State and Church to Massachusetts and there reform them at will. Massachusetts would be a piece of England such as all England ought to be." As Thomas Shepard wrote: "Could God have expected us to remain helpless in England, protesting futilely and only find a way to have filled the Prisons . . . when a wide doore was set open of liberty otherwise?"[35]

The adventure in fellowship between the senior and junior churches was underway, a process of sharing that was to produce the New England church. The men of the Bay began to realize that Robinson's people were to be cultivated rather than shunned. The eminent Cotton said that Robinson "was a man of the most learned, polished, and modest spirit of that way, and withal he might have said, so piously studious and conscientiously inquisitive after the truth, that it had been truly a marvel, if such a man as he, had gone on to the end a rigid Separatist."[36] This statement carried weight with the Bay colony.

Isaac Robinson, son of Master Robinson, who had been born in Leyden in 1610, came over on the *Lion*, arriving on November 2, 1631. He was a fellow passenger of John Eliot, who was to become the apostle to the Indians, and Margaret Winthrop, wife of Governor John Winthrop, with their children. The *Lion* was welcomed as she came ashore in Boston, the settlers rejoicing at the arrival of supplies as well as newcomers. The ship brought "a great store of provisions as fat hogs, kids, venison, poultry, geese, partridges, etc., so as the like joy and manifestation of love, had never been seen in New England."[37]

When Isaac reached Plimoth the rafters must have rung with rejoicing. He married the sister of Elder Faunce and moved to nearby Scituate. John Lathrop, leader of part of Henry Jacob's 1616 London church, arrived about this same time. Jacob had lived in Leyden at least seven years and had often been in the Green Gate house. When Isaac met Lathrop he decided he would follow him and the group from his London congregation to West Barnstable on Cape Cod. Lathrop in his diary states that "Isaac Robinson and my son Fuller joyned [the church] having their letter dismissive from the church at Plimoth unto us Nov. 7, 1636." Although Isaac moved in later years, he kept his church membership in Barnstable and returned there in his last years to live with a daughter.[38]

Whereas you are become a body
politic, using amongst yourselves civil
government, and are not furnished with any
persons of special eminency above the rest, to
be chosen by you into office of government; let
your wisdom and godliness appear.
—John Robinson

21 "WHEREAS YOU ARE BECOME A BODY POLITIC"

John Robinson believed that able men, chosen by the people, should lead the church. When accused of being an extremist in setting up a popular democratic church where everybody had a finger in the pie and things were too free and easy, he made three points.

First, the external government of the church is aristocratic, administered by "certain choice men." The people are to vote in the elections and decisions of the church. The elders, elected by the people, are to "propound and order all things in the church."

Second, the elders may lawfully and sometimes by necessity meet apart from the body of the church to deliberate on its welfare.

Third, women and children are not to vote, as critics contumaciously inferred, "but only men and them grown and of discretion."[1]

Robinson explained that there were three types of political theory: the monarchical, where supreme authority is in the hands of one; the aristocratical, where it is in the hands of a few select persons; and the democratical, where it rests in the whole body or multitude. All three of these forms have a place in the church. In relation to Christ it is a monarchy, in respect of the elders an aristocracy, and in respect of the body it is a popular state.[2]

By aristocratical government he meant leadership of educated ministers and laymen. We know that he opposed class domination in the Church of England and did not want it in a free church. His writings and the records of the Leyden-Plimoth church indicate that his church made advances in democratic practice over those that prevailed in the Mother Church. He described procedures of the Leyden church which included (1) the exercise of prophesying, (2) the choice of officers, and (3) censuring of offenders. As to prophesying, he stated that "the officers, after their ordinary teaching," give other members the opportunity to ask questions, to state doubts, and to exhort. Thus the people have a certain liberty, yet "the officers govern."

The pastor and officials were elected by church members. This formed a forward step in ecclesiastical government. The elders, chosen by the people, served as teachers and spiritual helpers of the minister. They should "be apt to teach in public assembly." Elected for life, they must take decisions to the people for final action. The elders were not the church and their function was purely moral.

277

Following the New Testament, deacons were also chosen by the congregation. A new significance was added to church membership due to the central importance of the covenant and the obligation placed upon each individual to be responsible for the good name of the church. Every member possessed the right to participate in its activities. The head of the church was Jesus and his power was communicated to every member of the church "and so makes every one of them severally kings and priests and all jointly a kingly priesthood."[3]

Wary of the evils of excommunication as practiced by former churches, he left the power of censure to the people, who were to follow the advice of Jesus: "If he refuses to listen to them, tell it to the church (Matthew xviii. 17)." Robinson taught "that the people have power to censure offenders: for they that have power to elect, appoint, and set up officers, they also have power, upon just occasion, to reject, depose, and put them down."[4]

The power of excommunication belonged to the congregation. In cases of discipline the officers consulted with the offender and then brought their suggestion to the people. Robinson compared the process of discipline to a session of the assize, where the procedure is determined by the law of the land, but where the jury's "power and sentence is of such force, as that the Lord Chief Justice himself and all the Bench with him, cannot proceed against it."[5]

Men may be constrained by the magistrates in outward acts such as justice and honesty, but in religious actions the proper guide is not civil authority, because these deeper aspects are attainable only by "faith and devotion in the heart of the doers."[6]

In speaking of the contrast between the civil magistrate and the church leader, he pointed out that in many things the bare authority of the civil magistrate requires submission, but this is not true of the church ruler. The civil magistrate can demand obedience, but the church officers should not assert similar authority. He limited the power of the church leaders to the right to persuade. And this right belongs to the people also.

It should be noted that Robinson disapproved of violence in all forms:

> Neither good intents, nor events, which are casual, can justify unreasonable violence: & withal, that by this course of compulsion many become atheists, hypocrites, & familists: & being at first constrained to practice against conscience, lose all conscience afterwards.[7]

He stated that the state should not enforce church attendance: "Considering that neither God is pleased with unwilling worshippers, nor Christian societies bettered nor the persons themselves neither, but the plain contrary. . . . Bags and vessels overstrained break, and will never after hold anything."[8]

Elected officers were "not lords over God's heritage," to rule like princes and magistrates over their subjects, but "ministers and servants of Christ." They were all "frail men." It was lawful for members, "doubtful of anything in the officer's administration, to propound their doubt for satisfaction." They had the right to admonish them of their duty and to go further and clear up problems.[9]

If ministers did not live up to the terms upon which they were chosen, the church, even "the meanest member thereof," was not bound to submit. Clergymen were not to be obeyed for the authority of the commander as the magistrates are, "but for the reason of the commandment, which the ministers are also bound in duty to manifest, and approve unto the consciences of them over whom they are set."[10]

These principles remain the basic structure of Congregationalism today, which possesses as democratic a polity as any segment of Christendom. Many denominations still operate under bishops, presbyteries, and firm dogmas. The Congregational Way remains a people's church, but each unit is led by representatives who are chosen to operate it for the members.

Three practices in the Leyden-Plimoth community tended to develop democracy. First, the leaders of the church were chosen by the people and responsible to the people. The governor also was elected by popular vote. This policy influenced later communities in New England to move toward government by the consent of the people.[11]

The second was the covenant principle of church membership. Through this form members were called to commital and to mutual trust. This compact bound all to care for one another in a community of sharing.[12] The Christian life was based on a covenant between the individual and God. Magistrates and monarchs were also bound to keep their covenant with God and the people. When they failed to live up to their pledges they forfeited their authority. If permitted to continue in office the community would suffer.[13]

The Pilgrims accepted the biblical theory that church and state should employ different officers and different methods because they performed separate functions. The church represented the kingdom of God on earth. The powers of its officers were purely spiritual because the kingdom was not of this world. The church should not carry on the will of God by force, but only by the weapons of the spirit: persuasion, admonition, and exhortation. The most extreme form of discipline to be employed was expulsion.[14]

Third, there was the granting of land in fee simple. Vernon L. Parrington has observed that the land system "threw the economics of the developing commonwealth on the side of local home rule and provided a substantial foundation for the erection of a democratic opposition to oligarchy." Instead of following the plantation system of Virginia or the patroon system of New York, the colony gave land to settlers so that they all had a stake in the economy.

They were granted freehold estates in "free and common socage." They were not obligated to serve some knight, who could compel them to attend the lord of the manor for forty days of each year in time of war. The authority of the squire was rejected. The system of inheritance by primogeniture was abolished. The ancient feudal system was broken.

The land-holding system of Plimoth encouraged a strong yeoman class and bred the qualities of the independent Congregational Way.[15] Daniel Webster wrote that the "parceling out and division of the lands fixed the future frame and form of the Plimoth government." This led to a great equality of condition, the true basis of a popular government.[16]

With the growth of Plimoth colony it was decided in 1636 to draw up laws. The governor and his assistants met with four men from Plimoth, two from Duxbury, and two from Scituate, to draft a body of laws called the "General Fundamental," which was adopted by the General Court of the freemen. This formed a constitution for the colony and the first bill of rights in America.[17] The preamble stated that the Pilgrims came "hither as free-born subjects of the Kingdom of England," and claimed "all and singular privileges belonging to such."[18]

"We think good that it be established for an act: That . . . no imposition of law or ordinance be made upon or by ourselves or others at present, or to come, but such as shall be made or imposed by consent" of the voters.[19]

Plimoth settlers brought with them English common law, the jury system, and the right of elected representatives of the people to appropriate or deny taxes. Most of them came from East Anglia where citizens had led the fight for parliamentary reform. At that time England had 149 capital crimes. Plimoth colony reduced this number to six. They were treason, murder, witchcraft, burning of ships and houses, sodomy, and rape. Adultery was to be punished, but they refused to make it a capital crime as the Bay colony did.[20]

The freemen were the voters. The first freemen were the forty-one signers of the compact. These included all male passengers except a few of the servants who were under bond to work for a certain master for a period of years to pay for their passage. Some of the hired workers did sign like John Alden, John Howland, Edward Doty, Edward Lester, and George Soule.[21]

Every year more were "admitted freemen" by the vote of the existing freemen. In order to qualify, a planter had to be at least twenty-one years old and of a good reputation. They elected each year the governor, the deputy governor, and, after 1680, the assistants and the secretary. They met at least once a year as a "court" or general assembly.

Opportunity to take part in political life existed for a majority of the adult males in the early days of the plantation. In 1633 four out of every five male taxpayers were or would be freemen. By 1643 one out of every two adult males enjoyed the freeman status. Plimoth Plantation had no property qualifications for its voters. Freemen could vote in the General Court and hold public office. They were required to meet for sessions of the court. As the colony grew, deputies were elected to represent the settlers. In 1638 the right to choose these deputies was extended to every man who had taken the oath of fidelity, who was head of a family, and who was a settled resident. This was a significant extension of the right of representation to a large number of the male taxpayers.[22]

Although the freemen were the minority, the plantation developed self-government and a government under law. The freemen alloted land to the settlers—to young men who needed farms and to newcomers who were approved. They gave the land and did not sell it. They did not try to make profit out of their people.[23]

Plimoth did not require proof of regeneracy for admission to the freeman status as Massachusetts did. Peregrine White, the first white child born in New England, was made a freeman in 1652, but he did not affiliate with the church in Marshfield until 1698.

The Massachusetts Bay colony passed a law in 1631 that restricted the franchise to members of the church, but Plimoth permitted nonmembers to vote. In 1635 the Bay colony made church attendance compulsory, but it was on a voluntary basis at the plantation.[24] Myles Standish did not share communion in the Fort Meeting House, but he was a freeman, a voter, and a pillar of the plantation. Most of the books in his library dealt with Puritan religion, and he owned "three olde Bibles and a testament." He left a legacy to "Mercy Robinson, who I tenderly love for her grandfather's sake." In spite of the fact that Robinson had rebuked him about the Wessagusset Indian affair, the captain developed into a loyal friend of the Leyden leader although he never became an actual member of his flock.[25]

The court was able to report that it did permit men "though of different Judgments, yett being otherwise orthodox" to become freemen.[26] Quakers were not admitted to citizenship but Baptists were.

Church and state lived together in relative harmony. It was the duty of the magistrates to see that religion was established and protected. The clergyman was not to deal in temporal affairs. Each by calling performed in his own sphere. Magistrates conferred with the clergy but made ultimate decisions of state.

In 1632 the congregation in Boston wrote to the elders and brethren of the churches in Plimoth and Salem for their advice as to whether one person might be a civil magistrate and a ruling elder at the same time. All answered in the negative. Evidence that church and state were distinct is found in the fact that the Royal Charter of 1629, which was given to the Bay, conferred no prerogatives on the church, and it did not include any ministers as grantees.

At the ecclesiastical synod held in 1648 in Cambridge the ministers declared: "As it is unlawful for the church-officers to meddle with the Sword of Magistrates, so it is unlawful for the magistrate to meddle with the work proper to church officers."[27] Ministers did not seek political office. Churchmen were not to undermine and destroy the authority of the magistrate unless he violated the word of the scriptures.

The Fort Meeting House was the center of the plantation. Here the people assembled on Sunday morning for worship, on Sunday afternoon for informal discussion, and at midweek for Bible study and more psalm-singing. A diversity of matters came up from

time to time before this cross section of the community, which included women as well as men and a good number who were not freemen. Affairs of the church were openly considered as were the problems of the colony. Also certain political decisions were shaped in these meetings. Minor offenders might be ordered by the "assistants" to appear before the church and be "admonished," that is, be lectured by Elder Brewster. In severe breaches of the law it could mean going to the Fort Meeting House in penitence to confess one's sins.

Plimoth achieved one first in civil government by establishing the first registry of deeds in the New World. This important legal achievement was emphasized during the residence in Holland. Following the Dutch example, the settlers required the registration of births, marriages, and deaths. They also demanded that every real estate transaction should be recorded.[28]

Plimoth Plantation realized another first in establishing marriage as a civil right. The settlers practiced Robinson's teaching that marriage should be removed from the exploitation of the church and placed in the hands of the magistrates. Marriage was not rooted in ecclesiastical dogma but in God's original commandment of creation. Robinson wrote:

> Considering how popish superstition hath so far prevailed, that marriage in the Romish church hath got a room amongst the sacraments, truly and properly so called, and by Jesus Christ the Lord instituted; the celebration and consecration whereof the patrons, and consorts of that superstition will have so tied to the priests' fingers, that by the decree of Evaristus the First, they account the marriage no better than incestuous, which the priest consecrates not.[29]

Marriage was not a sacrament of the church, but a contract between two persons and related to questions of property and inheritance. This made it the responsibility of the civil authorities, not the ministry. Marriage was to be treated seriously. It could not be carried out through the mere presence of the two involved. A public official was required. Certain responsible citizens were authorized to perform the ceremony. Those who joined themselves in matrimony were fined.[30]

Marriage by the magistrates was the Dutch practice and the Pilgrims adopted it, continuing until 1692, the year that Plimoth merged with Massachusetts.[31]

In 1635 when Edward Winslow was in England on his third mission for the colony, he was extended inhospitable treatment by Archbishop Laud even though he served as official ambassador of New Plimoth. The archbishop locked him up for seventeen weeks in the Fleet Prison and questioned him regarding his "teaching in the church publicly." Winslow replied that "some time (wanting a minister) he did exercise his gifts to help the

(pages 282-83, clockwise from top left)
Bradford House, Harlow House, Alden House, Howland House

284

edification of his brethren when they wanted better means, which was not often."

Laud upbraided him for his role in marriage by the laity. Winslow

> confessed that having been called to the place of magistracy, he had sometimes married some. And further told their Lordships that marriage was a civil thing and he found nowhere in the Word of God that it was tied to the ministry. Again, they were necessitated to do so, having for a long time together at first no minister; besides, it was no new thing for he had been married himself in Holland by the magistrates in their Statthouse.[32]

All this irritated the prelate from Canterbury, who did all he could to impede the Plimoth colony ambassador's undertakings in England. English friends finally intervened and secured his release. On the long homeward voyage the spirited Winslow brooded over this further insult to Plimoth Plantation.[33]

John Robinson had emphasized marriage as a pattern of the Christian life: "God hath ordained marriage amongst other good means for the benefit of man's natural and spiritual life."[34] He rejected the Roman Catholic exaltation of celibacy:

> This is, indeed, the very dregs of Popery, to place special piety on things either evil, or indifferent, at the best; as is abstinence from marriage, and the marriage bed; which is no more a virtue than abstinence from wine, or other pleasing natural things. Both marriage and wine are of God, and good in themselves.[35]

He stressed the importance of mutual love in marriage, stating that a man's love for his wife must be "like Christ's to his church; holy for quality and great for quantity"; and must be long-suffering although "her failings and faults be great."[36]

While upholding the necessity for mutuality in marriage, he reflected current skepticism on equality of the sexes: "Many graces and good things are requisite both for husband and wife, but more, especially the Lord requires in the man love and wisdom; and in the woman subjection. Eph. v 22-5"[37] Robinson also said that the husband should walk with his wife as a man of understanding, "that he might guide and go before her as a fellow heir of eternal life with him."[38]

He opposed the traditional view that women were "necessary evils":

> Not only heathen poets, which were more tolerable, but also wanton Christians, have nick-named women, necessary evils; but with as much shame to men as wrong to women, and to God's singular ordinance withal. When the Lord amongst all good creatures which he had made, could find none fit and good enough for the man, he made the woman a rib of him, and for a help unto him, Gen. ii. 20, 21: neither is she, since

the creation, more degenerated than he, from the primitive goodness. Besides, if the woman be a necessary evil, how evil is the man, for whom she is necessary![39]

He disagreed with Paul's statement that women should keep silence in the church. He stated that they were not to be debarred from speaking in the church, making confession of faith or confession of sin. They could "say amen to the prayers of the church, sing psalms vocally, accuse a brother of sin, witness an accusation, or defend themselves being accused." A woman could "reprove the church rather than permit it to go along in wickedness."[40] He pointed out that numerous women in the Bible had spoken publicly: Miriam, Deborah, Huldah, Anna, Jezebel, the Samaritan woman, and others.[41]

There was a woman deaconess in the Leyden church. She was honored in the congregation and "obeyed as a mother in Israel and an officer of Christ."[42] The Fort Meeting House also was served by deaconesses. A kindly matron may have been on hand during the long services to tickle restless children with a feather that was fastened to the end of her rod. Perhaps this gesture also served the beneficent purpose of reminding the pastor or elder to approach more rapidly the termination of his sermon or prayer.

A number of women were active in the early days of the plantation. Bridget Fuller, widow of Dr. Samuel Fuller, was midwife. She not only helped her husband with obstetrical cases, but made medicines from the herbs she gathered and were brought in to her herbshed by villagers who all cared lovingly for their herbs and "sallets" in the kitchen gardens around their houses. Bridget also did some tutoring of children after she came over from Leyden on the *Anne*. The *Old Colony Records* of February 11, 1635 state that "Benjamin Eaton, with his mother's consent, is put to Bridget Fuller being to keep him at school two years, and employ him after in such service as she saw good, and he may be fit for."

Elizabeth Warren was a large landowner who gave property to her numerous children and helped them build their homes. She was authorized by the General Court to succeed her husband, Richard Warren, as a purchaser. She bought lands in Little Compton, Rhode Island and Dartmouth, Massachusetts. She owned seven horses in 1652 and no doubt a good herd of cattle. She was famous for her purple dye. "Mistris Elizabeth Warren an aged widow aged above 90 years Came to her Grave as a shok of Corn fully Ripe" on October 12, 1673, having a flock of at least seventy-five grandchildren.[43]

The ordinaries or taverns were popular gathering places for a mug of ale or beer or a nip of aqua vitae or brandy. Some of these centers of conviviality were operated by women. Goodwife Knowles was brought before the court "for selling strong waters for five or six shillings a bottle that cost but 35 shillings the case." She was fined ten shillings to be bestowed on "ye poor of Plimoth."[44]

In certain church customs the Pilgrims were surprisingly pragmatic. They deliberately eliminated from their worship the pagan background of Lent, Easter, and Christmas, and removed adoration of the cross, relics, holy water, and the doctrine of purgatory. They were spartan in their practices regarding death in an effort to remove superstition from religion. They had observed how the church exploited people when sorrow and panic made them vulnerable. They repudiated the role of religion in efforts to control the human soul after its departure from the world. They rejected all dogma regarding what happened when man's spirit left his body, along with prayers for the dead. They adopted the French Protestant abolition of funeral prayers "to avoid superstition."

Ritual forms were eliminated at burials. The church bell tolled, when there was one; neighbors gathered around their minister and proceeded to the grave. Here they stood reverently and silently while earth was placed on the coffin. When Capt. John Alden (son of John Alden) died in 1697 he was buried with a military escort and Pastor Wiswall spoke at his grave, although no religious form is mentioned.[45]

In 1685, at the funeral of Pastor Adams of Roxbury, Pastor Wilson of Medfield prayed with the company before going to the grave; and this is the first instance known in these colonies. So late as 1774, when Joseph Howland was buried in Newport (the great-grandson of the Pilgrim Howland), Rev. Drs. Hopkins and Styles walked in the procession, but held no services, it not being the practice then for a prayer or address to be offered at a funeral.[46]

In their process of self-government the Plimoth settlers developed a ruling class made up of Brewster, Bradford, Winslow, Fuller, Standish, Cushman, Allerton, and others. It is fortunate that most of these key personalities were from Leyden and that they shared Master Robinson's thinking, for they escaped the corruptions of snobbery. "These men showed a judgment rare even among statesmen of great countries, when dealing with external enemies, internal sedition and the powerful neighbors of their own nation."[47]

Governor Bradford did not receive any salary until 1639 when it was voted to give him £20 a year. For many years thereafter he continued to entertain the assistants for meals at his own expense when they held their meetings. Chosen unanimously in May 1621 to the post of governor, he served thirty times for a one-year term, although there was a five-year period when he "by importunity gat off." *Of Plimoth Plantation,* the first major book in American letters, established him as one of the great writers of his time.

Thirty-five of the 102 *Mayflower* passengers were from Leyden, which would lead one to believe that they were a minority. But the passengers should be studied as families, as Dr. Samuel E. Morison reminds us. A number of the Leydenites were joined by relatives or servants in England. In that period dependent kinsmen and servants shared the religious and political views of their masters, so we can be sure that they were in sympathy with Leyden views. There were twenty-six heads of families on the ship. Half of these were from Leyden. There were twelve boys or men without families, and of these, five came from Leyden.[48] Furthermore, many of the *Mayflower* people who had come from English towns were related to the Leyden people by blood or conviction; consequently the company was more homogeneous than is commonly supposed.[49]

After the devastation of the Great Sickness, three of the six surviving non-Leyden family heads were Hopkins, Standish, and Warren. These three strangers were supporters of the plantation, as were John Alden, Gilbert Winslow, and Richard Gardiner.

Dr. H. M. Dexter has made a study of the Pilgrim community in Leyden showing:

Known members up until July 1620			298
Others associated more or less closely with them until this time or with the remaining members later			281
			579
Deduct those named more than once			106
The entire Pilgrim colony			473
The other English in Leyden 1609-81 of whom perhaps some belonged to the colony		169	
Deduct those named more than once		16	
		153	
			153
Total English colony likely to have been associated with the Pilgrims			626
Plimoth colonists from Leyden:			
on the *Mayflower*	35		
on the *Fortune*	4		
on the *Anne*	24		
on later ships	18		
Total	81[50]		

William Bradford could well have become lord and proprietor of the plantation colony like Penn and Baltimore of their colonies. But he remembered the pomposity of bishops and lords in England, and in contrast the simplicity and the strength of Robinson. Consequently, he avoided the pitfalls of some other governors and kept close to his people.

Bradford penned one of his verses on this theme:

Oh, how great comfort was it to see,
The churches to enjoy free liberty!

· · ·

A prudent Magistracy here was placed,
By which the Churches defended were and graced:

· · ·

Whilst things thus did flourish and were in their prime,
Men thought it happy and a blessed time,

To see how sweetly all things did agree;
Both in Church and State, there was an amity;
Each to the other mutual help did lend.[51]

As the Pilgrims crossed the Atlantic it was impossible for them to leave their heritage behind. They brought the Judeo-Christian Bible; the ethics of the Church of England; Anglo-Saxon law and learning; British clothing, books, and madrigals; Dutch cradles and Delftware; German, Swiss, and French hymns. A substantial number of artifacts have been found in the areas where their first houses stood. These serve as treasured mementoes of their material culture. Far more important, however, in the understanding of the Pilgrims and their influence in American history is their life style which was firmly rooted and grounded in spiritual precepts. On the shores of the New World, insights, attitudes, and practices were added to the culture of the Old World, and the imported patrimony was supplemented by new confrontations and obligations indigenous to frontier living. The Pilgrim experiment initiated new departures by evolving certain distinctive patterns of faith and practice on the American continent.

We should affect strife with none.
—John Robinson

22 "WE SHOULD AFFECT STRIFE WITH NONE"

In the acquisition of land the Pilgrim policy was to purchase from the Indians. They did not buy the original site of Plimoth Plantation because not one Patuxet Indian was alive with whom to deal except Squanto. Most of the land in Plimoth colony was, however, purchased from the tribes.[1]

The Pilgrims also endeavored to protect the rights of the Indians. Chief Massasoit gave them their lands at Plimoth, so Nathaniel Morton stated in his *New Englands Memoriall*. From that time on they insisted on paying the Indian owners. In order to safeguard the red man's rights, the General Court directed in 1643 that no one could buy land from an Indian without the approval of the court:

> Whereas it is holden very vnlawful and of dangerous consequence and it hath beene the constant custome from our first beginning That no person or persons haue or euer did purchase Rent or hire any lands herbage wood or tymber of the Natiues but by the Majestrates consent. It is therefore enacted by the Court that if any person or persons do hereafter purchase rent or hyre . . . without the consent and assent of the Court euery such person or persons shall forfait fiue pounds for euery acree.[2]

In negotiating with the natives for their land, payment usually consisted of implements, trinkets, or wampum. By current standards these amounts were extremely modest, but it should be remembered that the Indians wanted these items just as eagerly as the settlers desired the land and to them it was a fair exchange. Massasoit once sold 150 square miles of land for seven coats, nine hatchets, eight hoes, twenty knives, four mooseskins, and ten and one-half yards of cotton.[3] This appears on the surface to be a bargain for the Pilgrims, but they did not have enough coats for themselves, were often hungry, and their mooseskins and implements were precious items essential to their survival.

The Pilgrims and Puritans "did not push the New England Indian off his land," so Alden T. Vaughan contends. The myth of the early colonist as a landgrabber is one of the most persistent, for on the surface it has an immediate aura of validity. The red man once owned all the land, now he owns little or none; hence the Puritan must have tricked, cajoled, or forced the Indian out of his birthright.

But the Indian did not hold that the entire continent belonged to him; it was rather the white man who introduced the idea that it was a red man's continent that purchase alone could transform into the domain of the white. The Indian only knew that he had enough land for himself and his tribe; the remainder was as truly *vacuum domicilium* to him as it was to the Puritan. The native therefore did not object to the occupation of proximate territory by European settlers, so long as the immigrants came as friends rather than foes.[4]

This was evident from the attitude of the Wampanoags who displayed no hostility to the planters of Plimoth Plantation; and also the Massachusetts tribe did not object to the establishment of English communities around Boston Harbor. The sachems were willing to exchange title for a payment which brought them something they considered valuable. Deeds were drawn up and signed after the contents were translated by an interpreter. These deeds were then filed with an official of the colony. In real estate transactions full recognition of the Indians' title was required. A group of trustworthy men was appointed to arrange a sale. Deeds of all purchases were recorded. The Indians, after the example of the Pilgrims, also recorded in a colony record book the transactions of their buying and selling.

Josiah Winslow, son of Edward Winslow, wrote in 1676:

I think I can clearly say that, before these present troubles broke out, the English did not possess one foot of land in this colony but what was fairly obtained by honest purchase of the Indian proprietors. Nay, because some of our people are of a covetous disposition, and the Indians in their straits are easily prevailed with to part with their lands, we first made a law that none should purchase or receive as gift any land of the Indians without the knowledge and allowance of our Court. . . . And if at any time they had brought complaints before us, they have had justice impartial and speedy, so that our òwn people have frequently complained that we erred on the other hand in showing them overmuch favour.[5]

The Pilgrims established laws for protection of the rights of Indians. The Plimoth court treated English offenders against the Indians as severely as Indians who wronged white men. Capt. William Macomber was fined forty shillings and administered a public whipping for "abusing two old Indians" on the sabbath. And it is recorded that on March 5, 1667, "Joseph Bartlett for breaking the Kinges peace in striking of an Indian called Sampson, is centanced to pay a fine of 00/03/04."[6]

Arthur Peach, Thomas Jackson, Richard Stinnings & Daniell Crosse were indicted for murther & robbing by the heighway. They killed and robd one Penowanyanguis, an Indian, at Misquamsqueece, & took from him fiue fadome of Wampeux, and three coates of wollen cloth.[7]

The question was raised by "some of the rude and ignorant sort" as to whether it was proper that "*any* English should be put to death for the Indians." The court stood firm and English justice was upheld.[8] They were tried before a twelve-man jury.

Daniell Crosse made an escape, & so had not his tryall, but Peach, Jackson & Stinnings had sentence of death pnounced. vist, to be taken from the place where they were to the place from whence they came, and thence to the place of execucon, and there to be hanged by the neck vntill their bodyes were dead, wch was executed vpon them accordingly.[9]

Massasoit, chief of the Wampanoags, stood by the Pilgrims as their protector. When it was reported that this "friend was sick and near unto death," Winslow led a delegation from the planta-tion to visit his majesty. He found him suffering with constipation and proceeded to doctor him and save his life. The ingenious ambassador treated him with a physic and built up his strength with chicken broth. The sachem spoke in warm appreciation of this gesture of English friendship: "Now I see the English are my friends and love me; and whilst I live, I will never forget this kindness they have showed me."[10]

Hobomok was another Indian ally won by the Pilgrims, "a proper lusty man, and a man of account for his valour and parts amongst the Indians, and continued very faithful and constant to the English till he died." He became a devoted friend of Capt. Myles Standish and according to tradition lived for a time in the captain's house.[11]

Squanto developed into the indispensable guide of Plimoth Plantation. He was close to Governor Bradford, who described how on a voyage to Cape Cod

Squanto fell sick of an Indian fever, bleeding much at the nose (which the Indians take for a symptom of death) and within a few days died there; desiring the Governor to pray for him that he might go to the Englishman's God in Heaven; and be-queathed sundry of his things to sundry of his English friends as remembrances of his love; of whom they had a great loss.[12]

As noted in an earlier chapter, when the first Pilgrim conflict with the Indians occurred, Pastor Robinson wrote from Leyden and rebuked Captain Standish for taking the way of violence. This attitude of fair treatment marks an advanced position for the time. Robinson's contemporary, Richard Hakluyt, a cosmographer, an explorer, and a minister of the church, presented a strikingly different view. He warned the voyagers to Jamestown that they might have to beat God into the heads and hearts of the Indians:

To handle them gently, while gentle courses may be found to serve, . . . will be without comparison the best. But if gently polishing will not serve, we shall not want hammerers and rough masons enow—to square and prepare them to our Preachers' hands.[13]

In contrast, Deacon Robert Cushman gave a sermon at Plimoth Plantation on December 12, 1621 in which he spoke of the mutual friendship between the settlement and the Indians:

They [the Indians] were wont [reported] to be the most cruel and treacherous people in all these parts, even like lions; but to us they have been like lambs, so kind, so submissive, and trusty, as a man may truly say, many Christians are not so kind nor sincere. . . .

And though when we first came into the country, we were few, and many of us sick, and many died by reason of the cold and wet, it being the depth of winter, and we having no houses nor shelter, yet when there was not six able persons among us, they came daily to us by hundreds, with their sachems or kings, and might in one hour have made a dispatch of us, yet such fear was upon them, as that they never offered us the least injury in word or deed. . . .

And we, for our parts, through God's grace, have with that equity, justice and compassion carried ourselves towards them, as that they have received much favor, help, and aid from us, but never the least injury or wrong by us. . . . And when any of them are in want, as often as they are in the winter, when their corn is done, we supply them to our power, and have them in our houses eating and drinking, and warming themselves.[14]

Bradford tells the dramatic story of Dutch traders on the Connecticut River who went upstream to prevail upon the Indians to sell them furs rather than trade with the Pilgrims at their Windsor center. During a fearful epidemic some 950 Indians died, and the Dutch came south to the Pilgrim trading post at Windsor "spent with hunger and cold." They were welcomed and fed and "were very thankful for this kindness."[15]

In the spring the Indians around Windsor

fell ill of the small pox and died most miserably. . . . But of those of the English house [the Pilgrims at their Windsor trading post] though at first they were afraid of the infection, yet seeing their woeful and sad condition and hearing their pitiful cries and lamentations, they had compassion on them, and daily fetched them wood and water and made them fires, got them victuals whilst they lived; and buried them when they died. . . . And this mercy which they showed them was kindly taken and thankfully acknowledged of all the Indians that knew or heard of the same.[16]

In spite of these incidents of good will there were tensions and clashes. Some other settlements were not as fortunate as the Pilgrim colony. There were basic, unresolved conflicts between the Indian and the white man over control of the land "over

294

which the Indian had roamed at will for generations," so writes Ola E. Winslow.

> He still expected to roam over it, even after he had made little marks on the white man's pieces of paper, and to hunt and fish freely as before. But the white man spoiled all that: put up fences, cut trees, planted orchards, built mills, not because he wanted to spoil the land, but because he had a different notion of what it meant to own land and use it. Bitter situations came one after another.[17]

Some historians rationalize that the Indian's idea of land ownership differed from that of the Englishman's. Through a purchase agreement the native gave the newcomer the right to use the land but not the exclusive control of it. At any rate, whatever the philosophy about ownership, the steady expansion of the white man disturbed the Indian. The demand for land appeared to be insatiable and increased continually. Although the colony endeavored to regulate its purchases and protect Indian rights, the influx of settlers with their muskets decimated the game supply, and their cows and pigs raided native cornfields. The conduct of the aggressive planters destroyed the security the Indians had enjoyed.

The Pilgrims made no special effort to convert the Indians. It was not until 1667 when John Cotton, Jr. came from Boston to serve as minister that the first missionary outreach began. He started a program of preaching to the Indians of the colony. John Eliot of Roxbury was a strong ally in this endeavor. Philip of the Wampanoags, however, resented this proselyting evangelism. He once grasped a button on the coat of John Eliot and said that he cared no more for Christianity than for that button.[18] Philip had been in Plimoth at least once to hear Cotton preach. The zeal to win his people to the white man's ways irritated him as it did other Indian sachems, because they sensed that their culture as well as their land was threatened. John Cotton reported in his *Journal*: "I went to Josiah (Indian sachem of Matakeset) to preach to the Indians but because many of his Indians would forsake him and he would lose much tribute he would not hearken."

In 1665 Richard Bourne had been appointed superintendent of Praying Indians of the Colony. Five years later he was ordained pastor of the first Indian Congregational Church in Mashpee.

Governor Bradford and his associates in the early days had revealed statesmanship in dealing with the Indians. They managed to avoid the bloodshed and tragedy that occurred in other areas of the New World. But circumstances after their passing led to a break in the long period of peace they had enjoyed with the Indians. King Philip's war erupted in 1675.

Thirty-five years after the landing of the *Mayflower* the Quakers began to infiltrate the New England colonies. They formed a left-wing development in the Separatist movement. They repudiated "idol-temples," "steeple-houses," and the church bells, "like a market-bell, to gather the people that the priest may set forth his wares to sell." Even the Pilgrim Fort Meeting House was too formal for them. They rejected all ritual and an established ministry, holding that ordained clergy were unnecessary.[19]

Plimoth records refer to their "crying down of ministry and ministers." This did not set well with Robinson's followers, who believed strongly in an educated, specially trained ministry who taught the people. The Friends also refused to take public oaths and held little respect for the magistrates. This attitude undermined the Pilgrim deference for public authority and threatened to create anarchy.

As protesters and demonstrators, these followers of George Fox upset the apple cart of propriety by their strange actions and puzzling harangues. The congregation at Newbury was surprised one Sunday morning when a young matron walked into the meeting house quite in the nude "to show the people," she explained "the nakedness of their rulers." Another Friend invaded the Cambridge church bearing two bottles. He shouted to the startled minister, "Thus will the Lord break you in pieces!" as he shattered the bottles on the floor. These unconventional acts shocked Puritan tradition, and the Quakers were denounced as "madmen, lunaticks, daemoniacks."

The religious tolerance of the Pilgrims was limited. They passed legislation against the Quakers and other dissenters as did the Massachusetts Bay and other New World colonies—English, French, and Spanish. But at Plimoth there were evidences of sympathy which demonstrated that the Leyden spirit was still alive.[20]

The first law passed in 1657 by the colony began:

Whereas there hath several persons come into this Government commonly called Quakers whose doctrines and practices manifestly tend to the subversion of the fundamentals of Christian Religion, Church Order and Civil peace of this Government as appears by the Testimonies given in sundry depositions and otherwise. . . .

In June 1661 it was decreed that "Quakers and such like vagabonds" shall "be whipt with rods so it not exceed fifteen stripes" and "made to depart the government."[21] And because they challenged the authority of government and would take no oaths, it was enacted: "All such as refuse to take the oath of fidelity as Quakers shall have no vote nor shall be employed in any place of trust."

Certain Quakers were disturbers of the peace, emotional agitators who followed their strange "movings." A legislation was passed that "No Quaker or Rantor or any such corrupt person shall be admitted to be a freeman."[22]

The Quakers called themselves the "people of God" and claimed direct fellowship with the divine reality. Each individual could travel this direct route through guidance of the "inner light," so there was no place for a "hireling priesthood," for sermons or religious ceremonies. The Quaker invasion came at a time when Puritanism was threatened with secularization and dilution, and both the Puritan defenders and the Quaker missionaries displayed incivility and bitterness in this unhappy conflict. Their harping on the guidance of the "inner light" to direct their actions dismayed the Pilgrims who believed that the scriptures, reason, and conscience were the bases for judgment.

The Plimoth colony was upset by this influx and decreed the death penalty; but the law was passed late in their history and was never enforced. No Quaker was ever tortured or executed at Plimoth, although whipping and banishing from the colony were applied as penalties for disturbing the liberty of the people. These regulations were never popular. The Pilgrim conscience could not accept them and opposition caused them to fall into disuse. John Cotton stated that "the Pilgrims never made any sanguinary or capital laws against that sect [Quakers] as the colonies did."[23]

The fear and resentment that were generated by the coming of the Quakers unfortunately had to be faced soon after the more rigid Prence had succeeded Bradford as governor. He was less tolerant than his predecessor and was "a terrour to evill-doers." The second generation at the plantation had not been educated in England and broadened by experiences in Holland. They had not mingled with diverse people and been liberalized through association with the mores of other countries. They revealed ruder manners and less tolerance than their parents who had been trained under Robinson. In this second generation theology grew more dogmatic and social rules more constrictive.

The prejudice and recrimination marked a hiatus in the Robinsonian way of moderation, but in general the bark of these Plimoth anti-Quaker laws was worse than their bite. By 1690 several Friends' meetings had been established along the border of Rhode Island at Rehoboth and Swansea, at Dartmouth, and at Falmouth on Cape Cod.[24]

Thomas Prence as governor represented the extreme right as the Quakers did the extreme left. He said, as six Friends were banished in 1659, "in his conscience" all Quakers deserved "to be destroyed, both they, their wives and children, without pity or mercy." But he was a minority voice. Most of the Pilgrims rejected his violent views. They refused to follow the Bay Puritans in slicing off Quaker ears, branding them with hot irons, burning their books, and confiscating their property.

Quaker Humphrey Norton was "found guilty of divers horred errours, and was centanced speedily to depart." But he returned from Rhode Island and once again was brought before the General Court. Governor Prence charged the prisoner with "many offenses against God." Norton replied boldly: "Thou lyest, Thomas, thou art a malicious man. Thou art like a scolding woman, and thy glamorous tongue I regard no more than the dust under my feet."[25]

Refusing to take an oath before he testified, he was sentenced to be whipped. But he avoided punishment by refusing to pay the marshal the customary fee for a beating. After his release he sent a blistering letter to Governor Prence and to John Alden, who acquiesced in the governor's condemnation.

Puritan extremists advocated hanging for the troublesome Friends, and there were four executions in the Bay. But opposition was particularly strong to this in the old colony where the Pilgrims recalled the teaching of Master Robinson that there was some good in all sects: "There is hardly any sect so anti-Christian or evil otherwise, in church profession, in which there are not divers truly, though weakly led, with the spirit of Christ in their persons, & so true members of his mystical body."[26]

Evidently the Quakers found Plimoth somewhat more congenial than most other areas. Henry Fell, a Quaker, wrote in 1657 to Margaret Fell from Barbados: "In Plimoth patent there is a people not so rigid as the others in Boston, and there are great desires among them after the Truth."[27]

Plimoth may have been more lenient than other settlements because its settlers were accustomed to laymen speaking their minds freely, so they were not as agitated by the outpourings of these zealous newcomers.

In 1656, as the Quaker turmoil started to boil, Isaac Robinson was appointed by Governor Prence to a committee of three to attend the Quaker meetings to reason with them. A law was enacted the same year which stated:

Whereas some have deserved and others think it meet to permit some persons to frequent the Quaker meetings to endeavor to reduce them from the error of their Ways, the Court considering the premises do permit John Smith of Barnstable, Isaac Robinson, John Chapman and John Cooke of Plimoth or any two of them to attend the said meetings for the ends aforesaid at any time betwixt this Court and the next October Court.[28]

Isaac was, like his father, disinclined to bigotry and suppression. He had served as assistant governor and was one of the commissioners of Plimoth colony. And now as an inspector of Quaker heresies he revealed sympathy for them and openly declared himself for tolerance. Whereupon "in 1658 he fell under the displeasure of the commissioners because he would not set his hand to the laws which had been propounded to the several courts to be enacted against the Quakers."[29] He was disenfranchised, but his rights as a freeman were later restored by Gov. Josiah Winslow. It must have been a satisfaction for the son of Edward Winslow to uphold the charitableness of the son of Master Robinson.

James Cudworth of Scituate supported Isaac in his stand for tolerance. He had been a member of Henry Jacob's church in London. He said:

I thought it better so to do than with the blind world to censure, rail at, and revile when they neither saw their persons nor knew any of their principles. But the Quakers and myself cannot close in divers things, and so I signify to the Court that I am no Quaker. . . . But withal I tell you that as I am no Quaker, so I will be no persecutor.[30]

When Ann Hutchinson and her followers were banished from Massachusetts they made application to Plimoth for permission to settle upon the island of Aquidnick or Rhode Island, which was then within the Plimoth patent. The request was granted, "considering they were their countrymen and fellow-subjects that were thus distressed and destitute of habitation, although they held their errours in as great dislike as those from whence they came."

The hardships suffered by Quakers in Plimoth were moderate compared with the treatment administered in the Bay colony. During these stormy years of intolerance the pastor of the First Church in Boston announced from his pulpit that he would "carry fire in one hand and faggots in the other to burn every Quaker in the world." Plimoth was not guilty of this fanaticism. Robinson would have turned in his grave at this bigotry and vituperation! So would Brewster, Bradford, Winslow, and all the original saints of his church. The leavening power of his influence was still living.

Isaac Robinson explored Cape Cod, considered settling on Martha's Vineyard, but decided to buy land from the Indians and found the town of Falmouth. With thirteen other settlers he sailed around Cape Cod to Succoneset Shores, where he built the first house in Falmouth and became the leader of the village and the patriarch of Cape Cod.[31] In 1665 he was granted a license to keep a tavern in Succoneset.

Judge Sewall mentions in his *Journal* a journey to Martha's Vineyard (where Isaac lived for a time) in 1702:

Visit Master [Isaac] Robinson, who saith he is 92 years old; is the son of Master Robinson, pastor of the church of Leyden; part of which came to Plimoth. But to my disappointment he came not to New England, till the year [1631] in which Master Wilson was returning to England, after the settlement of Boston. I told him I was very desirous to see him, for his father's sake and his own. Gave him an Arabian piece of gold, to buy a book for some of his grandchildren.[32]

Prince wrote in his *Annals:* "His [Robinson's] son Isaac came over to Plimoth Colony, living to about ninety years, an agreeable man, whom I have often seen, and was left many posterity in the county of Barnstable." One son and numerous grandchildren of John Robinson came to enjoy the freedom of Cape Cod in the New World and the father's dream was realized in part.[33]

After a few trying years the Friends won out over the Plimoth colony establishment. The General Court declared that if the Quakers and other "rantors" would remove themselves to the western boundary all would be peaceful. From this time on no one was molested simply for holding Quaker beliefs. And the colony treasurer wiped off his books some £300 in fines that had been levied against these dissenters.[34]

It is too great arrogancy for any
man to think that he has so sounded the Word
of God to the bottom as precisely to set
down the church's discipline without error.
—John Robinson

23 "IT IS TOO GREAT ARROGANCY"

The staunch Dr. Samuel Fuller, who had helped carry the settlers through the first winter and had battled epidemics in Salem and Boston, the faithful deacon, was called upon to combat a plague of infectious fever in the summer of 1633. The disease swept away a large number of the Indians. Many of the settlers fell desperately ill and twenty persons died, including two valuable Leyden leaders, Deacons Thomas Blossom and Richard Masterson. The good doctor, after he had exhausted himself in caring for the sick, also perished with this fever.

Elder Brewster continued to remain a bulwark of the plantation until he died April 10, 1644. The plantation and its Fort Meeting House could never be the same without its elder statesman. Bradford mentioned in his journal that Brewster had always been "wise and discreet," "of a very cheerful spirit," "of an humble and modest mind, of a peaceable disposition." He disliked the haughtiness of those who paraded their fine clothes and riches. He bore the burden with the humblest, and during the first years "living many times without bread or corn many months together, having nothing but fish and often wanting that also."[1]

The foremost symbols of the Scrooby-Leyden odyssey had been lost in Robinson and Brewster. For five years Brewster's post as elder was not filled. Thomas Cushman, son of Deacon Cushman, who came over on the *Fortune* with his father, was then chosen for the position. Thomas had been left in care of Brewster and Bradford, while his father went back on a mission to England, and Bradford had adopted him after Deacon Cushman's death. Thomas Cushman took up the mantle of his illustrious predecessor for forty-two years, and proved "very studious & solicitous for the peace & prosperity of the church, & to prevent & heale all breaches."[2] Elder Cushman assisted the minister

not only in ruling, catechising, visiting, but also in publick teaching as Mr. Brewster had done before him. It being the professed principle of this church in their first formation "to choose none for governing elders but such as are able to teach." Which ability (as Mr. Robinson observes in one of his letters) other reformed churches did not require in the ruling elders.[3]

The Plimoth church had not been as fortunate in its choice of ministers as in its lay leaders. For more than ten years the Ley-

301

den fellowship had enjoyed Robinson's "able ministrie & prudente governmente." These had been the golden years. The people had been guided on a high level intellectually and spiritually, and they did not succeed in securing anything comparable to Robinson's leadership in Massachusetts. In spite of this dearth of qualified ministers, the church managed to survive.

In 1628 Isaac Allerton, while in England, found a "yonge man for a minister" and sent him over on the *White Angel* without consulting home base. When Mr. Rogers arrived the congregation was skeptical about his choice because they "had bene so bitten by Mr. Lyford as they desired to know ye person well whom they should invite amongst them." The newcomer proved to be an unfortunate candidate for it was "perceived, upon some triall, that he was crased in his braine." So the Pilgrims were forced to send him back at their expense in 1629.[4]

That same year Ralph Smith, a Cambridge graduate, was brought to Plimoth. He was ordained as the first pastor in 1629. "Yet he proved but a poor help to them in that, being of very weak parts," and. "a dull man."[5]

The most noteworthy episode during Smith's indifferent ministry was the arrival in Plimoth of Roger Williams who came to serve as teacher. His contribution to the colony and to New England is worthy of review. This graduate of Pembroke College, Cambridge, age twenty-seven, landed in Boston in 1631 on the *Lion* with Isaac Robinson. He was invited to the First Church, but he "refused to join with this congregation because they would not make a public declaration of their repentance for having communion with the churches of England while they lived there."[6]

The Salem church called the young man to serve with Samuel Skelton. The General Court warned this parish that Williams had "declared his opinion that the magistrate might not punish the breach of the Sabbath, nor any other offense, as it was a breach of the first table" of the ten commandments.

After a brief sojourn in Salem he departed for Plimoth where he hoped he would find a more Separatist outlook, but he was surprised to discover that Robinson's followers were not rigid Separatists. He learned that members of the Plimoth fellowship on trips to England visited Anglican churches and returned home without being condemned. Williams said it was wrong to hear Church of England padres and also that it was wrong to remain in a church that did not censure its members for such deviations. He stated that Plimoth should not require the oath of fidelity to their commonwealth of any who were unregenerate because the oath was invoked in the name of God and was therefore a sort of religious communion with others who took it. This caused the older members to shake their heads.

Others who could not share his eccentricities and enthusiasms stated that God had been pleased "to put a windmill in his head." Nevertheless, Williams passed some two years at Plimoth Plantation as teacher of the church. He stirred up considerable excitement in the colony, but he departed on his own to Salem to assume the post of teacher in 1635. He had by this time developed his idea of the separation of church and state so as to deny that a magistrate had power to require an oath and that the king had no right to grant a charter of lands in the New World since the land belonged to the Indians. He taught that the government had no authority to punish violations of the first four commandments, and he held that a man should not pray with his wife unless both were regenerate.[7]

The General Court refused the petition of Salem for further land grants because they had chosen Mr. Williams as their teacher, while he stood under question of authority, and so offered contempt to the magistrates.[8]

He sent a letter to his flock on August 16, 1635 announcing that he had cast off communion with the churches of the Bay since they were false and unclean; and that he would have nothing more to do with the folks of Salem unless they would join him in cutting loose from all the other churches of the colony.[9] The church could not go along with this extreme separation. John Cotton wrote in 1647: "It was well known that whilest he lived in Salem, he neither admitted, nor permitted any church members, but such as rejected all communion with the Parish Assemblies, so much as hearing of the Word amongst them."[10]

Williams refused to take communion with Governor Winthrop and his fellow churchmen because they were an "unseparated people." He urged them to "make public declaration of their repentance for having taken communion with the churches of England while they lived there."

This position, so contrary to Robinson's views and practices in Leyden and Plimoth, is difficult to reconcile with Williams' championship of religious liberty. He was more bent on trying to exclude the ungodly from the congregation than was Robinson and he demanded much stricter qualifications for membership. He asked candidates to renounce the Anglican church and promise to break with its corruptions. He refused to accept the baptism of any church as valid. He rejected his own baptism since it was performed by a false church, and was rebaptized.[11]

He set up such rigid requirements that the church was threatened with extinction because no members could be found who were able to meet his standards. He insisted that the church should possess a high degree of purity which other religious leaders considered impossible to realize. Winthrop says in his *Journal* that Williams "refused communion with all, save his own wife."[12]

Williams supported Robinson's idea that the church should choose the minister and that ordination by bishops was not necessary. He believed that the apostolic succession had been broken and that this extinguished the church. Robinson agreed only with the fact that the succession had been severed. He held that the church had survived this rupture. Both men taught that non-Christians had the right to hold public office and officials did not have to be church members.

Unfortunately, Williams' quixotic and headstrong nature had

stirred up the people of Salem and the Bay. He became obsessed with sympathy for the Indians and maintained in a tract that he published "that we have not our land by Pattent from the King but that the Natives are the true owners of it, and that we ought to repent of such a receiving it by Pattent."[13]

He wrote Bradford: "Why lay such stress upon your patent from King James? 'Tis but parchment. James has no more right to give away or sell Massasoit's lands, and cut and carve his country, than Massasoit has to sell King James' kingdom or send Indians to colonize Warwickshire."[14]

This heretical concept threatened the economy of the colonies and, coupled with his bizarre theology, led to his public trial before the General Court of the Bay where it was stated that "he holds forth four particulars:

First, that we have not our land by patent from the King but that the natives are the true owners of it, and that we ought to repent of such a receiving it by patent.

Second, that it is not lawful to call a wicked person to swear, to pray, as being actions of God's worship.

Thirdly, that it is not lawful to hear any of the ministers of the parish assemblies in England.

Fourthly, that the civil magistrates' power extends only to the bodies and goods and outward state of men.[15]

After an extensive hearing, during which the court consulted the prominent ministers of New England, he was ordered to depart from the jurisdiction of the Bay in a sentence passed in October 1635. This sentence was based on his attacks upon the authority of the magistrates and his insistence in defaming them and the churches of which they were members, in spite of all warnings to desist. The decree was revised to take effect in the spring, provided he would refrain from attempting to spread his opinions —a provision in which he failed to comply.

When the authorities heard that he was planning to lead a colony to Narragansett they feared that the "infection" might spread from there throughout the colony and they undertook to send him back to England. But Williams escaped in the middle of January and made his way through the snow-covered fields and woodlands to Rhode Island. During this wilderness journey he was "sorely tossed for fourteen weeks in a bitter winter season, not knowing what bread or bed did mean."

It was not Plimoth Plantation, as often thought, who engineered the exile of Williams. He was not forced to leave Plimoth. He was a "bull in a china closet" while he served there, but he won friends who respected his learning and courage. Bradford wrote of him:

Mr. Roger Williams, a man godly and zealous, having many precious parts but very unsettled in judgment, came over first to the Massachusetts; but upon some discontent left that place and came hither, where he was friendly entertained according to their poor ability, and exercised his gifts amongst them and

304

after some time was admitted a member of the church. And his teaching well approved, for the benefit whereof I still bless God and am thankful to him even for his sharpest admonitions and reproofs so far as they agreed with truth.

He this year began to fall into some strange opinions, and from opinion to practice, which caused some controversy between the church and him. And in the end some discontent on his part, by occasion whereof he left them something abruptly. Yet afterwards sued for his dismission to the church of Salem, which was granted, with some caution to them concerning him and what care they ought to have of him. But he soon fell into more things there, both to their and the government's trouble and disturbance. I shall not need to name particulars; they are too well known now to all, though for a time the church here went under some hard censure by his occasion from some that afterwards smarted themselves. But he is to be pitied and prayed for; and so I shall leave the matter and desire the Lord to show him his error and reduce him into the way of truth and give him a settled judgment and constancy in the same, for I hope he belongs to the Lord, and that He will show him mercy.[16]

Edward Winslow was another of Williams' defenders and he made it clear that Plimoth did not conspire to banish their "teacher." The founder of Rhode Island wrote of his friends in Plimoth after his departure:

Of the letter from my ancient friend, Mr. Winslow, then Governor of Plimoth, professing his own and others' love and respect to me, yet lovingly advising me (since I was fallen into the edge of their bounds, and they were loath to displease the Bay) to remove but to the other side of the water; and then he said I had the country free before me and might be as free as themselves, and we should be loving neighbors together; that the then prudent and godly Governor, Mr. Bradford, and others of his godly council, said that I should not be molested nor tossed up and down again while they had breath in their bodies [and] that great and pious soul, Mr. Winslow, melted and visited me at Providence, and put a piece of gold into the hands of my wife for our supply.[17]

Deacon Samuel Fuller also stood by this prophet, and left a clause in his will that two acres on Strawberry Hill were to go to his son "if Mr. Roger Williams refuse to accept them as formerlie he hath done."

William Brewster and others at the plantation remembered the erratic course that their old friend John Smyth had taken in Holland and he expressed the fear that Williams was headed for the byways that led so many nonconformists to extremes, that he "would run the same course of rigid Separation and anabaptistry which Mr. John Smyth, the sebaptist at Amsterdam had done."

The elder's apprehensions were vindicated. Williams did have himself rebaptized "by one Holyman" in Salem. He then baptized his baptizer and a handful of followers and so created the first

Baptist church in America. He then began to question his second baptism, as Smyth had done, and departed from his church as a "seeker," brushing aside all creeds and rituals.

Like Robinson, Williams was a product of a turbulent era of disputation. They were both independent and creative minds. The former escaped some of the extremes of the latter and was more of a constructive leader of men, more engaging as a personal friend and as a thinker whose wholesome philosophy wore well through the passing years.

Although more exclusive in his communion with other Christians and more stringent in his requirements for the holy life, Williams shared Robinson's defense of the individual conscience and his tolerance of diversity of opinion. Master Robinson would have enjoyed fellowship with him, if they could have met at the spring near the spot where Williams and his companions landed in 1636 to found Providence. He would have approved the inscription there: "Liberty is reserved for the inhabitants to fetch water at this spring forever."[18] And Williams would have commended Robinson for his words: "The hearing of the Word of God is not

"Edward Winslow"—painted by Robert Walker (London, 1651)

306

so inclosed by any hedge, or ditch, divine or human, made about it, but lies in common for all, for the good of all."

But the founder of the free colony of Rhode Island, with his passion for religious freedom, could not tolerate the erratic and iconoclastic Quakers. A number of his critics had embraced the way of the "inner light." So when George Fox reached his area in 1672 he sent him a challenge to debate at Newport. Fox had departed before Williams arrived, but three of his followers, John Stubbs, John Burnet, and William Edmundson, agreed to take on the redoubtable Baptist, who rowed all the way from Providence to Newport.

During the three-day debate, auditors heckled the "old man," who grew hoarse in the midst of the shouting, whereupon his opponents cried out that he was drunk. Following this exhausting encounter Williams returned to Providence to continue the argument. In the report that he wrote of this encounter he did not propose civil action against the assertive and reckless Friends. He had been accused by them of deserting his profession of tolerance and he admitted gamely: "You mind me again of my books against persecution, and yet myself a persecutor of my peaceable neighbors."[19]

Faced with the problems created by Smith and Williams, the church authorized Edward Winslow to discover "some able & fitt man for to be their minister" while he was on his 1635 mission to England.

He "procured a godly and worthy man, one Mr. Glover. But it pleased God when he was prepared for the voyage, he fell sick of a fever and died." Winslow then persuaded the Rev. John Norton, a graduate of Brewster's Peterhouse College, to visit Plimoth and look over the field before committing himself. He promised "to repay the charge laid out for him [which came to about £70] and to be at his liberty."[20]

He wrote "pure elegant Latin," was a "hard student," and "he would spend whole days in prayer." He remained about four months, "and was well liked of them and much desired of them; but he was invited to Ipswich, where so many rich and able men and sundry of his acquaintance so he went to them and is their minister." And here Bradford adds ruefully, "About half of the charge was repaid, and the rest he had for the pains he took amongst them." "His temper had a tincture of choler in it."[21]

Once again, the teaching in the meeting house was laid upon William Brewster. The Rev. John Rayner of Yorkshire, another Cambridge graduate from Magdalene College, had come to New England in 1635. He was brought to Plimoth, and proved to be "of a meek and humble spirit, sound in truth and every way unreprovable in his life and conversation. Whom after some time of trial they chose for their teacher, the fruits of whose labours they enjoyed many years with much comfort, in peace and good agreement." He was "an able, faithful, laborouse preacher."[22] During his ministry the first meeting house was built in 1648 to replace the Fort Meeting House.

In certain brief periods the Plimoth church enjoyed both a

307

minister and a teacher; at other times only a minister or a teacher.

During Rayner's regime as teacher, a minister was also invited in 1638—the Rev. Charles Chauncy, an eminent Cambridge scholar from Trinity College, who had served there as Greek lecturer. He was one of the most learned men who came to New England. He had at three different times been censured by the university or the archbishop. He recanted three times and retracted his recantation three times.[23] Bradford spoke of him as "a reverend, godly and very learned man, intending upon trial to chose him pastor of the church here, for the more comfortable performance of the ministry with Mr. John Rayner, the teacher of the same."

However, the erudite Chauncy stayed only until the latter part of 1641. He was a stickler for baptism by immersion,

> he holding it ought only be by dipping, and putting the whole body under water, and that sprinkling was unlawful. The church yielded that immersion or dipping [might] be lawful [as well as sprinkling] but in this cold country not so convenient. But they could not, or durst not, yield to him in this, that sprinkling (which all the churches of Christ do for the most part use at this day) was unlawful and an human invention, as the same was pressed. But they were willing to yield to him as far as they could, and to the utmost, and were contented to suffer him to practice as he was persuaded. And when he came to minister that ordinance he might so do it to any that did desire it in that way, provided he could peaceably suffer Mr. Rayner and such as desired to have theirs otherwise baptized by him by sprinkling or pouring on of water upon them, so as there might be no disturbance in the church hereunto.[24]

One can read between the lines the evidence of Robinson's moderation as reflected in the reasoning of Bradford, Brewster, and others. In the controversy the congregation reserved the right to choose and so the conflict between their two clergy was more or less resolved. Also the church laymen invited nearby ministers "to dispute the point with him publicly." Mr. Ralph Partridge came over from Duxbury and disputed "very ably and sufficiently; as also some other ministers within this government. But he was not satisfied." Unable to convince Chauncy through these public forums, "the church sent to many other churches to crave their help and advice in this matter, and with his will and consent sent them his arguments written under his own hand." Boston, New Haven, and other New England churches "all concluded against him. But himself was not satisfied therewith."[25]

Chauncy, "an exceeding plaine preacher," possessed the stature of Robinson when it came to scholarship, but he did harp on baptism by immersion, and he insisted that holy communion should be celebrated only in the evening. Neither of his pet ideas made much headway at the plantation where the people tolerated his eccentricities but demanded the right to choose how their children should be baptized and at what time they would celebrate the Lord's Supper.

He was strong on praying and fasting and set quite a stiff schedule of meditation for himself. He was ascetic in his Bible study and private devotion. The Pilgrims had not been accustomed to such otherworldliness in Master Robinson, who was warmhearted and down-to-earth.

Their scholar-minister moved to Scituate in 1641. Here he soon found himself involved in further debate about total immersion. Governor Winthrop relates in his *Journal* for 1642 that Chauncy caused one of his own twins to swoon while trying to immerse them. Following this mishap one anxious mother caught hold of the pastor and "near pulled him into the water" when he reached out to baptize her child.[26]

After his two failures to win the people of Plimoth and Scituate, Mr. Chauncy determined to return to England. As he was about to set sail in 1654, representatives of the board of overseers at Harvard College interviewed him. They explained that they had encountered trouble with their president, Henry Dunster, a graduate of Magdalene College, Cambridge, who had been forced to resign because he held "antipaedo-baptistical principles"; that is, he agreed with John Smyth, Thomas Helwys, John Murton, Roger Williams, and others in rejecting infant baptism. This seems a miniscule irritation to upset the dignitaries of a university, but as the citadel of Puritan orthodoxy, Harvard could not tolerate this departure from the truth. Dunster removed to Scituate where he got along with the Pilgrims and soon took over the pulpit vacated by Chauncy. The second president of Harvard was engaged by the overseers after he made a pledge that he would "forbear to disseminate or publish any tenets concerning the necessity of immersion in baptism and celebration of the Lord's Supper at evening." He was pleased to accept "without reluctance" the salary of £100 a year and to diligently serve the college.

President Chauncy set a pattern for piety. Rising at four every morning, he prayed for an hour, and then departed to a college hall to expound a chapter of scripture to the students, "with a short prayer before, and a long one after." He returned home to interpret another chapter to his family and conduct prayers. At eleven he retreated to his study for three quarters of an hour of meditation, and once again at four in the afternoon. In the evening he presented another exposition based on a Bible chapter with prayer, and went home to read one more Bible passage and to pray. He retired at nine after another hour of "secret Prayer."[27]

About this time the colony was stirred with news from England. Cromwell had defeated the forces of Charles I in Gainsborough in 1643. The next year he won a smashing victory over the Cavaliers at Marston Moor. This impelled Bradford to break forth in a pean of praise:

Do you not now see the fruits of your labours, O all ye servants of the Lord? That have suffered for His truth? . . . The tyrannous Bishops are ejected, their courts dissolved, their canons forceless, their service cashiered, their ceremonies useless and despised, . . . and all their superstitions discarded . . . and the monuments of idolatry rooted out of the land. And the proud and profane supporters and cruel defenders of these . . . marvelously overthrown. And are not these great things? Who can deny it? . . .

Anno Domini 1646   Hallelujah![28]

John Rayner, the Plimoth pastor, resigned in 1654 and moved to Dover, New Hampshire. The church again managed for some time without an established leadership. In 1667, after "perishing without vision" for some thirteen years, the son of the eminent John Cotton came to the Mother Church. He was offered a salary of £50 a year—one third to be paid in wheat or butter, an equal amount in rye, barley, or peas, and the remainder in Indian corn, and "so to continue till God in his Providence shall so impoverish the town that they shall be necessitated to abridge the sum."[29]

Plimoth's complete acceptance by the Bay was assured with John Cotton, Jr. as minister. The new era of Harvard-trained men promoted closer association among the Massachusetts churches as the Congregational Way evolved on New England soil.

Cotton, who had graduated from Harvard in 1654, was elected and ordained after eighteen months of trial at Plimoth in 1669. His distinguished father had known Robinson through his writings and mutual acquaintances and had followed his career with interest. The Pilgrims agreed to settle the young man even though he had, through youthful indiscretions, been temporarily excommunicated from his father's church. He was short, chubby, and ruddy-complexioned, eloquent and scholarly, "a man of strong parts." His sister had married Increase Mather, so he brought to New Plimoth the Harvard-Boston prestige and led the old church for thirty years into a period of fellowship with other communities in the Bay.

His coming vindicated the words of Master Robinson spoken in the summer of 1620: "There will be little difference between the unconformable [the nonseparating Puritan] ministers and you when they come to the practice of the ordinances out of the Kingdom." Furthermore, he urged "by all means to endeavour to close with the godly part of the Kingdom of England and rather to study union rather than division."[30]

The divisions of the Old World were not as clear-cut in the New World, where practicality took precedence over tradition. Robinson would have been pleased to see his company moving in the direction of cooperation with their neighbors.

To revive lagging religion in the colony, Cotton employed the catechisms used by Robinson in Leyden, written by his esteemed William Perkins: *The Foundation of the Christian Religion gathered into sixe Principles*. Robinson had added an appendix of forty-six questions and answers. Thus his edition was taken up again in an effort to quicken the lagging faith of his colony.

Under John Cotton's ministry in 1680 there was a prolonged discussion as to whether a psalm should be read before it was sung. During the argument the minister was asked to preach on the issue. He favored the prior reading of the psalm, but it was up to the church members to decide. And after due deliberation they voted to go along with his suggestion. They continued to use the *Psalm Book* by Henry Ainsworth, which they brought with them from Holland, until the end of the century, long after the *Bay Psalm Book* was used by the Bay churches.

Not all the tunes from Ainsworth's book were noteworthy for their harmony, and the selection was limited in range and variety. Some of the Pilgrims, like Robert Bartlett, hankered at times for old favorites they had grown to love in the Church of England, where organ and choir tended to give a boost to the theology of the hymn writer. Bored by the dullness of the Calvinistic music in the Plimoth Meeting House, Bartlett protested against the monotony of hymnody and was brought before the court on May 1, 1660:

At this Court, Robert Bartlett appeared, being summoned to answer for speakeing contemptuously of the ordinance of singing of psalms, and was convict of the fact and did in part acknowlidg his euill therein, promising that hee hoped it should bee a warning to him; on which the Court sharply admonished him, and required him that unto such as hee had soe appobriously spoken of the said ordinance he should acknowlidg his falt, which hee engaged to do as hee should bee minded of them, and soe hee was discharged.[31]

In nearby Salem another worshiper wrote on the panel of his pew his reaction to the psalm-singing in the parish:

Could poor David but for once
To Salem church repair,
And hear his Psalms thus warbled out,
Good Lord, how he would swear.[32]

The psalms of Ainsworth may appear dull to moderns as they did to some of the Pilgrims, but in content they are preferable to the emotionalism of revival hymns and gospel jazz that flourished in a later period. They at least possessed beauty, biblical foundation, and intellectual acceptability.

The compact village inside the stockade soon spilled out into the countryside. In the 1630's Plimoth changed into a straggling village. Settlers moved out to seek better land and to build larger houses. This geographic expansion led to the establishment of new communities. Scituate was first in 1636, with Duxbury following the next year. In 1639 four new towns sprang up: Barnstable, Sandwich, Taunton, and Yarmouth. Eventually there were twenty offspring in the colony.[33]

As the Pilgrim families left the stockade they built bigger homes—some gambrel-roof cottages common in the Netherlands and some the two-story saltbox type, many of which still grace the hills and valleys of New England. They were made of rough-hewn boards around a great central brick chimney and covered with clapboards or shingles. Walls were plastered with a combination of straw, shells and clay. Some had wooden paneling and wainscoting. These houses are sought after today by the most discriminating buyers.

Attractive furniture, now highly prized in the antiques market,

311

was imported on the numerous ships that came from England or fashioned by the colony carpenters. These artisans were capable of reproducing in oak, pine, or maple the beautiful pieces they had owned or seen in England and Holland: court cupboards, high chests, carved blanket chests, trestle, gateleg, and tavern tables, joined stools, benches, settles, and armchairs.

Authentic originals used by the Pilgrims are now in Pilgrim Hall, Plimoth, and they speak eloquently of the good taste of these early settlers. In spite of their privations they loved beauty and created it in their homes and gardens.

The dispersion from the Fort Meeting House was a hardship for the founders but a healthy movement in the development of New England. As Robinson's church in Leyden had been depleted of strength through its self-giving mission to New England, so the Fort Meeting House was grieved to see its saints acquire land and move to adjoining hamlets and establish their own churches. Governor Bradford recorded in 1644:

And thus was this poor church left, like an ancient mother grown old and forsaken of her children, though not in their affections yet in regard of their bodily presence and personal helpfulness; her ancient members being most of them worn away by death, and these of later times being like children

Bartlett House—showing influence of Dutch gambrel roof

312

translated into other families, and she like a widow left only to trust in God. Thus, she that had made many rich became herself poor.[34]

Troubled over the declining state of religion, the scattering of the original Plimoth Plantation over a wider territory, Bradford wrote in his *Journal* on a blank page opposite the eloquent letter of December 15, 1617, written by John Robinson and William Brewster, which they had addressed to the authorities in England pleading their cause:

O sacred bond, whilst inviolably preserved! How sweet and precious were the fruits that flowed from the same! But when this fidelity decayed, then their ruin approached. O that these ancient members had not died or been dissipated (if it had been the will of God) or else that this holy care and constant faithfulness had still lived, and remained with those that survived, and were in times afterwards added unto him. . . . I have been happy, in my first times, to see, and with much comfort to enjoy, the blessed fruits of this sweet communion, but it is now a part of my misery in old age, to find and feel the decay and want thereof (in a great measure) and with grief and sorrow of heart to lament and bewail the same. And for others' warning and admonition, and my own humiliation, do I here note the same.[35]

The despondent words of Bradford, as he watched disturbing change, were natural for one who was growing old and weary of the long contest. Although the outward decline of the Leyden spirit was apparent, it was cherished by yet unheralded men and women who were to preserve its vision. It was a trying transition to behold, but it was a form of expansion rather than a waning. The diaspora sent advocates of the way out into the surrounding countryside where the faithful preserved the inheritance.[36]

If in anything we err, advertise
us brotherly.
—John Robinson

24 "ADVERTISE US BROTHERLY"

With the increase in population and the coming of more heterogeneous groups, religious profession diminished and Plimoth Plantation was pressured to act in support of orthodoxy. Governor Prence tried to legislate goodness by enacting rules to regulate conduct. The court then passed laws to ban travel on the sabbath, prohibit "violent riding," punish dozing and playing during church services, and the smoking of tobacco near the meeting house. It was enacted: "That any psons that shalbe found smooking of Tobavco on the Lords day; goeing too or coming from the meetinges within two miles of the meeting house shall pay twelve pence for every such default to the Collonies use."[1]

One wonders how Elder Brewster would have reacted since his inventory indicates that he owned a "tobacco box," "pipes," and a store of "tobacco." In the earlier years of the plantation his cottage was close to the Fort Meeting House and one may be sure that he smoked there after services; and that he often joined William Bradford in his house as they enjoyed their long-stemmed clay pipes and drinks from the governor's "great beer bowl worth three pounds" which he had hospitably filled from his "brewing tub." As long as Brewster and Bradford were in power few bluenose excesses crept into the social life of the old colony.

There is evidence that some Pilgrim women also enjoyed the aroma of Sir Walter's blessed weed. Capt. James Cudworth, who championed the rights of the persecuted Quakers along with Isaac Robinson, stated in one of his letters from Scituate that his wife was so feeble that "when she is up she cannot light a pipe of tobacco, but it must be lighted for her; and until she has taken two or three pipes, for want of breath is not able to stir."[2]

Plimothians always took religion seriously and expected citizens to attend the Fort Meeting House, but church attendance was not compulsory. In the 1650's a tightening of the reins led to new regulations and restrictions, as the *Records of Plimoth Colony* testify:

Whosoever shall prophane the Lords day by doeing any servill worke or any such like abusses shall forfeitt for every such default ten shillings or be whipt.[3]

It is ordered that if any in any lazey slothful or prophane way doth neglect to com to the publick worship of God shall forfeit for euery such default ten shillings or bee publicly whipte.[4]

It was also stipulated that there should be a fine of twenty shillings or "else sit in the stockes foure houres" for traveling on the Lord's day "except they can give a sufficient reason for theire soe doeing."[5] Another ordinance stated:

That noe ordinary keeper in this Govrnent shall draw any wine or liquor on the Lords day for any except in case of necessitie for the reliefe of those that are sicke or faint or the like for theire refreshing; on the penaltie of paying a fine of ten shillings for every default.[6]

The Pilgrims' strict sabbath observances, however, were mild compared with those in England and elsewhere in the New World. For some time there had been a movement in England to strengthen the sabbath laws. In 1595 Nicholas Bownd, rector of Norton in Suffolk, wrote *The doctrine of the Sabbath, etc.* which gave voice to the widespread resentment of the worldly and pagan practices that prevailed. Magistrates should restrain men from working on Sunday. All recreations of honest character, all lawful delights enjoyed on other days must be abstained from on the seventh day. Feasting was wrong. People should abstain from needless worldly conversation. The day was to be sanctified by worship, common prayer, public reading of the scriptures, and celebration of the sacraments. Weekly attendance at church was mandatory in England and this duty was enforced by the state. Fines were imposed on absentees, but they were not exacted as a regular practice except from a known "Popish recusant."[7]

The authorities in Bermuda passed laws that required that all "Sabbath breakers" should be haled before the court who were found "absenting themselves from church, or leaving during service," or "by using any bodily recreation by gaminge, sportinge, or by doing any servile work as travelling, fyshinge, cutting of wood, digginge of potatoes, carryinge of burdens, beating of corne," etc.

The Genevan restraints at the Plimoth colony never reached the extremes practiced on Bermuda. The spying and tattling that impelled some holier-than-thou souls to report sinners to the Fort Meeting House was not indigenous to the soil of Plimoth. The Bermudian law stated that "church wardens and sydesmen shall dailie observe the carriage and lives of the people, and shall forthwithe informe the ministers of all such scandalous crymes as shall be comitted by any of them."[8]

In the Jamestown colony under Governor General De La Warr two church services were held every week for the work gangs with sermons every Sunday morning and afternoon, and attendance was compulsory. The penalty for three unexcused absences was death. There was no such iron regimen at the Fort Meeting House.

The court records of the early years reveal only a minimum of major crimes. They tell largely of efforts to protect the public welfare, of numerous land grants, of military service, of the problems and rights of indentured workers, and of misdemeanors

"Penelope Winslow" (wife of Josiah Winslow)—painted by Robert Walker (London, 1651)

such as drunkenness. (The Pilgrims countenanced the use of alcohol, but legislated against excess.)

The village enjoyed a little drama now and then like the one staged by an indentured worker who served Elizabeth Warren, the active businesswoman, who was the widow of Richard Warren. The *Plimoth Colony Records* of July 5, 1635 read:

> Thomas Williams, ye servant of widow Warren, was accused for spreading profane & blasphemous speeches against ye majestie of God, which wer these: ther being some discention between him and his dame, she, after other things, exhorted him to fear God & doe his duty; he answered, he neither feared God, nor the divell; this was proved by witneses, and confessed by himselfe. This, because ye courte judged it to be spoken in passion & distemper, with reprove did let him pass.[9]

New Plimoth did not enact laws regulating apparel. The Leyden Pilgrims had seen enough during the Millinery war in Amsterdam where the Ancient Brethren tried to outlaw frilly hats, ribbons, high-heel boots, and gay colors. They were a sober people, but they liked a touch of brightness in their costumes. As seekers after liberty they reached beyond the bounds set by the Geneva reformers.

A Plimoth law required each householder to prepare an inventory of his possessions. These inventories and last wills and testaments are on file today at the Registry of Deeds in Plimoth. Through their study we can gain some knowledge of the clothing, furniture, and household equipment in the Pilgrim homes. These records are long and detailed, covering several pages in most cases. Here are a few items from the inventory of William Bradford:

    a turkey-red grogram suit and cloak
    a cloth cloak faced with taffety and lined with baize
    a lead coullered suit with silver buttons
    a stuffe suit with silver buttons
    an old violett coullered cloake and an old green gowne
    a sad coullered suit
    2 hattes, a blacke one & a coullered one, and 4 fine shirts
    a red waistcoat
    a brewing tub
    a great beer bowle worth 3 pounds
    2 silver wine cups
    4 Venice glasses
    13 silver spoons
    64 pieces of pewter
    silver and pewter candlesticks
    a large library of books
    a 300 acre farm on Jones River
    a house with gardens and orchard at Plimoth
    investments in fur trading posts

"Josiah Winslow"—painted by Robert Walker (London, 1651)

His estate was valued at £900, or approximately $45,000.[10]

The following are samples from the extensive inventories of William Brewster:

caps: 1 wrought, 1 red, 1 laced, 1 white, 1 quilted [his hair must have been thinning]
3 waistcoats, 1 green waistcoat
1 blue cloth suit, 1 old suit turned
1 violet colored coat
1 pair leather drawers, a pair ye green drawers
1 doublet, 2 girdles
stockings and silk stockings
2 pair of gloves
1 pair of garters
3 pair of shoes
26 handkerchiefs
1 ruffle band, 6 bands
rugs, blankets, sheets, pillow cases, table cloths
curtains, 2 cushions, 1 green cushion
1 bedstead and settle
1 settle bed, a feather bed, bolster and pillows
1 little desk
1 little table
a table and form
1 little trunk
1 broad chest, 1 chest
chairs
1 candlestick & snuffer
1 lamp
1 pewter bottle, 2 pewter cups & spoon
1 silver beaker and spoon
earthen pot with sugar
tobacco case, tobacco box & tongs

In a second inventory made on his Duxbury house a value of £107 was established. Elder Brewster's library was meticulously catalogued by William Bradford and Thomas Prence and a valuation of £150 set upon it.

Before they died, most of the Pilgrims had collected a surprising amount of furniture, household equipment, and clothing in addition to their land, houses, livestock, and tools. These thrifty people initiated the tradition of the New England attic where everything was saved for the day when it might be needed again. These repositories are now a mecca for collectors of antiquities.

The settlers had learned in England the importance of owning their own land. As members of the plantation and as freemen they were granted land and bought land, reaching out through a wide area. Frugal and hard-working, a number of the Pilgrims managed to accumulate substantial holdings. Myles Standish left

A sixteenth-century hornbook—used by children to learn their ABC's

an estate valued at £258, about $15,000, which was considerable for the period.

During the process of producing a 350th anniversary commemorative stamp to mark the arrival of the *Mayflower* in Plimoth, the Office of the Postmaster General sent a sketch to the Plimoth 350th Anniversary Committee. Members were surprised to see a group of Pilgrims in the foreground, all in black with white collars, the men with black beards and black hats, with a black *Mayflower* in the background. The only touch of color was the blue of the sea and a band of orange for the sky.

In an interchange of letters the postal department replied: "The time-honored image of the Pilgrims is to place them in black and white clothing. Boughton's well-known painting of the Pilgrims going to church through the snow has them in black and white as well as the seventeenth century Dutch painter, who painted them going abroad." Evidently the designer of the stamp had seen only a black and white reproduction of the original.

The Boughton painting hangs in the hall of the New York Historical Society and anyone can see that the Pilgrims are dressed in browns, reds, and greens. In Pilgrim Hall, Plimoth there are a number of famous paintings, all in color: "The Embarkation at Delfshaven" by Robert Wier, "The Landing of the Pilgrims" by Henry Sargent, "The Landing of the Pilgrims" by Michael Corne, "The Signing of the Mayflower Compact" by Percy Moran, and "The First Thanksgiving" by Jennie Brownscombe. The English 350th anniversary stamp showed them in bright colors.

More persistent than the black garb misconception is the portrayal of the Pilgrims as simple people with only one university man in the group—William Brewster. College breeding was rare in any seventeenth-century community around the world. The possession of a college diploma does not guarantee that a man is educated nor does the lack of one prove that he is ignorant. By such a false standard most of the world's foremost minds could be classified as unlearned. Education is a matter of wisdom, judgment, and resourcefulness, of which the Pilgrims were endowed with a good supply. Most Pilgrims were above average for their time in knowledge of the Bible, (a fair test of the learned even today) and the literature and political affairs of their country. Many spoke two or three languages. Brewster and Bradford left libraries larger than the collection given by John Harvard to help start Harvard College.

The leaders of the colony proved to be sagacious builders and their settlement maintained loyalty to the tradition of learning. They deserve a good rating intellectually. It required intelligent people to plan two mass migrations, finance them, and make a go of it as a self-sustaining community against powerful odds.

Bradford, who created America's first literary classic, was an educated man. So was Winslow as the author of *Good News from New England*. So was Fuller. One can judge him by his library and his reception by Endecott and Winthrop. As for Cush-

320

man, one has his letters and his able address presented before Plimoth settlers in December 1621. The mental stature of a number of central figures at the plantation is clearly demonstrated in the facile flow of the letters of Allerton, Blossom, and Masterson. The portfolio of Pilgrim correspondence contains consistently fine Elizabethan English.

Forty-one of the *Mayflower* passengers signed their names to the compact. Most of them owned their own Geneva Bibles, which they had been trained to regard as their guidebook for living, and they felt a profound obligation to read the scriptures themselves.

The small Plimoth colony was fairly well supplied with books. Brewster's inventory lists 397: sixty-two in Latin and the balance in English. H. M. Dexter has classified them: expository, 98; doctrinal, 63; practical religion, 69; historical, 24; ecclesiastical, 36; philosophical, 6; poetical, 14; miscellaneous, 54. Four books were by John Robinson. Eleven had been printed in Leyden at

Elizabeth Paddy Wensley (1641-1731)—painter unknown

the Pilgrim Press. Bradford also owned a substantial library of about 400 volumes, including four by Robinson, two Bibles, "Calvine on the epistles in Dutch with Divers other Dutch bookes."[11]

Samuel Fuller's inventory lists twenty-six books in addition to his "Phisicke bookes," including three Bibles, a "psalme booke," and a book by Robinson.[12] William Bassett had eighteen books, including one title by Robinson.[13]

Richard Lauchford listed twenty-two books and two singing psalm books.[14] William Lumkin had three Bibles and other books.[15] Cuthbert Cuthbertson (Godbert Godbertson) owned "a great bible," a book in French, Dod on the commandments, a Bible, and a "psalme booke."[16] John Thorp possessed a Bible and a "psalme booke."[17]

Mary Ring owned one Bible, a "psalme booke," and five other religious works.[18] Peter Browne had a Bible.[19] Will Wright owned "one great Bible and a little Bible, 1 psalme booke" with seventeen other small books.[20] Stephen Hopkins listed "Divers bookes,"[21] Francis Cooke, "1 great Bible & 4 old bookes."[22] John Howland had "1 great bible" and some fifteen other volumes.[23] Steven Dean possessed a Bible and "other books."[24]

Of seventy inventories examined, only a dozen failed to mention printed works of some sort, usually Bibles, catechisms, and religious tracts.[25]

Books were expensive and not too common even in England. Not all books were listed in inventories, but those that were reveal a rather surprising quantity and indicate that learning was highly regarded. A study of the writings, letters, and books in the colony can be recommended to the skeptic.

The level of literacy in England was higher in the sixteenth century than commonly believed, according to a recent survey made by J. W. Adamson. His study contradicts the conception regarding the almost total lack of learning of fifteenth- and sixteenth-century England, stating "that it was by no means an illiterate society and that facilities for rudimentary instruction at least were so distributed as to reach even small towns and villages."

With the sixteenth-century, educational facilities spread and numerous new schools were opened due to the stimulus provided by the printing presses. There were some thirty editions of the Bible and fifty editions of the New Testament in English published in 1557. People must have been reading quite widely to sustain these Bible sales. In addition to the scriptures there was a substantial output of religious and secular books. Some 214 titles came from the presses in 1550, and the number increased with the outpouring of Puritan tracts and tomes.[26] Literacy continued to increase in seventeenth-century England, especially among the Bible-reading Puritans.

(page 322) A seventeenth-century Delft bowl • The cradle of Peregrine White—believed to have been brought from Holland • A seventeenth-century mortar and pestle • Chest—belonged to William Brewster

(page 323) A cabinet—belonged to William White • A chair—belonged to Myles Standish • A salt dish (c. 1635)—belonged to Edward Fuller • A press cupboard—belonged to the Alden Family

The supply of books at the plantation proves that the printed word was more than a status symbol. They were borrowed, read, passed around, and discussed by these alert people. During the long hours of darkness these serious writings were scanned in the firelight and candlelight and talked about in the homes of the villagers. The founders of Plimoth brought with them the torch of learning and helped keep it alive on the wilderness frontier.

The Pilgrims have been made a catch-all of resentments against all patterns of pharisaic religiosity: bigotry, witch-hunting, drabness, and grouchiness. What Edmund S. Morgan wrote of the Puritans applies to the Pilgrims as well:

> We have to caricature the Puritans in order to feel comfortable in their presence. They found answers to some human problems that we would rather forget. Their very existence is therefore an affront to our moral complacency; and the easiest way to meet the challenge is to distort it into absurdity, turn the challengers into fanatics.[27]

It has been a common practice to ascribe the ugly record of witchcraft and witch-hunting to the New England Puritan theology. The fact is that many non-Puritans such as Lord Bacon, James I, Sir Thomas Browne, and Thomas Hobbes believed in sorcery and witches.

In early New England a few witch cases came before the courts, but until the outbreak of 1692 not more than half a dozen executions took place. In that orgy some twenty-two victims were involved. Meanwhile, across the seas hundreds were killed in England during the seventeenth century. Matthew Hopkins, the Witch-Finder General, sent at least 400 to the gallows from 1645 to 1647. In Scotland there were 3,400 witches killed between 1580 and 1680. On the continent many thousands suffered death in the sixteenth and seventeenth centuries. In Alsace 134 witches and wizards were burned in 1582 on one occasion, the executions taking place on October 15, 19, 24, and 28.

Nicholas Remy (Remiguis) of Lorraine gathered the materials for his work on the *Worship of Demons,* published in 1595, from the trials of some 900 persons whom he had sentenced to death in the fifteen years preceding. In 1609, De l'Ancre and his associate are said to have condemned 600 in the Basque country in four months. The efforts of the Bishop of Bamberg from 1622 to 1633 resulted in 600 executions. The Bishop of Worzburg in about the same period put 900 persons to death. These figures from the study of George L. Kittredge help us look at Salem witchcraft in its true proportions as a minor tragic incident in the history of a terrifying superstition.[28]

It is fortunate for the New World that this outbreak did not occur sooner and last longer. The record of Plimoth Plantation stands as a tribute to Robinson's followers who resisted the epidemic of hysteria and decreed that there were to be no witch-hunts in the colony.

Increase Mather, president of Harvard College, said as late as 1692:

I am abundantly satisfied that there have been and are still most cursed witches in the land. More than one or two of those now in Prison have freely and credibly acknowledged their Communion and Familiarity with the Spirits of the Darkness; and have also declared unto me the Time and Occassion, with the particular circumstances of their Hellish Obligations and Abominations.[29]

His son, Cotton Mather, believed in the devil as a living personality: "A short and Black Man . . . no taller than an ordinary Walking-Staff; hee was not of a Negro, but of a Tawney, or an Indian colour; hee wore a High-Crowned Hat, with straut Hair; and had one Cloven-Foot."[30]

It is amusing that Mather made the devil not wholly white nor wholly black, but a sort of a shadowy in-between.

In the midst of the witch-hunting hysteria there was a heritage of tolerance and common sense that prevailed at Plimoth Plantation. Only two residents were accused of witchcraft—both of them from Scituate and both of them women. One was the case of Mrs. William Holmes.

Dinah Sylvester of Scituate brought the charge of witchcraft against the wife of William Holmes of Marshfield, who served as a lieutenant in Myles Standish's military. Lieutenant Holmes sued for slander and the case was brought to court on May 7, 1661 before Gov. Thomas Prence and his board of assistants, including William Colgare, John Alden, Josiah Winslow, Thomas Southworth, and William Bradford, Jr.

"What evidence have you to support your charge?" she was asked.
"She appeared to me as a witch," she answered.
"In what shape?"
"In the shape of a bear."
"How far away was the bear?"
"About a stone's throw from the path."
"What manner of tail did the bear have?"
"I could not tell as the head was towards me. . . ."[31]
"But the plot was too shallow, and whatever there was of Deviltry in it was thrown upon the one who made the Attempt."[32]

After Dinah's accusations were heard, the court acquitted Mrs. Holmes, and Dinah Sylvester was found guilty of slander. She was ordered to be publicly whipped and to pay Mrs. Holmes £5 or to openly confess her slander and repay Holmes' costs and charges. She made her public acknowledgment on May 9:

To the honored Court assembled; whereas I haue bin convicted in matter of defamation concerning Goodwife Holmes, I doe freely acknowlidg I haue wronged my naighbour, and haue sinned against God in soe doing; though I had entertained hard

thoughts against the woman; for it had bine my dewty to declare my grouns, if I had any, vnto some majestrate in a way
of God, and not to haue devoulged my thoughts to others, to
the woman's defamation. Therefore I doe acknowlidg my sin
in it, and doe humbly begg this honored Court to forgive mee,
and all other Christian people that be offended att it, and doe
promise, by the healp of God, to do soe noe more; and although I doe not remember all that the witnesses doe testify,
yett I doe rather mistrust my owne memory and submitt to
the evidences.

Dinah Siluester[33]

Plimoth's second case involving the charge of witchcraft was
that of Mary Ingham, wife of Thomas Ingham of Scituate, who
was accused of bewitching Mehitabel, daughter of Walter Woodworth. The *Plimoth Colonial Record* of 1666-67 reads:

Mary Ingham: thou art indicted by the name of Mary Ingham,
the wife of Thomas Ingham of the towne of Scittuate, in the
jurisdiction of New Plimoth, for that thou, haveing not the
feare of God before thyne eyes, hast, by the help of the divill,
in a way of witchcraft or sorcery, maliciously procured much
hurt, mischieffe, and paine unto the body of Mehittable Woodworth of Scittuate aforesaid, and some others, and particularly
causing her, the sd Mehittable to fall into violent fitts, and
causing greate paine unto severall ptes of her body at severall
times soe as she the sd Mehittable Woodworth hath bin almost
bereaved of her senses, and hath greatly languised to her much
suffering thereby, and the procuring of great greiffe, sorrow,
and charge to her parents; all of which thou hast procured and
done against the law of God, & to his great dishonor and contrary to our soverign lord the kinge, his crowne & dignities.
    The sd Mary Ingham did putt herselfe on the tryal of God
and the country, and was cleared of this indictment in process
of law, by a jury of 12 men whose names follow:
    Thomas Huckins, John Wadsworth, John Howland, (second)
Abram Jackson, Benaiah Pratt, John Black, Mark Snow, Joseph
Bartlett, John Richmond, James Talbot, John Foster, Seth Poe.

Gov. Josiah Winslow presided. The jury brought in the verdict
"not guilty and soe the said prisoner was cleared as above said."
Mary Ingham was acquitted and her accuser silenced.[34]
    The witch mania was promptly squelched in Plimoth and never
raised its head again. But it continued in other colonies until it
reached its peak in Salem in the summer of 1692. In the Bay between 1648 and 1692 twenty-two witches were hanged, one was
pressed to death, two died awaiting trial in a "stinking dungeon,"
and many others were condemned by a court of justice but spared
because witch-hunting came to an end in 1692.[35]

Bradford, Brewster, and other wise heads faced the dilemma of
how to restrain the frailties of man. When moral exhortation
failed, they were forced to resort to the regulations of the court.

327

Some of the court restrictions were petty in content and were intrusions on the dignity of the individual, and they were difficult to reconcile with the harmonious society of Leyden. However, Plimoth laws in most areas were not as stringent as those of the Bay colony.

In England the Congregationalists were a minority, struggling with king, bishops, Parliament, and fellow Puritans who held divergent views. They were considered radicals and innovators. Their main course had been the way of protest against the conventions set up and imposed by the Establishment. There had been no occasion to date for them to fix their standards. They were a rebel group who by force of circumstance appeared to oppose the status quo and were therefore suspect and subject to constant criticism.

But they were in a different position in New England. The state did not suppress them but rather afforded them protection. They had become the dominant system. This made it necessary for them to assume a conservative position—the outlook of conserver and protector. They were no longer the innovators who had to show cause for their departures from orthodoxy. The innovators were the Presbyterians, Anglicans, Baptists, and later the Quakers. So it became necessary to determine where they stood and to define their position. A conference of leaders was called and the Cambridge Platform was drawn up in 1646. It affirmed the basic Congregational concepts of the autonomy of the local church, the dependence of the churches upon one another for counsel, and the representative character of the ministry.[36]

It was about this time that a petition was presented to the General Court in Plimoth, requesting "full and free tolerance of religion to all men that will preserve the civil peace and submit unto the government," as Edward Winslow reported the request in a letter to Gov. John Winthrop, seeking his advice. There was to be "no limitation or exception against Turk, Jew, Papist, Arian, Socinian, Nicholaytan, Familist, or any other."

Bradford, Winslow, Prence, and Collier of the board of assistants opposed the measure, while it was supported by Standish, Browne, Hatherly, and Freeman. Action on it was buried through postponement. Acceptance of such a universal view was too much to expect at this point in history. These leaders felt that they could be overwhelmed by an influx of men who would be out of harmony with their views, who might provoke chaos in Massachusetts, so that the peace they had gained would be lost.

Although the Pilgrims had proved more lenient than the men of the Bay colony in many ways, they began to reveal a tendency to conform to the sterner attitudes of the latter. Tolerance did persist in the alleviating reactions in their treatment of the Quakers and those accused of witchcraft, but periodically the saints at the plantation slumped in their idealism.

Plimoth Plantation followed a loose relation between state and church. Bradford consulted with William Brewster "in all weighty matters." Once at the request of Gov. Richard Bellingham of Massachusetts he was asked to poll the Plimoth colony clergy on what constituted rape. There were a few occasions when Bradford and his successors, Winslow and Prence, made formal requests to the colony ministers for an opinion.[37]

Governor Bradford was a devoted churchman, but he handled the affairs of state on his own. For nine years there was no local minister to consult. The first two moderately successful pastors, Ralph Smith and John Rayner, were not too strong as leaders and carried little weight in civic affairs. The abler clergymen—Roger Williams, John Wilson, and Charles Chauncy—remained for very brief periods so that there was no dominant clerical figure.

The court preferred to handle problems relating to the church as they developed, without laying down a program of legislation. The church people approved the duty of the state to defend religion and to enforce uniformity in theory, but the Leyden Pilgrims had carried on a successful church in Holland without positive state support. In the New World they no doubt felt reluctant to surrender this system of voluntarism. Their church had done well in Leyden without government intervention. Why should it not do so in America? Plimoth was slower to use the authority of the magistrates in support of religion. "Its leaders were at first willing to allow more deviation than was permitted in Massachusetts, and before 1645 seemed reluctant to crush minor divergencies from orthodoxy," writes George D. Langdon.[38]

In the fateful year 1657, in which Bradford died and Prence took over, the barricade against heresy was strengthened by declaring that those who sought admission as freemen were to be placed on probation for an extended period, to "stand one whole yeare propounded to the Court." This was to make sure that no "corrupt" persons got in, like Quakers and Baptists. And as a rebuke to Anglicans it now became a crime to celebrate Christmas by "forbearing of labour, feasting, or in any other way."[39]

Not many Anglicans crossed over to Plimoth Plantation, but those who did worshiped in the Congregational churches and were welcomed to communion. There is a record of one Roman Catholic who visited the Plimoth colony—the Rev. Gabriel Druillettes, a Jesuit priest from Canada. He made the journey to New England hoping to persuade the confederation to declare war against the Mohawk Indians. On his way he stopped at the Plimoth trading post on the Kennebec River, which was in charge of John Winslow. He was entertained as an honored guest. Governor Bradford received him graciously when he came south to Plimoth for a Friday evening fish dinner in the 1650's, even though the Pilgrims made a point of not eating fish on Fridays.[40]

For the first thirty years or so, Plimoth Plantation did not turn away anyone who came in need of help. Even Thomas Weston, the chief troublemaker among the London Merchant Adventurers, arrived destitute in Plimoth after shipwreck in Ipswich. The Pilgrims took him in, equipped him with supplies, and loaned him £100 worth of beaver pelts. He "never repaid them anything but reproache and evil words."

Thomas Morton, another fortune-hunter, took over the deserted shacks left by Weston's men in Wollaston, calling their settlement Merrymount. He and his men frolicked with the Indian squaws, drank with the braves, and traded muskets for corn. Captain Standish had to disperse the settlement. Morton was shipped back to England, but he later showed up at Plimoth and was outwardly forgiven and cared for.

In the winter of 1626 the *Sparrowhawk*, with twenty-five passengers, was wrecked in Pleasant Bay, Cape Cod. The plantation shallop brought them to Plimoth where they were taken into the cottages. They stayed through the summer until a ship called to carry them to Virginia.[41]

In 1635 members of Pastor John Warham's church in Dorchester decided to move to the Connecticut River. They visited the Plimoth trading post at Windsor that was in charge of Jonathan Brewster. He extended them hospitality and helped them secure canoes and guides to explore the area. He was shocked when they announced that they were taking over Plimoth's land and building on it. Brewster pointed out that the Pilgrims had bought the land from the Indians in order to establish their fur trade, and that thousands of acres were available for their Dorchester colony. But the newcomers stuck to their purpose, assured that providence had so willed it.

During these confrontations two shallops of Dorchester settlers set out from Boston for the Connecticut post. Their boats were wrecked on Brown's Island in Plimoth Bay. Plimothians rushed to the scene and gathered in the victims and their possessions. A third boat that was carrying cargo to the Windsor site for the migrants was blown ashore off Sandwich. Once again the people of Plimoth salvaged the goods and turned them over to the owners.[42]

Obviously the Dorchester colonists must have been somewhat chagrined by these demonstrations of brotherliness. In due time, as they reflected upon their haste and avarice, they decided to forego their claim on the Pilgrims' land and to move on into the wilderness.

These instances demonstrate that Plimoth Plantation adhered to Robinson's motto—"Advertise us brotherly."

Somehow there are those who think that because the Pilgrims were serious about religion, they did not know how to have a good time. Any frontiersman is apt to be a realistic and earthy human being. He lives close to sun and soil, grappling with the elements of nature. And frontiersmen they were in the physical as well as the spiritual sense. Moreover, they were Elizabethans. They were not squeamish or pious. We can be sure they reserved some time for the gayer side of life. Even in a wilderness a woman will find a way to pretty up herself and her home and create some social activity for her family. People visited together and feasted with their friends. There were games for the youngsters and romancing for the teen-agers. Men hunted, smoked, and drank together. Women gossiped at their needlework parties. The elemental joys of life were theirs.

Love of music was part of the cherished heritage from the homeland. Edward Winslow mentioned that many of the Leyden congregation were "very expert in music," which indicates that they could do more than sing psalms and implies that some of them played instruments. Henry VIII composed melodies, Edward VI played the lute, Mary and Elizabeth the virginal, and Charles I the bass viol. John Milton, the son of a musician, was taught the organ. John Bunyan made his own flute. Robert Browne, the bold reformer of church ritual, was an expert lutist who instructed his parishioners in music. His son, Timothy, played the viol for psalm-singing. Bishop Jewell wrote to Peter Martyr about the love of the people for their psalms, mentioning that he heard 6,000 of them singing together at Paul's Cross.

Percy Scholes contradicts the long-standing concept that the Pilgrims were antimusical, antiart, and antipleasure.[43] They liked drums and used them to summon the people to worship. Every town in the colony was required to have its own drums. They made use of horns and trumpets. Jew's harps were a means of barter with the Indians. Musical instruments were seldom mentioned in the early inventories, but they are not necessarily 100 percent inclusive of possessions. A treble viall is listed in one. Judge Sewall speaks of "my wife's virginal," and also of trumpets, of dinner music, and of the musical programs that he attended.

Elnathan Chauncy, son of the Pilgrim pastor and president of Harvard, who had lived in Plimoth, made many references to music and dancing in his commonplace book while a student at Harvard. George L. Kittredge has commented that the items in this anthology "show no trace of the sullenness and severity so often alleged against our Puritan ancestors."

John Cotton stated in 1647 that although he objected to instruments in the church, they could be used in the home for psalm-singing. Music was commended by Increase Mather for its "great efficacy against melancholy."

There is a quaint ballad from the traditions of Plimoth Plantation that furnishes an example of the Pilgrims' affinity for music and also of their sense of humor. It is one of those anonymous folk creations that has come down through the generations.

The place where we live is a wilderness wood,
Where grass is much wanting that's fruitful and good:
Our mountains and hills and valleys below
Being commonly covered with ice and with snow;
And when the northwester with violence blows,
Then every man pulls his cap over his nose;
But if any's so hardy and will it withstand,
He forfeits a finger, a foot, or a hand.

When the spring opens we then take the hoe,
And make the ground ready to plant and to sow;
Our corn being planted and seed being sown,
The worms destroy much before it is grown;
And when it is growing, some spoil there is made
By birds and by squirrels that pluck up the blade;
E'en when it is grown to full corn in the ear
It is often destroyéd by racoons and deer.

And now our garments begin to grow thin,
And wool is much wanted to card and to spin;
If we can get a garment to cover without,
Our other in-garments are clout upon clout;
Our clothes we brought with us are often much torn,
They need to be clouted before they are worn;
But clouting our garments they hinder us nothing,
Clouts double, are warmer than single whole clothing!

If flesh be wanting to fill up our dish,
We have carrots and pumpkins and turnips and fish;
And, when we've a mind for a delicate dish,
We repair to the clam-bank and there we catch fish.
Instead of pottage and puddings and custards and pies,
Our pumpkins and parsnips are common supplies;
We have pumpkin at morning and pumpkin at noon,
If it was not for pumpkin we should be undoon.

If barley be wanting to make into malt,
We must be contented, and think it no fault;
For we can make liquor to sweeten our lips
Of pumpkins and parsnips and walnut tree chips.

Now while some are going, let others be coming,
For while liquor's boiling it must have a scumming;
But we will not blame them, for birds of a feather,
By seeking their fellows are flocking together.
But you whom the Lord intends hither to bring,
Forsake not the honey for fear of the sting;
But bring both a quiet and contented mind
And all needful blessings you surely will find.

Markets and fairs brought the people together during the early years of the plantation. This custom was formally established when, in 1639, "it was enacted by the Court that there shalbe a market kept at Plimoth every Thursday, and a faire yearly the last Wensday in May, & to continue two days and a faire at Dux-borrow the first Wensday in October yearly, & to continue two days for all cattell & comodyties."

Once a week on Thursdays it was always possible to break away from weeding the crops and feeding the stock, from spinning and churning, and go shopping at the public market. Each householder could carry along merchandise for barter and exchange: corn, beans, wine, a jar of jam, bread or cake, a bit of embroidery, woolen yarn, a piece of linen woolsey, a joint stool, a calf or shoat.

Late in May, when the glory of spring bathed New England in vernal beauty, every householder was on hand for the Plimoth "faire" to show chickens, ducks, and geese, all the barnyard animals, tempting concoctions of culinary skill, the crafts from spinning wheel and loom, samplers and quilts, woodworking, tin and pewter from the hands of skilled artisans, along with the first fruits of their vegetable and flower gardens.

This was an auspicious beginning for the surge of productivity that blessed the summer. And then the projects were set underway for the great Duxburrow (Duxbury) "faire" of early October when golden days crowned the plantation with the bounties of the harvest. All the countryside poured into the village closest to Mother Plimoth, eager to see what the year had brought forth in "cattell and comodyties," to measure one's own production against the best, to chat with friends from whom one had been separated during the teeming farming months, and to hear news of what momentous events had transpired in England, in Virginia, and in the Bay colony closer at hand.

Plimothians loaded their dories and sailboats and crossed over the bay to Duxbury, or jostled over the dirt roads in ox carts with their loads of children and exhibits for the "faire." Some made the journey through the fields and woods on horseback, and the intrepid on foot for they had no dread of the short hike of a mere ten miles.

A modern man dwells upon this scene with nostalgia, thinking of a summer's outing when the whole, beautiful natural world was there for the taking. No four-lane highways, no gaudy signs, no pushing crowds, no hot dog stands, no beach cabanas. It was all theirs: the virgin forest, the soft pine trails, the pure air, the glorious, unpolluted sea.

Life had its good moments for the Pilgrims.

Although a small segment of the Puritan migration, their remembrance is indelibly stamped on the American mind. Their name will always signify a special contribution. Young and old come in a steady stream from north, south, east, and west to look upon the spot where these Pilgrims stood. Men and women tell and retell to their children the epic of the ship, the shallop and the Rock, the Indian friendship, the Fort Meeting House, the Great Sickness, the labor, the debt payment, and the thanksgiving.

A few come to scoff. They can deride the Rock or paint it red, but they cannot erase the footprints of the Pilgrims from the shores of Plimoth Bay.

The Lord hath more truth and light
yet to break forth from His holy Word.
—John Robinson

25 "MORE TRUTH AND LIGHT"

John Robinson's writings include a substantial number of books, pamphlets, and letters. His major works were published in three volumes in London in 1851. The titles and dates follow in Appendix A.

Some of his titles went through numerous editions during his lifetime and after his death. Among the most popular were *The People's Plea for the Exercise of Prophecy* and *Justification of Separation*. Many copies were smuggled out of Holland into the Mother Country where they continued his attack on dogmatism and suppression.

He was involved in seeing his volume of *Essays* through the press when he faced his last illness. The first edition of this book came out in 1625 with other printings in 1628, 1642, and 1654. These essays reveal a wide range of reading in classical studies. He had been exposed to the humanist discipline which Erasmus and Colet introduced into England, and he had explored Latin, Greek, and Hebrew cultures. In addition to his frequent Bible references, he made mention of Aemilius, Ambrose, Anacharsis, Anselm, Antisthenes, Antonius, Aristotle, Arminius, Audaens, Augustine, Barrowe, Basil of Caesarea, Bastingius, Bernard, Beza, Bodinus, Boethius, Bucer, Calvin, Cassander, Cato, Celsus, Chrysostom, Cicero, Cyprian, Cyril, Dionysius, Donatus, Epictetus, Erasmus, Eusebius, Fox, Greenwood, Gregory of Nazianzus, Herodotus, Ignatius, Irenaeus, Jerome of Prague, Josephus, Knox, Lactantius, Diogenes Laërtius, Livy, Luther, Martial, Peter Martyr, Melanchthon, Morneus, Novitian, Patricius, Philo Judaeus, Pindarus, Plato, Penry, Plautus, Pliny, Plutarch, Polybius, Sallust, Seneca, Socrates, Suetonius, Tacitus, Terence, Tertullian, Thales, Udall, Ursinus, Vergil, Zwingli.

He referred to a number of his contemporaries (he had exchanged opinions with some of them): Ames, Ainsworth, Bancroft, Bernard, Bradshaw, Broughton, Bishop Carlton, Clyfton, Chaderton, Comenius, Euring, Gifford, Grotius, Bishop Hall, Hansbury, Helwys, Jacob, Francis Johnson, Franciscus Junius, Bauledomero Keckerman, Murton, Paget, Pareus, Matthew Parker, Robert Parker, Perkins, Piscator, Sadeel, Scaliger, John Smyth, and Archbishop Whitgift.[1]

Robinson's sixty-two essays cover such subjects as Marriage,

Peace, Envy, Flattery, Conscience, Modesty, Sobriety, Labour, Zeal, Health and Physic, Riches and Poverty, Books and Writing, Wisdom and Folly, Truth and Falsehood, Speech and Silence, Knowledge and Ignorance, Authority and Reason. They evidence good sense and a healthy ethical emphasis: "He that makes a bridge of his own shadow cannot but fall into the water." "Living springs send out streams of water, dead pits must have all that they afford drawn out with buckets."[2]

He repudiated the magic of prayer and abject dependence upon the divine: "For us to ask anything at the hands of the Lord which withal we do not offer ourselves ready instruments to effect and bring to pass, is to tempt God's power and to abuse his Goodness." He was shocked that people should neglect the help of physicians when they were ill and count on God to cure their pain and carry them through.[3]

He wrote of flattery and flowery speech: "As a woman over curiously trimmed is to be suspected, so is a speech." He lamented the state of mind of leaders who were

> accounting it not only needless curiosity, but even intolerable arrogancy, to call into question the things received by them from tradition. But how much better were it for all men to lay aside these and the like prejudices, that so they might understand the things which concern their peace, and seeing with their own eyes, might live by their own faith![4]

His writings, teachings, and his spirit of mediation exerted a major influence in the development of the liberal Congregationalism of the nineteenth and twentieth centuries. There were very few in his century who could share with him in the outreach of his practice of brotherhood. He was far ahead of his time in charity. The seed of a universal outlook existed in his mind. The expansion of his thought was due also to exposure to university figures in England and Leyden, nurture in an international atmosphere and in an interconfessional religious experience. These contacts, coupled with his open mind and genial personality, fostered attitudes of breadth which made him one of the great figures in the Puritan movement. He was one of the first to sense that variety and unity are possible in Christendom, and was one of the pioneers in the movement toward unity. He explained:

> Men are for the most part minded for, or against toleration of diversity of religion, according to the conformity which they themselves hold, or hold not with the country or kingdom where they live. Protestants living in the countries of Papists commonly plead for toleration of religion: so do Papists that live where Protestants bear sway: though few of either, specially of the clergy, as they are called, would have the other tolerated, where the world goes on their side. The very same is to be observed in the ancient Fathers, in their times: of whom, such as lived in the first three hundred years after Christ, and suffered with the churches, under heathen persecutors, pleaded

Archbishop John Whitgift (1530?—1604)

336

against all violence for religion, true or false: affirming that it is of human right and natural liberty, for every man to worship what he thinketh God: and that it is no property of religion to compel to religion, which ought to be taken up freely; that no man is forced by the Christians against his will, seeing he that wants faith, and devotion is unservicable to God: and that God not being contentious, would not be worshipped of the un- willing.[5]

His emphasis on the good life rather than on orthodox con- formity was a contribution to Congregationalism, which "holds that the formulation of creeds is the proper business of theolo- gians but not of Christians with little possibility of understanding them, and that the living doctrine is made known to us in the scripture and his continuing presence in the fellowship of the church."[6]

Robinson took a broad view of Christian doctrine which helped initiate the Congregational tradition of doctrinal tolerance. Robert Baillie, the Presbyterian, complained in the seventeenth century that Congregationalism had "become a uniting Principle." So in- stead of having led to parochialism and narrowness, "the path of Separatism has led into a large room, where by putting first things first, and only first things, men of varying intellectual gifts and judgments find it possible to be at one," so writes Geoffrey F. Nuttall.[7]

Always strong on fellowship, Robinson longed to be part of the koinonia that should gather people into harmony. While Robert Browne was, in a measure, the father of the Congregational idea, he was not the father of Congregational fellowship which de- veloped under Robinson and grew to be one of the dominant emphases of the Congregational Way.

Brownism and Barrowism soon disappeared, but the Robinson

Robinson's book Justification—*autographed by William Bradford*

philosophy of religion lives today as an irenic sector of the world church, placing strong emphasis on cooperation and unity.

Among the Puritan reformers Robinson is unique in that he did more than teach and write. He succeeded in organizing communities in Leyden and Plimoth that lived out his precepts. He was more than a theologian and author. He had the ability to bring people of kindred minds together, to inspire them to share his intellectual views.

William Ames was remembered over a hundred years or more for his writings on theology. Robert Parker and William Bradshaw died early, leaving no well-defined movement. Henry Jacob was lost in his move to Virginia, although members of his London congregation established a church in West Barnstable on Cape Cod. Robert Browne pioneered boldly but recanted. His associate, Robert Harrison, obscured his contribution through his quarrels with Browne. Francis Johnson ended his life under a cloud of dispute. John Smyth, Richard Clyfton, Henry Ainsworth, Thomas Helwys, and John Murton were all involved in the strife of the Ancient Brethren Church.

Robinson achieved a continuing immortality of influence through the efforts of followers who crossed to the New World. He did not realize his cherished goal and reach Plimoth, but his disciples succeeded in building a living memorial to his pursuit of truth and brotherhood: "We must acknowledge but one brotherhood of all."[8]

He was forced to live in what Roger Williams called "wonderful, searching, disputing and dissenting times." He was paid in adversity for his efforts as a reformer. A hunted exile, who had known loneliness and privation, he wrote wistfully of his hardships as he concluded his *Just and Necessary Apology:*

They who truly fear thee, and work righteousness, although constrained to live by leave in a foreign land, exiled from country, spoiled of goods, destitute of friends, few in number, and mean in condition, are for all that unto thee (O gracious God) nothing the less acceptable. Thou numberest all their wanderings, and puttest their tears into thy bottles. Are they not written in thy book? Towards thee, O Lord, are our eyes; confirm our hearts, and bend thine ear, and suffer not our feet to slip, or our face to be ashamed, O thou both just and merciful God. To him through Christ be praise, fore ever, in the church of saints; and to thee, loving and Christian reader, grace, peace and eternal happiness. Amen.[9]

His forty-nine years brought persecution and suffering, but he succeeded in out-living many of his contemporaries with whom he had been intimately associated in the cause of reformation: William Perkins died in 1602, Thomas Cartwright in 1603, John Smyth in 1612, Robert Parker in 1614, Richard Clyfton in 1616,

Thomas Cartwright (1535-1603)—Cambridge University Puritan scholar

John Robinson Memorial Window—from the English Reformed Church in Amsterdam

Paul Baynes in 1617, William Bradshaw in 1618, Francis Johnson in 1618, David Pareus in 1622, Henry Ainsworth in 1623, and Henry Jacob in 1624.

The dispersal of the faithful at Plimoth Plantation, which appeared to spell its diminution, was in reality a scattering of the mustard seed of faith into more distant places. There it took root and grew until every village in New England boasted its own church and schoolhouse. Transplanted into new soil, the idealism of the Green Gate and the Fort Meeting House lived on.

If Robinson could return in our time he would see the precepts of Scrooby, Leyden, and Plimoth expounded from the pulpits of little white meeting houses across the land and from scores of colleges that have been established in pursuit of "more truth and light": Harvard, Yale, Dartmouth, Bowdoin, Amherst, Williams, Wellesley, Mount Holyoke, Smith, Middlebury, Oberlin, Marietta, Illinois, Knox, Beloit, Carleton, Grinnell, Doane, Yankton, Pacific, Pomona, Talledega, Hampton, Howard, Fiske, Dillard, Tougaloo, and others.[10]

This would be reassuring to the scholar, who believed so ardently in learning, to discover that the Congregational Way still endures without the regulating formalism of dogma and ritual, that ethical emphasis keeps religion relevant to social need, that fellowship within Christendom is progressing.

The realization of the United Church of Christ in America, a major step in church union, achieved in 1961, brought together the Congregationalists with their British background of reform and the Evangelical and Reformed churches with their continental tradition which sprang from Luther and Calvin. Robinson's own achievements in intercommunion with European Christians was prophetic of this development.

He would find today that the Congregational Way is more inclusive than these who bear the name, that its precepts are practiced not only among Congregationalists, Universalists, and Unitarians, but also among Baptists, Reformed, Disciples of Christ, and many other fragments of the Holy Catholic Church that he upheld. To all of them Plimoth's Fort Meeting House has become a symbol of the unity of the spirit and the bond of fellowship.

And viewing this vista of Christendom's slow movement toward ecumenicity, he would be the first to admit that this growing realization of his hope of brotherhood was due to many of his fellow Puritans. They formed an unheralded and unremembered company: those who confronted kings and queens, bishops and torturers, in their stand for conscience. From the days of Tyndale, Bilney, Barrowe, Greenwood, and Penry to the last of the Pilgrims, who had just crossed over to America from shores of oppression, there was an unending line of those who shared his sacrifice.

The passing of 350 years has brought new appreciation of Robinson's role in the struggle for religious freedom. On July 24, 1891 a bronze tablet was placed on the outer wall of St. Peter's Church in Leyden. It bears this inscription:

In Memory of
Rev. John Robinson, M. A.
Pastor of the English Church Worshiping Over Against
This Spot, A.D. 1609-1625, Whence at his Prompting
Went Forth
THE PILGRIM FATHERS
To Settle New England
in 1620
- - - - - - - - -
Buried under this house of worship, 4 March, 1625
Aet. XLIX Years.
In Memoria Aeterna Erit Justus.
Erected by the National Council of the Congregational
Churches of the United States of America
A.D. 1891

On September 4, 1928 a memorial tablet was unveiled in the Baptismal Chapel of St. Peter's Church:

In Memory of
JOHN ROBINSON
Pastor of the English Church in Leyden
1609   1625
His Broadly Tolerant Mind
Guided and Developed the Religious Life of
The Pilgrims of the Mayflower
Of Him These Walls Enshrine All That Was Mortal
His Undying Spirit
Still Dominates the Consciences of A Mighty Nation
In the Land Beyond the Seas
This Tablet Was Erected By the General Society of
Mayflower Descendants in the
United States of America   A.D. 1928

Desirous of the extension of his brotherly views through the world, he stated belief in their ultimate triumph:

Religion is not always sown or reaped in one age. One soweth and another reapeth. John Huss and Jerome of Prague finished their testimony a hundred years before Luther, and Wycliffe well nigh as long before them; and yet neither one nor the other with the like success as Luther. And yet many are already gathered into the Kingdom of Christ; and the nearness of many more throughout the whole land, for the regions "white unto harvest," do promise *within less than a hundred years,* if our sins and theirs make not us and them unworthy of this mercy, a very plenteous harvest.[11]

The Pilgrim quest was not realized within the space of that hundred years, but a pilgrimage toward "more truth and light" was set under way, like the sailing of the *Mayflower,* that still enlivens the minds of men.

APPENDIXES

Appendix A

The Writings of John Robinson

1. Controversy with John Burgess recorded in Jones Ms. 30, Bodleian Library, Oxford. 1608-9

2. *An Answer to a Censorius Epistle,* a pamphlet in reply to a "monitory letter" from Joseph Hall, rector of Halstead. 1609

3. *A Justification of Separation from the Church of England,* a reply to Richard Bernard. Nov. 14, 1610

4. Letter to the church at Amsterdam concerning dismissal of members and the method of handling cases of discipline. 1610

5. Letter on Christian fellowship to William Ames, printed in *The Prophane Schisme of the Brownists.* 1611

6. *Testimonie of the Elders in the Church at Leyden,* written by Robinson and Brewster. 1612

7. *A Brief Answer to the Exceptions of Francis Johnson* against points in Robinson's *Justification of Separation,* printed in Henry Ainsworth's *Animadversion to Mr. Richard Clyfton.* 1612

8. A book of five pamphlets:
   Of Religious Communion Private and Public
   Of Flight in Persecution
   The Outward Baptism received in England Lawfully retained
   Of the Baptism of Infants
   A Survey of the Confession of Faith published in certain conclusions by the remainders of Mr. Smyth's Company 1613-14

9. *A Manumission to a Manuduction* or answer to a letter inferring public communion in the parish assemblies upon private communion with godly persons there. 1615

343

10. *Admonitio ad Lectorem* prefixed to Robert Parker's *De Politeia Ecclesiastica Christi.* 1616

11. *Seven Articles* sent to the Privy Council giving the judgment of the Leyden church on matters of religion, relating to their proposal to migrate to Virginia. 1617

12. Letter to Sir Edwin Sandys, written by Robinson and Brewster. Dec. 15, 1617

13. Letter to Sir John Wolstenholme with two declarations, written by Robinson and Brewster. Feb. 1618

14. *The People's Plea for the Exercise of Prophecy,* against Mr. John Yates. 1618

15. *Apologia Justa et Necessaria quorundam Christianorum,* later translated by Robinson as *A Just and Necessary Apology.* 1619

16. Letter to John Carver. June 14, 1620

17. *The Wholesome Counsel* Master Robinson gave that part of the Church whereof he was Pastor at their Departure, reported by Edward Winslow. July 1620

18. Letter to John Carver. July 27, 1620

19. *Certain Useful Advertisements* sent in a Letter unto the Planters . . . at their first setting sail from Southampton. July 1620

20. *Letter to the Church of God in Plymouth.* June 30, 1621

21. *Letter to William Brewster* on the faint prospects of Robinson joining him. 1623

22. *Letter to William Bradford* pleading for a moderate and Christian course with the Indians. Dec. 19, 1623

23. *A Briefe Catechism concerning Church Government,* an appendix to Mr. Perkins' *Six Principles of the Christian Religion.* 1623

24. *A Defence of the Doctrine propounded by the Synod of Dort.* 1624

25. *A Letter to the Church of Christ in London.* Apr. 5, 1624

26. *An Appeal on Truth's Behalf,* a letter to the elders and church at Amsterdam. Sept. 18, 1624

27. *Treatise on the Lawfulness of Hearing the Ministers of the Church of England.* 1624

28. *Observations Divine and Moral* (essays). 1625

29. *A Just and Necessary Apology of certain Christians commonly called Brownists or Barrowists,* English translation by Robinson.* 1625

---

*Walter H. Burgess, *John Robinson, Pastor of the Pilgrim Fathers* (London: Ernest Benn, Ltd., 1920), pp. 418-20.

Appendix B

The Mayflower Passengers
The names of those that came first in the year
1620 and were . . . the first beginners of all the
colonies in New England.

—William Bradford

*MR. JOHN CARVER
  (governor)
*Katherine, his wife
 Desire Minter and a maid
 John Howland; Roger Wilder
 Wm. Latham; *Jasper More
 MR. WM. BREWSTER; wife
  Mary
 Love; Wrestling (sons)
 Richard More and *his brother
 MR. EDWARD WINSLOW
*Elizabeth, his wife; *Ellen
  More
 George Soule; *Elias Storey
 WM. BRADFORD; *wife
  Dorothy
 MR. ISAAC ALLERTON; *wife
  Mary
 Bartholomew; Remember;
  Mary
*John Hooke
 MR. SAMUEL FULLER
  (physician)
*William Button (died at sea)
*JOHN CRACKSTON; son John
 CAPT. MYLES STANDISH;
  *wife Rose
*MR. CHRISTOPHER MARTIN;
  *wife

*Solomon Prower; *John
  Langmore
*MR. WM. MULLINS and
  *his wife
*Joseph; Priscilla
*Robert Carter
*MR. WM. WHITE; wife
  Susanna
 Resolved; Peregrine (sons)
 (Peregrine was born on the
  MAYFLOWER in Province-
  town harbor)
*Wm. Holbeck; *Edw.
  Thompson
 MR. STEPHEN HOPKINS
 Elizabeth, his wife
 Giles; Constance; Damaris
 Oceanus (born at sea)
 Edw. Doty; Edw. Lister
 MR. RICHARD WARREN
 JOHN BILLINGTON
 Ellen, his wife
 John; Francis
*EDW. TILLEY, *wife Ann
 Henry Sampson; Humility
  Cooper
*JOHN TILLEY; *his wife
 Elizabeth Tilley
 FRANCIS COOKE; son John

*THOMAS ROGERS
 Joseph, his son
*THOMAS TINKER
*wife; *son
*JOHN RIGDALE
*wife Alice
*JAMES CHILTON; *wife
 Mary Chilton
*EDW. FULLER; *wife
 Samuel, their son
*JOHN TURNER; two sons
 FRANCIS EATON
*Sarah, his wife
 Samuel, infant son
*MOSES FLETCHER
*JOHN GOODMAN
*THOMAS WILLIAMS
*DEGORY PRIEST
*EDMOND MARGESON
 PETER BROWN
*RICHARD BRITTERIDGE
*RICHARD CLARKE
 RICHARD GARDINER
 GILBERT WINSLOW
 JOHN ALDEN
*JOHN ALLERTON
*THOMAS ENGLISH
*WM. TREVOR, seaman
 . . . ELY, seaman†

---

*Died first year.

†*Picture Guide to Historic Plymouth* (Pilgrim Society, 1963). The names of the *Mayflower* passengers are spelled in various ways. Cf. William Bradford, *Of Plymouth Plantation*, ed. Samuel Eliot Morison (New York: Alfred A. Knopf, 1952), pp. 441-48.

NOTES

Chapter 1 "The World Is Waking"

1. Walter H. Burgess, *John Robinson, Pastor of the Pilgrim Fathers* (London: Ernest Benn, Ltd., 1920), pp. 10 ff.

2. Carl Bridenbaugh, *Vexed and Troubled Englishmen, 1590-1642* (New York: Oxford University Press, 1968), p. 282.

3. Mildred Campbell, *The English Yeoman in the Tudor and Stuart Age* (New York: A. M. Kelley, 1968), p. 57. Used by permission of Merlin Press. See also Bridenbaugh, *Vexed and Troubled Englishmen*, pp. 16-47 and Frank Aydelotte, *Elizabethan Rogues and Vagabonds* (New York: Clarendon Press, 1913), p. 14.

4. Campbell, *The English Yeoman in the Tudor and Stuart Age*, p. 36.

5. Ibid., p. 12.

6. Bridenbaugh, *Vexed and Troubled Englishmen*, p. 53.

7. Ibid., p. 99. See also *Colonial Society of Massachusetts Publication*, XLII, 185.

8. Campbell, *The English Yeoman in the Tudor and Stuart Age*, pp. 271-77.

9. William Gouge, *Of Domesticall Duties* (1622), p. 18.

10. In Allerdyce Nicoll, *The Elizabethans* (New York: Cambridge University Press, 1957), p. 77.

11. L. F. Salzman, *England in Tudor Times* (London: B. T. Batsford, Ltd., 1926), p. 97.

12. Philip Stubbes, *Anatomie of Abuses* (1595) in William Chappell, *Popular Music of the Olden Time* (Magnolia, Mass.: Peter Smith Publisher), p. 98.

13. Peter Laslett, *The World We Have Lost* (New York: Charles Scribner's Sons, 1965), p. 16.

14. Thomas Fuller, *The Holy State* (London, 1650), Book 2, chap. 28. Cf. *Essays on the Economic and Social History of Tudor and Stuart England* (New York: Cambridge University Press, 1961); Lawrence Stone, *The Crisis of the Aristocracy, 1558-1641* (New York: Oxford University Press, 1967); F. G. Emmison, *Elizabethan Life: Disorder* (England: Chelmsford Essex County Council, 1970).

15. In George M. Trevelyan, *English Social History* (New York: Harper & Bros., 1942), p. 129. Cf. Anthony Esler, *The Aspiring Mind of the Elizabethan Younger Generation* (Durham, N. C.: Duke University Press, 1966).

16. In Burgess, *John Robinson, Pastor of the Pilgrim Fathers*, pp. 20-21.

17. Ibid., pp. 23-25.

18. Alfred L. Rowse, *The England of Elizabeth* (New York: Macmillan, 1951), p. 21.

19. Thomas Wilson, *The State of England* (1601) in *The Puritan Revolution: A Documentary History*, ed. Stuart E. Prall (New York: Doubleday, 1968), pp. 7-8. Copyright 1968 Stuart E. Prall.

20. John Robinson, *Works* (London: John Snow, 1851), III, 131.

21. Laslett, *The World We Have Lost*, p. 113.

22. In W. B. Rye, *England as Seen by Foreigners in the Days of Elizabeth and James I* (New York: Benjamin Blom, 1867), p. 78.

23. Elizabeth Burton, *The Pageant of Stuart England* (New York: Charles Scribner's Sons, 1962), pp. 29-30.

24. Ibid., pp. 31 ff.

25. Salzman, *England in Tudor Times*, p. 49.

Chapter 2 "The New Philosophy Calls All in Doubt"

1. Walter H. Burgess, *John Robinson, Pastor of the Pilgrim Fathers* (London: Ernest Benn, Ltd., 1920), p. 34.

2. In H. P. Stokes, *Corpus Christi* (London: F. E. Robinson, 1898), p. 240.

3. In Michael Grant, *Cambridge* (New York: Reynal & Co., 1966), p. 112.

4. Ibid.

5. Stokes, *Corpus Christi*, p. 78.

6. Ibid., p. 79.

7. In Alfred L. Rowse, *The England of Elizabeth* (New York: Macmillan, 1951), p. 512.

8. Ibid., p. 512. Cf. Albert Peel and Leland Carlson (eds.), *Cartwrightiana* (London, 1951).

9. Cooper's *Annals,* III, 28-33.

10. Sylvester Horne, *The Separatists in the Universities* (London: Congregational Union of England and Wales, 1895), p. 28.

11. In W. F. Adney, *Early Independents* (London: Congregational Union of England and Wales, 1895), p. 11.

12. Burgess, *John Robinson, Pastor of the Pilgrim Fathers*, p. 50.

13. In F. J. Powicke, *Henry Barrowe the Separatist* (Cambridge: James Clarke & Co., Ltd., 1920).

14. Ibid.

15. In Champlin Burrage, *Early English Independents* (New York: Cambridge University Press, 1912), pp. 129-30. Cf. Donald J. McGinn, *John Penry and the Marprelate Controversy* (New Brunswick, N. J.: Rutgers University Press, 1966).

16. Ibid., pp. ii, 87.

17. George Johnson, *A Discourse* (Amsterdam, 1603).

18. W. H. Bartlett, *The Pilgrim Fathers—The Founders of New England* (Boston: Arthur Hall, Virtue & Co., 1853), p. 24.

19. William Perkins, *Works* (Cambridge, 1603), II, 11-12.

20. In Perry Miller, *The New England Mind* (Boston: Beacon Press, 1961), p. 85. Used by permission of Harvard University Press. Cf. William Haller, *Elizabeth I and the Puritans* (Ithaca, N. Y.: Cornell University Press, 1964).

21. In William Bradford, *Of Plymouth Plantation*, ed. Samuel Eliot Morison (New York: Alfred A. Knopf, 1952), pp. 7-8.

22. From *Puritan Political Ideas 1558-1794*, ed. Edmund S. Morgan, copyright © 1965, by The Bobbs Merrill Company, Inc., reprinted by permission of the publisher.

23. William Haller, *The Rise of Puritanism* (New York: Columbia University Press, 1938), pp. 54-82.

24. G. R. Elton, *Reformation Europe, 1517-1559* (New York: Harper & Row, 1966), p. 297.

25. D. B. Knox, *The Doctrine of Faith in the Reign of Henry VIII* (Naperville, Ill.: Alec R. Allenson, 1961), p. 138. Used by permission of James Clarke & Co., Ltd.

26. Craig R. Thompson, "The Bible in English," *Life and Letters in Tudor and Stuart England*, ed. Louis B. Wright and Virginia A. LaMar (Ithaca, N. Y.: Cornell University Press, 1962), p. 204. Used by permission of The University Press of Virginia.

27. In Roland H. Bainton, *Erasmus of Christendom* (New York: Charles Scribner's Sons, 1969), pp. 153-54.

28. Ibid., p. 141. See also Erasmus, *Paraclesis* (1516).

29. Thompson in Wright and LaMar, *Life and Letters in Tudor and Stuart England*, pp. 196 ff.

30. Ibid., pp. 195-97.

31. Thomas Hobbes, *English Works*, ed. William Molesworth (New York: Adler's Foreign Books, Inc., 1966), VI, 190.

Chapter 3 "Give Me Liberty to Know"

1. Joel Hurstfield, ed., *The Elizabethan Nation* (New York: Harper & Row, 1964), pp. 9-10.

2. Hilaire Belloc, *Elizabeth, Creature of Circumstance* (New York: Harper & Row, 1942), pp. 72-73.

3. J. R. Green, *A Short History of the English People* (New York: Harper & Bros., 1900), p. 400.

4. George M. Trevelyan, *English Social History* (New York: Harper & Bros., 1942), p. 100.

5. Henry Jacob, *In Defence of the Chvrches and Ministry of Englande* (Middelburg, 1599), p. 13.

6. H. M. C. Mss. of the Marquis of Bath, II, 7.

7. In Alfred L. Rowse, *The England of Elizabeth* (New York: Macmillan, 1951), p. 397.

8. L. F. Salzman, *England in Tudor Times* (London: B. T. Batsford Ltd., 1926), p. 97. Cf. R. G. Usher, *The Rise and Fall of the High Commission* (New York: Oxford University Press, 1913).

9. In Salzman, *England in Tudor Times.*

10. Hurstfield, *The Elizabethan Nation,* pp. 73-77.

11. Rowse, *The England of Elizabeth,* p. 393.

12. In W. F. Adney, *Early Independents* (London: Congregational Union of England and Wales, 1895), p. 85.

13. *Seconde Parte of a Register* (1586), II, 211. See Edmund S. Morgan, *Visible Saints: The History of a Puritan Idea* (New York: New York University Press, 1963), p. 6.

14. *Seconde Parte of a Register.*

15. In W. H. Frere and C. C. Douglas, *Puritan Manifestoes* (New York: Burt Franklin Pub., 1907), p. 110.

16. *Seconde Parte of a Register,* II, 157-62.

17. Ibid., p. 45.

18. Maurice Ashley, *England in the Seventeenth Century* (New York: Penguin Books, 1960), pp. 26-27.

19. In Allerdyce Nicoll, *The Elizabethans* (New York: Cambridge University Press, 1957), p. 53.

20. Thomas W. Mason, *New Light on the Pilgrim Story* (London: Congregational Union of England and Wales, 1920), p. 7.

21. In R. W. Dale, *History of English Congregationalism* (London: Hodder & Stoughton, 1907), pp. 165-66.

22. H. M. Dexter, *The Congregationalism of the Last 300 Years as Seen in Its Literature* (New York: Harper & Bros., 1879), p. 360.

23. Ibid.

24. Trevelyan, *English Social History,* p. 150.

25. George M. Trevelyan, *England Under the Stuarts* (New York: G. P. Putnam, 1930), p. 52.

26. Walter H. Burgess, *John Robinson, Pastor of the Pilgrim Fathers* (London: Ernest Benn, Ltd., 1920), pp. 36-37.

27. Ibid., p. 38.

28. Ibid., pp. 39 ff.

29. In Adney, *Early Independents,* p. 27.

30. Ibid., p. 29.

31. Ibid.

32. In Joseph Hunter, *Collection Concerning the Church of Congregational Separatists Founded at Scrooby* (London: John R. Smith, 1841), p. 51.

33. Ruth McKenney and Richard Bransten, *Here's England* (New York: Harper & Bros., 1950), p. 279.

34. F. J. Powicke, *John Robinson* (London: Hodder & Stoughton, 1920), p. 7.

Chapter 4 "I Will Make Them Conform"

1. In Joel Hurstfield, ed., *The Elizabethan Nation* (New York: Harper & Row, 1964), pp. 9-10.

2. John Knewstubs emphasized covenant theology in his Cambridge lectures, first published in 1578. See *Elizabethan Puritanism,* ed. Leonard J. Trinterud (New York: Oxford University Press, 1971), pp. 313 ff.

3. Thomas Fuller, *The Church History of Britain from the Birth of Jesus to the Year 1648* (New York: Oxford University Press, 1845), V, 294-95.

4. Ibid., V, 298.

5. Gustavus S. Paine, *The Learned Men* (New York: T. Y. Crowell, 1959), p. 1. Cf. Patrick Collinson, *The Elizabethan Puritan Movement* (London: Jonathan Cape, 1967), pp. 448-67.

6. In R. W. Dale, *History of English Congregationalism* (London: Hodder & Stoughton, 1907), p. 177.

7. In C. K. Akrigg, *The Jacobean Pageant* (Cambridge, Mass.: Harvard University Press, 1962), p. 306.

8. Stow's *Annals*, p. 840; Dale, *History of English Congregationalism*, p. 185.

9. Dale, *History of English Congregationalism*, p. 185.

10. James F. Stephen, *Commentaries on the Laws of England*, IV, 127.

11. Elizabeth Burton, *The Pageant of Stuart England* (New York: Charles Scribner's Sons, 1962), pp. 35-36.

12. In George M. Trevelyan, *England Under the Stuarts* (New York: G. P. Putnam, 1930), p. 105.

13. Arthur Wilson, *The History of Great Britain*. E. S. Turner, *The Court of St. James's* (New York: St. Martins Press, 1960), p. 117. Cf. J. R. Tanner, *Constitutional Documents of the Reign of James I, 1603-1625* (New York: Cambridge University Press, 1960).

14. Ibid., p. 106.

15. George F. Willison, *Saints and Strangers* (New York: Harcourt Brace Jovanovich, 1945), p. 462. Used by permission of the author. Cf. Christopher Hill, *Society and Puritanism in Pre-Revolutionary England* (New York: Schocken Books, 1964), pp. 145-218.

16. Maurice Ashley, *Great Britain to 1688* (London: B. T. Batsford, Ltd., 1964), II, 309 states that James I was a homosexual who fawned on his favorites and permitted his court to lose itself in intrigue and pleasure.

17. Champlin Burrage, *New Facts Concerning John Robinson* (Cambridge, Mass.: Harvard University Press, 1920).

18. Ibid., p. 3.

19. Ibid., p. 30.

20. Ibid., p. 71.

21. Ibid., pp. 74-76.

22. Henry Ainsworth, *Counterpoyson* (1608), p. 248.

23. John Robinson, "A Justification of Separation (1610)," *Works* (London: John Snow, 1851), pp. 51-52.

24. Robinson, "A Manvmission to a Manvdvction (1615)," *Works*, p. 2.

25. John Robinson used as a text for the title page of his "Justification of Separation," "God separated between the light and between the darkness (Gen. 1:14)."

Chapter 5 "As the Lord's Free People"

1. Adam Stark, *The History and Antiquities of Gainsborough* (London: Longmans, 1843), p. 316.

2. In J. H. Shakespeare, *Baptist and Congregational Pioneers* (London: National Council of Evangelical Free Churches, 1905), p. 129.

3. William Bradford, *Of Plymouth Plantation*, ed. Samuel Eliot Morison (New York: Alfred A. Knopf, 1952), p. 325.

4. Ibid., p. 325.

5. Fynes Moryson, *An Itinerary* (London, 1617), III, 61.

6. Bradford, *Of Plymouth Plantation*, pp. 325-26.

7. Ibid., p. 236.

8. Edmund F. Jessup, Rector, *The Mayflower Story* (Retford, Nottinghamshire: Wharton Ltd., 1969).

9. Bradford, *Of Plymouth Plantation*, p. 9.

10. Ibid.

11. Walter H. Burgess, *John Robinson, Pastor of the Pilgrim Fathers* (London: Ernest Benn, Ltd., 1920), pp. 79-80.

12. Carl Bridenbaugh, *Vexed and Troubled Englishmen, 1590-1642* (New York: Oxford University Press, 1968), p. 195.

13. John Robinson, *Works* (London: John Snow, 1851), III, 406.

14. In H. M. Dexter, *The Congregationalism of the Last 300 Years as Seen in Its Literature* (New York: Harper & Bros., 1879), p. 381.

15. Robinson, *Works*, III, 7.

16. William Bradford, *First Dialogue*.

17. Bradford, *Of Plymouth Plantation*, p. 10.

Chapter 6 "Stepping Stones unto Others"

1. William Bradford, *Of Plymouth Plantation*, ed. Samuel Eliot Morison (New York: Alfred A. Knopf, 1952), p. 11.

2. *The State of England Anno Dom 1600*, Camden Miscellany (London: Camden Society and Royal Historical Society, 1936), XVI, 42.

3. Bradford, *Of Plymouth Plantation*, p. 13.

4. Ibid., pp. 14-15.

5. Ibid., p. 13.

6. Ibid., p. 14.

7. Ibid., p. 15.

8. John Robinson, *Works* (London: John Snow, 1851), III, 71.

9. George Johnson, *A Discourse of Some Troubles* (Amsterdam, 1603), p. 79.

10. Ibid., p. 136.

11. Ibid.

12. William Bradford in Alexander Young, *Chronicles of the Pilgrim Fathers* (Boston: Little, Brown & Co., 1841), p. 453.

13. Robinson, *Works*, III, 412.

14. Ibid., p. 417.

15. In Christopher Lawne, *The Prophane Schisme* (1612), p. 83.

16. Ibid.

17. Bradford, *Of Plymouth Plantation*, pp. 357-59.

Chapter 7 "Truth Can Be as Little Restrained as Light"

1. In H. M. Dexter, *The England and Holland of the Pilgrims* (Boston: Houghton Mifflin Co., 1909), p. 383.

2. Ibid.

3. In F. J. Powicke, *John Robinson* (London: Hodder & Stoughton, 1920), pp. 127-28.

4. Ibid.

5. William Bradford, *Of Plymouth Plantation*, ed. Samuel Eliot Morison (New York: Alfred A. Knopf, 1952), p. 17.

6. *Les Delices de Leide* (1712), p. 1.

7. William Bradford, *Dialogue* in Alexander Young, *Chronicles of the Pilgrim Fathers* (Boston: Little, Brown, & Co., 1841), p. 441.

8. Bradford, *Of Plymouth Plantation*, p. 17.

9. John Motley, *The Rise of the Dutch Republic*, ed. G. W. Curtis (New York: AMS Press, 1900).

10. H. M. Dexter, *The Congregationalism of the Last 300 Years as Seen in Its Literature* (New York: Harper & Bros., 1879), pp. 384-85.

11. In Walter H. Burgess, *John Robinson, Pastor of the Pilgrim Fathers* (London: Ernest Benn, Ltd., 1920), p. 158.

12. Albert Eckhof, *Three Unknown Documents Concerning the Pilgrim Fathers in Holland* (The Hague: Nijhoff, 1920).

13. In W. H. Bartlett, *The Pilgrim Fathers—The Founders of New England* (Boston: Arthur Hall, Virtue & Co., 1853), pp. 72-73.

14. Winifred Cockshott, *The Pilgrim Fathers* (New York: G. P. Putnam, 1910), p. 124.

15. Adriaan J. Barnouw, *The Dutch, A Portrait Study* (New York: Columbia University Press, 1940), pp. 42-44.

16. George N. Clark, *The Seventeenth Century* (New York: Oxford University Press, 1966).

17. In B. H. Vlekke, *The Netherlands* (Boston, 1945), p. 37.

18. In Barnouw, *The Dutch, A Portrait Study*, p. 432.

19. In R. G. Brandt, *History of the Netherlands*, I, 384.

20. George M. Trevelyan, *England Under the Stuarts* (New York: G. P. Putnam, 1930), p. 50.

21. Motley, *The Rise of the Dutch Republic*, IV, 517.

22. Cockshott, *The Pilgrim Fathers*, p. 117.

23. New York Hist. Coll., 1888. Cf. Francis R. Stoddard, *The Truth About the Pilgrims* (New York: New York Society of Mayflower Descendants, 1952), pp. 9-10.

24. Arthur Lord, *Plymouth and the Pilgrims* (Boston: Houghton Mifflin, 1920), pp. 24-27.

25. Bradford, *Of Plymouth Plantation*, p. 86.

26. Douglas Campbell, *The Puritan in Holland* (New York: Harper & Bros., 1892), II, 492-95. In contrast with Campbell's emphasis on the Dutch influence on the Pilgrims, cf. H. T. Colanbrander, "The Dutch Element in American History," Annual Report of the American Historical Association (Washington, D. C., 1911); C. O. Bangs, "The Leiden Pilgrims in American History," Archives of Leyden; L. D. Geller, "Pilgrim Artifacts and Dutch Genre Painting," *Halve Maen*, Holland Society of New York, XIV, Oct. 1970, XV, Jan. 1971, which trace the influence of Dutch art on the Pilgrims.

27. J. A. van Doesten, *Thomas Blossom, English Printer at Leyden, 1550-1613* (Leyden: Leyden University Press, 1961).

28. A. G. H. Bachrach, *Sir Constantine Huygens and Britain, 1598-1687* (Leyden: Leyden University Press, 1962). Also in this Sir Thomas Browne Institute Series: Paul R. Sellin, *Daniel Heinsius and Stuart England* (Leyden: Leyden University Press, 1968). Reveal Dutch-English interrelations. Cf. John Keevil, *The Stranger's Son* (London: Geoffrey Bles, 1953). Dr. Baldwin Hemey, physician to James I, studied medicine at Leyden and presented a pipe organ to one of the Leyden University halls in appreciation of his debt to the Dutch.

29. In Young, *Chronicles of the Pilgrim Fathers*, pp. 23-24.

Chapter 8 "Conceit of Faith or Want of Love"

1. John Robinson, *Works* (London: John Snow, 1851), I, xxviii.

2. In Walter H. Burgess, *John Smith, the Se-Baptist* (London: James Clarke & Co., Ltd., 1911), p. 84.

3. Robinson, *Works*, III, 188.

4. Ibid.

5. Ibid.

6. Ibid., III, 55. Cf. "The Order of the Prophecy at Norwich in Anno 1575," *Elizabethan Puritanism*, ed. Leonard J. Trinterud (New York: Oxford University Press, 1971).

7. In H. M. Dexter, *The England and Holland of the Pilgrims* (Boston: Houghton Mifflin Co., 1909), p. 383.

8. From *The Music of the Pilgrims* by Waldo Pratt, pp. 8-13. ©Copyright 1921 Oliver Ditson Company. Used by permission.

9. Edward Winslow, *Hypocrisie Unmasked*, p. 91.

10. In Dexter, *The England and Holland of the Pilgrims*, p. 543.

11. William Bradford, *Of Plymouth Plantation*, ed. Samuel Eliot Morison (New York: Alfred A. Knopf, 1952), p. 19.

12. Robinson, *Works*, III, 467.

13. Ibid., III, 472-74.

14. In Christopher Lawne, *The Prophane Schisme*, p. 84.

15. John Robinson, *Apology* in Alexander Young, *Chronicles of the Pilgrim Fathers*, pp. 6, 8, 52-56.

16. Robinson, *Works*, II, 78, 84, 212, 460.

17. Ibid.

Chapter 9 "We Seek Enlightenment from Others"

1. William Bradford, *Dialogue* in Alexander Young, *Chronicles of the Pilgrim Fathers* (Boston: Little, Brown & Co., 1841).

2. *The Utter Routing of the Whole Army of All the Independents* (1646), cxii.

3. Peirce, *Vindication*, I, 170.

4. In Matthew Nethernus et al, Preface, *Life of William Ames* (Cambridge, Mass.: Harvard Divinity School, 1965).

5. John Robinson, *Admonitio ad Lectorem*, preface to Robert Parker, *De Politeia*.

6. John Robinson, *Works* (London: John Snow, 1851), III, 356-57.

7. Ibid.

8. Ibid., I, 33-34.

9. William Haller, *The Rise of Puritanism* (New York: Columbia University Press, 1938). p. 123.

10. Charles and Katherine George, *The Protestant Mind of the English Reformation, 1570-1640* (Princeton, N. J.: Princeton University Press, 1961, p. 160. Copyright© by Princeton University Press.

11. In Perry Miller, *The New England Mind* (Boston: Beacon Press, 1961), p. 248. Used by permission of Harvard University Press.

12. Edmund S. Morgan, *Roger Williams: The Church and the State* (New York: Harcourt Brace Jovanovich, 1967), p. 131.

13. Robinson, *Works*, III, 354-57.

14. Ibid., III, 356-57.

15. Ibid., I, 37.

16. In Christopher Lawne, *The Prophane Schisme*, pp. 47-54.

17. In Walter H. Burgess, *John Robinson, Pastor of the Pilgrim Fathers* (London: Ernest Benn, Ltd., 1920), p. 129.

18. John Robinson, *Manvmission*, William Ames, *Manvdvction*, Sig q 3.

19. William Ames, **The Marrow of Theology,** tr. John Eusden (Philadelphia: Pilgrim Press, 1968), pp. 9-14.

20. *Johannes in eremo* (London, 1695), p. 21.

21. In Champlin Burrage, *The Early English Dissenters in the Light of Recent Research, 1550-1641* (Cambridge: The University Press, 1912; reprinted, New York: Russell & Russell, 1967), pp. 281-86.

22. In H. M. Dexter, *The England and Holland of the Pilgrims* (Boston: Houghton Mifflin Co., 1909), p. 370.

23. Henry Jacob, *Principles & Foundations of Christian Religion*.

24. F. J. Powicke, *John Robinson* (London: Hodder & Stoughton, 1920), p. 94.

25. In Burrage, *The Early English Dissenters*, p. 293.

26. Ibid.

27. Robinson, *Works*, III, 446.

28. Ibid., II, 232.

29. In Benjamin Hanbury, *Historical Memorials Relating to the Independents & Congregationalists* (1879), I, 225.

30. Robinson, *Works*, III, 105.

31. John Cotton, *Way of the Congregational Churches Cleared* (London, 1642), pp. 7-9.

Chapter 10 "He Was Never Satisfied in Himself"

1. Perry Miller, *The New England Mind* (Boston: Beacon Press, 1961). Used by permission of Harvard University Press.

2. Thomas Hall, *Vindiciae Literarum* (London, 1665), p. 68. "How the Cobbler" was Samuel How.

3. Champlin Burrage, *The Early English Dissenters in the Light of Recent Research, 1550-1641* (Cambridge: The University Press, 1912; reprinted, New York: Russell & Russell, 1967), p. 100.

4. In Albert Peel and Leland Carlson, *The Writings of Robert Harrison and Robert Browne* (London: Allen & Unwin, 1953), see pp. 15-22.

5. Ibid., p. 415.

6. Ibid., p. 404.

7. Verne D. Morey, "History Concerns Itself" (Boston: Congregational Historical Society).

8. John Robinson, *Works* (London: John Snow, 1851), II, 121.

9. Ibid., II, 260.

10. Ibid., II, 171.

11. Ibid., III, 42.

12. In Edward Arber, *A Demonstration of the Truth* (London, 1880), p. 6.

13. Robinson, *Works*, III, 52-56.

14. Ibid., II, 13.

15. Ibid., III, 126-29.

16. In Williston Walker, *The Creeds and Platforms of Congregationalism* (Philadelphia: Pilgrim Press, 1960), pp. 22-23.

17. Robinson, *Works*, II, 132.

18. Ibid., III, 132.

19. In F. J. Powicke, *John Robinson* (London: Hodder & Stoughton, 1920), pp. 52-54.

20. Robinson, *Works*, III, 141.

21. Ibid., III, 363.

22. Ibid., II, 332.

23. *An Answer to John Robinson* in Edmund S. Morgan, *Visible Saints: The History of a Puritan Idea* (New York: New York University Press, 1963), p. 57.

24. Robinson, *Works*, II, 374-75.

25. William Haller, *The Rise of Puritanism* (New York: Columbia University Press, 1938), pp. 298-99.

26. Robinson, *Works*, II, 398.

27. Ibid., II, 397.

28. Haller, *The Rise of Puritanism*, p. 258.

29. Ibid., p. 117.

30. Carl Bridenbaugh, *Vexed and Troubled Englishmen, 1590-1642* (New York: Oxford University Press, 1968), p. 411.

31. A. T. Hart, *The Country Clergy in Elizabethan and Stuart Times* (London: Phoenix House, 1958), p. 69.

32. Bridenbaugh, *Vexed and Troubled Englishmen*, pp. 296-310.

33. Douglas Bush, *English Literature in the Earlier Seventeenth Century: 1600-1660* (2d ed.; New York: Oxford University Press, 1962). Cf. Charles and Katherine George, *The Protestant Mind of the English Reformation, 1570-1640* (Princeton, N. J.: Princeton University Press, 1961), p. 296.

34. William Bradford, *A Dialogue or 3rd Conference* (1652).

35. Ibid., p. 51.

36. Edward Winslow, *Hypocrisie Unmasked*, p. 96.

37. Ibid., III, 63-64.

Chapter 11 "Disputations in Religion Are Always Dangerous"

1. John Robinson, *Works* (London: John Snow, 1851), III, 159.

2. Ibid., II, 155-56.

3. Walter H. Burgess, *John Smith, the Se-Baptist, Thomas Helwys and the First Baptist Church in England* (London: James Clarke & Co., Ltd., 1911), p. 276.

4. Thomas Helwys, *History of Iniquity*, pp. 204-5, 212.

5. Burgess, *John Smith, the Se-Baptist, Thomas Helwys and the First Baptist Church in England*, pp. 282-85.

6. Ibid., pp. 284, 313-15.

7. John Robinson, *Defense of Doctrine of the Synod of Dort* (1624).

8. Walter H. Burgess, *John Robinson, Pastor of the Pilgrim Fathers* (London: Ernest Benn, Ltd., 1920), p. 150.

9. John Robinson, *Works* (London: John Snow, 1851), III, 235.

10. Prince, *Annals*, p. 87.

11. Burgess, *John Robinson, Pastor of the Pilgrim Fathers*, p. 147.

12. Robinson, *Works*, III, 237.
13. Ibid., I, 37-39.
14. Ibid., II, 160.
15. Ibid., III, 77-78, 97.
16. Ibid.

Chapter 12 "To Learn Better and Further"

1. John Robinson, *Works* (London: John Snow, 1851), III, 102.
2. Ibid., III, 353.
3. In G. O. McCulloch and G. J. Hoenderdaal, *Man's Faith and Freedom, The Theological Influence of Jacob Arminius* (Nashville: Abingdon Press, 1962), p. 97.
4. In H. M. Dexter, *The England and Holland of the Pilgrims* (Boston: Houghton Mifflin Co., 1909), p. 535.
5. C. K. Akrigg, *The Jacobean Pageant* (Cambridge, Mass.: Harvard University Press, 1962), p. 311.
6. In Daniel Plooij, *Pilgrim Fathers from a Dutch Point of View* (New York: AMS Press, Inc., 1932), p. 52.
7. William Bradford, *Of Plymouth Plantation*, ed. Samuel Eliot Morison (New York: Alfred A. Knopf, 1952), pp. 20-21.
8. Dr. G. J. Hoenderdaal, Leyden University.
9. Bradford, *Of Plymouth Plantation*, pp. 20-21.
10. Ibid.
11. In McCulloch and Hoenderdaal, *Man's Faith and Freedom*, pp. 95-96.
12. Ibid.
13. Ibid., p. 103.
14. Robinson, *Works*, I, 23.
15. George M. Trevelyan, *England Under the Stuarts* (New York: G. P. Putnam, 1930), p. 152.
16. Ibid., p. 154.
17. A. G. H. Bachrach, *Sir Constantine Huygens and Britain, 1598-1687* (Leyden: Leyden University Press, 1962), p. 17.
18. James L. Adams in G. O. McCulloch and G. J. Hoenderdaal, *Man's Faith and Freedom, The Theological Influence of Jacob Arminius* (Nashville: Abingdon Press, 1962), p. 104.
19. Bachrach, *Sir Constantine Huygens and Britain*, p. 77.
20. Bradford, *Of Plymouth Plantation*, p. 21.
21. Ibid.
22. In Dexter, *The England and Holland of the Pilgrims*, p. 563.
23. Robinson, *Works*.
24. Ibid., III, 455-56.
25. Bradford, *Of Plymouth Plantation*, pp. 19-20.

Chapter 13 "As if the Word of God Came unto You Alone"

1. From Dr. G. J. Hoenderdaal, Leyden University.
2. Hendrik Riemens, *The Netherlands* (New York: Eagle Books, 1944), pp. 32-34.
3. *Biblical Repository*, I, 253-57.
4. Riemens, *The Netherlands*, pp. 32-34.
5. Gerard Brandt, *History of the Reformation* (London: John Necks, 1722), p. 43.
6. Riemens, *The Netherlands*, p. 34.
7. John Robinson, *Works* (London: John Snow, 1851), III, 239.
8. Ibid., III, 40-41.
9. Ibid., I, 49.
10. Ibid., III, 39.
11. Ibid., III, 238.
12. Ibid., I, 274-75.

13. Edward Winslow, *Hypocrisie Unmasked* (London: 1646), p. 92.

14. Perry Miller, *The New England Mind* (Boston: Beacon Press, 1961), p. 93. Used by permission of Harvard University Press.

15. Winslow, *Hypocrisie Unmasked*, pp. 96-97.

16. In A. G. Dickens, *Reformation and Society in Sixteenth Century Europe* (New York: Harcourt Brace Jovanovich, 1966), p. 117.

17. *Cambridge Modern History* (Cambridge: Cambridge University Press, 1902-12), II, 373.

18. G. R. Elton, *Reformation Europe, 1517-1559* (New York: Harper & Row, 1966), p. 283.

19. James Moffatt, Introduction, *The Golden Book of John Owen*, p. 48.

20. Stefan Zweig, *The Right to Heresy*, trans. Eden and Cedar Paul (New York: Viking Press, Inc., 1936), pp. 23, 34, 45, 53.

21. Ibid.

22. Dickens, *Reformation and Society in Sixteenth Century Europe*, p. 180.

23. John Fiske, *The Beginnings of New England* (Boston: Houghton Mifflin Co., 1898), p. 56.

24. Robinson, *Works*, I, 67.

Chapter 14 "Imprisonment, Yea Death Itself, Are No Meet Weapons"

1. In Daniel Plooij, *Pilgrim Fathers from a Dutch Point of View* (New York: AMS Press, Inc., 1932), pp. 58-59.

2. Ibid.

3. Winifred Cockshott, *The Pilgrim Fathers* (New York: G. P. Putnam, 1910), pp. 149-50.

4. S. P. Dom. Ap. 12th, 1607, Vol. XXXIX.

5. William Bradford, *Of Plymouth Plantation,* ed. Samuel Eliot Morison (New York: Alfred A. Knopf, 1952), p. 326.

6. Rendel Harris and S. K. Jones, *The Pilgrim Press* (Cambridge: Heffner & Sons, 1922).

7. Ibid.

8. Cockshott, *The Pilgrim Fathers*, p. 152.

9. In Plooij, *Pilgrim Fathers from a Dutch Point of View*, p. 63.

10. Ibid.

11. *Sir Dudley's Letters to Secretary Naunton*, pp. 380, 386, 389.

12. Ibid.

13. In Harris and Jones, *The Pilgrim Press*. The authors state that the Pilgrim Press project was religiously motivated, "a religious act at the center of a new religion."

14. In Edward Arber, *The Story of the Pilgrim Fathers, 1606-1623* (London: Ward & Downey, 1897), p. 5.

15. In Champlin Burrage, *The Early English Dissenters in the Light of Recent Research, 1550-1641* (Cambridge: The University Press, 1912; reprinted, New York: Russell & Russell, 1967).

16. Plooij, *Pilgrim Fathers from a Dutch Point of View*.

17. Daniel Plooij and Rendel Harris, *Leyden Documents Relating to the Pilgrim Fathers* (Leyden, 1920).

18. Ibid.

19. *The Pilgrim Fathers*, Exhibition of Documents, etc., van Trupp, Leyden, 1888. A group of English churches was established in Holland under exiled Congregational Puritans like John Forbes, Thomas Hooker, John Davenport, Hugh Peters, Henry Jacob, and William Ames. They organized a Congregational synod among their independent parishes and developed a polity similar to that of John Robinson in Leyden. Their experiment was checked due to the interference of King Charles I. Their residence in the Netherlands provided an important training ground for the future leaders of New England. Raymond P. Stearns, *Congregationalism in the Netherlands* (Chicago: University of Chicago Press, 1940). The efforts of James I to control the Pilgrims and other English refugees in Holland and to interfere in Dutch affairs led to an unexpected denouement when his grandson, James II, was displaced by a Dutch king. William III, Protestant great grandson of William the Silent, who led the fight for independence of the Netherlands from Spain, overthrew Roman Catholic James II in 1688 and took over the throne of England. Maurice Ashley, *The*

Glorious Revolution of 1688 (New York: Charles Scribner's Sons, 1967). John Robinson III studied medicine at the University of Leyden. He must have associated with Henry Jacob, Jr., son of his father's colleague, who left Leyden in 1616 to found his Congregational church in London. Jacob sent his son back to Leyden where he studied Hebrew, Greek, and Latin under Daniel Heinsius and Thomas Erpenius, developing into an eminent scholar. Henry, Jr. returned to Oxford where he served on the faculty. He and John III may have met again in England. Paul R. Sellin, *Daniel Heinsius and Stuart England* (Leyden: Leyden University Press, 1968), pp. 23-24.

Chapter 15 "All Great and Honourable Actions Are Accompanied with Great Difficulties"

1. J. H. Adamson and H. F. Folland, *The Shepherd of the Ocean* (Boston: Gambit, 1969), pp. 402-53.

2. Goldwin Smith, *A History of England* (3d ed.; New York: Charles Scribner's Sons, 1966), pp. 297-300 for background on the Thirty Years' War (1618-48). James I's son-in-law, the Protestant Frederick Elector of Palatinate, was conquered in 1620 by Roman Catholic troops from the Spanish Netherlands. In 1623 Prince Charles journeyed with Buckingham to Madrid to negotiate Charles' marriage with the Spanish Infanta but returned in anger to England to urge war. This military expedition was poorly managed. Buckingham's "rabble of raw and poor rascals" fell apart in Walcheren, Holland.

3. Catherine Drinker Bowen, *The Lion and the Throne* (Boston: Little, Brown & Co., 1957), pp. 304-12, 423 explains how the Parliamentary conflict under James I influenced thought in Plymouth and New England. The Country Party opposed the Court Party. The Country Party was led by Sandys, Coke, Wentworth, Sackville, and others. James defended his right to "judge all and be judged by none." Edward Coke resisted his effort to govern by proclamation and by-pass Parliament and rebuked the king for defying law. Cf. Smith, *A History of England*, p. 294. On June 16, 1614 Sir Ralph Winwood wrote to Sir Dudley Carleton that he "never saw so much faction and passion as in the late unhappy Parliament, nor so little reverence of a King (James I)."

4. William Bradford, *Of Plymouth Plantation*, ed. Samuel Eliot Morison (New York: Alfred A. Knopf, 1952), p. 24.

5. Ibid., pp. 24-25.

6. Ibid.

7. Ibid.

8. Ibid., p. 26.

9. Ibid., p. 27.

10. Collection of New York Historical Society, 3d series, p. 111.

11. Williston Walker, *The Creeds and Platforms of Congregationalism* (Philadelphia: Pilgrim Press, 1960), p. 90.

12. Samuel E. Morison, *The Old Colony of New Plymouth* (New York: Alfred A. Knopf, 1956), p. 37. Copyright 1956 by Priscilla Barton Morison. Cf. Theodore K. Rabb, *Enterprise and Empire* (Cambridge, Mass.: Harvard University Press, 1967), pp. 147-64 re Merchant Adventurer Companies.

13. Bradford, *Of Plymouth Plantation*, p. 30.

14. Ibid., p. 353-56.

15. Ibid.

16. Ibid., pp. 32-33.

17. Ibid., p. 36.

Chapter 16 "We Are Well Weaned from the Delicate Milk of Our Mother Country"

1. *Jamestown, First English Colony* (New York: American Heritage), p. 10. Cf. Louis B. Wright, *The Elizabethan's America* (Cambridge, Mass.: Harvard University Press, 1962).

2. Ibid., p. 47. Cf. Earl S. Miers, *Blood of Freedom* (Colonial Williamsburg, Va., 1958), p. 39. A

census of Virginia, taken during the winter of 1624-25, counted only 124 persons in Jamestown, including adults, children, servants, and Negroes. There were 22 houses, 2 stores, a church, 181 cattle, 1 horse, 209 swine, and 121 goats. Promoters of the Virginia colony soon discovered that men who came "to get something and then to return to England will breed a dissolution, and so an overthrow of the Plantation." Cf. Samuel E. Morison, "The Plymouth Colony and Virginia," *Virginia Magazine of History and Biography*, LXII, Apr. 1954, 147-65.

3. John Smith, *A Description of New England* (American Tract Society, 1898), p. 19.

4. In Daniel Plooij and Rendel Harris, *Leyden Documents Relating to the Pilgrim Fathers* (Leyden, 1920).

5. Edward Winslow, *A Brief Narration*, p. 357.

6. Ibid.

7. In William Bradford, *Of Plymouth Plantation*, ed. Samuel Eliot Morison (New York: Alfred A. Knopf, 1952), p. 357.

8. Winslow, *A Brief Narration*, pp. 382 ff.

9. In Bradford, *Of Plymouth Plantation*, pp. 40-41.

10. Ibid., pp. 40-41.

11. Ibid., pp. 42-44.

12. Ibid., p. 36.

13. Plooij and Harris, *Leyden Documents Relating to the Pilgrim Fathers*.

14. Ibid.

15. Bradford, *Of Plymouth Plantation*, pp. 44-45.

16. Ibid., pp. 44-45.

Chapter 17 "They Knew They Were Pilgrims"

1. In William Bradford, *Of Plymouth Plantation*, ed. Samuel Eliot Morison (New York: Alfred A. Knopf, 1952), p. 47.

2. Ibid.

3. Edward Winslow, *Hypocrisie Unmasked* in Alexander Young, *Chronicles of the Pilgrim Fathers* (Boston: Little, Brown & Co., 1841), p. 358.

4. Bradford, *Of Plymouth Plantation*, p. 48.

5. Winslow, *Hypocrisie Unmasked*, p. 348.

6. Bradford, *Of Plymouth Plantation*, p. 47.

7. In Winslow, *Hypocrisie Unmasked*.

8. Bradford, *Of Plymouth Plantation*, p. 49. Cf. Crispin Gill, *Mayflower Remembered—A History of the Plymouth Pilgrims* (New York: Taplinger, 1970).

9. Bradford, *Of Plymouth Plantation*, p. 49.

10. Ibid., pp. 49-50.

11. Ibid., pp. 368-70.

12. Ibid., pp. 369-71.

13. Ibid., pp. 56-57.

14. Ibid., p. 54.

15. Ibid., p. 53.

16. Ibid.

Chapter 18 "What Could Now Sustain Them but the Spirit of God and His Grace?"

1. Thomas J. Fleming, *One Small Candle* (New York: Norton, 1964), pp. 66-67.

2. William Bradford, *Of Plymouth Plantation*, ed. Samuel Eliot Morison (New York: Alfred A. Knopf, 1952), p. 59.

3. Ibid., p. 75. Cf. Samuel E. Morison, "The Mayflower Destination and the Pilgrim Fathers' Patents," *Colonial Society of Massachusetts*, XXXVIII, 1959, 387-413.

4. Bradford, *Of Plymouth Plantation*, pp. 75-76. Cf. W. S. Nickerson, *Land Ho! 1620* (Boston: Houghton Mifflin Co., 1931); H. L. Osgood, *The American Colonies in the 17th Century* (New

York: Peter Smith, Publisher, 1930), I, 291, states that the Mayflower Compact was the first example of the "Plantation covenant" which was to be used many times "in the land of the covenants ecclesiastical and civil."

5. *A Guide to Plymouth* (Plymouth: Pilgrim Society). Regarding *Mayflower* passengers see Hubert K. Shaw, *Families of the Pilgrims* (Boston: Massachusetts Society of Mayflower Descendants, 1956).

6. Williston Walker, *The Creeds and Platforms of Congregationalism* (Philadelphia: Pilgrim Press, 1960).

7. Bradford, *Of Plymouth Plantation*, pp. 61-62.

8. Ibid., pp. 69-72.

9. Ibid., pp. 61-62. Regarding previous explorations of Plymouth, see Henry F. Howe, *Early Explorers of Plymouth Harbor, 1525-1619* (Plimoth Plantation and the Pilgrim Society, 1953) and Darrett B. Rutman, "The Pilgrims and Their Harbor," *William & Mary Quarterly*, 3d ser. 3, XVII, Apr. 1960, 164-82.

10. Bradford, *Of Plymouth Plantation*, p. 77.

11. Ibid., p. 114. Cf. Mourt's *Relations* (1622).

12. Ibid., p. 85. Cf. R. C. Anderson, "Have the *Mayflower's* Masts Been Found?" *Mariners' Mirror*, XIX, 1933; Alan J. Villiers, *Give Me a Ship to Sail* (New York: Charles Scribner's Sons, 1959), pp. 164-71.

13. Bradford, *Of Plymouth Plantation*, p. 95.

14. Ibid., pp. 374-75.

15. Ibid., p. 130.

16. Edward Winslow, *Good News from New England*.

17. John Robinson, *Works* (London: John Snow, 1851), Essays.

18. Bradford, *Of Plymouth Plantation*, p. 97.

19. Ibid., pp. 120-21.

20. Ibid., p. 375.

21. Ibid., pp. 376-77.

22. Ibid.

23. J. F. Jameson, ed., *Narratives of New Netherlands, 1609-1664* in *Original Narratives of Early American History* (New York: Charles Scribner's Sons, 1909), pp. 102-15.

24. Bradford, *Of Plymouth Plantation*, pp. 142-43.

25. Ibid., p. 174.

26. Ibid., p. 171-72.

27. Ibid., p. 113.

28. Sidney V. James, *Three Visitors to Early Plymouth* (Plymouth: Plimoth Plantation, 1963), pp. 29-30.

29. Jameson, *Narratives of New Netherlands, 1604-1664,* pp. 102-15. For description of Plimoth Plantation Village see Charles R. Strickland, "The Architecture of Plimoth Plantation," *Manuscripts,* IX, Fall 1957, 246-51; Richard M. Candee, "A Documentary History of Plymouth: Colonial Architecture," *Old Time New England,* LIX, Jan.-Mar. and Apr. 1969, 56-69, 105-11; LX, Oct.-Dec. 1969, 37-53; *Massachusetts Historical Society Collection,* 1st Ser., III, 54.

Chapter 19 "They Gathered Up Their Spirits"

1. Edward Winslow, *Hypocrisie Unmasked* in Alexander Young, *Chronicles of the Pilgrim Fathers* (Boston: Little, Brown & Co., 1841), pp. 90-95.

2. Ibid.

3. William Bradford, *Dialogue* in Young, *Chronicles of the Pilgrim Fathers.*

4. Winslow, *Hypocrisie Unmasked*, p. 98.

5. Ibid.

6. Ibid.

7. Ibid., p. 99.

8. John Cotton, *Way of the Congregational Churches Cleared* (London, 1642), p. 14.

9. In William Bradford, *Of Plymouth Plantation*, ed. Samuel Eliot Morison (New York: Alfred A. Knopf, 1952), pp. 179-80.

10. In Young, *Chronicles of the Pilgrim Fathers*, p. 452.

11. Bradford, *Of Plymouth Plantation*, p. 181.

12. In Walter H. Burgess, *John Robinson, Pastor of the Pilgrim Fathers* (London: Ernest Benn, Ltd., 1920), p. 303.

13. Winslow, *Hypocrisie Unmasked*.

14. The Pieterskerk, Leyden.

15. In Burgess, *John Robinson, Pastor of the Pilgrim Fathers*, p. 359.

16. Bradford, *Of Plymouth Plantation*, p. 278.

17. *Bradford, Dialogue*, p. 452.

18. Bradford, *Of Plymouth Plantation*, pp. 17-19.

19. Thomas Prince, *Chronological History of New England* (Boston, 1736), p. 238.

20. Burgess, *John Robinson, Pastor of the Pilgrim Fathers*, pp. 348 ff.

21. Albert Eckhof, *Three Unknown Documents Concerning the Pilgrim Fathers in Holland* (The Hague: Nijhoff, 1920).

22. In H. M. Dexter, *The England and Holland of the Pilgrims* (Boston: Houghton Mifflin Co., 1909).

23. George F. Willison, *Saints and Strangers* (New York: Harcourt Brace Jovanovich, 1945), p. 341.

Chapter 20 "It Is Not by Good and Dainty Fare"

1. Ruth A. McIntyre, *Debts Hopeful and Desperate* (Plymouth: Plimoth Plantation, 1963), pp. 52-65.

2. George F. Willison, *Saints and Strangers* (New York: Harcourt Brace Jovanovich, 1945), p. 261.

3. McIntyre, *Debts Hopeful and Desperate*, pp. 52-65.

4. William Bradford, *Of Plymouth Plantation*, ed. Samuel Eliot Morison (New York: Alfred A. Knopf, 1952), pp. 194-96.

5. In Samuel E. Morison, *The Old Colony of New Plymouth* (New York: Alfred A. Knopf, 1956), p. 108. Copyright 1956 by Priscilla Barton Morison.

6. Willison, *Saints and Strangers*, p. 454.

7. In Bradford, *Of Plymouth Plantation,* pp. 75-76.

8. Carl Bridenbaugh, *Vexed and Troubled Englishmen, 1590-1642* (New York: Oxford University Press, 1968), p. 447.

9. Darrett B. Rutman, *Husbandmen of Plymouth* (Boston: Beacon Press, 1967), pp. 4-13.

10. Bernard Bailyn, *The New England Merchants in the 17th Century* (Cambridge, Mass.: Harvard University Press, 1955), pp. 14-25. Cf. "Aptucxet, a Trading Place of the Pilgrims," *Business Historical Society Bulletin*, VIII, 1934, 108-11.

11. McIntyre, *Debts Hopeful and Desperate*, p. 67.

12. Morison, *The Old Colony of New Plymouth*, p. 130.

13. Ibid.

14. In Bradford, *Of Plymouth Plantation*, p. 376. The efforts of Charles I to govern without Parliament led political liberals to back the Puritans. This resulted in more stubborn efforts to check the monarch and more determined plans to seek freedom in New England. Samuel E. Morison, *The Oxford History of the American People* (New York: Oxford University Press, 1965), p. 64.

15. In Cotton Mather, *Magnalia Christi Americana* (London, 1702), III, 11.

16. In Bradford, *Of Plymouth Plantation*, pp. 223-24.

17. Alan Simpson, *Puritanism in Old and New England* (Chicago: University of Chicago Press, 1955), p. 15.

18. Perry Miller, *Orthodoxy in Massachusetts, 1630-60* (Cambridge, Mass.: Harvard University Press, 1933), ch. 4.

19. William W. Sweet, *Religion in Colonial America* (New York: Cooper Square Publishers, Inc., 1942).

20. In Bradford, *Of Plymouth Plantation*, pp. 224-25.

21. In Alexander Young, *Chronicles of the Pilgrim Fathers* (Boston: Little, Brown & Co., 1841), p. 296. The Bay settlement was launched by a group of Cambridge alumni who met secretly in the summer of 1629 and signed an agreement to set out for New England. During the first half of 1630 their exodus began, due in considerable measure to conflict with their king and archbishop. Morison, *The Oxford History of the American People,* p. 65. Cf. Charles E. Banks, *The Winthrop Fleet* (Boston: Houghton Mifflin Co., 1930). Cf. John E. Pomfret and Floyd M. Shumway, *Founding the American Colonies, 1583-1660* (New York: Harper & Row, 1970), p. 161.

22. William Rathband, *A Briefe Narration of some Church Courses* (1644), pp. 54-55.

23. Edward Winslow, *Hypocrisie Unmasked*, p. 92.

24. Ibid.

25. In Young, *Chronicles of the Colony of Massachusetts Bay*, p. 441.

26. In Bradford, *Of Plymouth Plantation*, pp. 235-36.

27. John Winthrop, *Journal* (1908), pp. 92-94.

28. Massachusetts Historical Society, Series III, p. 74.

29. Ibid.

30. Harris, *Memorials*, pp. 53-57.

31. Larzer Ziff, *The Career of John Cotton* (Princeton, N. J.: Princeton University Press, 1962), p. 200.

32. Edmund S. Morgan, *The Half Way Covenant Reconsidered, Puritanism in 17th Century Massachusetts*, ed. David D. Hall (New York: Holt, Rinehart & Winston, Inc., 1968), pp. 96-107.

33. William Bradford, *Dialogue* in Young, *Chronicles of the Pilgrim Fathers*, p. 426.

34. John Cotton, *Way of the Congregational Churches Cleared* (London, 1642), p. 12.

35. In Miller, *Orthodoxy in Massachusetts*, p. 100. Cf. Kenneth B. Murdock, *Literature and Theology in Colonial New England* (Cambridge, Mass.: Harvard University Press, 1949).

36. Cotton, *Way of the Congregational Churches Cleared,* p. 82.

37. John Winthrop, *Journal* (Boston: 1825), I, 63-67.

38. West Barnstable Congregational Church Records.

Chapter 21 "Whereas You Are Become a Body Politic"

1. John Robinson, *Works* (London: John Snow, 1851), III, 42.

2. Ibid., III, 277.

3. Ibid., I, 41-42.

4. Ibid., III, 61.

5. Ibid.

6. Ibid., III, 277.

7. Ibid., I, 139. Cf. R. H. Bainton, "Congregationalism from the Just War to the Crusade in the Puritan Revolution," *Andover Newton Theological School Bulletin*, XXXV, No. 3, Apr. 1943, regarding the Puritan shift from respect for the king to resistance to the crown.

8. John Robinson, *Essays*, p. 7.

9. H. M. Dexter, *The England and Holland of the Pilgrims* (Boston: Houghton Mifflin Co., 1909), p. 554.

10. Robinson, *Works*, III, 61.

11. Charles M. Andrews, *The Colonial Period of American History* (New Haven, Conn.: Yale University Press, 1964), I, 299.

12. Vernon L. Parrington, *Main Currents in American Thought*, Vol. I, *The Colonial Mind, 1620-1800* (New York: Harcourt, Brace, 1927), p. 22.

13. Edmund S. Morgan, *Puritan Political Ideas* (Indianapolis: Bobbs Merrill, 1966), p. xx-xxv.

14. Ibid.

15. Parrington, *The Colonial Mind, 1620-1800*, p. 22. Cf. George M. Trevelyan, *Illustrated History of England* (London: Longmans, Green & Co., 1958), p. 439. New England was democratic in

spirit because the Saxon township was brought over from East Anglia. Squireship was left behind. "Abundant land, divided up into freeholds among all who were ready to clear it of trees and till it with their own hands, was the firm basis of the original North American democracy."

16. Parrington, *The Colonial Mind, 1620-1800*.

17. John A. Goodwin, *The Pilgrim Republic* (Boston: Houghton Mifflin), p. 402. Cf. George L. Haskins, "The Legal Heritage of Plymouth Colony," *Essays in the History of Early American Law*, ed. David H. Flaherty (Chapel Hill, N. C.: University of North Carolina Press, 1969). Also William Lambarde, *Eirenarcha: Of the Office of the Justices of the Peace* (London, 1592). This book was found in the library of William Brewster in Plymouth. Many of its principles were applied in Plimoth colony. The coat of arms of Sir William Cecil (secretary of state under Elizabeth) appears on the cover of this volume. It is believed that the book came into the possession of Brewster when he left the employ of Lord Davison and returned to Scrooby. It is now in Pilgrim Hall, Plymouth. Cf. William Dunkel, *William Lambarde, Elizabethan Jurist (1536-1601)* (New Brunswick, N. J.: Rutgers University Press, 1965); D. C. Parnes, *Plymouth and the Common Law (1620-1775)*, (Plymouth: Pilgrim Society, 1971).

18. In Samuel E. Morison, *The Old Colony of New Plymouth* (New York: Alfred A. Knopf, 1956), p. 152. Copyright 1956 by Priscilla Barton Morison.

19. *Plymouth Colony Laws* (1623), p. 8.

20. Ibid., p. 12.

21. Morison, *The Old Colony of New Plymouth*, p. 148.

22. George D. Langdon, Jr., *William and Mary Quarterly*, 3d Ser., XX, No. 4, Oct. 9, 1963, 521.

23. Morison, *The Old Colony of New Plymouth*, p. 171.

24. Parrington, *The Colonial Mind, 1620-1800*, p. 18.

25. George F. Willison, *Saints and Strangers* (New York: Harcourt Brace Jovanovich, 1945), p. 336.

26. *Plymouth Colonial Records*, pp. 4, 85-86.

27. In Williston Walker, *The Creeds and Platforms of Congregationalism* (Philadelphia: Pilgrim Press, 1960), p. 42. Cf. on church and state relations: Horace E. Ware, "Was the Government of the Massachusetts Bay a Theocracy?" *Publication of the Colonial Society*, X, 1904-6, 151-80; Aaron Seidman, "Church and State in the Early Years of the Massachusetts Bay Colony," *New England Quarterly*, XVIII, 1945, 211-13; and J. M. Bumsted, "A Well Bounded Toleration: Church and State in Plymouth Colony," *Journal of Church and State*, X, Spring 1968, 265-76.

28. Morison, *The Old Colony of New Plymouth*, p. 166.

29. Robinson, *Works*, III, 45.

30. John Demos, *The Little Commonwealth: Family Life in Plymouth Colony* (New York: Oxford University Press, 1970), p. 162.

31. Goodwin, *The Pilgrim Republic*, p. 576.

32. D. K. Winslow, *Mayflower Heritage* (New York: Funk & Wagnalls, 1951), pp. 71-73. Used by permission of George G. Harrap & Co. Ltd.

33. Ibid.

34. Robinson, *Works*, I, 239.

35. Ibid., I, 237.

36. Ibid., I, 20.

37. Ibid., I, 240.

38. Ibid., I, 240.

39. Ibid., I, 236.

40. Ibid., II, 215-16.

41. Ibid., III, 57, 317.

42. William Bradford, *Of Plymouth Plantation,* ed. Samuel Eliot Morison (New York: Alfred A. Knopf, 1952).

43. *Old Colony Records*.

44. Ibid.

45. Goodwin, *The Pilgrim Republic*, p. 589.

46. *Life and Records of John Howland of Rhode Island*, p. 491.

47. Morison, *The Old Colony of New Plymouth*, p. 179.

48. Ibid., p. 38.

49. Samuel E. Morison, *By Land and by Sea* (New York: Alfred A. Knopf, 1953), p. 239.

50. Dexter, *The England and Holland of the Pilgrims,* p. 650-52.

51. William Bradford, Massachusetts Historical Collection, 1st Series, III, 1810, 79-80.

Chapter 22 "We Should Affect Strife with None"

1. Samuel E. Morison, *The Old Colony of New Plymouth* (New York: Alfred A. Knopf, 1956), p. 239. Copyright 1956 by Priscilla Barton Morison.

2. *Plymouth Colony Records,* II, 41.

3. Ibid., 5, 106.

4. Alden T. Vaughan, *New England Frontier: Indians and Puritans* (Boston: Little, Brown & Co., 1965), p. 327. Cf. Chester E. Eisinger, "The Puritan Justification for Taking the Land," *Essex Institute Historical Collections,* LXXXIV, 1948, 131-47.

5. In Winifred Cockshott, *The Pilgrim Fathers* (New York: G. P. Putnam, 1909), p. 271.

6. *Plymouth Court Orders,* p. 161.

7. Ibid.

8. Edwin Powers, *Crime and Punishment in Early Massachusetts, 1620-92* (Boston: Beacon Press, 1966), p. 302. Cf. Catherine Martin, "An Ethnohistorical Survey," *Occasional Papers in Old Colony Studies,* No. 2, Dec. 1970, Plimoth Plantation.

9. *Plymouth Court Orders.*

10. Edward Winslow, *Good News from New England* in Alexander Young, *Chronicles of the Pilgrim Fathers* (Boston: Little, Brown & Co., 1841), ch. 20.

11. William Bradford, *Of Plymouth Plantation,* ed. Samuel Eliot Morison !(New York: Alfred A. Knopf, 1952), p. 48.

12. Ibid., p. 111.

13. In George F. Willison, *Saints and Strangers* (New York: Harcourt Brace Jovanovich, 1945), p. 376.

14. In Young, *Chronicles of the Pilgrim Fathers,* pp. 258-67.

15. Bradford, *Of Plymouth Plantation,* p. 14.

16. Ibid.

17. Ola E. Winslow, *John Eliot, Apostles to the Indians* (Boston: Houghton Mifflin Co., 1968), p. 109. Cf. Douglas E. Leach, *Flintlock and Tomahawk: New England in King Philip's War* (New York: Macmillan, 1958).

18. George D. Langdon, Jr., *Pilgrim Colony* (New Haven, Conn.: Yale University Press, 1966), p. 158; John Cotton, *Journal.*

19. Willison, *Saints and Strangers,* p. 376. Cf. George Fox in Samuel Groom, *A Glass for the People of New England* (London, 1676), p. 31; clergy were labeled "priests" and "professors".

20. *Plymouth Colony Records,* XI, 100-101.

21. Ibid., 129-30.

22. Ibid.

23. Roland G. Usher, *The Pilgrims and Their History* (New York: Macmillan, 1918), p. 216.

24. Morison, *The Old Colony of New Plymouth,* p. 165.

25. In John A. Goodwin, *The Pilgrim Republic,* pp. 482-83; *Plymouth Colony Records.*

26. John Robinson, *Works* (London: John Snow, 1851), I, 42.

27. *Plymouth Colony Records,* III, 159.

28. In William Brigham, *The Compact with the Charter and Laws of the Colony of New Plymouth* (Boston: Dutton & Wentworth, 1836), p. 125.

29. Goodwin, *The Pilgrim Republic,* pp. 277-90.

30. In Thomas W. Mason, *New Light on the Pilgrim Story,* p. 37.

31. Rufus M. Jones, *The Quakers in the American Colonies* (New York: Russell & Russell, 1962), p. 60.

32. Ibid.

33. Thomas Prince, *Annals,* p. 238.

34. Langdon, *Pilgrim Colony,* pp. 72, 76.

Chapter 23 "It Is Too Great Arrogancy"

1. William Bradford, *Of Plymouth Plantation*, ed. Samuel Eliot Morison (New York: Alfred A. Knopf, 1952), p. 327.

2. In George F. Willison, *Saints and Strangers* (New York: Harcourt Brace Jovanovich, 1945), p. 444.

3. In John Cotton, *An Account of the Church of Christ in Plymouth, The First Church in New England*, Massachusetts Historical Society Collection, III, 107-15.

4. Bradford, *Of Plymouth Plantation*, p. 210.

5. Ibid., p. 210.

6. John Winthrop, *Journal*, I, 62-63.

7. Edmund S. Morgan, *The Puritan Dilemma: The Story of John Winthrop* (Boston: Little, Brown & Co., 1958), pp. 15-33.

8. Bradford, *Of Plymouth Plantation*.

9. Williston Walker, *The Creeds and Platforms of Congregationalism* (Philadelphia: Pilgrim Press, 1960), p. 109.

10. John Cotton, *Works*, II, 106.

11. Edmund S. Morgan, *Roger Williams, The Church and the State* (New York: Harcourt Brace Jovanovich, 1968), p. 33.

12. Ibid., pp. 33-34.

13. *Publications of the Narragansett Club*, I, 324.

14. Ibid.

15. In Perry Miller, *Roger Williams* (New York: Athenaeum, 1962), p. 93. Cf. John Gannett, *Roger Williams, Witness Beyond Christendom* (New York: Macmillan, 1970); Alan Simpson, "How Democratic Was Roger Williams?" *William and Mary Quarterly*, 3d Ser., XIII, 1956, 53-67.

16. Bradford, *Of Plymouth Plantation*, p. 257.

17. Address by C. S. Bradley, "150th Anniversary of the Landing of the Pilgrims" (1891), p. 148.

18. Roger Williams, *Complete Writings* (1963), pp. 41, 228. Dr. Samuel Fuller left a note with his will: "Whatsoever Mr. Roger Williams is indebted to me upon my books for physick I freely give him," indicating that he had another loyal friend in Plymouth.

19. In Miller, *Roger Williams*, p. 245.

20. Bradford, *Of Plymouth Plantation*, p. 284.

21. Ibid.

22. Ibid., p. 297.

23. Ibid., p. 317.

24. Ibid., p. 313.

25. Ibid., p. 314.

26. Ibid., p. 314.

27. Samuel E. Morison, *Three Centuries of Harvard* (Cambridge, Mass.: Harvard University Press, 1936). Cf. Charles Chauncy, *God's Mercy, shewed to his people in giving them a faithful ministry, and schools of Learning* (Cambridge, 1655).

28. Bradford, *Of Plymouth Plantation*, p. 352.

29. John Cotton, *Plymouth Church Records*.

30. In Edward Winslow, *Hypocrisie Unmasked*, p. 98. Cf. *An Apologeticall Narration* (London, 1643), ed. Robert S. Paul (Philadelphia: Pilgrim Press, 1963).

31. *Plymouth Court Order*, III, 188.

32. Thomas J. Wertenbaker, *The Puritan Oligarchy* (New York: Charles Scribner's Sons, 1947), p. 130.

33. John Demos, *William and Mary Quarterly*, 3d Ser., XXII, No. 2.

34. Bradford, *Of Plymouth Plantation,* p. 334.

35. Ibid., p. 334 (see footnote).

36. John Norton exhorted New Englanders "alwayes to remember that Originally they are a Plantation Religious," *The Heart of New England* (1659), p. 58; Peter N. Carroll, *Puritanism and the Wilderness* (New York: Columbia University Press, 1969), p. 116. Cf. Samuel E. Morison, *The*

Oxford History of the American People (New York: Oxford University Press, 1965), p. 61 states "Puritanism was essentially and primarily a religious movement; attempts to prove it to have been a mask for politics or money-making are false as well as unhistorical."

Religious motivation was certainly central in creating the Scrooby-Leyden-Plimoth community. With the increasing migration to the New World other factors contributed in the shaping of New England Congregationalism: the economic, political, social, geographic, intellectual, and spiritual. See Darrett B. Rutman, *American Puritanism: Faith and Practice* (New York: J. B. Lippincott, 1970), p. 130. Cf. Philip J. Creven, Jr., "Historical Demography, Colonial America," *William and Mary Quarterly*, 3d Ser., XXIV, 1967; D. E. C. Eversley, *Population in History—Essays in Historical Demography* (London, 1965); Ray A. Billington, *The Reinterpretation of Early American History* (San Marino, Calif., 1966); Kai T. Erikson, *Wayward Puritans, A Study in the Sociology of Deviance* (New York: John Wiley & Sons, 1966); Christopher Hill, *Society and Puritanism in Pre-Revolutionary England* (New York: Shocken Books, 1964).

Chapter 24 "Advertise Us Brotherly"

1. In William Brigham, *The Compact with the Charter and Laws of the Colony of New Plymouth* (Boston: Dutton & Wentworth, 1836), p. 158.

2. In Samuel E. Morison, *The Old Colony of New Plymouth* (New York: Alfred A. Knopf, 1956), p. 158. Copyright 1956 by Priscilla Barton Morison.

3. *Plymouth Colony Records* (1623-82), p. 57.

4. Ibid., p. 58.

5. In Brigham, *The Compact with the Charter and Laws of the Colony of New Plymouth*, p. 113.

6. Ibid., p. 137.

7. George M. Trevelyan, *English Social History* (London: Longmans, Green & Co., 1942), p. 180. Cf. William Lambarde, *Eirenarcha* (London, 1592), pp. 202, 396, written by the English jurist who was a justice of the peace in Kent. He listed the law of England which stated that people who failed to attend church on Sundays and holy days were subject to a fine of twelve pence. This rule was in effect long before the Pilgrims established their colony. They should not be wholly blamed for the strictness that was brought over from the mother country.

8. In James T. Adams, *The Founding of New England* (Boston: Little, Brown & Co., 1963), p. 112.

9. *Plymouth Colony Records*, I, 35.

10. "Pilgrim Inventories," Pilgrim Hall, Plymouth.

11. In *Massachusetts Historical Society Publication* (1880), pp. 38 ff.

12. *Mayflower Descendants*, II, 8-9.

13. Ibid., pp. 16, 62.

14. Ibid., I, 83.

15. Ibid., 12, 139.

16. Ibid., I, 151-57.

17. Ibid., I, 158.

18. Ibid., I, 31-34.

19. Ibid., I, 79.

20. Ibid., I, 97.

21. Ibid., II, 14.

22. Ibid., II, 25.

23. Ibid., II, 73.

24. Ibid., II, 74.

25. John E. Pomfret and Floyd M. Shumway, *Founding the American Colonies* (New York: Harper & Row, 1970), p. 115.

26. H. S. Bennett, *English Books and Readers, 1475-1557* (New York: Cambridge University Press, 1952), pp. 19-29. Cf. Lawrence Stone, "The Educational Revolution in England, 1560-1640," *Past and Present*, XXVIII, 1964.

27. Edmund S. Morgan, Preface, *The Puritan Dilemma—The Story of John Winthrop* (Boston:

Little, Brown & Co., 1958). Cf. Darrett B. Rutman, *Winthrop's Boston* (Chapel Hill, N. C.: University of North Carolina Press, 1965).

28. George L. Kittredge, *Witchcraft in Old and New England* (New York: Russell & Russell, 1958), p. 368. Cf. Perry Miller, *The New England Mind,* Vol. 2, *From Colony to Province* (Cambridge, Mass.: Harvard University Press, 1967), ch. 13.

29. In Edwin Powers, *Crime and Punishment in Early Massachusetts, 1620-92* (Boston: Beacon Press, 1966), pp. 455, 457.

30. Ibid.

31. *Plymouth Colony Records*, III-IV, 211.

32. Samuel Deane, *History of Scituate*, p. 152.

33. *Plymouth Colony Records*, III-IV, 211.

34. *Plymouth Judicial Acts*, 1666-67.

35. Powers, *Crime and Punishment in Early Massachusetts, 1620-92*, p. 530.

36. Williston Walker, *The Creeds and Platforms of Congregationalism* (Philadelphia: Pilgrim Press, 1960), p. 185.

37. George D. Langdon, Jr., *Pilgrim Colony* (New Haven, Conn.: Yale University Press, 1966), pp. 59-60.

38. Ibid.

39. *Plymouth Colony Records*.

40. R. G. Thwaites, *Jesuit Relations and Allied Documents* (Cleveland, 1897), XXXVI, 91.

41. "*Sparrowhawk*—A Seventeenth Century Vessel in Twentieth Century America," *American Neptune*, XIII, Jan. 1953, 51-64; Pilgrim Society, Plymouth, 1969.

42. John A. Goodwin, *The Pilgrim Republic* (Boston: Houghton Mifflin Co.), pp. 392-93.

43. Percy A. Scholes, *Puritans and Music in England and New England* (New York: Oxford University Press, 1934), pp. 33-40. Cf. Marshall Knappen, *Tudor Puritanism* (Chicago: University of Chicago Press, 1939), pp. 431-33; Goldwin Smith, *A History of England* (New York: Charles Scribner's Sons, 1966), p. 266; Maurice Ashley, *Great Britain to 1688* (London: B. T. Batsford, Ltd., 1969), pp. 397-400.

Chapter 25 "More Truth and Light"

1. John Robinson, *Works* (London: John Snow, 1851), I.

2. Ibid., I, 301.

3. Ibid., I, 142.

4. Ibid., I, 23.

5. Ibid., I, 40.

6. Geoffrey E. Nuttall, *The Puritan Spirit* (London: Epworth Press, 1967), pp. 63-64.

7. Ibid.

8. Robinson, *Works*, II, 60.

9. Ibid., III, 79.

10. Mildred L. Sharkey, *The Congregational Way* (New York: Doubleday & Co., 1966). Cf. Douglas Horton, *The United Church of Christ* (New York: Nelson, 1962) and Albert Peel, *A Brief History of English Congregationalism* (London: Independent Press, 1953).

11. Robinson, *Works*, III, lxxiv. One of the outstanding leaders in the Virginia colony was named John Robinson. His ancestor, Christopher Robinson, who settled in Virginia about 1666, was the son of John Robinson of Hewick Manor, near Cleasby in the northern part of Yorkshire. Christopher Robinson had a brother, John (1650-1722) who served as Bishop of Bristol and London, as ambassador to Sweden, and as England's representative at the Congress of Utrecht in 1712. Virginia's John Robinson was born in Middlesex County of the colony February 3, 1704. He lived in King and Queen County on an estate called Mount Pleasant. He was a member of the House of Burgesses from 1736 to 1765, serving as Speaker of the House and treasurer of the colony from 1738 to 1765. For many years he was considered the most influential man in Virginia. He died May 11, 1766. (This information came through the courtesy of Edward M. Riley, director of research, Colonial Williamsburg.) Two John Robinsons from the same home base in England, and undoubtedly cousins, provided leadership for the first two colonies in America.

Followers of the Congregational Way pioneered in creating the first woman minister. On September 15, 1853 Antoinette L. Brown, a graduate of Oberlin College, was ordained at South Butler, Wayne County, New York. Robert F. Fletcher, *History of Oberlin College,* pp. 290-94.

With the passing years the Congregationalists have developed close ties of cooperation with the Remonstrant Brotherhood. The followers of Arminius and Episcopius and those of Perkins and Robinson now work together in close Christian fellowship.

INDEX

Brewsters.

fear, 3624, Johnathan 109
122, 167, 192, 204, 330, PAtience,
Gerj, William 14, 30-31, 33
27, 64, 66-73, 81, 83, 87, 89, 90
04, 98, 109-10, 113, 118, 121-23, 148
152, 165, 181, 183, 186-92, 196-97
199-201, 203-6, 208-11, 213-14,
235, 245-46, 250, 263, 269, 270,
284, 287, 299, 301, 305, 3018
313, 315, 318, 320, 321, 327-28.

369

371